WEEK LOAN

ousing and

*of related interest*

**Cultural Competence in the Caring Professions**
*Kieran O'Hagan*
ISBN 1 85302 759 6

**Settlements, Social Change and Community Action**
**Good Neighbours**
*Edited by Ruth Gilchrist and Tony Jeffs*
ISBN 1 85302 764 2

**Immigration Controls, the Family and the Welfare State**
**A Handbook of Law, Theory, Politics and Practice for Local Authority,**
**Voluntary Sector and Welfare State Workers and Legal Advisors**
*Steve Cohen*
ISBN 1 85302 723 5

**Housing and Social Exclusion**
*Edited by Fiona E Spiers*
ISBN 1 85302 638 7

**Social Care and Housing**
*Edited by Ian Shaw, Susan Thomas and David Clapham*
ISBN 1 85302 437 6
*Research Highlights in Social Work 32*

**Race, Culture and Ethnicity in Secure Psychiatric Practice**
**Working with Difference**
*Edited by Charles Kaye and Tony Lingiah*
ISBN 1 85302 696 4

**Housing Options for Disabled People**
*Edited by Ruth Bull*
ISBN 1 85302 454 6

**Welfare and Culture in Europe**
**Towards a New Paradigm in Social Policy**
*Edited by Prue Chamberlayne, Andrew Cooper,*
*Richard Freeman and Michael Rustin*
ISBN 1 85302 700 6

**Meeting the Needs of Ethnic Minority Children**
*Edited by Kedar N Dwivedi and Ved P Varma*
ISBN 1 85302 294 2

# 'Race', Housing
# and Social Exclusion

*Edited by*
*Peter Somerville and Andy Steele*

Jessica Kingsley Publishers
London and Philadelphia

First published in the United Kingdom in 2002 by
Jessica Kingsley Publishers Ltd,
116 Pentonville Road, London
N1 9JB, England
and
325 Chestnut Street,
Philadelphia PA 19106, USA.

*www.jkp.com*

© Copyright 2002 Jessica Kingsley Publishers Ltd

**Library of Congress Cataloging in Publication Data**
A CIP catalog record for this book is available from the Library of Congress

**British Library Cataloguing in Publication Data**
A CIP catalogue record for this book is available from the British Library

ISBN 1 85302 849 5

Printed and Bound in Great Britain by
Athenaeum Press, Gateshead, Tyne and Wear

# CONTENTS

*Theoretical considerations*

*Housing experiences + needs*

*This book is dedicated to the memory of Valerie Karn*

*Chapter 1*

# Introduction

## Peter Somerville and Andy Steele

Social exclusion is now a very popular theme in political and academic discourse. Recent books on the topic have included Room (1995), Jordan (1996), Levitas (1998), Oppenheim (1998), Madanipour, Cars and Allen (1998), Byrne (1999) and Somerville (2000). Specifically on housing and social exclusion, we have seen Spiers (1999), Anderson and Sim (2000) and a special issue of *Housing Studies* (1998). As is now well known, the salience of the term 'social exclusion' derives from its use within the European Union. Its origins, however, predate this policy development by a considerable period of time. As pointed out by Ratcliffe in Chapter 2 of this volume, the concept of exclusion has long been used in relation to racial discrimination. Apartheid in South Africa was arguably a form of social exclusion, and the Nazis practised exclusionary 'ethnic cleansing' long before this latter term was invented. What has happened in more recent years can be characterised, to some extent, as a 'de-racialisation' of the concept of social exclusion and its generalisation to a wide range of types of social relations. Whether or not this marks a theoretical and political improvement is a matter of debate. Most commentators appear to have concluded that the concept is useful for signalling the existence of a problem, or type of problem, but needs to be treated with caution when it comes to devising an adequate explanation of that problem.

Berghman (1995) identified the two distinctive elements of the concept of social exclusion as being its comprehensiveness and its dynamic character. 'Comprehensiveness' signifies that social exclusion operates in all areas of society, and 'dynamics' refers to the idea that exclusion implies a relationship between excluders and excluded which is being continually re-negotiated (as opposed to poverty which can be interpreted as a purely static property of poor people). The dynamic character of social exclusion has been explored by Weberian sociologists in the past (Parkin 1979) and is in the process of being rethought today in a variety of useful ways (Byrne 1999; Jordan 1996, 1998; Walker and Leisering 1998). The comprehensive nature of social exclusion, however, is problematic, mainly because of its inherent vagueness and ambiguity. For example, does it mean that similar dynamics of exclusion take place in employment, housing, education, health and so on and, if so, what exactly are these dynamics? Or does it mean that groups of people who are said to be socially excluded experience that exclusion in similar ways, that what they have in common as excluded groups is more important than what separates them? Or does it mean that any given excluded group will be excluded in a variety of respects, all of which have to be taken into account in order to understand and deal with the social exclusion as a whole? Or, finally, does it mean that the different ways in which people are socially excluded are all linked up together, and that these linkages need to be understood as a whole in order to solve the problem?

This book looks specifically at social exclusion in housing. It is not contended that the dynamics of housing exclusion are similar to those for other sets of social relationships. Indeed, one of the themes of the book is that exclusion in housing has characteristics that make it quite different from other spheres of social activity. The book also concentrates on issues of 'race'. Whilst explicitly recognising that members of certain racial and ethnic groups may also belong to other socially excluded groups, it is not argued that the basis of exclusion is necessarily similar in the different cases. For example, a black woman may experience social exclusion both as a woman and as a black person but this does not mean that the characteristics shared by sexism and racism are more important than what distinguishes them. The multi-dimensional character of social exclusion, however, by which is meant the tendency for socially excluded individuals to be excluded from a number of different life chances (housing, health, education, employment, leisure and so on) and on the basis of a number of different categories ('race', gender, class, 'ability', sexuality and so forth), is acknowledged in this book and attempts are made to show some of the connections between 'race' and housing and other social categories and types of life chances. The implications of these connections are taken up and discussed further in Chapter 17.

The book aims to provide an up-to-date picture of the evidence and debates on 'race' and housing and social exclusion, at least in Britain. The general approach is to explore the differential character of social exclusion as it affects different minority ethnic groups in different areas and to identify, wherever possible, the dynamics of this social exclusion. Although there is an attempt to clarify the state of theory in this area (Chapter 2), the book does not adopt a single clear theoretical perspective. There is, however, a common thread of theory running through most of the contributions and that has to do with the old dichotomy between 'choice' and 'constraint'. The general argument is that housing outcomes for minority ethnic groups are the product of 'constrained choices' on the part of individual households within these groups. One of the contributors, David Robinson, has expressed the purpose of the book in this regard thus: 'The challenge for research and policy is...to understand and address the processes through which discrimination constrains minority ethnic communities from expressing and satisfying their housing need' (Chapter 6, p.96).

The notion of constrained choice, however, is inevitably vague in the absence of both a theory of choice and a theory of constraints – it could, for example, be used to characterise the position of any individual in the housing market, regardless of colour or culture. There is a need to identify precisely the nature of the constraints (or 'choice/constraint' dynamics) which are responsible specifically for racial exclusion in housing, on top of the other constraints to which ethnic minorities may be subject. In Chapter 2 of this volume Ratcliffe suggests that these additional constraints include the following:

- the 'common sense knowledge' of ethnic preferences, and racist steering of ethnic choices, by housing market professionals
- the failure of the housing market to respond to cultural needs other than those of the rich and of the majoritarian nuclear family norm
- the effects of racial disadvantage in employment and education
- discrimination by state and housing agencies; for example, in urban renewal
- exclusion from certain residential areas ('White Highlands') due to racist harassment.

These constraints involve a powerful combination of subjective, institutional and structural racism (Ginsburg 1992) (see also Robinson in this volume) but the articulation of this combination varies not just from one ethnic group to another but from one individual to another within any particular ethnic group. Taking the dynamics of social exclusion seriously entails a rejection of the idea that racism is monolithic and affects different ethnic groups in the same way or even different individuals in the same way within a given ethnic group. A key purpose of the book is then to convey an impression of the differential character of these effects. Clearly, there can be no simple model of the dynamics of racial exclusion in housing, although this conclusion does not rule out the possibility of a variety of models applicable to different circumstances.

Ratcliffe, in Chapter 2 of this volume, makes an important distinction between inclusion and integration. Individuals may be socially included in the sense of not being subject to systematic discrimination or disadvantage but may choose to develop in their own way, within their own ethnic groups, and therefore not necessarily work with or live alongside members of other ethnic groups. The key point here, however, is that individuals should be capable of exercising such a choice: in other words, social inclusion in this sense requires empowerment (Somerville 1998). Social inclusion in the absence of empowerment – for example, where individuals do not have the choice over whether to be included or not – is no more than incorporation or assimilation into the dominant group. The approach taken in this book rejects this Durkheimian interpretation of social inclusion, while recognising that this is contested terrain (Levitas 1996). We would argue that, simply because it is a dynamic process, genuine social inclusion must involve change for the majority group or groups as well as for the minorities becoming included. For this reason, we would disagree with the claim made by Anderson and Sim (2000) that empowerment approaches represent an alternative to approaches based on social inclusion. To be sure, empowerment is not the same as inclusion but it is a pre-requisite for it.

Apart from Durkheimian functionalism, the other theoretical approach rejected by this book is that of essentialism, according to which individuals can be adequately categorised in terms of their membership of particular groups such as ethnic groups or social classes. Our view is that categories such as ethnicity, class, gender, disability and nation are socially constructed or 'imagined' (Anderson 1983) entities. To define people's characteristics and needs by reference to such categories is therefore to reify the social groupings concerned, reducing human diversity to the dried-up labels which are typical of 'race-thinking' (Husband 1982). If there is any general character to social exclusion at all, it consists precisely in the process whereby individuals are so labelled by more powerful others as a prelude to, and as a justification for, discriminating against them. Ironically, as a means of defence against such discrimination, individuals may well develop their own collective identities which can then, in turn, become oppressive of individuals, though this is not an issue explored in this book.

As Ratcliffe notes, none of the above argument should be taken to imply that we are necessarily in favour of taking a 'postmodern turn' in our understanding of social exclusion. Whilst acknowledging the utility of postmodernism for criticising essentialist assumptions, our argument is not that social categories such as 'race' or ethnicity are imaginary or arbitrary but rather that they are imagined and, consequently, socially real and patterned. An important theme in the book relates to the questioning of the 'banal nationalism' (Billig 1995) of the majority ethnic group. This emerges perhaps most clearly in the context of Northern Ireland (Chapter 15) where the legitimacy of that majority is most strongly challenged. The concept of 'ethno-nation' (Wallerstein 1979) has been invented in order to distinguish an ethnic group with a national identity within its country of residence from the minority ethnic groups which are the focus of this book and whose national aspirations, if any, lie outside the country in which they have settled. On the basis of this concept, it could be argued that the dynamics of racial exclusion relate to the conflict between a majority 'ethno-nation' and a set of minority ethnic groups. The inevitable consequence of such a conflict, given the overriding power of the majority group, must be either the assimilation or encapsulation (Crow and Allan 1994, p.81) of the minority groups. The discussion of Northern Ireland, however, suggests that the assumption of a relatively homogeneous dominant 'ethno-nation' may be at best simplistic and at worst a gross distortion of reality. Here the majority ethnic group does not appear to have a national identity at all while the largest minority ethnic group does.

In general, as with racism, nationalism is not monolithic but subject to substantial change over the course of time; for example, in response to the mass immigration of people who do not belong to the majority ethnic group. Because the latter group is itself typically extremely diverse, with a highly fluid sense of its own culture and identity, there is always potential for it to accommodate itself to newcomers rather than vice versa. The result can be an increasingly multi-cultural, multi-national and diversity-tolerant society. We hope that this book can make a small contribution towards this end.

## The structure of the book

After Ratcliffe's discussion of theoretical considerations in Chapter 2, the remainder of the book can be divided into three parts. The first part (Chapters 3–8) is concerned with the housing experiences and housing needs of black and minority ethnic (BME) groups in Britain in general and with how those needs are being met (or not met) and how they could be met by housing organisations. The second part (Chapters 9–13) deals with the housing experiences and aspirations of specific groups of people such as refugees and asylum seekers, BME women, young people and older people. This part also contains an important chapter on how black and minority ethnic groups might be involved and empowered. The third part (Chapters 14–16) provides comparable information about the housing conditions and experience of BME groups in specific locations in other countries such as Scotland, Northern Ireland and a number of other countries in the European Union.

In Chapter 3, Bowes and Sim provide an overview of housing conditions for different minority ethnic groups over the UK as a whole. They show in detail how a dialectic between 'choice' and 'constraint' determined the housing outcomes in different cities and in different tenures for groups as diverse as Chinese, Pakistanis, Indians and Black Caribbeans. Racist harassment is identified as a particularly important constraint but, in spite of this, there is evidence that better-off members of some groups such as Pakistanis have begun to move out of their inner-city enclaves. For lower-income households, however, conditions have barely improved and, in some cases, have got worse because of reduced support for marginal home-owners, continuing high unemployment, poor health, increasing incidence of racist harassment and continuing difficulties of access to good quality social rented accommodation in areas where black and minority ethnic people want to live.

The chapter by Gidley, Harrison and Tomlins (Chapter 4) reviews current understanding of housing need among BME groups. The authors acknowledge the increasing complexity in this area and, in particular, the growing diversity of preferences and circumstances within and between minority ethnic groups. They point out that, although 'choice' has become more differentiated, the constraints to which minority ethnic groups are subject, in terms of racism and lack of well-paid employment, have continued to affect all such groups. The authors report the findings of their own research on African/Caribbean, Chinese, Pakistani, Indian and Bangladeshi households in Sheffield, and on Vietnamese households in London. Although revealing considerable detailed evidence of poor housing conditions, the authors are cautious about using this evidence to draw conclusions about the nature and degree of need experienced by different minority ethnic groups and how exactly that need should be met. They do not feel, however, that the current lack of information should deter policy makers and housing providers from taking appropriate action on the basis of consultation with local BME communities and working in partnership with them. Two important points that they make are that the demand for culturally sensitive services implies a need for the involvement of (more) organisations run by minority ethnic people themselves; and that the common preference of minority ethnic households to continue living in the private sector requires a range of policy responses including care and repair, shared ownership and support for minority ethnic businesses and sub-contracting.

In Chapter 5, Phillips and Unsworth focus on the social rented sector and examine its role in meeting the needs of minority ethnic households. Traditionally, this sector has been conceptualised as a constraint upon such households (Henderson and Karn 1987) but the authors show how it can also be used to enhance housing choice. In essence, they provide a detailed illustration of specific barriers or constraints on minority ethnic choices in the housing market and how these can be removed. They review the history of official attempts to extend choice in this area and report on a recent survey of relevant local authority and housing association policy and practice. The findings are not very encouraging, with local authorities lacking political will and resources and housing associations continuing to stereotype black and minority ethnic housing demand as being confined to their original areas of settlement. On the positive side, however, practice in Bradford and by BME-led associations has shown the importance of 'ethnic clustering', involving the rehousing of networks of members of the same ethnic group rather than isolated individual households, for successful relocation outside of areas of established residence. It appears that local authorities are often aware of the need to cater for the locational aspirations of BME households but to meet such need can be problematic for them because of the resulting loss of population from inner-city areas, possibly undermining the authority's policies on urban regeneration. The chapter concludes with a number of suggestions and recommendations for helping to ensure that the locational preferences of minority ethnic households are met.

Robinson continues the focus on the social rented sector in Chapter 6. He is concerned to examine the nature of the system of constraints which is, at least in part, responsible for the disadvantaged position of minority ethnic groups in the housing market. Using Ginsburg's (1992) typology of subjective, institutional and structural racism, he shows how racism in housing has affected adversely, and continues to so affect, the life chances of minority ethnic households. Practices that have long been condemned and are often presumed to have been abandoned, such as word-of-mouth recruitment, continue to be widespread. Other forms of indirect discrimination, such as more restrictive allocations to homeless households (where minority ethnic households are more likely to be homeless) and the effects of racist harassment (limiting their locational choices) continue to be of major significance. In addition, aspects of structural racism such as the effects of the right to buy, the residualisation of council housing and the devaluation of housing need as a political issue, have exacerbated the position of many minority ethnic communities. The response to the problems of minority ethnic households by social housing providers such as local authorities and housing associations has been generally half-hearted, complacent, dilatory and minimalistic. Nevertheless, demand for social housing among minority ethnic households is increasing, and the response from mainstream housing organisations may, in some cases, be becoming more sensitive and more appropriate. Evidence for the latter comes from certain 'housing plus' initiatives and 'community lettings' types of approach, although these initiatives themselves are all too often the source of new forms of racist exclusion.

In Chapter 7, Harrison looks at the history and contribution of BME housing associations to meeting housing need and combating social exclusion. He provides an up-to-date assessment of the current funding position of these associations, their role within the housing association movement and their prospects for development in the future. He suggests a number of ways in which the activities of such associations could be expanded in order to provide a better service to minority ethnic households, including facilitating house renovation and owner-ship and meeting specialised housing and housing-related needs. He concludes that, although there are continuing severe constraints, especially financial constraints, on BME-led associations, reflecting a continuing reality of structural racism, there is still scope for grass-roots resistance and genuine community development.

The focus of Chapter 8 is specifically on BME employment in social housing organisations. Somerville, Steele and Sodhi show that, although the representation of BME groups in such organisations has improved considerably over the last ten years, they remain concentrated in the lowest level jobs, with hardly any at all in top positions except in the case of BME-led housing associations. The authors analyse the nature of the institutional racism that produces this situation, considering issues of core values, competence and managerial autonomy. They question common assumptions about what counts as good management and discuss current approaches to combat racism within employing organisations by changing their cultures. The authors report on their own research for the Housing Corporation, which was concerned with identifying the barriers to progress of BME staff within housing associations. They focus on key aspects of career progression such as recruitment and selection, promotion, training and staff development, and staff appraisal, and conclude that most mainstream registered social landlords (RSLs) fall well short of practice that could be regarded as fair to BME groups. Failure to recognise, let alone welcome, cultural diversity appears to be the most common fault within such organisations. The authors end their chapter by suggesting a number of courses of action that RSLs could take in order to remedy the situation, including a re-interpretation of Best Value principles so as to be directly applicable to racial equality objectives.

Chapters 9–13 concentrate on issues of housing and social exclusion as they relate to specific categories of BME people in specific circumstances. In Chapter 9, Gill emphasises the diversity of experience of BME women and is concerned to demonstrate how this diversity has been largely ignored by theoretical and political debates that have been dominated by white and male perspectives. Gill is particularly critical of much of the current discourse around social exclusion for its lack of recognition of the realities of racism, sexism and disablism. She takes up some of the key themes of earlier chapters in the book, such as structural and institutional racism and the differential patterns of 'constrained choices' among different BME groups, and uses these to explain why BME women are particularly disadvantaged. She shows how a variety of housing policies and practices have had, and continue to have, detrimental effects on women, especially lone mothers, and these effects have served to compound the disadvantage already suffered by BME women on account of their 'race' or ethnicity. She also stresses the inadequacy of our current knowledge and understanding of the experiences and needs of BME women and the need for further research in this area. She concludes with an assessment of how far the government's social exclusion agenda is likely to be able to meet their needs, arguing that area-based policies are not necessarily the best way forward here and that resources need to be targeted more explicitly on BME communities and on women in particular within those communities. She is most concerned that the government's commitment to 'traditional' family values will exacerbate the already severe exclusion of lone parents and their children and the problems experienced by women suffering domestic violence.

Young BME people are the focus of Chapter 10. Steele concentrates in particular on homelessness and reports on findings from his own research in Nottingham and Oxford. He notes how BME young people are far more likely than white youngsters to become homeless and he documents how services that have been set up to assist young homeless people too often fail to cater for the needs of those who come from BME communities. He cites examples of culturally insensitive decisions made by such services, stemming from 'colour-blindness' and lack of understanding. He points out that it is not just an issue of having too few BME staff within such organisations but also of services being managed and delivered in ways that are inappropriate for meeting the needs of BME young people. He describes a positive action befriending scheme that aims to address some of these needs and, while accepting that this scheme may be successful in its own terms, suggests that it is not an ideal solution to the problem. What is more importantly required, so he argues, is that mainstream services for young homeless people should change so as to become far more aware of young BME people's needs and how best to meet them. This is, after all, the option that most BME people themselves would prefer to see developed.

Patel and Patel consider the position of older Asian people in Chapter 11. The authors aim to let the elders speak for themselves as far as possible and this results in a chapter with a style that is rather different from the others in this book. The logic of the approach is that housing services should be determined by the elders themselves. The authors are at pains to emphasise the many obstacles that Asian elders have overcome in migrating to the UK and making a life for themselves in this country. This chapter is, in a sense, a celebration of their achievements. The changing character of Asian culture is discussed and, in particular, the ambivalence that many Asian elders feel towards this change. For example, the increased opportunities for their children bring with them the risk that those children may not be there for them if they are ever to need help on a long-term basis. The authors are critical of policy approaches which are based on the opinions of self-appointed 'community leaders' and argue for a more 'bottom-up' approach founded on working with Asian elders in their own cultural settings and building up, in an organic manner, organisations that are controlled by Asian elders themselves. They believe that this group has a rich diversity of experience and opinions that is not being taken into account in current policy and practice but also a good deal of experience in common in terms of the racism and disadvantage that they have historically encountered and resisted.

Chapter 12, by Gayle, also has a unique style, being concerned with the processes by which BME people gain influence and control over their housing conditions. He reviews current national policy in this area and describes the recent development of collective organisation among BME tenants and residents at national level. He points to the powerful obstacles that have prevented BME collective organisation over the years and suggests ways in which these obstacles may be overcome. He then links participation and empowerment with regional development and area regeneration and discusses the possible implications of these links for the future. The chapter concludes with a number of case studies that provide concrete illustrations of how BME people can empower themselves through participation in housing processes.

In Chapter 13, Pearl and Zetter examine the plight of refugees and asylum seekers. This could be regarded as an extreme product of social exclusion based on national or ethnic origins. Pearl and Zetter point out how access to housing is a key issue for this group and explain how government policy has failed to address their needs and exacerbated the exclusion to which they have already been subjected. The authors provide a detailed critique of the relevant legislation, in particular the Immigration and Asylum Act 1999, showing how measures such as the replacement of cash benefits by a voucher system, and the enforced dispersal of asylum applicants away from areas of high demand, will be neither fair nor effective in operation. They explain this ill-judged law as pandering to the racist prejudices of large sections of the British electorate, attempting to minimise government expenditure for those who are not British citizens, and deterring potential asylum seekers from applying in the future. They show that housing providers generally are not equipped to respond to the needs of this group and the result is likely to be a continuing failure to provide an effective and equitable response to the group's special needs. Ironically, this failure may be perceived as a success by racists and English nationalists if it leads to a decline in asylum applications.

Chapters 14–16 are devoted to a consideration of the housing needs and preferences of BME groups outside England, which is the main focus of all the other chapters. Chapter 14, for example, looks in particular at the housing conditions of Pakistani, Indian and Chinese households in inner Glasgow and, specifically, at those households living in 'Below Tolerable Standard' (BTS) accommodation. Kearns reports the findings of a recent survey by himself and Littlewood which shows that minority ethnic households in this area are far more likely than white households to be living in overcrowded conditions, to have lived in BTS housing for much longer, to have mobility-related housing needs, and to have problems in affording their housing costs. Kearns also cites evidence of BME households wanting to move outside of current areas of settlement and a readiness among some Pakistani households to move into social rented housing. He concludes that there is an opportunity here for housing associations in particular to provide suitable accommodation close to as well as within areas of BME residence in order to ease problems of overcrowding and enable new household formation. Currently, however, BME households in inner Glasgow have little or no knowledge of housing associations, and Scottish Homes' development strategy takes no account of their widening locational aspirations.

Chapter 15, by Mackay and Glackin, is concerned with the housing experiences of Travellers and Chinese in Northern Ireland. The chapter explains the different character of legislation and policy in the province as it affects minority ethnic groups. The authors point out that the Irish themselves are an ethnic minority within the UK and that Northern Ireland is deeply divided along ethnic lines, with an extraordinarily high degree of residential ethnic segregation. These realities serve to bring home to the typically unselfconscious English reader that the concept of an ethnic majority is a deeply problematic one. The record of the Northern Ireland Housing Executive, however, in pursuing consistently a non-discriminatory policy in housing allocation, has reinforced rather than reduced the level of segregation between the two main ethnic groups. In this context, it is hardly surprising that numerically far smaller ethnic groups, such as Irish Travellers and Chinese, should be regarded with outright intolerance and hostility and their needs almost universally ignored.

Van Kempen and Özüekren consider the housing experiences of minority ethnic groups in EU countries in Chapter 16. They point out that the numerically largest groups come from Mediterranean countries such as Turkey and Morocco and that numbers are increasing in most, but not all, countries. They argue that, since World War II, new immigrants have passed through three main stages: 'labour migration', coinciding with living in boarding houses and lodgings; 'family reunification', coinciding with a move to less desirable rented (and some-times owner-occupied) accommodation; and 'settlement', coinciding with an improvement in housing conditions by a diversity of means. Overcrowding con-tinues to be a widespread and serious problem for minority ethnic groups in all countries, though not as severe as it has been in the past. Housing quality gener-ally varies considerably from one country to another but, in every case, the condi-tions for minority ethnic groups are worse than those for the ethnic majority.

## References

Anderson, B. (1983) *Imagined Communities: Reflections on the Origin and Spread of Nationalism.* London: Verso.

Anderson, I. and Sim, D. (eds) (2000) *Social Exclusion and Housing: Context and Challenges.* Coventry: Chartered Institute of Housing.

Berghman, J. (1995) 'Social exclusion in Europe: Policy context and analytical framework.' In G. Room (ed) *Beyond the Threshold: The Measurement and Analysis of Social Exclusion.* Bristol: Policy Press.

Billig, M. (1995) *Banal Nationalism.* London: Sage.

Byrne, D. (1999) *Social Exclusion.* Buckingham: Open University Press.

Crow, G. and Allan, G. (1994) *Community Life: An Introduction to Local Social Relations.* Hemel Hempstead: Harvester Wheatsheaf.

Ginsburg, N. (1992) 'Racism and housing: Concepts and reality.' In A. Rattansi and R. Skellington (eds) *Racism and Antiracism.* London: Sage.

Henderson, J. and Karn, V. (1987) *Race, Class and State Housing: Inequality and the Allocation of Public Housing in Britain.* Aldershot: Gower.

*Housing Studies* (1998) 'Special issue: Housing and social exclusion.' *Housing Studies 13*, 6.

Husband, C. (ed) (1982) *'Race' in Britain.* London: Hutchinson.

Jordan, B. (1996) *A Theory of Poverty and Social Exclusion.* Cambridge: Polity Press.

Jordan, B. (1998) *The New Politics of Welfare: Social Justice in a Global Context.* London: Sage.

Levitas, R. (1996) 'The concept of social exclusion and the new Durkheimian hegemony.' *Critical Social Policy 16*, 1, 5–20.

Levitas, R. (1998) *The Inclusive Society? Social Exclusion and New Labour.* Basingstoke: Macmillan.

Madanipour, A., Cars, G. and Allen, J. (eds) (1998) *Social Exclusion in European Cities: Processes, Experiences and Responses.* London: Jessica Kingsley Publishers.

Oppenheim, C. (ed) (1998) *An Inclusive Society – Strategies for Tackling Poverty.* London: Institute for Public Policy Research.

Parkin, F. (1979) *Marxism and Class Theory: A Bourgeois Critique.* London: Tavistock.

Room, G. (ed) (1995) *Beyond the Threshold: The Measurement and Analysis of Social Exclusion.* Bristol: Policy Press.

Somerville, P. (1998) 'Empowerment through residence.' *Housing Studies 13*, 2, 233–257.

Somerville, P. (2000) *Social Relations and Social Exclusion.* London: Routledge.

Spiers, F. (ed) (1999) *Housing and Social Exclusion.* London: Jessica Kingsley Publishers.

Walker, R. and Leisering, L. (1998) 'New tools: Towards a dynamic science of modern society.' In L. Leisering and R. Walker (eds) *The Dynamics of Modern Society.* Bristol: Policy Press.

Wallerstein, I. (1979) *The Capitalist World-Economy.* Cambridge: Cambridge University Press.

*Chapter 2*

# Theorising Ethnic and 'Racial' Exclusion in Housing

### Peter Ratcliffe

*[handwritten: Social exclusion → Apartheid racism]*

## Introduction

Before entering the housing debate, it is important to examine the roots of the key concept of the current volume: social exclusion. Many of the prominent UK commentators in the field of 'race' and ethnicity have long used the idea of exclusion to refer to discriminatory forces and practices, and more broadly to racism(s) and racialisation processes (Banton 1983; Miles 1982, 1993). Enslavement, apartheid and other forms of rigid 'racial' segregation, such as 'Jim Crow' in the United States, have also been seen as forms of exclusion. For rather more obvious reasons, immigration controls and the treatment of refugees and asylum seekers have attracted the same 'label', or social construct (Bader 1997).

The concept attracted little general attention by social scientists, however, until it was co-opted by European Union policy makers and politicians in the early 1990s, and more recently (in 1997) by the UK government under Tony Blair. It now took on a very different guise. No longer was it a term referring to very specific processes: it now assumed a much broader, and distinctly more nebulous, guise. Indeed, in many ways it arguably developed into what was little more than a rhetorical gesture, a soundbite. As such, it threatened to blur the lines of theoretical debate and thereby, more significantly, to reduce the possibility of effective policy formulation.

Tony Blair established the Social Exclusion Unit (SEU) at Number 10 Downing Street and urged local authorities to develop policies to address 'social exclusion' in their patches. Tapping into the latter concerns, the University of

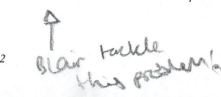
*[handwritten: Blair tackle this problem!]*

Warwick's Local Government Centre established, in 1999, a network of local authorities committed to tackling 'it'. The UK's premier funding body for the social sciences, the Economic and Social Research Council (ESRC), currently lists 'social inclusion and exclusion' as a thematic priority area and funds the new Centre for Analysis of Social Exclusion (CASE) at the London School of Economics.

Significantly, the latter development coincided with the termination of funding for the Centre for Research in Ethnic Relations (CRER), the only ESRC core-funded body focusing exclusively on matters of 'race' and ethnicity. The question is: does this matter? Are not the issues more effectively addressed in a more explicitly holistic way? This chapter will argue that they are, but that sociological perspectives on 'exclusionary processes' (and, importantly, exclusionary *states*) should be distinguished sharply from the political rhetoric. It argues further that an appreciation of these theoretical concerns demonstrates that policy-making requires a more nuanced approach than is currently evident.

## 'Social exclusion': Soundbite as universalising discourse?

The argument for a global, holistic approach to social inequality is clearly strong. After all, social divisions ostensibly grounded in 'race', ethnic/cultural, gender and class differences clearly intersect, and experiences of education and of the labour and housing markets are theoretically inter-related in significant ways. Our concern with the 'social exclusion' paradigm is not with its theoretical rationale, but with its contemporary manifestations in the political and policy-making spheres. 'Joined-up policy-making', so overtly espoused by Blair's government, is to be applauded. In practice, however, there appear as yet to be few signs of an overarching strategy behind the soundbites of 'on-message' politicians and 'spin-doctors'. Indeed, there is evidence of confused thinking and a lack of focus. In this respect, the UK government is not alone: much EU discourse suffers from the same problem. There are also significant signs of a lack of 'ideological break' from earlier (more conservative) philosophies, as will be demonstrated below.

The focal point of social exclusion in EU debates has tended to be labour market concerns, in particular unemployment levels (Levitas 1996; Madanipour, Cars and Allen 1998). In a very obvious way, those outside the formal economy are 'excluded' from the economic and social benefits which accrue from paid employment: it impacts on their 'social citizenship' status (Marshall 1950; Morris 1994). Arguably, however, the principal underlying concern is one of social control: hence the identification of those who appear to have rejected mainstream cultural values. So, the concerns are not so much about poverty *per se*, but about an alleged *culture* of poverty. These are the 'dangerous classes' referred to by Lydia Morris (1994). Importantly, they are more often than not the 'White Tribe' identified so effectively by Darcus Howe in the television documentary series of the same name (Howe 2000). Here, the massive increase in levels of CCTV surveillance was seen as the official response to both economic 'exclusion' and the loss of social identity of the (white) working class.

These examples illustrate a key problem with the dominant model of exclusion (in the UK context at least), namely, a tendency to pathologise (and therefore implicitly disempower) whole communities. In rather obvious ways, they are seen to *exclude themselves* from mainstream society, which (importantly for our present concerns) is the case for some minorities, although for different reasons – for example, because they wish to follow a different path culturally. Although rejected by the majority of left-of-centre politicians, Charles Murray's depiction of the 'New Victorians' (see Lister 1996) has had a major influence on UK debates about urban inequality (indeed more than would be admitted by the Blair administration). Murray's analysis of poverty problematises black culture and the black family by focusing, for example, on the incidence of female-headed households and the (alleged) lack of a paternal role model. It resurrects the pathologising, 'victim blaming' discourse outlined by Lawrence (1982).

It also intersects with debates about educational underachievement (highly disputed theoretical terrain – see, for example, Troyna 1988) and the relatively high school 'exclusion' rates of black males (Smith, Smith and Wright 1997), suggesting that both stem from a failure of effective socialisation combined, importantly, with a rejection of local social norms. These are seen as the central features of an 'underclass' – the 'self-excluded'. They are now joined in the eyes of many commentators by a new underclass, the 'Bangladeshis'. The publication of the results of the third PSI study (Jones 1993), showing the poor overall educational performance of this group, initiated an intense debate about the possibility of the creation of another 'dangerous (under)class' threatening the social stability of urban Britain. A contemporary television documentary, made by the BBC for its *Panorama* series and entitled 'Underclass in Purdah', laid the blame for the Bangladeshis' plight firmly at their own door. They 'left English society at the front door' of their homes, excluding themselves from it by virtue of their 'excessive' level of contact with the home country, with overseas trips, for example, hampering the education of their offspring.

What this evidences is a highly racialised terrain, with certain groups seen as choosing to opt out of crucial obligations associated with 'social citizenship'. In some accounts this is viewed as a spatial/territorial phenomenon relating to 'excluded neighbourhoods' (Gilroy 1996; Sibley 1995), in others it takes on a more localised interpretation relating to the incursion of the private into the public domain – as with the Bangladeshis (see also Rex 1996, pp.18–25). A parallel literature in the United States talks about the 'outcast ghetto' – the ghetto of the excluded (Marcuse 1996).

The key point to note here is that, at the hands of politicians and urban policy makers, all of these analyses have a universalising tendency: they stigmatise/stereotype whole communities. Crucially, they also fail to comprehend the intersection of ethnicity with other key aspects of social identity, most notably gender, class and wealth/economic position. But in an important sense, they obscure the 'race' issue as well. By suggesting that exclusion is at least partly a result of 'choice', external, structural forces and institutional factors are de-emphasised. As a consequence, policy makers can 'see' urban problems as universally rooted in poverty and life perspective. Arguably as a result of this, there is some evidence of a tendency in the UK to see social exclusion as a 'race'- or ethnicity-neutral problem: hence a reversion to 'colour-blind' policy solutions.

Exclusion is therefore seen as at least as much (perhaps even more) a white rather than a black phenomenon. Thus, educational 'exclusion' is tackled by *general* targets and league tables; schools and their management being held responsible for children failing to meet certain performance criteria. Success, as measured by a minimum of five GCSE passes at grades A to C, becomes the notional passport to future 'inclusion' in the labour market. The school, as the 'passport authority', recognises that class and poverty are important factors in a child's performance, but finds it increasingly difficult to argue its case with a government whose position is that some poor children succeed (therefore it is schools which fail the rest). Meanwhile, the sources of 'literal' exclusion (suspension and expulsion) are researched (Gillborn and Gipps 1996) but remain somewhat detached (in both theoretical and policy terms) from broader '*social* exclusion' discourse (Ratcliffe 1999a). Thus, joined-up policy-making in theory fails to result in joined-up policy in practice. The 'race' factor is, along with ethnicity and cultural difference, marginalised.

Widely varying educational and labour market experiences face those from different class and ethnic backgrounds. The same is true of housing market position (which is, of course, partially linked to success – or failure – in these other spheres). The question for this chapter is: how do we explain these differences? We address this question first by looking briefly at the empirical evidence (later chapters will cover this in more detail). What then follows is a review of the theoretical literature, pointing in particular to the obvious *lacunae*. But we begin by asking an apparently obvious, even trite, question. In what sense can we argue that 'race', ethnicity or cultural background influences housing position?

## 'Race', ethnicity and housing position

All the evidence points to wide disparities in housing position between the UK's white majority and minority communities. Successive English House Condition Surveys have pointed to disproportionately high levels of the latter groups (and particularly South Asians) in the worst properties. Confirmed by data from the 1991 Census of Population and numerous housing needs studies, overcrowding is also seen to be a serious problem amongst those identified as being of Pakistani or Bangladeshi origin (Ratcliffe 1997). Households of African (or Black) Caribbean origin are more likely to be found in social housing. With the exception of London-based Bangladeshis, South Asians on the other hand exhibit extremely high levels of home ownership (higher even than amongst whites). Of the latter 'groups' it is Indian households who fare better in terms of both housing quality and location. Pakistani households (and Bangladeshis living outside the metropolis) are disproportionately concentrated in run-down pre-1919 terraces in inner urban areas. Levels of concentration and segregation (from whites) are much higher for the South Asian groups (especially Pakistanis and Bangladeshis) than for Africans and African Caribbeans.

What are we to make of this? Is there something about being of African Caribbean origin which propels one to rent and/or is there something within South Asian culture which accounts for the extremely high propensity to own property? Is there a meaningful cultural or religious explanation for residential patterns? Surely, one might argue, all minority households are subject to similar structural constraints, i.e. exclusionary forces such as racism and discriminatory practices, therefore the explanation for differences must be located elsewhere, for example in mechanisms of choice? The answers are complex, invoking a number of different levels of argument.

We defer the discussions about choice and constraint to the next section, focusing here on the internal logic of the questions themselves. All the latter entail the reification of ethnic categories, and the summation of individuals/households into 'groups'. They then necessarily invoke essentialist explanations, for example, that there is something intrinsically 'Asian' or 'African Caribbean' about a particular approach to the housing market. Everyday, common-sense explanations do this routinely: housing professionals will tell you that South Asians prefer to buy property rather than rent (unlike African Caribbeans). Not only does the empirical evidence seem to confirm the theory, minority residents when interviewed will repeat the mantra. But, as argued by Carter and Green (1996), sociologists need to produce explanations that question these common-sense understandings.

They are correct in criticising the implied, crude causality in some of the social science literature of the 'race' and housing/education/employment/health/policing/etc. variety. They are also correct to point out the dangers of reifying 'ethnic group' categories that are part of (state) bureaucratic data gathering processes such as the decennial censuses. But, the *sociological* literature has long recognised these problems, and they fail to recognise that it is now social scientists who are in many ways responsible for driving the census agenda forward.

It is clear that the census categories do not reflect 'ethnicity' in any way that sociologists would acknowledge (Ratcliffe 1996a). The 'groups' so formed are in fact loose collectivities of people who have accepted a given label (out of a limited range of possibilities), have been allocated it by another member of the household, or have acquired it during the coding process (having defined themselves, or been defined, in some other fashion). There is in fact a fatal contradiction here. The point of the 'ethnic group' question is to assess the impact of exclusionary forces, or more specifically to assess the effectiveness of current anti-discrimination legislation, essentially the Race Relations Act 1976. It therefore asks for 'self-defined ethnicity' when the key issue has to do with *ascribed* identity: how respondents are 'seen' by others. Inevitably, therefore, use of the data in our analyses in a sense merely constitutes a heuristic solution to a fairly intractable problem.

Given that the resulting collectivities are inevitably heterogeneous, any conclusions referring to 'ethnic groups' need to be highly circumscribed. The addition of a question on religion in the 2001 Census (which has been the subject of recent research by the Office for National Statistics – Rainford 1997) may help to refine what is currently a fairly crude measure, but those looking for a sociologically sound fix on ethnicity will be disappointed. As we saw above, however, differences between the housing market location of existing 'groups' are clear: the question is what they tell us.

If we use ethnicity as the sole variable in the causal chain (thereby implicitly prioritising choice/agency) we are indeed lured into speculations about the meaning and significance of (say) home ownership to those of a particular heritage. What, for example, is it about 'Asian' culture, familial obligations or even religious traditions that result in a high value being put on ownership? Might it not have more to do with the social relations of production and distribution in the Indian sub-continent, knowledge of which migrants bring with them (thus illustrating the embeddedness of social relations in economic processes)?

The solution to the apparent riddle lies in the rejection of mono-causal explanations. Migrant populations have radically different wealth and class distributions, and different age/gender distributions. They also arrive at different times, settle in different parts of the country, and so on. Controlling (statistically) for a number of these factors suggests a number of weaknesses in explanations based on ethnicity alone. Peach and Byron (1993) show that, controlling for class and gender/household structure and property type, African Caribbean council tenants display at least as high a propensity to exercise their 'right to buy' (under the Housing Act 1980) as South Asians. Using the Sample of Anonymised Records (SARs) from the 1991 Census (1% of households), Ratcliffe (1997, pp.135–138) demonstrates that much of the variation in housing tenure between 'Black Caribbeans' and South Asians disappears if one controls simultaneously for social (occupational) class and household structure.

So as not to throw out the proverbial baby with the bath water, we would not wish to suggest that 'ethnicity', in whatever interpretation, plays *no* part in decisions about housing. That would be absurd. The point is simply that we should tread carefully, and avoid forms of essentialism that reify 'ethnic groups' and generate stereotyping narratives of housing market attitudes and behaviour. As implied above, it would also be naive to assume that household decisions/strategies are invariably effective in determining market position: they are clearly mediated by external exclusionary forces. And one of those exclusionary forces stems from the social reproduction of 'common-sense knowledge' of ethnic preferences by housing market professionals and fellow social scientists. This clearly implies that we need to look in more detail at the dynamics of the structure–agency dualism.

## Theorising 'racial'/ethnic exclusion in housing

The principal theme in the '"race" and housing' literature can be summarised very simply: the 'choice–constraints' debate. As there is a plethora of accounts in the literature (see, for example, Ratcliffe 1999b; Smith 1989, 1991) there is no need to develop the issue here in detail. Suffice it to say that the proponents of the 'constraints' school argue that the housing position of minorities results from a variety of external forces, mainly to do with the discriminatory behaviour of individuals and the actions/policies of housing market institutions and exchange professionals. Thus, structural constraints take theoretical primacy over individual choices. The latter are seen by the 'choice school', on the other hand, as having much greater efficacy than is recognised by those adopting the former perspective. Minority groups are seen as approaching the housing market in ways that satisfy particular needs, social obligations and aspirations. It is simply wrong, they would argue, to ignore culture, identity and agency at the level of individuals and/or households.

Many of the earlier accounts could be seen as placing far too little emphasis on issues of wealth, class and gender. It is obviously the case that the possession of capital and/or a high income means that housing choices can more easily be realised, irrespective of external constraints. There may nevertheless be other, sometimes less tangible, constraints in the form of concerns as to the wisdom of certain relocation plans. The safety of one's family (from racist harassment) is clearly a key element of the equation, even amongst relatively affluent migrants planning to move into 'white' suburbia (Basu 1997). Arguably, one of the principal weaknesses of the choice–constraints model, however, is that it provides an overly static form of explanation.

It was largely this reservation that led Sarre, Phillips and Skellington to investigate the applicability of Giddens' structuration theory (see Sarre *et al.* 1989) to this problem. The benefit of this new approach was seen to lie in its more dynamic and fluid treatment of the structure–agency dualism. In particular, it promised an analysis that reconceptualised the choice–constraint relation in the form of a dialectic. Structural features would feed through to, and impact upon, the realm of household decision-making, and aspects of the latter would in turn influence evolving structural forms. By way of an example, the sort of discriminatory behaviour exhibited by mainstream (invariably white-run) estate agents (described in the next section) might create a niche for minority entrepreneurs. The entry of these new professional 'actors' operating new 'rules', or codes of practice, *by definition* changes the institutional terrain facing potential minority customers, leading in turn to the possibility of changing spatial patterns. Subsequently, both the entry of new business competitors and the changing residential map can be expected to affect the ways in which mainstream exchange professionals and companies deal with clients of minority origin.

Both the choice–constraints and structuration approaches clearly invoke 'grand narratives' which rely on the presumed presence of structures within which actors undertake certain transactions, material/cultural or otherwise. The set of assumptions underlying this paradigm, however, has been challenged in the recent past by post-structuralism and the 'postmodern turn'. Although this has yet to make a direct impact on the 'race' and housing debate (or, for that matter, that concerning exclusionary processes), these ideas do have rather obvious implications not only for theory construction, but also for policy formulation in this area.

There is an important sense in which postmodern approaches intersect with the concerns of critical realists. Both begin by problematising the reification of 'ethnic groups' (or 'races') implicit in those analyses which fail to explore, or even question, the ontological status of ethnic categories. Both also question essentialist assumptions about (say) what it means to be 'Indian' or 'Muslim', and reject the implied fixity of social, cultural and religious norms. Where the postmodern accounts part company with those of the realists, however, is in rejecting overarching accounts of the global structural dynamics of discriminatory processes. They are not, of course, denying that exclusionary forces exist, they are simply questioning the idea that we can derive simple explanatory accounts based on the actions/experiences of putative 'groups'. Multiple identities are associated with a multiplicity of (changing and unpredictable) preferences and strategies resulting in action frameworks and transactional scenarios with unpredictable outcomes. The (relative) certainty of outcomes within structuralist accounts therefore dissolves into the realm of uncertainty and 'unknowability'. Critical realists, on the other hand, argue that it is possible to uncover underlying structural forces, so long as we delve beneath the veneer constituted by the world of appearances.

## Dimensions of exclusion in the housing sphere

Whatever theoretical approach one adopts, however, one thing is clear. The achievement of social citizenship rights in the housing sphere varies enormously in all contemporary Western societies. How we assess these 'variations' depends both on our interpretation of levels of rights and on how we 'slice' respective populations. We saw earlier that in the UK, working within the categorical schema of the 1991 Census of Population, certain patterns emerged. Different ways of slicing the minority population (and indeed of *defining the boundaries* of the 'minority' population) might produce somewhat different pictures, but evidence of exclusionary processes/practices permits a number of general substantive propositions, which might serve as a basis for assessing patterns of difference.

'Exclusion' can be seen as involving a number of distinct, but inter-related dimensions. For simplicity, we see these as threefold: cultural, material and spatial.

The first of these is probably the least recognised in the literature. Here, the *cultural* needs and aspirations of minority citizens are ignored or rejected. This is difficult, and also highly contested, terrain in that it is also an area where essentialism and 'ethnic managerialism' (Law 1996) are distinct dangers.

Simple points would be that the property market needs broadly to reflect cultural differences in the use of, and need for, space. The Western nuclear family model cannot be assumed as an appropriate basis for household projections, and thus expected demand in terms of property size and design. In fact, the recent growth in numbers of single-person households (Office for National Statistics 1999) means that it no longer 'works' even in relation to the majority population. A crucial point then emerges from a consideration of the most common cultural stereotype of 'Asian' communities. It is clear that the 'nuclear model' cannot be assumed as universally inapplicable to those, e.g. Muslims, who are routinely characterised as retaining, and wishing to retain (in perpetuity?), the extended/joint family system (Ratcliffe 1996b). This has implications for projections of property size requirements, and may also herald a need to rethink assumptions about other aspects of '(South) Asian' culture such as the need for separate social space for males and females, and the lack of (separate) housing provision for older people, and even young adults.

Further issues explored rather belatedly relate to Islamic attitudes to housing finance and welfare (Dwyer 2000; Hamzah and Harrison 2000). Closely related, then, to housing provision are such matters as planning and environmental health. This in many ways takes us far beyond the scope of the current chapter, but policy decisions here involve a variety of issues from the provision of separate institutional facilities (e.g. schools), to the control of noise pollution (especially noisy parties), the provision and siting of places of worship (including, importantly, appropriate space within offices, factories and prisons), and the investigation of minority-run businesses (perhaps especially food outlets). These raise difficult issues, which invariably invoke competing claims from various sections of citizenry to the maintenance of spatial integrity and socio-cultural autonomy in the use of space (CRE 1994).

*Material* inequalities in housing position arising from exclusionary processes are rather more obvious. However we divide the minority population, these groups are disproportionately concentrated in the poorer sectors of the housing stock: successive English House Condition Surveys amply attest to this point, as noted earlier. Part of the explanation, but only part, arises from poverty and (occupational) class position (themselves often a function of a myriad of exclusionary processes associated with educational provision and the labour market). Much more (of the explanation) lies in the initial/early treatment of those who came to Britain after World War II (as significant upward housing mobility implies the subsequent acquisition of substantial income/capital).

In the public sector, as is well known (Ratcliffe 1997; Smith 1989), residence requirements and the assessment of housekeeping standards denied access to good quality (or indeed *any*) accommodation and led to concentrations in low demand stock. Direct, and indirect, discrimination by individual landlords and estate agents restricted access to good quality private rented housing. The refusal to provide loan finance on the part of high street banks drove many into the hands of loan sharks and the fringe banking sector, who then typically imposed interest rates well above base rate and short repayment periods. Then, purchasers often suffered the additional burden of paying a 'colour tax' (Fenton 1977) for poor property as there was inflationary pressure at the cheaper end of the market simply due to the presence of these new buyers.

Once in poor property, and often saddled with large outgoings, there was little money to maintain the physical fabric of the property, this having an obvious impact on potential resale values and, importantly, on wealth transmission to successive generations (Ward 1982). Without substantial additional investment from the public purse, such houses would deteriorate inexorably from serious disrepair into unfitness (CRE 1994; Ratcliffe 1992, 1996b). Unfortunately, there is a significant and growing body of evidence to suggest that minorities have consistently failed to benefit from urban renewal policy since the 1960s.

The 'colour-blind' veneer of policy formulation has concealed a variety of discriminatory practices in service delivery. If renewal investment had gone to areas and properties truly on the basis of need, minorities would have benefited significantly. But, from the outset, racialised politics at a localised level ensured that this 'trickle down' process did not happen. Rex and Moore (1967) reported that black areas were excluded from clearance schemes in Birmingham in the 1960s because key actors in the local authority took the view that a white backlash might follow the rehousing of displaced blacks in new property. When clearance gave way to renewal under the Housing Act 1974, and poor areas were designated as Housing Action Areas (HAAs) or General Improvement Areas (GIAs), minority communities were now rightly included. Once again, however, this did not mean that they automatically benefited by inward investment.

Ratcliffe (1981) showed that few minority households knew that their house was in such an area, vital if they were to be in a position to acquire grants for renovation work. The employment of ethnic minority officers (EMOs) under Section 11 funding (from the 1966 Local Government Act) to act as a bridge between the local authority and these communities failed to result in the latter's empowerment for a number of reasons (Ratcliffe 1992). Decisions were taken concerning the prioritisation of work, which often left minority households at the end of the queue. Given finite funds, and the relatively short life of HAAs and GIAs, the end of the queue was often never reached. And, as anger surrounding the 'urban rebellions' in Handsworth in 1985 demonstrated, local people felt that their needs had been consistently ignored by the 'white bureaucracy' which governed the city. Not only had there been little evidence of meaningful improvement to the built environment, but also any work that was done involved outside (white) contractors and non-local labour. Thus, few of the benefits of investment had 'trickled down' to local people (West Midlands County Council 1986).

These concerns lead directly to the third strand in the exclusion debate, dealing with *spatial* issues. Strictly speaking, the debate begins with the 'exclusion' of intending migrants from the UK, and on the terms of entry for those who are not turned away. This, and the associated question of refugees and asylum seekers, will be addressed elsewhere in this volume. In the current context, suffice it to say that exclusion relates directly to the definition of 'the other' (Cohen 1994): those who do not (and could not) count as 'we', as British. These identity issues therefore clearly intersect with forms of cultural 'exclusion' alluded to above. Resettlement strategies seeking to minimise conflict surrounding absorption implicitly attach, or re-attach, cultural values to space and territory. These are frequently contested as majority society claims territorial rights and rejects the 'other': local authorities protect the interests of existing residents, and central government responds by dispersing migrants and their families irrespective of their wishes. Most recently, under the Asylum Act of 1993, housing rights are formally removed.

Spatial 'exclusion' is most commonly addressed in the literature as stemming from processes of 'racial' steering. Local authorities, via housing officers, subvert the project of 'housing choice' by suggesting to minority applicants those areas where they might settle best; for example, by living alongside those of a similar 'identity' (Henderson and Karn 1987). Exchange professionals in the private sector have been seen routinely to engage in similar behaviour in both the rental and owner-occupier markets. As we saw earlier, one way of subverting this process is for minorities to use alternative search strategies involving minority-run agents and financial institutions or 'word-of-mouth' information (Phillips and Karn 1992).

The latter processes do not necessarily by themselves lead to significant falls in levels of spatial segregation, but these are in any case nowhere (and for no 'groups') as high in the UK as they are routinely for African Americans in the United States (Peach and Rossiter 1996). There is, furthermore, continuing evidence of suburbanisation, and even ex-urbanisation, of some groups (Rees and Phillips 1996). This does not yet involve widespread incursion into the 'White Highlands', or into the hostile territory of the 'White Tribe' (Howe 2000). In most cases, it entails a modest expansion of the better-off middle classes into wards contiguous to those comprising the traditional settlement areas (Phillips and Karn 1992). The major reason for this is clear. To choose to relocate in a pre-dominantly white area would be to risk 'exclusion' in the form of racist harass-ment.

These very different, if inter-related, forms of 'exclusion', raise key questions for the remainder of this chapter, and the volume as a whole. To talk in general, global terms about 'exclusion' or 'exclusionary processes' clearly risks theoretical imprecision and, more importantly, ill-formulated policy responses to serious problems. We wish to contend that a more nuanced approach to policy formation needs to be followed; an approach which recognises the multi-dimensional and multi-faceted nature of 'exclusion'. So, how might policy address 'racial exclu-sion' in housing?

## The policy response to aspects of 'racial exclusion' in housing: Equal opportunities or managing diversity?

Combating these various aspects of exclusion will entail a number of quite distinct means; these in turn being associated with a series of rather different ends. One's approach in practice will therefore depend on

(a)   what one considers to be the (appropriate) obverse of exclusion

(b)   the underlying theoretical diagnosis of the forms and causes of 'exclusion'.

Combating exclusion via anti-discrimination law, for example, implies a concern with tackling those actions and processes that reduce housing options. The end in view is the generation of a housing market characterised by 'non-exclusion'. Although it creates a legal context within which (*theoretically* speaking) minority households may be 'included' as equals, it is not inclusionary *per se*. The latter would imply a more proactive policy strategy, taking into account the various dimensions of exclusion outlined in the previous section. Integration, which is often (wrongly) elided with inclusion, entails a very different social project once again. Taken literally, it would imply a political 'end', which may not accord with the wishes of minority communities. Those who believe in the positive virtue of integration, and this undoubtedly includes many, perhaps most, liberal social scientists in North America, are usually thinking about spatial integration. Although the stated aim is 'social integration' and the minimising of social conflict (and, laudably, recognises the fallacy of the doctrine of 'separate but equal'), it is nevertheless a highly value-laden approach. It ignores the possibility of a myriad of 'cultural projects' of minority communities, and is thereby potentially disempowering.

Most policy makers would probably espouse an approach that *in theory* recognises the highly diverse nature of contemporary societies, and acknowledges that citizens have certain (common and inalienable) rights that may nevertheless be interpreted and exercised in very different ways. In other words, people exercise social agency in ways that reflect different interpretations of needs and different aspirations. This is very much in accord with an explicitly *inclusivist* agenda. It implies respect for difference, and an acceptance of the idea that, subject to the fulfilment of certain basic social, moral and ethical obligations, people have the right to express a distinct identity, which may vary from the local norm. In the truly inclusive society, however, this overt espousal of 'otherness' would not be seen as a form of 'self-exclusion'.

The question is: how does one frame a policy blueprint that facilitates such an inclusivist agenda? In the past, the conventional answer has been to introduce Equal Opportunities Policies (EOPs). Here, the underlying assumption is that 'equal' does not imply 'the same'. So, it quite properly recognises that people entertain different agendas. In practice, however, it invariably does so by focusing on *group needs*. It is in this sense that policy formulation is contingent on theoretical position. The focus on group needs clearly points towards 'ethnic managerialism' (Law 1996), and the reification of social collectivities such as 'Indian', 'African Caribbean', and so on. Thus monitoring schemes, *when they are instituted*, tend to focus on the position and achievements of these 'groups' *vis-à-vis* the white majority population. The problems stemming from this essentialist position are all too obvious. One simply has to look at the term 'white' and reflect on the range of identities encompassed by this undifferentiated 'we'. Inherent weaknesses then become accentuated when reflecting on the policy implications of (simultaneously) recognising the salience of intersecting divisions such as class, gender, sexual orientation, disability, and so on.

It is precisely this dilemma that lures policy makers towards the 'postmodern turn'. Here, difference rules. A respect for the argument that essentialism is misguided both in imposing sameness on the different, and in fixing culture and ethnicity temporally, has led to a rejection of policies based on common identity (Mason forthcoming). The core of the problem is reflected in the Janus-faced character of Britain's 'ethnic group' question in the decennial census. This purports to measure self-defined identity, but appears to be more about categorising individuals by putative 'race' (by focusing on differences based on phenotype).

The key issue is that individuals are rarely discriminated against on the basis of their *self-identity*, but on their *ascribed identity*; that is, on how they are seen by others. It is this grand narrative of 'otherness' and perceived difference that results in the inequalities which monitoring and other measures seek to expose and then redress. It is vital, therefore, that an inclusivist strategy deals with the implications both of difference and of the external imposition of sameness.

## Concluding thoughts: Towards an inclusive housing policy

The evidence outlined in this chapter, and explored in more detail later in the volume, suggests major disparities in housing position between majority and minority sections of UK society, and between different sub-sections of the latter (irrespective of how these 'sub-sections' are conceived). But there is also considerable variation *within* ethnic groups/collectivities when (occupational) class and gender issues are considered (Modood *et al.* 1997; Ratcliffe 1997). Taking the 'broad brush approach', it is nevertheless the case that the relatively poor position of minorities (in terms of housing space, quality, type and location) is not simply a function of economics and class location. Nor is it primarily a matter of 'choice'. As has been argued above, structural constraints in the form of a variety of exclusionary processes have contributed, and continue to contribute, massively to housing outcomes.

So, what would constitute an inclusionary housing policy? The first step on a very difficult road would be to listen much more effectively than hitherto to the stated needs and aspirations of *all* sections of the community. Attitudes to different housing options are not static; nor are those of housing and planning professionals. We need a much more effective dialogue between consumers and providers. We need also to move beyond crude ethnic stereotypes which tell us, for example, that Asians prefer owner-occupation, value the maintenance of extended families, look after their elders, and like to cluster in certain urban locations; and that African Caribbeans look to social housing and retain a matri-focal family model. Cultural hybridity is after all part of a constantly shifting cultural map. The development of mixed tenure estates, shared ownership schemes, and the wider use of Housing Plus initiatives to make social housing more acceptable to a wider citizenry, as well as dealing with exclusionary practices, both overt and covert, would constitute a good start.

The overarching imposition of (however well-meaning) policies of (say) spatial integration is also a mistake, certainly in the absence of strong evidence to show that these are welcome to minority communities themselves. They may lead to ever-greater disempowerment, unless introduced as a part of a wider, and multi-faceted, strategy of consensual community development. And, as argued at the end of the previous section, policy makers need constantly to bear in mind the dual considerations of individual/household choice and the panoply of structural constraints restricting the efficacy of agency.

Finally, one should be constantly aware that housing is only part, if a very important part, of a much bigger picture. Strategies ensuring 'non-exclusion', or even 'inclusion', in housing market terms will ultimately have little effect without attention to broader exclusionary processes in education, work and other institutional areas.

## Note

1.    'Jim Crow' featured in a traditional minstrel song in the US. The phrase 'Jim Crow' was then applied to the rigid system of legal segregation in the Southern States.

## References

Bader, V. (ed) (1997) *Citizenship and Exclusion.* Basingstoke and London: Macmillan.

Banton, M. (1983) *Racial and Ethnic Competition.* Cambridge: Cambridge University Press.

Basu, D. (1997) 'Accounts of the experiences of "racial" harassment of middle class Asians.' Personal communication.

Carter, B. and Green, M. (1996) 'Naming difference: Race-thinking, common sense and sociology.' In C. Samson and N. South (eds) *The Social Construction of Social Policy: Methodologies, Racism, Citizenship and the Environment.* Basingstoke and London: Macmillan.

Cohen, R. (1994) *Frontiers of Identity: The British and the Others.* Harlow: Longman.

CRE (1994) *Environmental Health and Racial Equality.* London: Commission for Racial Equality.

Dwyer, P. (2000) 'British Muslims, Welfare Citizenship and Conditionality: Some Empirical Findings.' RAPP Research Working Paper 2. Leeds: Department of Sociology and Social Policy, University of Leeds.

Fenton, M. (1977) 'Asian Households in Owner Occupation: A Study of Patterns, Costs and Experiences of Households in Greater Manchester.' SSRC Working Papers on Ethnic Relations 2.

Gillborn, D. and Gipps, C. (1996) *Recent Research on the Achievements of Ethnic Minority Pupils.* London: HMSO.

Gilroy, R. (1996) 'Building routes to power: Lessons from Cruddas Park.' *Local Economy*, November, 248–258.

Hamzah, M. bin, and Harrison, M. (2000) 'Islamic Housing Values and Perspectives: Insights from Influentials in Malaysia.' RAPP Research Working Paper 1. Leeds: Department of Sociology and Social Policy, University of Leeds.

Henderson, J. and Karn, V. (1987) *Race, Class and State Housing: Inequality and the Allocation of Public Housing in Britain.* Aldershot: Gower.

Howe, D. (2000) *The White Tribe*. TV documentary series made by Channel Four, first screened in January 2000 (narrated and researched by Darcus Howe).

Jones, T. (1993) *Britain's Ethnic Minorities*. London: Policy Studies Institute.

Law, I. (1996) *Racism, Ethnicity and Social Policy*. Hemel Hempstead: Prentice Hall/Harvester Wheatsheaf.

Lawrence, E. (1982) 'In the abundance of water the fool is thirsty: The sociology of black pathology.' In Centre for Contemporary Cultural Studies (ed) *The Empire Strikes Back: Race and Racism in 70s Britain*. London: Hutchinson (now reprinted by Routledge).

Levitas, R. (1996) 'The concept of social exclusion and the new Durkheimian orthodoxy.' *Critical Social Policy 46*, 16, 5–20.

Lister, R. (ed) (1996) *Charles Murray and the Underclass: The Developing Debate*. London: Institute of Economic Affairs.

Madanipour, A., Cars, G. and Allen, J. (1998) *Social Exclusion in European Cities: Processes, Experiences and Responses*. London: Jessica Kingsley Publishers.

Marcuse, P. (1996) 'Space and race in the post-Fordist city: The outcast ghetto and advanced homelessness in the United States today.' In E. Mingione (ed) *Urban Poverty and the Underclass: A Reader*. Oxford: Blackwell.

Marshall, T.H. (1950) *Citizenship and Social Class and Other Essays*. Cambridge: Cambridge University Press.

Mason, D. (forthcoming) 'Equality, opportunity and difference: the limits of the diversity paradigm.' In E. Beitenbach, A. Brown, F. Mackay and J. Webb (eds) *Gender Equality and the New Politics*. Basingstoke: Macmillan.

Miles, R. (1982) *Racism and Migrant Labour*. London: Routledge and Kegan Paul.

Miles, R. (1993) *Racism after 'Race Relations'*. London: Routledge.

Modood, T., Berthoud, R., Lakey, J., Nazroo, J., Virdee, S., Smith, P. and Beishon, S. (1997) *Ethnic Minorities in Britain: Diversity and Disadvantage*. London: Policy Studies Institute.

Morris, L. (1994) *Dangerous Classes: The Underclass and Social Citizenship*. London: Routledge.

Office for National Statistics (1999) *Social Trends*. London: The Stationery Office.

Peach, C. and Byron, M. (1993) 'Caribbean tenants in council housing: "Race", class and gender.' *New Community 19*, 3, 407–423.

Peach, C. and Rossiter, D. (1996) 'Level and nature of spatial concentration and segregation of minority ethnic populations in Great Britain, 1991.' In P. Ratcliffe (ed) *Social Geography and Ethnicity in Britain: Geographical Spread, Spatial Concentration and Internal Migration (Ethnicity in the 1991 Census, Volume 3)*. London: The Stationery Office.

Phillips, D. and Karn, V. (1992) 'Race and housing in a property owning democracy.' *New Community 18*, 3, 355–369.

Rainford, L. (1997) *2001 Census Testing Programme: Report on the Ethnic Group and Religion Question Test Carried Out in March 1997*. Unpublished. London: Office for National Statistics (Social Survey Division).

Ratcliffe, P. (1981) *Racism and Reaction: A Profile of Handsworth*. London: Routledge and Kegan Paul.

Ratcliffe, P. (1992) 'Renewal, regeneration and "race": issues in urban policy.' *New Community 18*, 3, 387–400.

Ratcliffe, P. (1996a) 'Social geography and ethnicity: A theoretical, conceptual and substantive overview.' In P. Ratcliffe (ed) *Social Geography and Ethnicity in Britain: Geographical Spread, Spatial Concentration and Internal Migration (Ethnicity in the 1991 Census, Volume 3)*. London: The Stationery Office.

Ratcliffe, P. (1996b) *'Race' and Housing in Bradford: Addressing the Needs of the South Asian, African and Caribbean Communities*. Bradford: Bradford Housing Forum.

Ratcliffe, P. (1997) '"Race", ethnicity and housing differentials in Britain.' In V. Karn (ed) *Employment, Education and Housing Among the Ethnic Minority Population of Britain (Ethnicity in the 1991 Census, Volume 4)*. London: The Stationery Office.

Ratcliffe, P. (1999a) '"Race", education and the discourse of 'exclusion': A critical research note.' *Race, Ethnicity and Education 2*, 1, 149–155.

Ratcliffe, P. (1999b) 'Housing inequality and "race": Some critical reflections on the concept of "social exclusion".' *Ethnic and Racial Studies 22*, 1, 1–22.

Rees, P. and Phillips, D. (1996) 'Geographical spread: The national picture.' In P. Ratcliffe (ed) *Social Geography and Ethnicity in Britain: Geographical Spread, Spatial Concentration and Internal Migration (Ethnicity in the 1991 Census, Volume 3)*. London: The Stationery Office.

Rex, J. (1996) *Ethnic Minorities in the Modern Nation State: Working Papers in the Theory of Multi-Culturalism and Political Integration.* Basingstoke and London: Macmillan.

Rex, J. and Moore, R. (1967) *Race, Community and Conflict: A Study of Sparkbrook.* London: IRR/Oxford University Press.

Sarre, P., Phillips, D. and Skellington, R. (1989) *Ethnic Minority Housing: Explanations and Policies.* Aldershot: Avebury.

Sibley, D. (1995) *Geographies of Exclusion: Society and Difference in the West.* London: Routledge.

Smith, G., Smith, T. and Wright, G. (1997) 'Poverty and schooling: Choice, diversity or division?' In A. Walker and C. Walker (eds) *Britain Divided: The Growth of Social Exclusion in the 1980s and 1990s.* London: Child Poverty Action Group.

Smith, S.J. (1989) *The Politics of 'Race' and Residence: Citizenship, Segregation and White Supremacy in Britain.* Cambridge: Polity Press.

Smith, S.J. (1991) '"Race" and Housing in Britain.' Paper prepared for the Joseph Rowntree Foundation 'Race' and Housing Workshop, University of York, 4–5 April.

Troyna, B. (1988) 'Paradigm regained: A critique of "cultural deficit" perspectives in contemporary educational research.' *Comparative Education 24*, 3, 273–283.

Ward, R. (1982) 'Race and Residence in Britain: Approaches to Differential Treatment in Housing.' Monographs in Ethnic Relations 2. Birmingham: Research Unit on Ethnic Relations, University of Aston.

West Midlands County Council (1986) *A Different Reality: An Account of Black People's Experiences and their Grievances Before and After the Handsworth Rebellions of September 1985.* Birmingham: WMCC.

*Chapter 3*

# Patterns of Residential Settlement among Black and Minority Ethnic Groups

## Alison Bowes and Duncan Sim

## Introduction

Patterns of black and minority ethnic (BME) settlement in the UK show significant concentrations in certain towns and cities and in certain parts of the country.
Within those locations, there are further concentrations in particular areas, and
the patterns created appear to be far from random. There would therefore appear
to be distinctive factors involved in the residential choices made by minorities
that may be different from the majority, 'white', population. This chapter
examines these patterns of residential settlement, focusing especially on the
decision-making processes of households. In particular, there is a focus on the
ways in which the patterns reflect the impact of external constraints on the preferences of the individual actors concerned.

There is considerable research which suggests that housing preferences and
strategies are largely irrelevant for disadvantaged groups in society, such as BME
groups, whose housing is often determined by forces outside their control. For
example, local authority housing has been allocated in a discriminatory way
(CRE 1989; Henderson and Karn 1987), building societies and estate agents
have been shown to exhibit racist procedures (Cater 1981; CRE 1988, 1990),
and housing association policies have been criticised (CRE 1993; Dalton and
Daghlian 1989). Such findings have questioned earlier work, such as Dahya
(1974) and Werbner (1979), which suggested that the housing patterns of South
Asians were the result of choice based on cultural preferences, a position which
appears to stereotype South Asians. Ballard (1992), on the other hand, has
attacked the determinism of approaches that have portrayed Britain's BME popu-

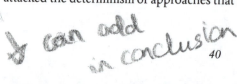

*can add*
*in conclusion*

lation as pawns, unable to resist the forces that control their lives. While we must accept that there are considerable limitations on housing choice, we recognise, with Sarre, Phillips and Skellington (1989), Ballard (1992) and Peach (1998), the importance of the role played by individual householders as a vital component influencing life-style and life chances.

The issue of choice and the existence of barriers to freedom of choice in housing has long been a matter of concern in the US. Some of the earlier studies of why families move allow us to draw inferences about how they approach it and the strategies adopted, but one of the most influential pieces of work (Rossi 1955) deliberately avoided the complexities confronting minority ethnic households and none was interviewed.

American research has also focused on institutional barriers to access, particularly regarding black families seeking to move into so-called 'white' areas. Much of this research, however, has examined the institutions rather than the families concerned, for example Biochel et al. (1969), who interviewed realtors in Pittsburgh. A contemporary study by Denton (1970) interviewed apartment owners in an attempt to explore their attitudes to letting to black tenants. There is also a literature in the US that has examined issues of racial segregation within the housing market (Taeuber 1983).

In the US, as in the UK, researchers have now begun to explore the housing problems of minority ethnic families with reference to the families themselves. An important study by Leavitt and Saegert (1990), for example, focused on black families in Harlem who had bought apartments cheaply from the city council. Interviews were conducted with the households themselves, in which they were encouraged to describe their housing histories.

Such qualitative work, which focuses on action by the householders themselves, is an important missing element in much minority ethnic research. We would argue, like Sarre et al. (1989), Leavitt and Saegert (1990), Ratcliffe (1998) and Peach (1998), that this omission means that the realisation (or otherwise) of preferences, the consequences of various actions for success and failure, and the cumulative results of actions in facilitating or restricting choice, have not been fully understood.

Fenton (1999) argues that, in many societies, ethnic differences may be linked to ideologies about racial superiority or inferiority, and racism may result, associated with 'political domination and economic exploitation' (p.69). Ethnicity and social exclusion can therefore be linked and research on minority ethnic housing has produced much evidence of this. Ethnicity may be an important factor in influencing choice in that people may express particular cultural preferences. Alternatively, stigmatisation of and discrimination and racism towards minority groups may be key constraining factors in housing choice, as harassment in particular areas may deter people from living there.

This chapter examines the settlement patterns of minority ethnic groups within the UK and seeks to explain them in terms of the choices available to minority households and the constraints that they encounter. The chapter focuses on employment and housing tenure, which form the basis of constrained choice, before discussing some key issues, including harassment, finance and the availability of houses of differing types and quality. Factors influencing the choices that households seek to make, such as household structure and personal circumstances, are also covered. Thus, the influence of choice, the operation of constraints and the ways in which households deal with such constraints demonstrate the interactions between household preference, housing provision and the exclusionary processes involved. Our analytical focus is on social actor agency within structural constraints. Phillips and Karn (1992) and Peach (1998) have noted that, though more structurally focused and more culturally focused explanations for minority ethnic housing patterns and experiences have competed with one another, recent work has increasingly acknowledged that minority ethnic groups face a range of structural constraints and opportunities, some of which may be culturally based, and that research needs to demonstrate how these operate for individuals and households.

## Existing patterns of black and minority ethnic settlement

Black and minority ethnic settlement[1] has a long history in Britain, with the earliest settlement clusters tending to be in major ports, such as London, Liverpool, Cardiff and Bristol. Generally speaking, however, the main influx of minority ethnic settlers came after World War II and this has produced a quite distinctive geography. As Phillips (1998) has described, regional concentrations emerged, particularly in the larger metropolitan areas such as London and the West Midlands, but also in smaller industrial towns in the East Midlands and the north west of England, often allied to the textile industry:

> This uneven distribution mirrored the restricted range of employment opportunities open to the migrants upon arrival and was subsequently reinforced by chain migration, which gave rise to clusters of immigrants of similar local and regional origins. At the local level, a pattern of inner-city clustering, overcrowding and housing deprivation was reproduced throughout most of the immigrant reception centres. (Phillips 1998, p.1683)

The most comprehensive data on the current patterns of settlement are those derived from the 1991 Census. The highest concentrations of minority ethnic people in the UK are in the metropolitan areas, particularly in industrial areas and south east England. Thus, 20.2 per cent of the population of Greater London and 14.6 per cent of the West Midlands is minority ethnic, compared to the British average of 5.5 per cent (Owen 1992). The lowest concentration is in the north of England (1.2% of the total).

Different minority groups are often concentrated in quite distinct geographical locations. The Black Africans and Black Caribbeans tend to be over-represented in London and the West Midlands and under-represented elsewhere. There are also concentrations of Black Caribbeans in Bristol, Nottingham, Manchester and Leeds, and of Black Africans in Cardiff, Liverpool, Manchester, Leeds and Sheffield.

Of the South Asian groups, the Indians have their highest concentration in London, while there are significant concentrations in both the West and East Midlands and a smaller presence in north west England. The largest single district population is in Leicester. The Bangladeshis are highly concentrated in London, with 44 per cent of all Bangladeshis living in inner London alone. There are smaller groupings in Birmingham, Oldham, Luton, Bradford and Sandwell (Rees and Phillips 1996).

The Pakistani population is much more widely spread. The largest communities are in the West Midlands and West Yorkshire, while there is also a significant Pakistani presence in Manchester and the north west of England, South Yorkshire, Glasgow, Luton and Slough, as well as London. To a large extent, this is connected with the distribution of the textile industry, where many Pakistani families initially secured employment.

The Chinese, like the Bangladeshis, are concentrated in London but are also spread across the country, with a significant presence in Liverpool, Birmingham, Manchester and Glasgow. This may reflect their involvement in the catering industry, with its wide dispersal of establishments (Bailey, Bowes and Sim 1994; Rees and Phillips 1996).

While it may be inadvisable to generalise about settlement patterns involving such disparate ethnic groups, nevertheless there does seem to be significant clustering in declining industrial centres, where the worst economic and social conditions occur. There is also clustering in central London and in affluent commuter towns – often in the south east – where some job opportunities have occurred. Owen (1995) suggests that there is a clear pattern of relative exclusion of minority ethnic groups from the successful parts of the British economy, where growth is mainly occurring, and a tendency for concentrations in areas of decline. Modood (1997), however, emphasises that the situation is not clear-cut and varies across ethnic groups.

The 1998 estimates of the minority ethnic population show little change in patterns of concentration from 1991 and Schuman (1999) has sought to explain the persistence of such concentrations in terms of the 'choice' and 'constraint' theories. He summarises these by pointing out that the

choice theory argues that ethnic minorities may prefer to live within concentrations of their own group, for reasons of social support, and shared linguistic, cultural and religious traditions. The constraint theory argues that ethnic minority groups have often been prevented from moving outside certain geographical areas by their economic position, by lack of information about housing opportunities elsewhere, and by discrimination or fear of discrimination. (Schuman 1999, p.36)

Both theories suggest that the settlement patterns of minority ethnic groups are characterised by a degree of immobility, and this is as likely to apply to population patterns within towns and cities as between them. Thus, as well as being located in particular types of towns, minorities are often concentrated in particular areas within those towns. This chapter, through interviews with minority ethnic households, explores the extent to which these households felt they were exercising a 'choice' over their housing and expressing a positive locational preference, and the extent to which households saw themselves as 'constrained' in terms of the housing which they felt was actually available to them. The views of households are then interpreted and discussed in the context of wider patterns and policies.

## The basis of constrained choice

Patterns of housing inequality have their origins in the period following World War II and the arrival in the UK of black migrant labour in substantial numbers. Rex and Moore (1967) painted a bleak picture of the housing then occupied by BME households and the sometimes open discrimination practised by private landlords. There was, however, a belief that such inequalities were due to the newcomer status of the incoming population and that household circumstances would improve with increasing assimilation (Patterson 1965). To an extent, this has happened but there is considerable variation between different minority groups. Black Africans and Caribbeans appear to have been successful in accessing social rented housing while many Indian households appear to have moved into relatively good quality owner-occupied housing. Other South Asian groups remain located in the inner city, however, and have moved relatively little over the last forty years or so.

## Employment and housing

The settlement pattern of minorities remains closely linked to the employment opportunities available at different points during the post-war period. In the 1950s, large numbers of South Asian migrants found employment in the textile industries of Lancashire and Yorkshire, as well as in more isolated cities like Dundee where the jute trade had given the city a direct link with India. In some places, where there was a quantifiable labour shortage in particular employment sectors, recruitment campaigns in Commonwealth countries encouraged people to move to the UK. Many doctors and nurses entered the health service in this way; while in cities like Glasgow, South Asians were encouraged to fill vacancies in public services, notably on trams and buses. Later, in the 1960s, job opportunities in expanding industries such as motor manufacturing led to new concentrations of minorities in towns like Luton (Goldthorpe *et al.* 1969).

In some instances, minority ethnic households have become self-employed, often in retailing or catering, and there is a noticeable concentration of Chinese households in catering, for example (Baxter and Raw 1988). As the size of the minority ethnic population has increased, however, it has not been possible for all the younger members of the minority communities to obtain employment in family businesses. Combined with a decline in industries such as textiles, this has led to high levels of unemployment and Phillips (1998), for example, shows how unemployment levels among younger, British-born, Pakistanis and Caribbeans have reached extremely high levels. Thus many black people are at greater risk of poverty and unemployment than white people and levels of exclusion are greater. Many minority families are becoming trapped in areas of economic decline.

Amongst the self-employed, there have been severe economic problems. Bowes, Dar and Sim (1998) discovered that a number of Pakistani households in their study had experienced repossession of their home. In nearly all of these cases, the loss of the house was linked with business failure, where the house had been used as security for business loans: when the business failed, the family became homeless. Third, Wainwright and Pawson (1997), in a study for Scottish Homes, concluded, first, that minority ethnic households had larger monthly mortgage repayments than white households and, second, that those in paid employment found it easier than those in self-employment to meet their repayments. Thus minority ethnic households with their own businesses were particularly likely to have mortgage arrears.

The one minority group that appears to be doing relatively well economically are the Indians and Robinson (1988) has drawn attention to the expanding Indian middle class. Many are employed in the professions and a number have moved into suburban detached and semi-detached housing, in contrast to other South Asian groups who are still largely located in inner cities.

### Housing tenure

The tenure pattern of minority ethnic groups varies considerably. Data from the 1991 Census show that the Black Caribbean population, together with the Bangladeshis, have a higher representation within the social rented sector (43–50% of the groups concerned). In contrast, only 10 per cent of Indians and 12 per cent of Pakistanis are in these tenure categories (Ratcliffe 1997). There are also regional variations. Dorling (1997) shows, for example, that in Glasgow, Indian and Chinese households are substantially over-represented in owner-occupation, whereas they, together with the Black African and 'Other-Other' groups, are under-represented in council renting. In some of the London boroughs, the situation is reversed with greater over-representation in local authority housing and under-representation in the private sector. It is important, therefore, to avoid tenure stereotyping, as the tenures occupied by minorities will be as varied as the majority, white, population.

These variations in the tenure patterns of the different minority groups raise certain questions. While minorities may have successfully gained access to social rented housing, have they done so on terms of equality with the majority population and is their housing therefore of reasonable quality? Where minorities are occupying accommodation, either rented or owned, in the private sector, does this result from a positive decision to do so, or is it due to difficulties in gaining access to alternative tenures such as social renting? Does the tenure pattern of minorities therefore reflect constraints in the housing system?

There is research that shows that those groups who do achieve access to social rented housing do not in fact achieve access to the full range of property types. Henderson and Karn's (1987) work in Birmingham, for example, showed that West Indians tended to receive older housing, were more likely to be offered flats and had their area preferences met less often than white applicants. The situation was exacerbated by the transfer system and the cumulative effect was the production of an entrenched pattern of racial inequality and growing segregation.

Similar studies in Tower Hamlets (Phillips 1986) and Nottingham (Simpson 1981), and in local authorities investigated by the Commission for Racial Equality (CRE) such as Liverpool (CRE 1989), have all suggested that housing allocations were discriminatory (see Robinson in Chapter 6 of this volume).

Although knowledge of social rented housing is still sometimes sketchy and confused, there is evidence that minority ethnic groups increasingly see it as a tenure of choice. In a study of Pakistani housing careers, Bowes *et al.* (1998) discovered that half of their sample had at some point applied for council housing – yet Pakistanis have traditionally been regarded as having an overwhelming preference for home ownership. Ratcliffe (1996) obtained similar results in Bradford, where Pakistanis increasingly expected to move into social renting. That the rate of application is not reflected in actual Pakistani tenancies suggests, *inter alia*, that when offers of accommodation have been made, they have been regarded as unsuitable.

The ability of local authorities to house minorities has been affected by the right-to-buy, with larger, good quality housing being amongst the most likely to be sold. The residualisation of the stock has led to most allocations now being made in less popular estates, where minorities may feel isolated. Perhaps as a result, many minority households have begun to turn towards the housing associations, many of which are smaller than local authorities and operate in areas where minorities wish to live (Harrison and Law 1997). They seem therefore to be viewed as being more sensitive to minority ethnic needs, particularly the BME associations, which are now significant landlords in many areas (Cabinet Office 2000). The 1991 Census showed that 3.1 per cent of the population as a whole was housed in the housing association sector but, for minorities, the figure rose to 5.3 per cent (Owen 1992). By the mid-1990s, Housing Corporation data suggest that lettings to minorities in England had risen to around 11 per cent although, in Scotland, the proportion has fallen.

South Asian groups are located primarily in owner-occupied housing but much of it is in poor condition (Ballard 1996; Ratcliffe 1996). The 1991 Census showed that Pakistani and Bangladeshi owners in England tended to be concentrated in terraced housing, and were more likely than other owners to lack central heating, bathrooms and inside toilets. Pakistanis and Bangladeshis had particularly low incomes, so those who did enter owner-occupation were doing so at the lower end of the market. In contrast, Indians and African Asians appeared to be in a better position, and were as likely as white people to occupy detached or semi-detached houses (Lakey 1997).

It is unclear to what extent groups like the Pakistanis have 'chosen' to locate in relatively poorer quality housing. It is certainly true that some households have 'chosen' to live in the inner city, but this may be due to experiences of harassment elsewhere and an inability to access alternative, suitable housing. Living in poor housing is unlikely to be a positive choice and Ratcliffe (1996) and Third *et al.* (1997), among others, demonstrate that the widely held belief that South Asians prefer home ownership is not necessarily true and many are reluctant owner-occupiers. Choice of tenure is influenced by the constraints imposed in regard to other tenures as well as by the more positive attributes of owning.

## Emerging constraints

The process of minority ethnic decision-making in respect of housing appears to be one of complexity, operating at quite distinct levels. Issues such as employment and the availability of housing of different tenures influence the general choice of location, in regard to town or neighbourhood. But the choice of a specific house is subject to various constraints such as safety and the fear of harassment, the availability of finance and issues of house type. In taking these factors into account, it appears that minority ethnic households are exercising considerable care in their choice of house – to an extent which households from the majority white population would probably find less necessary. This section therefore considers the influence of these specific constraints.

### Harassment

Racial harassment can take many forms, from simple name-calling or the daubing of graffiti to personal attacks and life-threatening incidents such as arson. It can occur in any location but seems to be prevalent where minority ethnic families are fairly isolated, for example on peripheral housing estates; in the inner city, there may be 'safety in numbers'.

The experience or fear of harassment and the perception of some areas as unsafe leads many minority ethnic households to refuse offers of housing in these localities. Indeed, Bowes, Dar and Sim (1997) suggested that a number of minority households indulged in trade-offs between particular areas and particular houses or in some cases, between different tenures. They interviewed Pakistani households who had given up secure tenancies in the social rented sector and moved to overcrowded privately rented property, simply in order to feel safe. Similarly, Sarre *et al.* (1989) found a general reluctance by minorities to move to certain suburban areas, even though the housing was of high quality, because of incidences of racial harassment in those areas.

Shaw (1988) has also suggested that minority households indulge in trade-offs. She suggests that the characteristics of certain houses, such as size, are extremely important in decisions about accommodation, but perhaps more important was the fear of racism and harassment if the family moved from a familiar area. Racist incidents, she found, led to households opting for safe areas in preference to more appropriately sized housing. Thus many minority households are denied the range of housing opportunities afforded to white households and are forced into certain housing strategies that reflect this.

Many social landlords have traditionally allocated houses on a 'colour-blind' basis. Such policies are perhaps understandable historically, but are based on spurious assumptions of cultural homogeneity and take insufficient account of the diversity of housing needs. Such policies have led to black families being offered houses on predominantly white estates, where they become isolated. Research by Love and Kirby for the Department of the Environment (1994) drew attention to the need, not only to tackle harassment when it occurred, but also for preventative measures in relation to racial violence and harassment. Such measures could range from community development work such as the encouragement of residents' and tenants' associations, to improvements in the design of estates to prevent crime. They suggested that communication of the landlord's policies to tenants and other residents, and campaigns to educate and raise awareness, also had a role to play.

Bradford provides a useful example of a local authority where proactive, preventative work is currently taking place (Bowes *et al.* 1998). There is evidence that the council is succeeding, in its Canterbury estate, south west of the city centre, in creating an environment within social rented housing where minority households feel relatively safe. The estate has been modernised and there is strong tenant involvement. Because it is relatively close to the city centre, it has proved to be a fairly popular destination for minorities. This suggests, first, that the city council has succeeded, through a mixture of careful allocations, refurbishment work and community development, in creating a satisfactory environment for minorities. Second, minority households have made a positive choice to live there precisely because it is seen as 'safe'.

The need for greater sensitivity in allocations to minorities suggests that a community lettings approach is one that may sometimes be appropriate. Recent research (Griffiths *et al.* 1996) defines such lettings as social housing allocation policies which operate alongside, or in place of, a consideration of housing need and take account of the potential tenant's contribution to that community in which the vacancy has occurred. (JRF Findings no.171, p.2, summary of Griffiths *et al*.'s research)

The researchers point out that allocation policies are frequently a compromise between meeting needs, making best use of housing stock, avoiding social polarisation and helping to engender more balanced communities. They suggest that, when allocations are made, there may be benefits in giving preference to households who actually want to live in an area, as well as those who have particular needs. It may therefore be appropriate in dealing with minority ethnic households, who have specific needs in relation to house size and type, and in relation to safety and freedom from harassment. Such allocations may help to engender feelings of safety and identify a particular area as one in which minority households may make a positive choice to live.

## Finance

Previous research within the minority ethnic communities has identified a reluctance on the part of many individuals to borrow money from banks and building societies. In the early 1980s, for example, only around two-thirds of Caribbean and Asian mortgage or loan holders used a building society as their main source of finance, compared with more than three-quarters of white borrowers (Lakey 1997). Many preferred to rely on informal networks of friends and relatives. Shaw (1988) has described the operation of savings clubs known as kametis or 'committees', whereby individual households pay in at a rate they can afford, eventually retrieving their savings after an agreed period. Many households have used this system to save for the deposit on a house or perhaps even the whole asking price. The operation of these 'committees' is not unlike the early terminating building societies, although there is normally a strong degree of anonymity involved.

Bowes *et al.* (1998) showed, in their study of Pakistanis, that attitudes to mortgages were very varied. Some households made use of building societies and banks and this would confirm the view that building societies were increasingly being used by minorities (Lakey 1997). For others – particularly devout Muslims who formed a small proportion of respondents – such borrowing was out of the question for religious reasons, and they preferred to make private arrangements. These findings are similar to those of Herbert and Kempson (1996), in their study of credit use and minority ethnic groups.

An important reason for the historic reluctance to use building societies and preference for private saving is the rather negative image which some banks, building societies and estate agents have within the minority communities. Sarre *et al.* (1989) found that a number of estate agents stereotyped Asians as being unreliable and devious where property transactions were concerned, and two openly admitted excluding Asians from their services. This echoed the findings by the CRE (1988, 1990), identifying discrimination by estate agencies in London and Oldham. In 1996/97, a case in the Glasgow area involved an Asian family who claimed they had been prevented from viewing a house in a wealthy city suburb by the estate agents concerned and who later sued for damages, with CRE support. They won their case on appeal and received enormous publicity within Scotland. The term 'blacklining' was coined to suggest that certain areas were being unofficially delineated by estate agents as inappropriate for minority ethnic settlement (Bowes *et al.* 1998).

In fact, the evidence relating to the exclusion of minority households from the processes of mortgage finance and house exchange is extremely unclear. While there may be considerable use of estate agents and financial institutions by the households concerned, there does seem to be some discrimination within the system. The houses that are bought by minority ethnic households may not therefore be entirely a matter of choice but may also result from 'steering' by estate agents and mortgage lenders towards particular areas.

## House type and quality

A major issue for some minority ethnic groups is that of overcrowding. Census data show that the average size of white households in 1991 was 2.4 but this rose to 2.6 for black groups, 3.0 for the Chinese, 3.8 for Indians, 4.8 for Pakistanis and 5.2 for Bangladeshis. For South Asian groups, the situation is sometimes complicated by the presence of two households living within the same house; such 'extended' families may result from the presence of two or more different generations.

Within the social rented sector, the provision of larger housing, which would allow these needs to be met, has not generally been given a high priority. As a result, few council houses are large enough and local authorities are in any case affected by the right to buy which, by reducing available stock, has frustrated their attempts to match houses and households in many areas. As a result, there is often severe overcrowding and Harrison *et al.* (1996) have estimated that 31 per cent of Pakistanis and Bangladeshis are one or more bedrooms below the required bedroom standard, as defined by the General Household Survey. Given the youthful age structure of these groups, it is likely that the living conditions in these households will deteriorate further as younger members grow older and demand more space.

Within the housing association sector, there is the added problem that the average size of new housing has declined since the 1988 Housing Act and the introduction of mixed funding. Research by Walentowicz (1992) showed that there was a measurable fall in space standards between the old and new funding regimes and further work by Karn and Sheridan (1994) has confirmed this trend. It is increasingly difficult for associations to build larger houses for minority ethnic applicants without breaking the cost limits set by funders for new developments and associations must therefore seek to gain extra grant allocations from the Housing Corporation, Scottish Homes or the Welsh Office.

Minority ethnic groups living in the social rented sector may live in overcrowded conditions but score relatively well on basic amenity levels. Groups like the Pakistanis, however, who are more likely to be housed in the private sector, are often in poor quality accommodation. A high rate of owner-occupation, far from painting a positive picture of achievement, often masks the fact that these dwellings are at the bottom of the market, frequently in serious disrepair (Ratcliffe 1997). Ballard (1996, p.144) notes that Census data confirm that Pakistanis 'enjoy a substantially inferior quality of housing compared with that occupied by the indigenous majority', while they are far more likely than anyone else to 'be living in overcrowded circumstances, as well as in houses which lack central heating'. Harrison (1995) also refers to the poor quality of Pakistani and Bangladeshi housing, while Ratcliffe's (1996) work in Bradford refers (p.40) to the 'particularly poor quality of the properties occupied by the Pakistanis and Bangladeshis'.

These findings suggest that either Pakistani households have found great difficulty in accessing good quality accommodation or, alternatively, in improving sub-standard housing with grant assistance. Living in poor housing is unlikely to be a positive choice but households may, at some point, have been forced into making compromises over their housing choices, accepting poor quality inner city property, partly because of low income levels and partly in return for a relatively safe living environment. Thus many minority ethnic groups are able to exercise only limited choice over their housing, because of the influence of forces beyond their control.

There is, however, some evidence of population movement out of the inner cities, and into better quality housing. Werbner (1979) noted the outward movement of Manchester's Pakistani population from initial areas of settlement into inner suburban neighbourhoods, a process which tended to be accompanied by business success. Those who moved first were able to establish themselves as the elite of the community by virtue of their wealth and control of institutions, although they suffered some disruption of their social life by moving out of the inner city. Gradually, however, other migrants followed them and the centre of gravity of the whole community began to shift outwards.

Some minority ethnic households have succeeded in moving even further from the inner city in search of appropriate housing and there is evidence of the increasing suburbanisation of the minority population. In 1989, for example, a study of minority ethnic housing problems in Glasgow (Bowes, McCluskey and Sim 1989) showed that many families were moving outside the city boundary into suburban local authority districts, as well as into new private housing estates within the city. This shift was later confirmed by the 1991 Census. (For further discussion of these changes, see Phillips and Unsworth in Chapter 5 of this volume.)

Home ownership can therefore provide a route into the suburbs, particularly for more affluent minority families, and Phillips (1998) notes the increasing numbers of Asian businessmen securing good quality, high status, detached housing. Sometimes, however, purchasers have had to pay high prices to secure property in these areas, a payment dubbed a 'colour tax' (Phillips and Karn 1992). In a number of cities now, researchers have noted an outward movement of minority ethnic households. In Bradford, for example, Ratcliffe (1998) has found evidence of two conflicting tendencies, with some households wishing to stay in traditional minority locations, while others have expressed a willingness to shift to newer suburban housing. He points out that it is easy to overstress the demand for owner-occupation, however, as many households are increasingly looking towards the social rented sector, in contrast to the stereotype.

## Making choices

While issues such as harassment exercise an important influence on locational choice, individual households have specific needs, which also affect the choices that they make. Some minority ethnic groups have particular household structures which affect the suitability of certain forms of housing, while there are various personal circumstances – such as domestic violence and relationship breakdown – which are also important. This section considers these specific and individual constraints, which influence the choices that minority households make.

## Household structure

Family size and household structure vary across the different minority ethnic groups. Family sizes have tended to fall in the UK over the years and Caribbean and African Asian households are of similar sizes to the white population; Chinese families are, on average, slightly smaller. Pakistani and Bangladeshi households, however, stand out not only as being larger but also as having a different structure (Berthoud and Beishon 1997).

For white people – and for Caribbeans – most adults cease to live with their parents once they have family responsibilities of their own. Even in the case of elderly people, who have become more dependent as they have got older, only a relatively small proportion (about 13 per cent of those in their sixties and seventies) share a household with their son or daughter. But as many as one-fifth of South Asian couples live with (one of) their families and a high proportion of Asian elders live with a son or daughter. There are therefore significantly more 'joint' households, involving more than one generation, among South Asians than among other ethnic groups (Berthoud and Beishon 1997). We have already seen how this larger household size limits the housing stock that can be accessed by South Asian households; the structure of the household has a similar effect.

Some households have sought to overcome the problem by living in more than one house, a solution that works if the houses are adjacent or in close proximity to each other. Bowes *et al.* (1998) interviewed a household in Glasgow where the family owned two tenement flats, one above the other, and had constructed an internal staircase between the two. A Bradford household had recently occupied two neighbouring houses, with an elderly couple living in one and their daughter and family next door; in describing this situation, the interviewee spoke of only one household. But such solutions are not always possible. Another issue relates to the demand within some families for men and women to have separate accommodation within the house; this is difficult, given the size constraints of the property available.

It is possible that the presence of older relatives within the larger household is symptomatic of a lack of housing for minority ethnic older people, but the evidence is inconclusive. There is an increasing body of work that has examined the housing needs of minority ethnic older people (reviewed in Blakemore and Boneham 1994), and Bright (1996) has studied the experiences of minority older people who are living in sheltered accommodation. It may be, however, that a greater priority for many households is the provision of accommodation that would allow older people to live with their families if they so wish. In these cases, it would be more appropriate to assist the households to extend existing accommodation and to provide appropriate social services support for older people within the household, rather than to provide specialist accommodation, separate from families.

There is also a need for housing and social services to become more aware of and sensitive to the 'special' needs of minority communities. Ratcliffe (1998) draws attention to the high levels of disability and long-term sickness within the South Asian population in Bradford, with many of the cases requiring housing solutions. Nazroo (1997) suggests that health problems are greater for Pakistanis, Bangladeshis and Caribbeans than for white people; such problems are closely related to socio-economic status, which is in turn affected by housing circumstances, including overcrowding, access to amenities and so on.

Bowes *et al.* (1998) note that, for the Pakistani population, continuing relationships with family in Pakistan also had an impact on households. It was commonplace for family members to be called back to deal with family affairs there and a household head could be absent for many months. If this led to a drop in family income, it could lead to a forced house move. Family links with Pakistan also led to much visiting from Pakistan to Britain and, in discussing whether their housing was adequate for their needs, survey respondents would refer to the need for space for visitors.

## Personal circumstances, gender and family break-up

Although minority ethnic communities are often highly concentrated, there are some indications that this is changing. Some younger people are now moving out of the family home and neighbourhood and we have already referred to the suburbanisation of the minority populations. In some cases, individuals make a conscious choice to move away from areas of minority settlement, which they see as too segregated from the white population (Bowes, Neale and Sim 1997). The behaviour of this younger generation is not homogeneous, however, and where attitudes to traditional values and behaviour are changing, the change is very uneven (Ahmad 1996). Research by the authors would confirm these variations in behaviour.

In many respects, the personal circumstances of minorities are as varied as in the majority population. For example, within the minority ethnic communities, as in the white communities, there are a number of households who have experienced domestic violence, relationship breakdown, separation and divorce and these events have led to house moves and to cases of women living alone. There is evidence that women in these circumstances often live in relatively poor accommodation and have few resources to allow them to compete effectively in the housing market. Many are in social rented housing and are open to harassment (see Gill in Chapter 9 of this volume).

There has been little research on domestic violence as experienced by minority ethnic women in Britain or on the policy response, although Harvie (1991) and Mama (1996) are exceptions. Mama, in her analysis of black women's experiences of domestic violence, attributes many of them to patriarchy, with many women inexperienced in running a home alone, and less likely to be economically independent.

In one sense, the situation of such minority ethnic women or lone-parent households is little different from comparable white households. There is evidence that lone-parent households generally are poorly served by allocation systems, and often end up in poor quality housing in low demand areas (Power and Tunstall 1995). Minority ethnic lone parents often suffer a double disadvantage, however, because many lack knowledge of the options open to them. As well as becoming cut off from circles of support within their communities, a number experience racism within refuges (Harvie 1991), and so the issues of safety for minority ethnic women and lone parents are more complex than for white women, and access to rehousing more restricted.

Within traditional married couple families, women appear rarely to be as influential in making decisions as their male partners, and this appears to be the case in relation to the existing family home, as well as to future moves. These gender issues have been explored by Robinson (1993), who argued that some minorities, notably the Pakistanis, were highly mobile, moving across the country in search of employment opportunities. However, men were more mobile than women and single Pakistani men were almost four times more likely to migrate over long distances than single women. Robinson suggests that, within Islamic culture, women would be expected to remain with their extended household, caring for parents and siblings. Thus, for Pakistanis, migration is often a survival strategy rather than a route to social mobility, and Pakistani households still tend to end up in poor quality accommodation.

## Conclusions

This chapter demonstrates that the settlement patterns of minority ethnic groups in the UK are the result of a complex set of circumstances, relating to the interaction of choices and constraints.

In many respects, owner-occupation appears to be the favoured tenure of most minority groups and this may be linked to flexibility of location, ability to move in search of work and ability to change household arrangements to suit preferences. Home ownership, however, has been and continues to be problematic for many, especially those located in the inner city where house conditions can be poor. There is evidence that these problems have become worse over recent years, as there has been less support available for renovation and repairs to older property. Thus, it is important to acknowledge that some minority ethnic home ownership is 'reluctant', arising through lack of choice (Third *et al.* 1997).

The financing of owner-occupation still relies to some extent on families and friends but building society mortgages are widely used. Like white households, minorities sometimes faced problems with repayments and subsequent repossession. There are a number of examples where this has been linked to business failure.

Statistics which indicate low levels of council-house occupancy among minority ethnic groups tend to mask higher levels of experience of council housing, which are often temporary. Moves in and out of council housing are partly dictated by personal circumstances, partly by prevailing views about the nature of the tenure and the experiences that may be expected by those who take it on, and partly by the operation of the system itself. There is evidence that local authority housing is still operating to exclude many minorities. Key issues include the size and location of housing, allocations systems which may be discriminatory, and ethnic monitoring which remains patchy and ineffective. In some respects, housing associations, particularly BME-led associations, seem to have a more positive reputation amongst minority ethnic groups.

Some of the problems experienced by minority households might also be experienced by white households in similar circumstances. Other problems, however, are explicitly related to minority ethnicity and the racism that is linked with it (Fenton 1999). Racist harassment is the most striking example of this. Distance from community support is also a factor for some households and, for women alone, the difficulty is even greater.

Despite attempts in the past to tackle the problem of harassment, it has proved persistent. Policy approaches need to include not only support for those who experience harassment and action against perpetrators but also preventative action, including joint working with other agencies (Seager and Jeffery 1994). Sensitive allocation policies, for example, might avoid the situation of minority families being offered housing in 'unsafe' areas. There is no doubt that the continuing prospect of harassment affects minority ethnic housing choices and strategies, restricting them considerably. An important component of truly sensitive policy must be to tackle factors that make an area 'unsafe', especially racism.

Thus, because a significant number of minority ethnic households have been excluded from access to the housing which they need and want, so many of the locational choices described in this chapter are severely constrained. There is, therefore, a need to continue to explore the implications and effects of a range of policies on minority ethnic groups. The change of government in 1997 and the apparent commitment by New Labour to address issues of social inclusion, coupled with high profile investigations into racial incidents such as the Stephen Lawrence case, have combined to give the needs of excluded minorities a higher policy profile. It is important to try and take advantage of the opportunities offered by this apparent momentum for policy change.

## Note

1.  It is acknowledged that the use of terminology denoting minorities is problematic. The term 'black and minority ethnic' (BME) is used as it refers to sections of the population in relation to the 'majority ethnic' population, and to those that may experience discrimination and inequality on account of skin colour, heritage, way of life, language or religion. The categories that we use, such as 'Pakistani', are Census categories and do not necessarily reflect people's views of themselves.

## References

Ahmad, W. (1996) 'Family obligations and social change among Asian communities.' In W. Ahmad and K. Atkin (eds) *'Race' and Community Care.* Buckingham: Open University Press.

Bailey, N., Bowes, A. and Sim, D. (1994) 'The Chinese community in Scotland.' *Scottish Geographical Magazine 110,* 2, 66–75.

Ballard, R. (1992) 'New clothes for the Emperor? The conceptual nakedness of the race relations industry in Britain.' *New Community 18,* 3, 481–492.

Ballard, R. (1996) 'The Pakistanis: Stability and introspection.' In C. Peach (ed) *Ethnicity in the 1991 Census. Volume Two: The Ethnic Minority Populations of Great Britain.* London: HMSO.

Baxter, S. and Raw, G. (1988) 'Fast food, fettered work: Chinese women in the ethnic catering industry.' In S. Westwood and P. Bhachu (eds) *Enterprising Women. Ethnicity, Economy and Gender Relations.* London: Routledge.

Berthoud, R. and Beishon, S. (1997) 'People, families and households.' In T. Modood, R. Berthoud, J. Lakey, J. Nazroo, S. Virdee, P. Smith and S. Beishon *Ethnic Minorities in Britain: Diversity and Disadvantage.* London: Policy Studies Institute.

Biochel, M. *et al.* (1969) 'Exposure, experience and attitudes: Realtors and open occupancy.' *Phylon 30,* 325–337.

Blakemore, K. and Boneham, M. (1994) *Age, Race and Ethnicity: A Comparative Approach.* Buckingham: Open University Press.

Bowes, A., Dar, N. and Sim, D. (1997) 'Tenure preference and housing strategy: An exploration of Pakistani experiences.' *Housing Studies 12,* 1, 63–84.

Bowes, A., Dar, N. and Sim, D. (1998) *'Too White, Too Rough, and Too Many Problems': A Study of Pakistani Housing in Britain.* Housing Research Report 3. Stirling: University of Stirling.

Bowes, A., McCluskey, J. and Sim, D. (1989) *Ethnic Minority Housing Problems in Glasgow.* Glasgow: Glasgow City Council.

Bowes, A., Neale, J. and Sim, D. (1997) *The Housing Preferences and Needs of Minority Ethnic Commuters to Renfrew.* Local Research Report. Edinburgh: Scottish Homes.

Bright, G. (1996) *Caring for Diversity. The Housing Care and Support Needs of Older Black and Ethnic Minority People.* London: Odu Dua Housing Association.

Cabinet Office (2000) *Minority Ethnic Issues in Social Exclusion and Neighbourhood Renewal.* London: Cabinet Office.

Cater, J. (1981) 'The impact of Asian estate agents on patterns of ethnic residence: A case study in Bradford.' In P. Jackson and S. Smith (eds) *Social Interaction and Ethnic Segregation.* London: Academic Press.

CRE (1988) *Racial Discrimination in a London Estate Agency. Report of a Formal Investigation into Richard Barclay and Co.* London: Commission for Racial Equality.

CRE (1989) *Racial Discrimination in Liverpool City Council. Report of a Formal Investigation into the Housing Department.* London: Commission for Racial Equality.

CRE (1990) *Racial Discrimination in an Oldham Estate Agency. Report of a Formal Investigation into Norman Lester and Co.* London: Commission for Racial Equality.

CRE (1993) *Housing Associations and Racial Equality.* London: Commission for Racial Equality.

Dahya, B. (1974) 'The nature of Pakistani ethnicity in industrial cities in Britain.' In A. Cohen (ed) *Urban Ethnicity.* London: Tavistock.

Dalton, M. and Daghlian, S. (1989) *Race and Housing in Glasgow. The Role of Housing Associations.* London: Commission for Racial Equality.

Denton, J. (1970) *Report of Consultant.* San Francisco: National Committee against Discrimination in Housing.

Dorling, D. (1997) 'Regional and local differences in the housing tenure of ethnic minorities.' In V. Karn (ed) *Ethnicity in the 1991 Census, Volume Four.* London: HMSO.

Fenton, S. (1999) *Ethnicity. Racism, Class and Culture.* Basingstoke: Macmillan.

Goldthorpe, J., Lockwood, D., Bechhofer, F. and Platt, J. (1969) *The Affluent Worker in the Class Structure.* Cambridge: Cambridge University Press.

Griffiths, M., Park, J., Smith, R., Stirling, T. and Trott, T. (1996) *Community Lettings: Local Allocations Policies in Practice.* York: Joseph Rowntree Foundation.

Harrison, M. (1995) *Housing, 'Race', Social Policy and Empowerment.* Aldershot: Avebury.

Harrison, M. and Law, I. (1997) 'Needs and empowerment in minority ethnic housing: Some issues of definition and local strategy.' *Policy and Politics 25,* 3, 285–298.

Harrison, M., Karmani, A., Law, I., Phillips, D. and Ravetz, A. (1996) *Black and Minority Ethnic Housing Associations. An Evaluation of the Housing Corporation's Black and Minority Ethnic Housing Association Strategies.* Source Research Report 16. London: The Housing Corporation.

Harvie, L. (1991) 'Sexual violence and the voluntary sector: Asian women and wife abuse.' In A. Bowes and D. Sim (eds) *Demands and Constraints: Ethnic Minorities and Social Services in Scotland.* Edinburgh: Scottish Council for Voluntary Organisations.

Henderson, J. and Karn, V. (1987) *Race, Class and State Housing: Inequality and the Allocation of Public Housing in Britain.* Aldershot: Gower.

Herbert, A. and Kempson, E. (1996) *Credit Use and Ethnic Minorities.* London: Policy Studies Institute.

Karn, V. and Sheridan, L. (1994) *New Homes in the 1990s. A Study of Design, Space and Amenity in Housing Association and Private Sector Production.* Manchester/York: University of Manchester/Joseph Rowntree Foundation.

Lakey, J. (1997) 'Neighbourhoods and housing.' In T. Modood, R. Berthoud, J. Lakey, J. Nazroo, S. Virdee, P. Smith and S. Beishon *Ethnic Minorities in Britain: Diversity and Disadvantage.* London: Policy Studies Institute.

Leavitt, J. and Saegert, S. (1990) *From Abandonment to Hope. Community-Households in Harlem.* New York: Columbia University Press.

Love, A.-M. and Kirby, K. (1994) *Racial Incidents in Council Housing: The Local Authority Response.* London: HMSO.

Mama, A. (1996) *The Hidden Struggle: Statutory and Voluntary Sector Responses to Violence Against Black Women in the Home.* London: Whiting and Birch.

Modood, T. (1997) 'Employment.' In T. Modood, R. Berthoud, J. Lakey, J. Nazroo, S. Virdee, P. Smith and S. Beishon *Ethnic Minorities in Britain: Diversity and Disadvantage.* London: Policy Studies Institute.

Nazroo, J. (1997) 'Health and health services.' In T. Modood, R. Berthoud, J. Lakey, J. Nazroo, S. Virdee, P. Smith and S. Beishon *Ethnic Minorities in Britain: Diversity and Disadvantage.* London: Policy Studies Institute.

Owen, D. (1992) *Ethnic Minorities in Great Britain: Settlement Patterns.* 1991 Census Statistical Paper No.1. Coventry: CRER, University of Warwick.

Owen, D. (1995) 'The spatial and socio-economic patterns of minority ethnic groups in Britain.' *Scottish Geographical Magazine 111,* 1, 27–35.

Patterson, S. (1965) *Dark Strangers: A Study of West Indians in London.* London: Tavistock.

Peach, C. (1998) 'South Asian and Caribbean ethnic minority housing choice in Britain.' *Urban Studies 35,* 10, 1657–1680.

Phillips, D. (1986) *What Price Equality?* GLC Housing Policy Report 9. London: Greater London Council.

Phillips, D. (1998) 'Black minority ethnic concentration, segregation and dispersal in Britain.' *Urban Studies 35,* 10, 1681–1702.

Phillips, D. and Karn, V. (1992) 'Race and housing in a property owning democracy.' *New Community 18,* 3, 355–369.

Power, A. and Tunstall, R. (1995) *Swimming Against the Tide: Polarisation or Progress on 20 Unpopular Council Estates.* York: Joseph Rowntree Foundation.

Ratcliffe, P. (1996) *'Race' and Housing in Bradford: Addressing the Needs of the South Asian, African and Caribbean Communities.* Bradford: Bradford Housing Forum.

Ratcliffe, P. (1997) '"Race", ethnicity and housing differentials in Britain.' In V. Karn (ed) *Ethnicity in the 1991 Census, Volume Four.* London: HMSO.

Ratcliffe, P. (1998) '"Race", housing and social exclusion.' *Housing Studies 13,* 6, 807–818.

Rees, P. and Phillips, D. (1996) 'Geographical spread: The national picture.' In P. Ratcliffe (ed) *Ethnicity in the 1991 Census, Volume Three.* London: HMSO.

Rex, J. and Moore, R. (1967) *Race, Community and Conflict: A Study of Sparkbrook.* Oxford: Oxford University Press.

Robinson, V. (1988) 'The new Indian middle class in Britain.' *Ethnic and Racial Studies 11,* 4, 456–473.

Robinson, V. (1993) '"Race", gender, and internal migration within England and Wales.' *Environment and Planning A 25,* 1453–1465.

Rossi, P. (1955) *Why Families Move.* Glencoe, ILL: Free Press.

Sarre, P., Phillips, D. and Skellington, R. (1989) *Ethnic Minority Housing: Explanations and Policies.* Aldershot: Avebury.

Schuman, J. (1999) 'The ethnic minority populations of Great Britain – latest estimates.' *Population Trends 96,* 33–43.

Seager, R. and Jeffery, J. (1994) *Eliminating Racial Harassment: A Guide to Housing Policies and Procedures.* London: Lemos.

Shaw, A. (1988) *A Pakistani Community in Britain.* Oxford: Basil Blackwell.

Simpson, A. (1981) *Stacking the Decks: A Study of Race Inequality and Council Housing in Nottingham.* Nottingham: Nottingham Community Relations Council.

Taeuber, K. (1983) *Racial Residential Segregation, 28 Cities, 1970–1980.* Madison, WIS: University of Wisconsin.

Third, H., Wainwright, S. and Pawson, H. (1997) *Constraint and Choice for Minority Ethnic Home Owners in Scotland.* Research Report 54. Edinburgh: Scottish Homes.

Walentowicz, P. (1992) *Housing Standards After the Act. A Survey of Space and Design Standards on Housing Association Projects in 1989/90.* Research Report 15. London: National Federation of Housing Associations.

Werbner, P. (1979) 'Avoiding the ghetto: Pakistani migrants and settlement shifts in Manchester.' *New Community 7,* 3, 376–389.

*Chapter 4*

# The Housing Needs of Black and Minority Ethnic Groups

## Glen Gidley, Malcolm Harrison and Richard Tomlins

There has been increasing recognition in recent years of black and minority ethnic (BME) housing needs, and numerous investigations of these needs. Housing need, however, is a complex and potentially contested concept, and many conceptual and practical difficulties can arise for local studies. The 'traditional' indicators of housing need within minority communities – such as overcrowding or lack of self-contained accommodation – remain extremely important, providing continuing evidence of severe conditions. This chapter, however, looks beyond them, to include other features from the landscape of housing experiences, and to explore methodological issues. As we shall indicate, researching needs is a complicated process, which should be understood in its particular political and organisational environments. Examples below come especially from recent work in Sheffield, and from a study of the needs of communities of Vietnamese origin in London, but we also engage with broader debates. Our conclusions are that needs studies can be extremely useful, but that their limitations should be acknowledged. It can be difficult to move from needs to policy prescriptions.

## Meanings, definitions and choices

The evaluation of needs plays significant roles in the housing policy arena. For example, local authorities have a duty to assess housing need, and are now being expected to include policies covering BME needs within housing strategies (DETR 1998). Yet need is difficult to pin down, and the way it is approached or measured varies according to the setting. Although the concept of need has been discussed frequently at a general level by scholars (see particularly Doyal and Gough 1991; Percy-Smith 1996; Ware and Goodin 1990), this has not resolved potential problems about its practical use. Indeed, need perceived in abstract terms is problematic in many organisational environments. Policy makers must consider exactly *what* is needed, and *why,* alongside available means of responding (if any). They also operate in political contexts. Four matters in particular will be highlighted now.

### Contexts and policy environments

The kinds of needs searched for, prioritised or analysed often reflect specific policy options, established concerns of professional practice and resource constraints. Researchers, practitioners and politicians make choices about meanings and coverage, with the issues being as much political as technical. Conditions and preoccupations in particular policy environments can be crucial. With respect to housing allocation, for example, criteria used may have related to an 'ideology of need' (or structured set of concepts and values) which itself was grounded partly in what was available and on what terms (for discussions, see Spicker 1987, 1989, pp.121–127). As Spicker indicates, the idea of need effectively may have been subject to interpretation 'according to the measures available to meet it' (1989, p.122). For investment planning, attempts to quantify housing need have been influenced by an assumption that what was required was an evaluation of where and how far there was a shortfall or 'conditions deficit' (Harrison and Law 1997, p.288; Gidley, Harrison and Robinson 1999); but this reflected beliefs about the desirability of specific solutions. Chosen indicators have reflected policy preferences, but have not necessarily directly measured need itself.

In practice, there is today a wide choice of targets which a local needs study may address (Gidley *et al.* 1999; London Research Centre and Lemos and Crane 1998, p.3, 1.3), reflecting diverse political environments. Immediate objectives might include assessing the housing difficulties of households with particular characteristics, assessing physical deficiencies of dwellings, measuring failures of supply or affordability, assessing claims to priority for support or accommodation, analysing broader issues linked to collective notions of need (such as those implicit in ideas about community regeneration and capacity-building), or examining equality of opportunities, fairness and cultural sensitivity of treatment. There is also the aim of discovering people's preferences. Along with these diverse orientations come numerous options for methods, from physical surveys to focus groups. Underlying an exercise may be political or organisational goals such as deriving priorities to inform a strategy, underpinning a bid for funds, rationing accommodation, improving services, providing a 'technical' rationale for a particular way forward, delaying or preparing for an immediate difficult action, increasing the 'user-led' dimension of practice, and so forth. Defining or predicting unmet needs is not only about setting an agenda for action, but can be about legitimating that agenda; the specific context may be crucial for the meanings given to need.

## Changing practices

Approaches to needs have become more complex. Housing provision has been altering, with some blurring of public, voluntary and private sectors, stock transfers, care packages, and so on; while faith in local authority housing has weakened. Projections of shortfalls are complicated by regional variations, some areas showing severe shortages whilst others appear to have a housing surplus (although this does not prove absence of 'housing need'). Preoccupations with numerical predictions have in any case become supplemented by other more 'cultural' approaches. Fordham et al. indicate a shift since the earlier post-war years (when the imperative might have been simply to build more houses), the current focus being on issues of housing of the wrong type or quality, and a continuing need for subsidised housing (1998, p.6). They also note that, during the last five years or so, studies of housing need have been carried out by most local authorities (see pp.6, 15–16). (For a relevant review see Cole and Goodchild 1995.) The research agenda is further complicated through increased interest in community care clients, elders, minority ethnic housing needs, and user involvement. Research by Tomlins et al. indicates that London boroughs have begun to consider producing BME strategies, and that local authorities may be acknowledging the desirability of moving to more sophisticated housing needs studies (Tomlins et al. 2000, pp.41–43). Acknowledgement of more particularised needs raises detailed questions about deficiencies of provision. Developing explicit strategies may require specialised needs studies, reaching beyond traditional social renting boundaries. One complication is that prioritising subsidised social rented housing can appear inappropriate as a way forward for certain minority ethnic groups who are in hardship. This is part of a larger issue concerning social renting, what it can offer, how it is perceived, and the 'fit' in terms of dwelling sizes, conditions and locations.

## Cultural sensitivity and specific community needs

It is important to be alert to specific conditions experienced by minority ethnic households, and to the issue of cultural sensitivity, both in respect of the defining of needs and household responses to provision (see for instance Bright 1996, pp.23–25). There are certainly questions to consider about people's relationships with (or knowledge of) existing services, and about the sensitivity of agencies. There may be hidden deprivations or problems of access, where absence of apparent demand appears to justify not providing a sensitive service, while non-provision in turn depresses demand (Johnson *et al.* 1998, p.58). More generally, diversity of preferences or circumstances within and between minority ethnic groups (Karn and Phillips 1998; Lakey 1997) may mean limitations not only in focusing on an overall category of BME households, but also in using general 'Asian' or 'Black African/Caribbean' categories (London Research Centre and Lemos and Crane 1998, pp.16–17).

One issue that may apply across minority ethnic groups, however, concerns constrained choice. The need for secure possession unthreatened by harassment is a key one; restricted choice may result from racism as well as from economic constraints. Knowing the limited alternatives, some households may place value on being within their own community, irrespective of poor conditions (Shah and Williams 1992, p.63). For certain communities there may be advantages in policy having a strong private sector emphasis (including a concern with low cost home ownership), given a lack of interest in social renting and the very rational reluctance to go to some white-dominated estates. There may be perceptions of council housing having a negative utility which outweighs the experience of living in poor physical conditions within another tenure (Harrison and Law 1997, pp.291–293; although see Third, Wainwright and Pawson 1997).

## Preferences

The emphasis given to household preferences may vary. An apparently 'technical' producer-determined needs definition might rely less on having to enter the terrain of desires, and seek universalistic measures to apply to households in a comparative way. Yet for households themselves, needs may be hard to distinguish from preferences, and universalistic technical approaches focused on quality and use of dwellings might undervalue cultural or religious issues, concerns about some types of costs (such as exposure to harassment), and preferences about area or tenure. The latter can be complicated by interplay between potentially negative views of social renting as a 'welfare' tenure, the ethnicity of the housing provider, and variable perspectives related to resources and individual experiences (Johnson *et al.* 1998, pp.13–14). Qualitative work with households and other informants may be suggested to discover key issues and complement measures of physical conditions, or to reduce dangers that assumptions based on a 'white norm' will remain unchallenged within apparently technical appraisals. Such research nonetheless raises questions about subjectivity, representativeness and selection. There can also be very practical problems; as Shah and Williams put it, some people 'do not easily reveal their hardships or even their lifestyles' (1992, p.62). When information is forthcoming, further questions might arise about how seriously felt a problem or need is, and about the bearing housing may have upon it. For example, we might ask how severe the asthma/respiratory problems of certain households are, and how far housing circumstance is a causative factor. It might also be problematic to research preferences and intentions relating to future moves, future household changes or adaptations to dwellings, so as to use findings in policy discussions. For instance, a household might have mixed views about the prospects of an older person continuing to live with younger relatives, or have unattainable aspirations about locality choice, or possess little information about adaptations, their costs and funding. A person's preferences may also shift over time with age, housing circumstances, networks, and so forth.

In a world with fewer resource constraints, official thinking about needs might well focus heavily on people's preferences for particular housing 'careers', packages or solutions, and on mechanisms for empowering housing consumers collectively or individually. In fact first steps have been taken in these directions in response to challenges from disabled people. Today their housing needs are likely to be discussed in the light of the notion of achieving independence, and with reference to community care (Crawford and Foord 1997; Oldman 1998, pp.69–70; Watts and Galbraith 1998). Earlier assumptions about segregated provision – and about predetermining need from a medicalised perspective on individual impairments – have been displaced; disabled people have shifted the debate towards rights, choices and the reduction of disabling barriers. A stress on disabled people's choices raises further questions about defining need. From a 'user' perspective, being an owner-occupier might become an important 'need' (Joseph Rowntree Foundation 1995; King 1998), although some professionals might confine this to the realm of desires.

## Research in Sheffield

Research sponsors may emphasise particular issues and look for direct policy implications from researchers, but it is important to recognise the limitations as well as the merits of needs studies. Recent research in Sheffield illustrates the complex agenda that can be set for a study of minority ethnic housing needs and some of the strengths and difficulties of such research. The project was funded by Housing Corporation grant through a locally-based housing association and ran in co-operation with the local authority. The agenda was influenced not only by the desire to establish some priorities within housing policy but also by difficulties previously experienced in the city over establishing a registered BME housing association. The research considered priorities in the conventional sense of housing needs but also in terms of options for organisational arrangements to provide and manage housing (see Gidley *et al.* 1999). It was clear from initial exploratory work (Harrison and Bhanu 1997) that selectivity would be inevitable (given the resources), that mixed methods might be appropriate and that an audit of institutional performance might help identify weaknesses in agency responses to minorities. In addition, the notion of 'housing plus' was deployed, given the importance of linking up with needs outside direct provision of housing.

The cornerstone of the research was a survey of 323 households with 1900 members. Interviews were undertaken in 1997/1998 by interviewers recruited from local communities. The sample was assembled through door-to-door enquiries, known meeting points such as community centres and other informal means. The survey focused in particular on housing and allied issues for African/Caribbean, Chinese and South Asian households but sought some subdivision beyond this. In the event it proved more straightforward to distinguish Pakistani, Indian and Bangladeshi households than adequately to subdivide the African/Caribbean group. A good mix was achieved amongst respondents in terms of gender, age, ethnicity and tenure. Just over half the survey households were owner-occupiers, although the proportion varied by ethnic groups and age. There were low numbers in paid employment, very low weekly income levels, and high numbers dependent on benefits (and possibly some doubts about take-up, for instance amongst Chinese). The researchers also carried out focus group work, analysed previous reports, undertook an audit of provision of housing services to minority ethnic people in the city and completed a study of 'housing plus' gaps and options via meetings with key informants. The audit was to obtain (as far as time allowed) a picture of services that agencies claimed to be providing to minority communities.

Household surveys provide useful information but do not necessarily generate a set of straightforward and detailed recommendations. The carrying out of such a survey, however, may increase interest and awareness about housing problems and thus have 'political' effects unrelated to its precise findings. The Sheffield survey proved productive. It illustrated or confirmed some problems that were already suspected to be important, revealed preferences and dissatisfactions, and pointed towards some 'new' issues. The findings could be (and were) brought back into the policy arena, where implications of the data would be a matter for debate. In recognition of diversity, analyses focused on drawing a picture of household experiences within each main 'community' or category. This was acceptable with policy makers keen to recognise the particular experiences and preferences of the different communities. Even so, analysis revealed that respondents shared some common experiences with regard to a number of issues.

Within all communities the research found a relatively high incidence of long-term impairment, illness or health problems, with a particularly high incidence evident within South Asian households. Reports of difficulties around the home were recorded, related to health problems and disability (for example, with stairs, bathroom and kitchen). Few people, however, were receiving help from formal support services to counter such problems and few were living in suitably adapted accommodation. (On illness and disability, see Ratcliffe 1996 for Bradford, pp.ix, 53–74.) There was also considerable experience of harassment, with a large minority of respondents (particularly women) feeling under threat whilst living in current accommodation.

As far as mobility was concerned, 51 per cent of survey households said that they would like to leave their current accommodation, but in only 19 per cent of cases were some or all of the household actively looking to move. The main reasons for wanting to move were the need for a bigger home or a concealed household's need for independent housing. Very few households expressed a need to move to specially designed or adapted housing for people with long-term health problems or impairment, despite many people suffering from difficulties in their current accommodation. It was not clear how far reticence regarding moving reflected genuine wishes to stay put, or limited awareness of available options. It may be added that many appeared reluctant to live on council estates but were on very low incomes and experiencing high levels of unemployment. This challenges the traditional approach to needs that assumes that those who can afford to buy will do so satisfactorily, while those who cannot will be catered for through social renting. Perhaps access to owner-occupation had been achieved at the expense of space or conditions, or through income pooling by many household members.

A substantial minority of respondents expressed dissatisfaction with the standards of their accommodation, although the majority were apparently satisfied with most aspects of it. Problems with the overall size of homes and available bedroom space were often mentioned: 11 per cent of respondents shared a living room with another household, 12 per cent a kitchen, 11 per cent bathroom/toilet facilities and 8 per cent a bedroom. Problems with physical conditions were common and, in particular, with condensation and damp. Most physical and structural problems were more prevalent among owner-occupiers, of whom 20 per cent reported rain coming through their roofs, 33 per cent problems with damp, 42 per cent problems with condensation and 21 per cent problems with plumbing and drainage. These findings are unsurprising given the low numbers of respondents in paid employment, the low weekly income levels reported, the high level of dependency on benefits and, consequently, the limited resources among many home-owners to maintain and repair their property. Despite the incidence of housing-related problems, relatively few households had sought help or advice and, among those who had, few had approached the council or a housing association, reliance instead being on family and friends, advice and community centres. There had been limited uptake of available services, with relatively little use of the council's housing department or housing associations for assistance. This appeared to have reflected a language barrier reported by many respondents but also a possibility that the information that did exist in community languages was not readily accessible.

## Limitations and difficulties?

This study shares with others the general limitation that households' conditions and experiences do not necessarily measure need as such or provide a direct guide for improved provision. There were also practical methodological limitations. Resource constraints precluded linking the household survey to a parallel 'independent' professional appraisal of dwelling conditions, although such links might have been beneficial (see London Research Centre and Lemos and Crane 1998, p.33). When sampling, it was impossible to satisfy all possible objectives for coverage (relating to localities, minority groups, age groups, etc.). Even without other complications, the 'black and minority ethnic' category embraced such diversity that selectivity was inevitable. Although previously-reported work on specific Sheffield communities proved helpful, the focus groups were not numerous or successful enough to fill all gaps, or to cover separately groups in temporary accommodation or supported housing schemes. These can be seen as part of the potential 'missing' households in a survey of this type. As for locating and interviewing an appropriate sample, this depended on meeting quotas through a 'snowball' approach. The survey relied on local community interviewers with language skills, and informants and interviewers became involved in the selection process. Results from such a survey cannot be representative of minority ethnic populations in a strict statistical sense, so that findings become more like a set of extensive insights into the kinds of circumstances that exist for households in targeted groups. The methods used do not achieve the depth of concentrated qualitative research such as a life-history interviewing technique (Bowes, Dar and Sim 1997). Findings, however, indicate problems and their severity, albeit that questions asked may reflect researcher preoccupations, however carefully considered. Given a compressed timescale, there was limited scope for starting with the interviewees' own perspectives across a wider canvas.

Despite constraints on the work undertaken in Sheffield, we should recall the significance of environment before judging methods. As we have argued, context is crucial. Analyses from a substantial household survey can confirm and offer specific instances of known problems, reveal new ones, and suggest some interrelationships. Policy makers do not necessarily require a strictly representative picture of the extent of a difficulty, although they must be kept aware of data limitations. In effect, a method's usefulness is not merely evaluated by reference to statistical reliability, but by reference to the roles that findings are expected to play in a specific political/organisational environment.

Another aspect of the Sheffield approach to needs was to engage with and in some ways empower community members. This was seen as important by local agencies, especially since the research was to help 'kick-start' development of a discrete BME housing strategy. Using the local skills and knowledge of interviewers drawn from the communities contributed to the process of engagement, as did discussing options and research details with minority ethnic informants and advisers, although the researchers anticipated that voices might diverge as well as agree. There are limits, however, on emancipatory research empowering local people. There will usually be differences between advocacy and 'independent' research, and a research team must tread carefully between the competing interests of different groups and agencies. Furthermore, involvement of local people is prone to self-selection.

Another target was to make contacts to review 'housing plus' (for the relevance of housing plus to needs studies see London Research Centre and Lemos and Crane 1998, pp.6–9). Work of this type is likely to depend for a sample on a mix of reputational and organisational information, to locate useful interviewees with experience (and with some representative roles in respect of their organisational bases). Informants indicated issues and priorities, the most helpful discussions often being about particular local circumstances. Looking at needs in 'housing plus' terms, however, not only required giving weight to matters indicated by informants; the research team was making interpretations about ways forward. This illustrates a more general point, namely, that a recommendation on meeting needs is usually going to involve some judgement about selecting priorities and key issues, even when founded on extensive consultations. The solution of offering policy options for debate does not entirely resolve this, although it can help.

## Vietnamese households

Reference to a second recent study enables us to highlight additional points. This London research was commissioned by An Viet Housing Association to inform its business plan and help achieve its mission of providing a 'safe haven' in the form of good quality housing, especially for refugees from Vietnam and South East Asia (Tomlins *et al.* 2000). The study reflected the vision of a housing service going beyond bricks and mortar, and took account of the necessity for housing to generate emotional and cultural security in addition to providing shelter. Refugees from Vietnam and their dependents were the main focus. Four main methods were used: synthesis from general literature; data analyses from existing statistical sources; an investigation of the extent to which housing strategy statements of London boroughs took account of minority communities (and particularly the Vietnamese population); and focus groups with community members and workers. Some elements paralleled the Sheffield approach. The work on London boroughs (supplemented with material on local health strategies) had something in common with the audit in Sheffield, although it also connected directly with identifying issues that might be relevant for the housing association's future strategy. Both studies explored existing sources and both recognised 'housing plus' issues. The London research, however, made more use of focus group findings and concentrated on relatively under-acknowledged target groups. As in Sheffield, empowerment was considered; the focus groups exercise was designed in such a way as to help generate confidence in the research process and play a part in capacity-building.

A background issue was the small size of the Vietnamese population, which affected availability of data. The limitations of official statistics here highlight a general lack of sensitivity to diversity in official data collection, which means that evaluating need often requires community-based approaches. There is also an overlap between Vietnamese and Chinese identities, complicating matters. Nonetheless, certain characteristics could be noted, including a tendency for older relatives to live with younger families, low levels of employment and high dependence on social renting. Perhaps some households are 'trapped' in council accommodation, with children continuing to live with parents and elders after having formed partnerships in probably overcrowded dwellings. It can also be argued that the Vietnamese in essence remain a refugee community, requiring the psychological as well as physical security of good quality housing and support services, which may well be best provided by a minority ethnic organisation dedicated to this purpose. Refugee groups have rarely been consulted by mainstream service providers, yet may lack the 'street knowledge' needed to challenge the approaches of these agencies. The Vietnamese community's needs may to an extent be hidden because of its relatively small size or disconnection from standard services, while dispersed settlement can inhibit provider responses. Central government initially contributed to dispersal by strategies aimed at avoiding geographical concentration, creating circumstances where households might seek subsequent remigration into particular areas to facilitate community-building (for examples of housing association roles here, see Tomlins *et al.* 2000). At local level, some boroughs today have targets for the involvement of BME registered social landlords (RSLs) in housing development, and there is also growing interest in identifying community care needs of BME communities. Even so, most local housing strategies fail to appreciate the complex nature of the Vietnamese and Chinese communities, leading to either no specific policies or inappropriate policy assumptions.

Housing need for Vietnamese households is not simply about bricks and mortar but nonetheless, as with other minorities, there are specific design issues. Physical requirements might include good kitchen ventilation and a powerful extractor fan, as well as specifications related to religious and cultural observances difficult to cater for via standard concepts of need. There may be a wish for a sacred space to use as an altar and for avoiding placing a toilet near the front door. Strong demand for a garden connects with uses such as entertaining and exercise, and with the opportunity to grow herbs and exotic vegetables. Beyond physical provision, there is interest in supplementary housing-related services, and connections with health, mobility, vulnerability to isolation, harassment, physical and cultural security and self-sufficiency. A key concern is for some community facilities for support, with the required facilities varying at different stages in life cycles. Nearness to Vietnamese or other people of South East Asian descent, and to shared facilities, can be crucial, as is the presence of family members. Concerns about harassment may restrict neighbourhood choice as well as influencing daily activities and dwelling design issues. Focus group informants acknowledged benefits of social renting and the sector's variations. They suggested that councils were 'safe' and relatively cheap landlords but buildings were of lower quality than those of RSLs and repairs could be difficult. Housing association accommodation could be seen as 'nicer', newer, better quality and often with a garden, but more expensive and with smaller rooms. There was some preference for rented accommodation run through a Vietnamese association with staff competent in language and cultural terms, and this was more specific than a desire for a generic minority ethnic RSL. Although exchange arrangements might make it feel slightly easier for council tenants to move, lack of ownership generally meant a brake on choice, and possibly on the ability to reunite families.

What this study brings out particularly well is the distinctive, and perhaps hidden, nature of needs, related to the histories and social circumstances of the households. Their perspectives are influenced by problems of communications, isolation and harassment. There are also some collective needs that might have implications for housing plus services and for the types of provider organisations that would be most beneficial.

## Conclusions

It has been suggested by Cole and Goodchild (1995, p.55) and by Hawtin (1996, p.98) that assessments of need are more of an art than an exact science. Furthermore, not only is need hard to define precisely, but needs indicators may not connect straightforwardly with policy prescriptions. Yet there is certainly a strong case for studies focused on minority ethnic households' housing needs. The qualifications must be that limitations of techniques and data should be kept in mind, and that any links to policy development should be reasonably clear and realistic. A survey should not occur in isolation, but should form part of an ongoing process of enquiry, consultation, and discussion. A mix of methods may have advantages. Researchers may synthesise from information already present (albeit scattered) within local housing agencies as well as collecting new data. It is certainly useful to gather material illuminating households' difficulties, or deficiencies in agency activity (particularly through audit). It is also well worth trying to connect findings to development of a minority ethnic housing strategy within a local authority. On the other hand, there is no magic research formula that ends the necessity for political debate and prioritisation or makes further, more specialised enquiries redundant.

Recent years have seen increasing awareness of household diversity and heightened demands for sensitivity to user perspectives. These trends have implications for needs studies (and there is scope for further involvement of local people themselves in processes of survey and analysis). Yet so long as resources have to be rationed by service providers, there will continue to be a requirement for measures of urgency and comparative circumstances. Needs studies that explore housing conditions through measures of poor standards and restricted choices, with a view to improving circumstances of the most disadvantaged, fit well with general ideas about meeting 'basic needs' in a universalistic manner (Doyal and Gough 1991). It may be possible, however, to make comparisons or measure circumstances using a wider range of variables than in the past. Of course, attempts to 'measure' remain subject to problems, even where there might be agreement about the important indicators. Professional assessments of individuals' housing needs certainly vary (for example, in community care contexts – Joseph Rowntree Foundation 1998). Nonetheless, there are specific indicators worth considering in relation to minority ethnic communities in particular, related to distinctive aspects of housing experience. Harassment, isolation or communications problems should be on the agenda, alongside more traditional benchmarks. Surveys and other techniques may bring out under-recognised issues, so there should be research space to facilitate this. It should not be assumed too readily that an absence of take-up of a service is definitive proof that there is no need for anything extra (see Harrison 1999, on 'non-participation' amongst homeless people). A general awareness of possibilities of institutional racisms is essential, implying ongoing monitoring of the suitability and 'fit' of service provision.

Households' views may be researched explicitly and collective expressions of 'voice' can also be considered. Using preferences information, however, remains complicated. Preferences might be influenced strongly by the extent or limitations of awareness about options and their costs. From the Sheffield household survey, there seemed to be a preference for staying in existing homes in respect of households for whom a possible move to adapted or specially designed accommodation might have appeared an issue. Furthermore, households' locality preferences may be contingent on numerous factors, including cost, other people's locations (Bowes *et al.* 1997, pp.71–72, 79) and (potentially) parallel activities by agencies and community-based organisations; for instance, community development and anti-harassment work. There is one long-standing matter in the domain of preferences, however, on which we can be definite. The preference for culturally sensitive services not only has implications for practices among mainstream providers but also strengthens the case for involving organisations run by minority ethnic people.

Needs studies may be expected to help generate or legitimate policies but available policy levers may not be capable of meeting identified needs. Ideally, agencies could develop more comprehensive local overviews, going beyond traditional preoccupations with supplying and rationing dwellings to let. Yet there can be constraints on what is on offer. Households may be in hardship but, if they wish to continue in the private sector, prospects for improvement may be restricted. Care and repair has been one avenue but others, such as shared ownership, have appeared limited or difficult to develop. In effect, there do not seem to have been many strong policy levers or forms of support related to private sector residence. The 'housing plus' dimension is difficult here. For instance, the viability of developing minority ethnic businesses or sub-contracting – if desirable – in the setting of private markets is very different from doing so within a council estate which has a large capital programme. Some avenues for community capacity building are opened by having substantial estate investment. It might be questioned how far this assists minority ethnic communities and firms when many large estates contain few black households. Minorities may be marginalised, albeit unintentionally.

Where policy potentially can connect with needs, it may be limited by lack of resources. If people wish to move to social rented dwellings in particular localities, land supply may be a constraint (as in Sheffield). Another example concerns minority ethnic elders, who might benefit from a range of assistance, including more support at home and better access to sheltered accommodation. Once recognised, such needs could generate large programmes. The policy response might be to prioritise a new project that 'shows willing' rather than being able to adjust mainstream services rapidly across the board. In some places, a well-regarded 'flagship' sheltered scheme has been created but this might not always be the best solution (for issues, see Whittingham 1998) or prove adequate on its own. If demand could be predicted, a carefully targeted sheltered scheme might seem desirable, allied with enhanced outreach services and additional large family dwellings, but a comprehensive strategy would be expensive.

We can conclude by observing that not only is there a strong case for continuing to update analyses of needs, to embrace minority ethnic households more fully, but there are also significant problems in connecting with policies and practices. Unless these are confronted, sophisticated needs studies will not bring all the benefits hoped for and may become perceived at the grass roots as tokenistic enterprises.

# References

Bowes, A., Dar, N. and Sim, D. (1997) 'Tenure preference and housing strategy: An exploration of Pakistani experiences.' *Housing Studies 12*, 1, 63–84.

Bright, G. (1996) *The Housing Care and Support Needs of Older Black and Ethnic Minority People.* London: Odu Dua Housing Association.

Cole, I. and Goodchild, B. (1995) 'Local housing strategies in England: An assessment of their changing role and content.' *Policy and Politics 23*, 1, 49–60.

Crawford, G. and Foord, M. (1997) 'Disabling by design.' *Housing Review 46*, 5, September/October, 98–100.

DETR (1998) *The Housing Investment Programme: 1998 Guidance Note for Local Authorities.* London: Department of the Environment, Transport and the Regions.

Doyal, L. and Gough, I. (1991) *A Theory of Human Need.* Basingstoke: Macmillan.

Fordham, R., Finlay, S., Gardner, J., MacMillan, A., Muldoon, C., Taylor, G. and Welch, G. (1998) *Housing Need and the Need for Housing.* Aldershot: Ashgate.

Gidley, G., Harrison, M. and Robinson, D. (1999) *Housing Black and Minority Ethnic People in Sheffield.* Research Report. Sheffield: Centre for Regional Economic and Social Research, Sheffield Hallam University.

Harrison, M. (1999) 'Theorising homelessness and "race".' In P. Kennett and A. Marsh (eds) *Homelessness: Exploring the New Terrain.* Bristol: Policy Press.

Harrison, M. and Bhanu, B. (1997) 'Report on Sheffield Housing Needs Study.' Unpublished. Leeds: Department of Sociology and Social Policy, Leeds University.

Harrison, M. and Law, I. (1997) 'Needs and empowerment in minority ethnic housing: Some issues of definition and local strategy.' *Policy and Politics 25*, 3, 285–298.

Hawtin, M. (1996) 'Assessing housing needs.' In J. Percy-Smith (ed) *Needs Assessments in Public Policy.* Buckingham: Open University Press.

Johnson, M. with Powell, D., Owen, D. and Tomlins, R. (1998) *Minority Housing and Social Care Needs in Warwickshire.* Coventry: Centre for Research in Ethnic Relations, University of Warwick.

Joseph Rowntree Foundation (1995) 'Housing needs of people with physical disability.' *Housing Research Findings 136.* York: JRF.

Joseph Rowntree Foundation (1998) 'Assessing housing needs in community care.' *Findings* (March). York: JRF.

Karn, V. and Phillips, D. (1998) 'Race and ethnicity in housing: A diversity of experience.' In T. Blackstone, B. Parekh and P. Sanders (eds) *Race Relations in Britain: A Developing Agenda.* London: Routledge.

King, N. (1998) 'Buying is an option for folk like Tony.' *Housing Today*, 7 May, 82, 17.

Lakey, J. (1997) 'Neighbourhoods and housing.' In T. Modood, R. Berthoud, J. Lakey, J. Nazroo, P. Smith, S. Virdee and S. Beishon *Ethnic Minorities in Britain: Diversity and Disadvantage.* London: Policy Studies Institute.

London Research Centre and Lemos and Crane (1998) *Assessing Black and Minority Ethnic Housing Needs.* London: Housing Corporation.

Oldman, C. (1998) 'Joint planning – why don't we learn from the past?' In I. Shaw, S. Lambert and D. Clapham (eds) *Social Care and Housing.* London: Jessica Kingsley Publishers.

Percy-Smith, J. (ed) (1996) *Needs Assessments in Public Policy.* Buckingham: Open University Press.

Ratcliffe, P. (1996) *'Race' and Housing in Bradford.* Bradford: Bradford Housing Forum.

Shah, L. and Williams, P. (1992) *The Housing Needs of the Asian Elderly in Cardiff.* Research Report. Cardiff: Centre for Housing Management and Development, University of Wales College of Cardiff.

Spicker, P. (1987) 'Concepts of need in housing allocation.' *Policy and Politics 15*, 1, January, 17–27.

Spicker, P. (1989) *Social Housing and the Social Services.* Coventry and Harlow: Institute of Housing and Longman.

Third, H., Wainwright, S. and Pawson, H. (1997) *Constraint and Choice for Minority Ethnic Home Owners in Scotland.* Scottish Homes Research Report 54. Edinburgh: Scottish Homes.

Tomlins, R., Johnson, M., Line, B., Brown, T., Owen, D. and Ratcliffe, P. (2000) *Needs of the Communities of Vietnamese Origin in London: A Report for the An Viet Housing Association.* Coventry: Centre for Research in Ethnic Relations, University of Warwick.

Ware, A. and Goodin, R. (eds) (1990) *Needs and Welfare.* London: Sage.

Watts, V. and Galbraith, C. (1998) 'Living independently.' In R. Bull (ed) *Housing Options for Disabled People.* London: Jessica Kingsley Publishers.

Whittingham, R. (1998) 'Sheltered accommodation for Asian elderly: Some lessons to be learnt?' Unpublished paper presented to Housing Studies Association conference, York, April.

*Chapter 5*

# Widening Locational Choices for Minority Ethnic Groups in the Social Rented Sector

Deborah Phillips and Rachael Unsworth

## Introduction

The social rented sector[1] plays an important role in the housing of minority ethnic households. This is particularly true for African-Caribbean households, 45 per cent of whom are housed by local authorities or housing associations according to the 1991 Census, compared with 24 per cent of white households. The South Asian and Chinese population have traditionally found this tenure less attractive than low cost home ownership, with only 14 per cent of South Asians and 17 per cent of Chinese living in social housing in 1991. There is, however, evidence that, while not necessarily a tenure of first choice, social housing may become an increasingly important housing alternative for young, newly forming Asian households in the next decade (Phillips and Harrison 2000; Ratcliffe 1996).

The social housing experience has nevertheless been highly variable for the minority ethnic population over the post-war years. A wealth of research points to the differential treatment of minority ethnic housing applicants when compared with whites, which has led to a restricted range of housing options for black minority ethnic (BME) groups in particular (Karn and Phillips 1998). This has resulted in the over-representation of African-Caribbean and Asian tenants in poorer housing and unpopular, deteriorating (often inner city) neighbourhoods. The marginalisation of these tenants, along with other socially excluded white groups, has been exacerbated by the commodification and residualisation of the social rented housing sector over the last two decades (Cole and Furbey 1994; Malpass 1996; Mullins 1998). BME tenants have not benefited from council house sales to the same extent as the better housed white population (Peach and Byron 1993), and financial cutbacks in construction and maintenance programmes have reduced the options for transfer for those who remain. In addition, the fear and experience of racial harassment have helped to reinforce the pattern of minority ethnic segregation in poor locations (Chahal and Julienne 1999), with many applicants opting for established areas of ethnic settlement in the inner city; a bounded choice reflecting a trade-off between the community support derived from clustering and the possibility of better housing options elsewhere (Phillips 1998).

The persistent concentration, segregation and deprivation of BME tenants within the social rented sector and the tendency for many minority ethnic appli-cants to opt for inner city living presents housing providers with some important challenges. First, as the number of minority ethnic households grows, it is likely to prove difficult to satisfy demand for the restricted inner city core areas of ethnic residence. There will therefore be increasing pressure to rethink allocation policies in order to provide minority ethnic applicants with housing opportuni-ties outside the established clusters. We are certainly beginning to see some outward movement of minority ethnic households in a number of cities. Although this has so far mostly been confined to the private housing sector (Phillips 1998), an emerging ethnic presence in new parts of the urban housing structure may encourage other ethnic households to consider a wider range of options. Second, the changing housing aspirations of younger minority ethnic households will, evidence suggests, lead to a growing demand for housing in the ethnically mixed areas near to the ethnic cores as well as beyond (Phillips and Harrison 2000). However, there can be very real constraints on successfully inte-grating ethnic households into new areas of settlement, especially where racial harassment is a problem (Hawtin, Kettle and Moran 1999).

Housing policy would certainly seem, at least on the face of it, to be moving in the direction of opening up 'choice' for social tenants. The Housing Green Paper published in April 2000 talks of modifying the existing 'prescriptive' social housing allocations system in order to give tenants a greater say in their housing outcomes. More specifically, the Housing Corporation's 'Black and Minority Ethnic Housing Policy', published in May 1998, is structured around issues of BME empowerment and the development of locally based housing strategies to promote racial equality and meet BME housing needs and aspirations. The climate for widening the locational choices hitherto available to minority ethnic groups within social housing (and for considering strategies to enable this) would therefore seem to be right, especially when set against the back-cloth of Tony Blair's pledge to tackle 'social exclusion'.

Nevertheless, past attempts to promote minority ethnic group mobility within the social rented sector have highlighted the difficulties associated with disrupting the traditional patterns of ethnic settlement in deprived and over-crowded areas, however well intentioned. One of the first institution-led schemes to widen housing choice was introduced under the auspices of the Greater London Council's far-reaching anti-racist programme of the mid-1980s. This explicitly aimed to widen the options of Bengalis applying for social housing in the council-dominated housing market of the London Borough of Tower Hamlets (Phillips 1987). Breaking with a long history of racially discriminatory allocations policies and practices within the borough (Phillips 1986), Bengali applicants were presented with housing options beyond the well established, highly segregated ethnic cluster in the deprived areas of Spitalfields and Brick Lane. However, most of the offers made to Bengalis in non-traditional areas of settlement were rejected for cultural reasons and because of the very real (and well founded) fear of racial harassment. A legacy of discrimination, which had cemented the tendency towards ethnic clustering in the west of the borough, coupled with the council's failure to tackle racial harassment, brought a minimal redistribution of tenants under this mobility initiative. A decade later, the London Borough of Lewisham uncovered similar difficulties in trying to persuade more of its black (mainly African-Caribbean) tenants to move into better quality estates beyond the traditional ethnic cluster in Deptford. A survey of Lewisham council housing applicants once again revealed the power of established community links with particular localities, as well as the fear of racial harassment, to inhibit movement away from relatively deprived and overcrowded areas of minority ethnic settlement (Phillips 1993).

This past evidence, together with more recent pilot schemes (e.g. Hawtin *et al.* 1999), indicates that there is a need for sensitive and well-tuned policies to support minority ethnic households now wishing to move to non-traditional areas within the social rented sector. The social, cultural and institutional forces promoting clustering are still strong, and thus widening the locational choices of minority ethnic groups is far from straightforward. There are justifiable reasons for minority ethnic households to resist opportunities to move away from the established areas of concentration: a sense of familiarity, a community infrastruc-ture, a feeling of safety for a population fearing harassment. There is, neverthe-less, evidence of changing housing aspirations. For example, a recent report from

Birmingham City Council (1998) concluded that there was 'a strong desire amongst Birmingham's black and minority ethnic communities to move to outer city areas' (p.1). The relatively poor environment of the inner city was thought to be the significant push factor; the potential for improving living conditions was the chief pull. Similarly, focus group research amongst Bradford's African-Caribbean and South Asian populations conducted in 1999/2000 indicated that some younger members of these groups are prepared to consider living in a much wider range of areas than their parents. Many displayed ambivalent attitudes towards remaining within the traditional areas of settlement for their group, seeing both advantages and disadvantages associated with living there, but some explicitly wished to escape both the social and cultural confines, and the deteriorating environment of the established ethnic clusters. One young Bangladeshi woman who we interviewed in Bradford explained her reasons for wanting to move in the following terms: 'I've had my education in this country. I don't want the [ethnic] culture to dictate how I am to live my life.' Another argued: '[The inner ethnic cluster], it's like a village, and that's the very reason why I don't want a house in this community…because everyone knows your business.'

The young residents of central Bradford were also clearly aware of and keen to escape from the stigma and the wider structural disadvantages associated with living in deprived, multi-racial inner city areas. Exclusion from job opportunities was uppermost in their minds. However, while some clearly wanted to escape the social labelling, the environmental deprivation and the strictures of community living by moving outwards, most were loath to move too far away. Residents of the clustered Bangladeshi and Pakistani communities explained:

> I don't want to be bang in the middle of the heart of the Bangladeshi community, but yet I don't want to be too far away. (Bangladeshi woman)

> My family say you can move, but don't move too far away. (Pakistani male)

> You can't really move that far if you want your children to be brought up religiously, that's the main restriction for most people I think…especially if you haven't got any transport. (Bangladeshi woman)

> I want to move out a bit, but don't want to move right far away from my parents and all. I want to stay nearby. (Pakistani male)

It is against this background of ambivalence about clustering in the traditional ethnic areas that this chapter is set. Our young Bradford minority ethnic focus group participants, while aspiring to home ownership, saw the social rented sector as a more viable housing option in the short term and a possible route out of the inner city. We therefore aim here to evaluate the extent to which the social rented sector is promoting and supporting opportunities for mobility amongst the younger and older members of the BME populations living in Britain.

The findings presented in this chapter are based on a national survey of local authority housing departments and housing associations (BME-led and 'mainstream' associations) operating in 14 urban localities in England with significant concentrations of BME households.[2] The research was undertaken in 1999. The aim of the survey was to look at the priority given to widening ethnic choice, at the type of strategies developed, at the scale of implementation and how successful they have been. Semi-structured telephone interviews were conducted with officers involved in strategic housing policy work and/or minority ethnic issues in 10 out of the 14 local authorities. Interviews were also completed with personnel[3] in 22 of the 32 registered social landlords (RSLs) approached. Together, the RSLs included in the survey were responsible for nearly 150,000 properties. The BME associations interviewed ranged in size from less than 10 units to over 2500, and represented 16 per cent of the total BME-managed/owned social rented property. The mainstream associations included both small community-based housing associations and large national organisations.

The findings from the survey indicate that the resources and political will to devise and implement institution-led initiatives to widen locational choices for minority ethnic groups are often lacking. There was no evidence of a widespread attempt or commitment to promoting the idea of, or opportunities for, outward movement into new locations. Most local authorities in the towns and cities with the highest levels of BME population recognised that outward movement was beginning, but there was great variation in the level of knowledge of processes, pace and outcomes of change. While many of those interviewed acknowledged that this issue is likely to become more important over time, few institutions were actively addressing it; they had other more pressing concerns at the top of their agenda. There were, however, some notable exceptions to this, which provide examples of good practice and a framework for developing strategies for widening choice.

## Progress by housing associations in opening up wider choice

Although the balance of social housing in England is provided by local authorities, other landlords account for about one-fifth of this sector. Housing associations are the most significant of the smaller landlords, and their relative importance as social housing providers increased dramatically throughout the 1990s. Their growth may be largely attributed to stock transfers from local authorities to housing associations (250,000 homes were transferred between 1988 and 1996 – Mullins 1998), although the scale of this process has varied from region to region. The housing association sector is also significant because it has provided the focus for new-build activity in social housing in recent years, and has seen the emergence of a flourishing black housing movement in the form of BME-led associations (Harrison 1995).

Housing associations play an important role in the housing of BME groups, particularly through the BME-led associations. RSLs house a disproportionately high number of African-Caribbean tenants; for example, according to the 1991 Census 10 per cent of households of Black-Caribbean, Black-African and Black-Other origin lived in this sector, compared with 3 per cent of white, 3 per cent of South Asian and 4 per cent of Chinese households. Importantly, BME-led RSLs have provided the main access points into the social rented sector for the South Asian population (Harrison 1995).

The fundamental contribution of BME-led associations stems from the fact that the needs of minority ethnic groups are their primary concern, not just an after-thought or one duty among many, as they are for the mainstream associations (Karn and Phillips 1998). However, they are still relatively small in number (117 in 1999) and in size (more than half of them own/manage less than 100 properties). Furthermore, the properties owned or managed by BME-led housing associations tend to be located within the main inner areas of ethnic settlement, and as yet there is no strong trend of acquiring property in outer city or suburban locations. It is also true that much of the property owned/managed by mainstream RSLs is located within the inner urban areas, although there is more potential for mobility in these associations. Indeed, as significant stock transfers look certain to continue,[4] both from local authorities to housing associations and from mainstream to BME-led associations, the potential for presenting minority ethnic groups with wider housing choices will grow. It is therefore important to examine the attitudes of this part of the social housing sector towards opening up new locations to BME tenants.

*Allocation policies – reinforcing existing patterns*

Many associations operating in areas of BME concentration experience disproportionately high levels of BME applications (and nominations from the local authority waiting list) for properties in the poorer, inner city areas of established ethnic clustering. The precise requests by some BME applicants for particular streets within the inner city help to reinforce the idea that all people of BME origin wish to live close to their community and would be unwilling to consider moving to other areas. Our survey revealed that this stereotyped view of BME demand is still widely held by those in the housing association sector, and continues to underpin the allocation process in a way that has changed little since the 1980s (Henderson and Karn 1987; Phillips 1987). The allocations practices of many housing associations thus clearly serve to reinforce the established patterns, or at least do not facilitate the outward migration, of minority ethnic households within the social rented sector. As one interviewee in a mainstream housing association in the West Midlands said: 'I'm not sure we have any views on BME people moving out.' It was simply not an issue on their agenda.

Staff working for the mainstream housing associations that we interviewed were mindful of their race equality obligations in the allocations process. This was, however, generally very narrowly conceptualised and operationalised in terms of a simple target system. It was assumed that as long as an association could demonstrate that their annual lettings were in line with the ethnic make-up of the locality, then this was sufficient to discharge their racial equality obligations. The implementation of targets has become a major plank of the Housing Corporation's BME strategy and a key indicator against which housing association performance is measured (NHF 1998). At the time of our survey in 1999, the Federation of Black Housing Organisations' view was that only a small number of mainstream RSLs were showing any real commitment to meeting their targets for housing BME people (*Housing Today* 1999a). Our interviews revealed that even when this commitment was evident, the targets were being implemented in an uncritical manner. There was little consideration, for example, of the possible failings of the 1991 Census in enumerating the BME population and its housing demand. Even more worrying, given the uneven pattern of minority ethnic settlement, there was little awareness of the effects of geographical scale on the setting of targets. One large association set its targets at local authority level because the computer system used to record lettings could only cope with this level of spatial detail. The question of whether an association in an area of low BME residence should set a low target for BME allocations, thereby institutionalising and perpetuating the low representation of minority ethnic groups in that area, was rarely addressed.

The survey also revealed a lack of data on the geography of BME households living in RSL properties. Associations monitor lettings but do not have an overview at any given time of their tenant profile; they do not have trend data on how the tenant profile has changed (by area) over time; there are no maps showing properties held/managed in relation to the BME concentrations and socio-economic indicators of affluence/deprivation and exclusion. Housing associations commonly carry out tenant satisfaction surveys, but not housing needs surveys. Several interviewees were embarrassed about the lack of monitoring information available and the lack of attention given to the issue of opening up wider choices of location. They nevertheless acknowledged that the issue of changing BME locational choices was likely to be of growing importance. BME-led organisations operating in the heart of Huddersfield and Birmingham, for example, were clearly aware of the increasing potential for movement into ethnically mixed areas adjacent to the inner city and saw links through common housing registers as a mechanism for facilitating this in the future. One large, national mainstream RSL was also conscious of the need to introduce a more culturally sensitive framework for assessing minority ethnic housing demands in order to capture changing locational preferences.

## Strategies and actions aimed at opening up choice of location

The potential for widening BME groups' locational choices within the housing association sector is therefore limited by the spatial concentration of existing stock and, importantly, the lack of plans to acquire housing in non-traditional areas, as well as the scant attention devoted to policies for widening minority ethnic group housing choices. There were nevertheless some important initiatives being undertaken. Several key strategies for opening up opportunities and supporting minority ethnic applicants wishing to move into non-traditional areas were identified, which we examine below.

### ESTABLISHING SETTLEMENT CLUSTERS

The positive attributes of ethnic clustering (which may be social, cultural and sometimes economic) as well as the defensive motives for doing so have been well documented (Phillips 1998). Failure to acknowledge the continuing importance of this undoubtedly contributed to the failure of earlier experimental initiatives to widen minority ethnic choices, as for example in the London Borough of Tower Hamlets case cited earlier. Our focus group research in Bradford underlined not only the importance of clustering, but also the fear of isolation in an 'all-white' area. This was as true for African-Caribbean, Pakistani and Bangladeshi youngsters currently living within the inner city as for older people in these groups. Issues related to a sense of well-being, security and identity were raised. It was widely agreed by Pakistanis and Bangladeshis, for example, that 'you don't want to be the only Asian family living on the block'. One Asian youngster said 'I'd be a bit uncomfortable if you're the only black face', and another explained 'the white people living [on outer estates]...you do get a lot of stick off them'. Meanwhile an African-Caribbean woman summed up the views expressed by many participants in her focus group when she said: 'I wouldn't be comfortable in an all-white area. I want my children to see their image around them. I think that's very important.'

Our national survey revealed that several organisations implementing strategies for widening minority ethnic locational choice had constructed their initiatives around the development of new settlement clusters. One BME association (400 units), which provides purpose-built and converted accommodation for South Asian families across north west England, had responded to the problems posed by a shortage of land in established areas of ethnic concentration by creating 'settlement nodes' of families in more outlying areas. This organisation's view was that some Asian households will be prepared to move if they are supported, both by the housing institution and by having other families of a similar origin close by. Access to cultural facilities, schools and health services is given careful consideration before families are offered the chance to settle. The chief executive acknowledged that the success of such schemes rests on a significant investment in terms of interagency initiatives and tenant support. The introduction of specialist training for wardens for the new clusters has been an important feature of this initiative and has served to provide employment, skills and sustained support for the newly settling families.

Similar initiatives had been introduced in the Midlands and South Yorkshire. For example, a relatively small BME association (320 units) had promoted a scheme to support African-Caribbean settlement in an outlying area, although most of its housing development was inner-city-based. One mainstream community-based RSL (750 units) was also endeavouring to acquire property in non-traditional areas in recognition of changing minority ethnic group aspirations. In this case, the aim was to create small settlement nodes both on the fringes of existing areas and in more distant locations, although there was a strong emphasis on maintaining links to the established community. Again access to appropriate schools was recognised as an important issue.

Another housing association recognised the potential for encouraging outward migration by creating clusters of voids so that several households could be transferred simultaneously. The financial implications of keeping properties empty are, however, an obvious deterrent, particularly for smaller social landlords.

COMMUNITY LETTINGS

One large mainstream association, with properties across the north of England, was notable for its attempts to move away from policies based on 'equal opportunities' towards an approach which aims to foster diverse communities through community lettings. This transition was rooted in a recognition of the importance of social interaction and the support inherent in the development of ethnic (and other social) clusters. The approach went hand-in-hand with other strategies, which sought to move beyond fulfilling simple ethnic quotas. For example, a review of the indirectly discriminatory effects of priorities within the allocations system was being undertaken, and the quality of inter-agency support for ethnic tenants was being evaluated.

TRUST/REPUTATION

The success of new initiatives to widen minority ethnic housing choices is dependent upon social landlords gaining the confidence and trust of BME households. This has particular implications for:

- whether minority ethnic households will apply to particular RSLs because of their reputation as 'white' associations

- the areas BME applicants will consider when making their choice of locations.

Evidence suggests that minority applicants may restrict their locational choices upon application, because they feel that they will be excluded from certain areas (Hawtin *et al.* 1999). Our survey uncovered one northern BME-led association that had achieved a high level of minority ethnic tenancies in properties located outside the city centre. The director believed that the potential for further outward movement existed. It was felt that the reputation of this association for being sensitive to BME needs had helped to counteract any potential negative considerations about moving out of the inner city.

Several of the mainstream RSLs included in our survey were taking steps to improve their image with the BME populations in their locality through establishing contacts with local community groups. There are certainly significant barriers to be eroded. It is clear that BME-led associations are more readily trusted to serve the housing needs of the BME communities and, very importantly, to provide long-term support for them as tenants (Harrison 1995; Phillips and Harrison 2000). The visible presence of minority ethnic employees in an RSL can help to boost the confidence of the local minority ethnic population in that organisation. To date, however, the employment of BME staff in mainstream

RSLs has been seriously lacking (*Housing Today* 1999b). A commitment to improving recruitment has become a key strand of the Housing Corporation's 'Black and Minority Ethnic Housing Policy'.

## Local authority awareness of and strategies supporting outward movement

Local authorities' awareness of, views on and policies relating to the outward movement of BME groups contrasts in several respects with the situation in the housing association sector. Local authorities have an overview of the entire area within their jurisdiction and a responsibility to manage the area in an integrated way – especially as sustainable development criteria become increasingly threaded through policies and activities. Linked to this 'new urban agenda' (Pugh 1997), various UK government policy strands are encouraging a multi-agency approach in which housing is seen as an element of the wider issue of quality of life. In addition, local authorities have property in a wide variety of urban locations, some of which may be difficult to let. Ironically, given the widespread exclusionary allocation policies of the past, some northern authorities facing problems of low demand (often on peripheral estates) now see the growing interest in social housing from minority ethnic groups as a possible solution to their problems. Attracting potential tenants to a wider range of locations dovetails with (although is not necessarily inspired by) their race equality commitments.

Local authorities have a statutory duty to assess housing needs and define local priorities. In a small number of authorities, housing needs surveys have uncovered a desire, or at least a willingness, by a significant number of households to consider moving to other areas. Birmingham City Council (1998), for example, has undertaken very detailed research into BME access to housing in its outer city areas, which contrasts with the general needs surveys conducted by most authorities. This council's research revealed considerable potential for outwards mobility from both Asians and African Caribbeans.[5] Similarly, a housing needs survey in Bradford revealed that up to 40 per cent of BME households would be prepared to consider moving outside the main areas of ethnic concentration, although 70 per cent of South Asian respondents felt it was at least fairly important to move to an area which contained those of similar ethnic background (Ratcliffe 1996). As indicated earlier, there were also clear limits on the distance that many households would be prepared to move. In the wake of these findings, Bradford Council commissioned research into opening up access to the social rented sector for South Asian households, particularly in relation to outer estates.

Overall, our survey revealed that most of the local authorities in areas of significant BME presence were aware of the need to widen the choice of location for minority applicants, even though data on the strength of minority ethnic group aspirations for outward movement and the level and pace of movement were often lacking. There was some sensitivity about being seen to be putting pressure on people to move; many respondents were mindful of the discredited ideas of encouraging cultural assimilation by spatial mixing. In any case, local authorities have a responsibility for improving the physical environment as well as the social and economic sustainability of inner city areas; large-scale outward migration would work against such goals. Regeneration efforts include refurbishing housing stock, reconverting sub-divided properties and developing shared equity schemes after clearance of unfit stock.

Most authorities were at least aware of the need to remove barriers to movement so that BME households could more effectively exercise their locational choices, although two out of the ten local authorities interviewed showed little awareness of the salient issues. Policies for widening choices were not, for the most part, very well developed in any authorities, though six of them were implementing at least some of the following strategies:

- tackling racism on outer estates to counteract their negative reputation

- marketing outer estates more actively to a wider range of potential tenants

- taking a more integrated approach to housing management by involving BME groups as well as all relevant agencies in policy review, development and implementation

- looking ahead to new housing land beyond established BME areas and considering land allocation for social infrastructure, for example, for the construction of a mosque in Hamilton, Leicester.

## Discussion and conclusions: Informed housing choices

In 1999, the housing minister Nick Raynsford stated that he would like social tenants to be able to make more 'informed choices' about where they live (*Housing Today* 1999c). In launching the Housing Green Paper in April 2000, he reiterated that message when he said that the government's proposals for a review of the social housing allocation system were 'about providing people with options, and giving them more control over their lives'. If this is to be more than rhetoric for BME tenants, then there are a number of key issues to be tackled.

Our research has identified clear shortcomings in institutional attitudes, policies and practices for widening BME locational choices within the social rented sector. Indeed, for some local authorities and RSLs, the issue of opening up minority ethnic choices was simply not on the agenda. It must be acknowledged that there are difficulties in bringing about the outward movement of BME households via the social rented sector. Vacancies occur less frequently in the more popular areas, and so it is a slow process to change the mix of people in the more desirable areas and to change the stigma and poor reputations of low-demand areas – whether inner or outer city. Providing the support essential for widening ethnic choices can also be expensive in terms of time and finances; this may be especially difficult for smaller RSLs. Some interviewees were wary of the extra management costs that might be incurred if households were encouraged to move into untested areas, only to request to be rehoused after a short time. This has been the experience in small-scale schemes in Liverpool and Bracknell, and in Birmingham.

Nevertheless, despite these difficulties, if the social rented sector is to provide a culturally competent service to its local BME population, then a range of issues must be considered as a framework for policy and action:

1.  The changing aspirations of BME groups, which are neither fully documented at the local scale nor acknowledged, need to be understood. Birmingham City Council's (1998) research recorded the prevalence of stereotypical views expressed by representatives of the housing organisations it surveyed and noted that while large numbers of BME people may indeed prefer to live in inner ethnic areas, 'an appreciation of the dynamic nature of settlement patterns is vital to avoid the view that certain areas somehow "naturally" constitute districts where black and minority ethnic groups wish to live' (p.6).

2.  Institutional cultures in many local authorities and mainstream RSLs are not conducive to the delivery of a culturally competent service. Too many organisations view their responsibilities in terms of narrowly defined ethnic targets and quotas, employ very few minority ethnic staff and, according to a recent report, are merely 'marking time on equal opportunities' (*Housing Today* 1999b). There are currently only two BME chief executives of mainstream housing associations.

3.    At present, the uneven distribution of the housing stock owned/managed by the RSLs (with its inner-city bias) presents limited opportunities for widening locational choices for BME groups. This points to the potential importance of stock transfers for broadening the range of opportunities offered by RSLs, especially if acquisitions were to be in areas just beyond the established ethnic cores. This would seem to be of particular relevance for the BME-led associations, who have often gained the confidence and trust of their local minority ethnic populations. Further supportive partnerships between BME-led and mainstream housing associations could provide the support needed for the newer and less experienced organisations.

4.    Research has emphasised the continuing importance of a sense of belonging, group identity and 'local connections' for both younger and older households, minority ethnic and white groups, when trading off locational options (Phillips and Harrison 2000). These social and cultural links help to cement the bonds of minority ethnic groups with inner city areas (irrespective of their negative attributes) and reinforce the desire to move into areas where there are 'people like them' (whether this is viewed in terms of race, class or other social factors). BME groups face the additional fear of isolation associated with racial harassment. The indications are that minority ethnic movement into non-traditional areas is most successful when families are settled in clusters. This may mean the adoption of policies affording a measure of priority to BME households wishing to move into areas identified as destinations for 'supported outward relocation'. It also requires an investment of time in identifying suitable sites in terms of transport communications, access to religious and community facilities and services, such as suitable schools, in advance of moves. Inner-city regeneration is also a high priority for meeting the needs of those who do not wish to move out.

5.    Improved communication and consultation with BME groups is crucial to instilling a climate of trust and confidence in the responsiveness of social landlords. Despite a stated commitment to tenant consultation and involvement enshrined in local authority 'Tenant Compacts', many tenants (both minority ethnic and white) still often feel that their social landlords do not understand their needs, aspirations or problems (Phillips and Harrison 2000). BME

households particularly fear being dumped in an isolated area and being left to fend for themselves.

6.    There is no doubt that the South Asian minorities in particular retain a strong preference for home ownership. There are, nevertheless, very real economic constraints on these households achieving this goal. Exploring ways in which a mix of affordable home ownership and social renting could be achieved in preferred areas of settlement could be a valuable way forward. The greater emphasis since 1998 on 'Mixed and Flexible Tenure' (MFT)[6] options in the Low Cost Home Ownership programme has been widely acclaimed by housing policy analysts and by the Joseph Rowntree Foundation as a positive step towards greater choice and flexibility for low income households (Terry and Joseph 1998). This reform has the potential to integrate tenures within designated neighbourhoods, thus helping to combat the stigma of social housing areas, and to give greater financial choice to low income households. However, according to a Housing Corporation report (1998), minority ethnic groups often have a poor level of knowledge about the low cost housing options available to them through such schemes.

BME groups may well have positive reasons to cluster as well as more negative reasons for not being able to express a higher grade choice or fearing to move away from their community. But it should not be assumed that these are the permanent areas of preference. Similarly, the extensive web of discrimination and disadvantage faced by BME people should not be overlooked. The social rented sector cannot open up housing choice on its own; it is a matter that goes far beyond the housing sector itself. Housing market position and residential location are closely bound up with a group's life chances and identity. Residential deprivation is associated with wider social exclusion and stigma, which has repercussion for exclusion from other life-chances, especially in relation to work. More open-minded, far-sighted policies and dedicated, co-ordinated implementation by local authorities and housing associations would help to allow a closer correlation between socio-economic potential and housing consumption. Removing barriers to movement rather than trying to engineer a new BME geography is the most enlightened approach and the one that is most likely to result in positive outcomes.

## Notes

1.  We define social rented housing as 'not-for-profit', publicly subsidised housing. This definition encompasses local authorities, registered social landlords and other voluntary sector housing organisations.

2.  These localities were Birmingham, Coventry, Wolverhampton, Nottingham, Derby, Leicester, Rochdale, Sheffield, Bristol, Kirklees, Liverpool, Bedford, Leeds and Bradford. With some misgivings, London was excluded from the sample because of the enormous scale and complexity of the urban structure and its administration.

3.  The designation of the personnel interviewed ranged from development director to research and information officer, chief executive to lettings officer. Inevitably, their views will have reflected their role, seniority and experience of their institution.

4.  The Housing Green Paper published in April 2000 envisages a programme of stock transfers from local authorities at the rate of 200,000 homes per annum from 2001/02.

5.  Nearly two-thirds of African Caribbeans stated a desire to move and of these, only 28 per cent wanted their next home to be in the inner city; 72 per cent preferred an outer-city or out-of-Birmingham location. Around half the Asian respondents had a wish to move and, of these, 65 per cent of the people aged under 60 and 42 per cent of older respondents expressed a greater preference for outer-city or out-of-Birmingham locations.

6.  MFT schemes include tenants, shared owners and full owners. All have the opportunity to alter their tenure if their circumstances change. Shared owners can either increase or reduce the share of the property they own.

## References

Birmingham City Council (1998) *Black and Minority Ethnic Communities' Access to Outer City Housing*. Birmingham: Birmingham City Council.

Chahal, K. and Julienne, L. (1999) *The Experience of Racist Victimisation*. York: Joseph Rowntree Foundation.

Cole, I. and Furbey, R. (1994) *The Eclipse of Council Housing*. London: Routledge.

Harrison, M. (1995) *Housing, 'Race', Social Policy and Empowerment*. Aldershot: Avebury.

Hawtin, M., Kettle, J. and Moran, C. (1999) *Housing Integration and Resident Participation: Evaluation of a Project to Help Integrate Black and Minority Ethnic Tenants*. London: Housing Corporation.

Henderson, J. and Karn, V. (1987) *Race, Class and State Housing*. Aldershot: Avebury.

Housing Corporation (1998) *A Critical Evaluation of the Low Cost Home Ownership Programme*. London: Housing Corporation.

*Housing Today* (1999a) 'Associations Told to Meet BME Targets.' 17 June.

*Housing Today* (1999b) 'Associations Are Failing BME Staff.' 2 September.

*Housing Today* (1999c) M. Weaver (author) 'Raynsford Unveils Plans for Allocations Shake-Up.' 23 September.

Karn, V. and Phillips, D. (1998) 'Race and ethnicity in housing: A diversity of experience.' In T. Blackstone, B. Parekh and P. Sanders (eds) *Race Relations in Britain: A Developing Agenda*. London: Routledge.

Malpass, P. (1996) 'The unravelling of housing policy in Britain.' *Housing Studies 11*, 459–70.

Mullins, D. (1998) 'More choice in social rented housing.' In A. Marsh and D. Mullins (eds) *Housing and Public Policy*. Buckingham: Open University Press.

NHF (National Housing Federation) (1998) *Equality in Housing: Code of Practice*. London: NHF.

Peach, C. and Byron, M. (1993) 'Caribbean tenants in council housing: "Race", class and gender.' *New Community 19*, 407–423.

Phillips, D. (1986) *What Price Equality? A Report on the Allocation of GLC Housing in Tower Hamlets*. GLC Housing Research and Policy Report, 9. London: Greater London Council.

Phillips, D. (1987) 'The rhetoric of anti-racism in public housing allocation.' In P. Jackson (ed) *Race and Racism*. London: Allen and Unwin.

Phillips, D. (1993) 'Report on the Housing Preferences of Black and White Applicants for Housing in the London Borough of Lewisham.' Unpublished report submitted to the London Borough of Lewisham.

Phillips, D. (1998) 'Black minority ethnic concentration, segregation and dispersal in Britain.' *Urban Studies* *35*, 10, 1681–1702.

Phillips, D. and Harrison, M. (2000) 'Access to Social Rented Housing: Findings from the Bradford Focus Groups.' Unpublished report to Bradford Metropolitan District Council.

Pugh, C. (1997) 'Habitat II: Editor's introduction.' *Urban Studies 34*, 10, 1541–1546.

Ratcliffe, P. (1996) *Race and Housing in Bradford.* Bradford: Bradford Housing Forum.

Terry, R. and Joseph, D. (1998) *Effective and Protected Housing Investment.* York: Joseph Rowntree Foundation.

*Chapter 6*

# Missing the Target?

## Discrimination and Exclusion in the Allocation of Social Housing

### David Robinson

Housing is a key determinant of opportunity and housing policy has long been employed to achieve social goals. A key instrument used to achieve social objectives in housing has been council housing (Clapham 1989), assisted more recently by increased activity within the housing association sector. Through allocation policies that assign property to people in housing need, council housing and housing associations have a time-honoured role in the freeing of disadvantaged people from poverty, poor living conditions and the threat of homelessness (Robinson 1998). However, evidence that this role is being performed in a discriminatory manner has long been accumulating. First, research evidence has pointed to the 'undeserving' status often conveyed on minority ethnic households regardless of their housing need, which served to largely exclude minority ethnic communities from the sector. Second, although the social rented sector has opened up to minority ethnic households since the 1960s, it has become clear that minority ethnic households are more likely to be allocated less popular properties in less desirable neighbourhoods. It is these racialised inequalities in the operation of allocation systems in the council housing and housing association sectors, resulting in the exclusion of minority ethnic communities from many of the opportunities offered by social housing, that are the focus of this chapter.

## Choice, constraint and forms of exclusion

There are two principal forms of exclusion visited upon minority ethnic house-holds through discriminatory practice in the allocation of social housing. First, the proportion of some minority ethnic communities living in social housing is relatively small. For example, only 12 per cent of Pakistani households currently reside in the social rented sector, compared to 21 per cent of white households (ONS 2000). This is despite Pakistani households experiencing higher rates of unemployment and poverty than the white population. Second, although some minority ethnic communities have a higher reliance on the social sector – for example, 54 per cent of Bangladeshi and 50 per cent of black households rent from a social landlord (ONS 2000) – they are typically living in less desirable properties than white tenants. Analysis of the 1991 Census reveals that across Britain, while 28 per cent of white local authority tenants were living in semi-detached properties, only 3 per cent of Black-African and 4 per cent of Bangladeshi tenants were doing so. Conversely, while 73 per cent of Black-African and 67 per cent of Bangladeshi tenants were living in purpose-built flats, only 35 per cent of white tenants were doing so (Howes and Mullins 1997).

Efforts to explain the exclusion of minority ethnic communities from oppor-tunities offered by social housing have centred around the relative importance of choice and constraint. Those promoting the importance of choice have rallied against the portrayal of minority ethnic households as pawns, unable to resist or control the forces shaping their lives (Ballard 1992), and highlighted the impor-tance of cultural preferences in shaping housing outcomes. In particular, research has focused on choice as exercised by South Asian communities. Dahya (1974), for example, studied housing outcomes among the Pakistani community in Bradford and concluded that a preference for owner-occupation reflected a desire to have a realisable asset, together with a conscious withdrawal from 'British' culture in order to construct an 'ethnic village'. Other writers have pointed to negative attitudes among some minority ethnic groups, particularly South Asian households, to council housing (see for example Ratcliffe 1981), and the idea of an 'Asian' housing preference for owner-occupation appears to have become an accepted stereotype, or at least a convenient excuse for the relative under-repre-sentation of Indian and Pakistani communities in local authority and housing association sectors.

In contrast, studies of housing constraints have suggested that the housing outcomes of minority ethnic communities are determined by forces outside their control. For example, local authority housing has been allocated in discriminatory ways, racist practices have been revealed among estate agents, building societies and builders and housing association practices have been criticised (Bowes, Dar and Sim 1998).

The convention to emerge from this debate is to regard minority ethnic housing outcomes as the product of 'constrained choice' – choices made within a greater system of constraints than those facing the white majority communities (Tomlins 1999). The challenge for research and policy is therefore to understand and address the processes through which discrimination constrains minority ethnic communities from expressing and satisfying their housing need. This chapter traces efforts to rise to this challenge and discusses why racialised inequalities in the allocation of social rented housing remain a cause for concern, despite the social rented sector increasingly being viewed as part of the problem of, rather than the solution to, social exclusion.

## Discrimination and exclusion in the allocation of social rented housing

While the Race Relations Act of 1968 outlawed more overt forms of discrimination, such as 'Whites Only' notices, more subtle forms of discrimination have remained within housing allocation systems (Hebbert 1999). The constraints facing minority ethnic households in making their housing choices have been categorised in three ways: the action or inaction of key individuals, such as council and housing association officers, sometimes referred to as *subjective racism*; the effect of policies and administrative processes of housing agencies, such as a council or housing association, referred to as *institutional racism*; and aspects of national processes, provided or condoned by the state, that underpin or reinforce racialised inequalities, often referred to as *structural racism* (Ginsburg 1992). Evidence of all three forms of discrimination in the allocation of council and housing association accommodation, either through deliberate intent, inaction or omission, has revealed the processes by which minority ethnic households have been and continue to be regularly excluded from access to one of the traditional tools for tackling the problems of poverty and poor living conditions.

### The action of individuals: Subjective racism

Individual gatekeepers have played a significant role in limiting the housing opportunities available to minority ethnic households. As far back as the 1960s, Rex and Moore (1967) pointed to subjective discrimination within the council housing allocation procedure, hidden beneath a thin veneer of formal justice. The point is well illustrated by their exposé of the role played by the housing visitor in 1960s Birmingham. Every applicant for council housing was seen by a housing visitor, whose job it was to make an assessment of their circumstances. On the basis of this assessment the desirability of each applicant was graded, applicants regarded as undesirable being refused a place in new council housing and placed in a 'slum' property. Although councillors and housing officers insisted that no discrimination operated, Rex and Moore observed significant inequalities in the experience of minority ethnic applicants, who typically ended up in 'slum' properties, rather than new council houses. They concluded that housing visitors are not 'so free of prejudice that a coloured skin is not taken to imply low domestic standards' (Rex and Moore 1967, p.27). The racist views of individual officers were informing the grading of minority ethnic applicants and, in turn, determining the quality of the accommodation offered to these households.

There is no reason to believe that the stereotyping, fed by prejudice, that labels whole communities as deserving or undeserving, does not continue to shape the allocation of housing to minority ethnic applicants, particularly in situations where the workplace culture or organisational practice provides space for racism to flourish. Housing associations, for example, are free to determine priority and allocate housing how they see fit. Freedom allows flexibility and therefore sensitivity to particular needs but, as Niner (1987) points out, freedom can also provide an opportunity for racism to thrive unchecked. Even within organisations with well developed equality programmes and non-discriminatory operating systems, discriminatory stereotyping can still exist to the disadvantage of minority ethnic households. Jeffers and Hoggett (1995), for example, show how, even when the judgements of individual officers are based on the best intentions, stereotyping of particular groups can lead to discrimination through efforts to make 'sensitive' allocations involving the matching of applicants to areas to which they are assumed to be best suited. Such stereotyping has also been recorded in local authority nominations practice, some registered social landlords (RSLs) reporting a reluctance among local authorities to nominate minority ethnic households to stock outside 'minority ethnic areas' (Robinson, Iqbal and Harrison 2000).

*The effect of policy and process: Institutional racism*

The phrase 'institutional racism' has been the subject of much debate in recent years, not least following the deliberations and report of the Stephen Lawrence Inquiry. Whether or not the Metropolitan Police Service is institutionally racist became a point of heated debate, with the Commissioner of the Service appealing against such a conclusion, not least because 'the average member of the public will assume the normal meaning of those words. They will assume a finding of conscious, wilful or deliberate action or inaction to the detriment of ethnic minority Londoners' (Macpherson 1999, para. 6.46). The report, however, took care to distinguish between overt individual racism and institutional racism, defining the latter as:

> The collective failure of an organisation to provide an appropriate and professional service to people because of their colour, culture, or ethnic origin. It can be seen or detected in processes, attitudes and behaviour which amount to discrimination through unwitting prejudice, ignorance, thoughtlessness and racist stereotyping which disadvantage minority ethnic people. (Macpherson 1999, para. 6.34)

Institutionalised racism, as so defined, is a charge that can be levelled at housing agencies and, indeed, has been for many years.

A series of local studies of 'race' and council housing conducted during the 1970s and 1980s documented a number of institutional processes causing minority ethnic applicants for council housing to wait longer for an offer of housing than white applicants, and often to be offered inferior accommodation (CRE 1984a; Phillips 1986; Simpson 1981). These included the inadequate provision of dwellings that meet the needs of minority ethnic households; formal local policies that create access problems for minority ethnic applicants, such as dispersal policies and managerial landlordism involving racialised criteria for determining applicant worth and the type of offer 'deserved'; pressure on staff to fill vacancies quickly and minimise the difficulties of managing multi-ethnic estates; and failure to tackle harassment by white tenants on better estates.

Henderson and Karn's (1987) study of racism and the allocation of council housing in Birmingham illustrated how these and other institutionally racist practices are created and maintained through the various stages of the allocation process. Starting at the beginning of the process, they identify a number of specific policies that exclude or disadvantage minority ethnic applicants, including the disqualification of applications from most single people, owner-occupiers, joint families and many unmarried couples. The justification for these policies was support for 'traditional' families in need, assumed-to-be-married couples living in private rented accommodation. However, minority ethnic applicants were at the time more likely to be low-income owner-occupiers and more likely to be single, particularly in the early post-war decades. Furthermore, the exclusion of unmarried couples particularly affected African-Caribbean applicants, while the splitting of joint families impacted disproportionally on South Asian households.

Moving on to the offer of accommodation, Henderson and Karn noted how minority ethnic applicants were being funnelled into the worst properties by the desire of officers to let properties as quickly as possible and to limit management headaches. Therefore, the preference of white applicants for the suburbs produced a tendency for minority ethnic households to be offered inner-city vacancies because housing officers assumed white applicants would reject such offers. A recent study uncovered similar practice in the RSL sector, if for slightly different reasons; some RSL officers recounting how, although they support applicants if they are insistent in their choice of area, effort is made to steer minority ethnic applicants away from traditional white areas where racial harassment is considered likely (Robinson *et al.* 2000).

One response is the imposition of allocation quotas or 'sensitive lettings', which are increasingly being revisited in the attempt to create so called 'balanced communities'. Emphasis has been placed on equality of opportunity and public accountability through transparent lettings criteria but, judging by the lessons of the past, a real danger is that organisational distinctions between deserving and undeserving will become more racialised. Henderson and Karn (1987), for example, revealed a dispersal policy under which five properties either side of one allocated to a minority ethnic household were automatically reserved for white applicants. The council justified the policy as a means of avoiding the concentration of minority ethnic tenants in the inner city and encouraging movement into the suburbs. Rather than promoting ethnic harmony, however, the policy appeared to be more an accommodation of racist pressure. Henderson and Karn point out that the policy was introduced at the very time a group of white tenants on one estate was threatening a rent strike in response to the allocation of a property to a minority ethnic household.

Many of the policies highlighted by Henderson and Karn and others have now been formally abandoned. Their effects, however, are still being felt by minority ethnic households condemned to live in less attractive council housing or excluded from the sector altogether (Ginsburg 1989). Research also continues to highlight common practices in council and housing association allocation processes, which, although appearing fair and impartial, disguise the housing need of minority ethnic communities and prevent it from being met in the social rented sector.

Housing associations often limit demand by not advertising, relying instead on word of mouth to draw applications. Doing so is likely to exclude households with less 'street knowledge', people who have lived outside the area and people without access to informed support and advice (Spicker 1991). Minority ethnic households also appear to be disadvantaged because of the route they often take into social housing. Jeffers and Hoggett (1995), for example, examined housing allocations in Haringey and Lambeth, two boroughs that had instigated high profile attempts to counter discrimination by limiting individual officer discretion. They revealed, however, that minority ethnic applicants were still disadvantaged in the allocation process because of their over-representation within the homeless stream, homeless households being limited in the number of offers they can refuse and typically being considered less deserving of better quality accommodation than applicants with other housing needs.

Racial harassment in and around the home remains a corrosive force in the lives of many minority ethnic households and evidence suggests that harassment restricts minority ethnic housing choices. First, the experience or expectation of harassment can deter people from taking housing in certain areas (Bowes *et al.* 1998). Phillips (1986, 1993), for example, details how institution-led efforts to widen the options for minority ethnic applicants for social housing in the London boroughs of Lambeth and Lewisham, by offering accommodation beyond the traditional ethnic cluster, were undermined by the legacy of discrimination and most of the offers made were rejected for cultural reasons, including the fear of harassment. Indeed, it appears that minority ethnic households can become involved in a trade-off between certain areas and particular properties, often moving to less suitable accommodation in order to live in an area where harassment is perceived to be less likely (Bowes, Dar and Sim 1997). Second, racial harassment restricts the housing choices of minority ethnic households by influencing the actions of social landlords. As discussed above, some allocation officers, for example, continue to steer minority ethnic applicants away from traditional white areas. This practice might be well intentioned. Landlords have attempted to allocate housing on a 'colour-blind' basis, but the result can be to isolate minority ethnic households on white estates without adequate support and assistance to deal with problems related to isolation and racial harassment. If unable or unwilling to provide necessary support and assistance, steering applicants to traditional areas may therefore appear a sensible strategy for limiting the experience of harassment and ensuring a positive housing outcome. The result, however, is the restriction of choice and the reinforcement of existing patterns of residential segregation.

Tackling racial harassment is therefore vitally important if 'choice' in the social rented sector is to be opened up, as the recent Housing Green Paper demands. The aspirations of, particularly younger, minority ethnic households are changing, with more expressing the desire to live in ethnically mixed neighbourhoods (Birmingham City Council 1998; Hawtin, Kettle and Moran 1999). Pakistani households, for example, increasingly regard social rented housing as a tenure of choice (Bowes *et al.* 1998; Ratcliffe 1996). Racial harassment continues to be allowed to exert a restrictive influence on the choices of minority ethnic households, however. Although there have been increasing numbers of evictions of tenants for racial harassment, it still appears more common for the victim to be moved rather than the offender (Skellington 1996). A recent national review of the use of legal remedies by social landlords to deal with neighbour nuisance found that only 50 per cent of local authorities will always take action in racial harassment cases and 14 per cent will never take possession action, although they might attempt other forms of resolution, such as mediation (Nixon, Hunter and Shayer 1999).

The failure of provision to recognise the changing aspirations of minority ethnic households appears to explain the tendency for new schemes intended to provide housing opportunities for minority ethnic households to be developed in what are considered 'traditional' minority ethnic neighbourhoods. Interviews with RSL staff suggest that a common assumption is that minority ethnic households have an automatic preference for locations with a relatively high proportion of households from the same ethnic group, where there might be culturally sensitive services and shopping facilities, and local minority ethnic owned businesses providing job opportunities not available in the wider labour market (Robinson *et al.* 2000). RSL reticence to develop new schemes outside 'traditional' areas also appears to be informed by concerns about expected problems with racist abuse, harassment and violence from the local population, which could undermine the commitment of minority ethnic tenants and precipitate management headaches. Many RSLs are therefore choosing not to develop outside 'traditional' minority ethnic neighbourhoods, viewing such a move as a risk not worth taking.

### Structural racism

As the Social Exclusion Unit (SEU 2000a) report on minority ethnic issues and social exclusion acknowledges, people from minority ethnic communities disproportionately experience various aspects of social exclusion. While experiences vary between minority ethnic groups, they are more likely than the rest of the population to live in deprived areas, have low incomes, be unemployed, live in inadequate or unsuitable housing, experience poor health and be the victims of crime (SEU 2000a). Racism is central to these experiences. Long-established images of different minority ethnic communities have come to be taken as fact, through repeated expression in mass media and their constant reassertion by hostile political and social movements (Harrison 1999). Aligned with individual prejudices, these images represent a powerful force shaping the perceptions and stereotypes that underpin racialised inequalities in the provision of opportunities and allocation of resources.

Looking at labour market experiences, for example, rates of unemployment are higher among minority ethnic communities regardless of qualifications, place of residence, gender or age (Modood 1997). A CRE study found that among young people, white job applicants are up to three times more likely to get interviews than people from South Asian communities with similar qualifications and five times more likely than 'Black' applicants (CRE 1996). Once in the workforce, evidence also suggests that racial discrimination limits the progress of minority ethnic employees. The TUC (2000), for example, report that the proportion of minority ethnic employees with higher level qualifications increased during the 1990s but that the gap between the proportion of minority ethnic employees and white employees in senior and managerial positions widened.

National housing policy has disadvantaged minority ethnic households by failing to account for, and even exacerbating, the impact that racism has on the range of social and economic factors that affect minority ethnic households. In particular, policies have tended to reward more economically advantaged households, while the economic inequalities faced by minority ethnic communities continue (Modood 1997). The Right-to-Buy programme is a prime example.

Minority ethnic communities have been less able to take advantage of right-to-buy policies, because of lower incomes and racialised allocations that have limited access to the more attractive, suburban estates most suitable for purchase and likely to provide a source of capital accumulation (Ward 1981). The increased social polarisation between owners and renters, and between owners whose property provides a source of capital accumulation and those whose property cannot store wealth, as Ward (1981) points out, was therefore closely aligned with racialised inequalities in allocation procedures that supported the segregation of minority ethnic households into less desirable properties and locations.

Meanwhile, through the sale of council housing, allied with limited spending on new building or the maintenance and rehabilitation of remaining stock, households unable or unwilling to buy have been presented with a housing opportunity declining in size and quality. Local authorities lost, for example, many of their larger properties through Right-to-Buy. Although housing associations have emerged as the main providers of new social housing for rent, following the introduction of the mixed funding regime in the Housing Act 1988 they have struggled to build within the Housing Corporation's grant limits the larger dwellings needed by some minority applicants and housing association properties have, in fact, been getting smaller (Walentowicz 1992). The social rented sector has consequently been increasingly unable to respond to the problem of overcrowding, which disproportionally affects minority ethnic households and, in particular, Pakistani and Bangladeshi communities (Modood 1997).

The lessons of Right-to-Buy well illustrate how disadvantages that are the legacy of past racist practices can be reproduced by what appears, superficially at least, to be non-discriminatory policy. It also highlights the failed logic that, as Smith (1987) points out, assumes racialised inequalities can be tackled through the eradication of racial discrimination, rather than recognising and responding to these inequalities across the whole range of economic and social (and housing) policy. The experiences of minority ethnic households not only differ in degree but also in kind from those of the majority ethnic population. Their interests are therefore not always best served by policies addressed to the general. The following section explores exactly how policy has responded to evidence of racism in the allocation of housing.

## Tackling discrimination: Limiting exclusion?

An important watershed in the recognition and response to racialised inequalities in the allocation of social housing was the CRE's report on Hackney London Borough Council in 1984 (CRE 1984b). Drawing on statistical information, the CRE report demonstrated that 'race' was a key factor in shaping differential housing outcomes and laid down a series of requirements for reform. These modest recommendations centred around administrative procedures, including record-keeping and ethnic monitoring of applicants, review and revision of allocation practice, staff training in 'race' relations and the appointment of a senior officer to lead the implementation of race equality policies. The CRE's Hackney reforms were criticised by some as minor administrative reforms unlikely to impact significantly on the experiences of minority ethnic households without a sea change in the social climate that feeds racism (see Jacobs 1985). Hackney, however, was held up as a typical example of local authority practice and the reforms demanded by the CRE were implemented in housing departments across the country. Indeed, the Hackney reforms continue to be presented as the essence of good practice. For example, the CRE Codes of Practice for the elimination of racial discrimination in the provision of housing and housing services issued during the 1990s emphasised the need for an equal opportunities policy, staff recruitment and training and ethnic record-keeping and monitoring.

A survey of housing agencies in Sheffield found that the majority operate *equal opportunity policies* that satisfy the basic requirements demanded by the Race Relations Act 1976, the Sex Discrimination Act 1975 and the Disability Discrim-ination Act 1995, to outlaw discrimination against employees and service users on the grounds of 'race', ethnic origin, nationality, gender or disability (Gidley, Harrison and Robinson 1999). There was little understanding, however, of the translation of policy into practice and the effectiveness of mechanisms employed to eradicate unlawful discrimination. Although aspects of good practice were identified, there was limited evidence of policies being widely advertised or vig-orously integrated into practice by housing organisations within the city. Neither was there any evidence of assessment procedures informing the ongoing revision of targets and methods of implementation (Gidley *et al.* 1999). It therefore seems unlikely that these equal opportunity programmes mounted a serious challenge to the unconscious ethnocentric stereotypes and culturally defined differences that have informed the institutional processes and the actions of individual officers responsible for the allocation of housing.

*Staffing and training initiatives* have been at the heart of reforms employed by housing organisations to tackle discriminatory assessments of housing need. This approach has focused on eradication of the historic processes that underpin dis-crimination through training and staffing issues. Training is vital to limit the impact of subjective racism, given the continuing reliance of the allocations process on officer discretion, while under-representation of particular communi-ties challenges an organisation's ability to recognise fully and respond adequately to the requirements of particular groups and sends damaging signals to current and potential minority ethnic tenants (Gidley *et al.* 1999). Training for housing staff at all levels was advocated by the CRE report in Hackney, and the impor-tance of a culturally diverse organisation in responding to the needs of a multi-ethnic society and current under-representation is recognised in recent guidance and statements from a variety of sources. For example, the Housing Cor-poration's recent black and minority ethnic (BME) housing policy statement points to the need to respond to under-representation of minority ethnic members on RSL governing bodies, for RSLs to review recruitment levels of minority ethnic staff and to develop and maintain opportunities for the career development of minority ethnic staff, who are particularly under-represented at senior levels (Housing Corporation 1998).

Despite the warm words, the provision and effectiveness of staff training on black issues remains in doubt and evidence suggests that minority ethnic communities continue to be under-represented among the staff of many council housing departments and RSLs. Somerville and Steele (1999) surveyed all housing organisations in the north west of England. Interviews with black staff members revealed deep concerns about the under-representation of black people within their organisations and evidence that recruitment and selection practices, although fair in theory, were considered unfair in practice; for example, as a result of judgements made by interview panels. Respondents also reported how in some organisations black staff were often taken on to deal with 'Black' issues, resulting in job segregation that could impact on promotion opportunities. A lack of training for all staff on black issues was also reported.

*Monitoring* is essential to review progress on equal opportunity commitments, policy implementation and the need for changes to strengthen and reinforce practice. Monitoring is only of value, however, if it is employed to check what is going wrong and to identify how it might be put right (Henderson and Karn 1987). Although there is no doubt that in these days of performance measures and target setting housing organisations are bound into the monitoring culture, whether or not the data collected are put to any meaningful application remains to be proven.

Recent research in Sheffield found that most RSLs did little other than fulfil their obligation to forward detailed information on lettings and allocations to the Housing Corporation. Why RSLs are not making more of the rich data at their disposal is not clear, although many referred to practical difficulties in putting their hands on the data and complained about time and resources to analyse the data being a luxury they could not afford (Gidley *et al.* 1999). More recently, a national survey of RSLs found wide variations in practice regarding ethnic monitoring of lettings and allocations (Robinson *et al.* 2000). At one end of the spectrum were the majority of RSLs that undertook ethnic monitoring infrequently and only across their whole stock. In contrast, a minority of RSLs, driven by organisational level commitments, local authority demands and key staff members with the time and relevant skills, reported regularly with scheme and/or estate level data and included information on refusals, terminations and transfers. Good practice was undermined, however, by performance being measured against targets that reflected little other than staff expectations about whom they would house, rather than an appreciation of whom they should be housing, given the local population profile and the relative housing needs of various communities.

The various programmes and initiatives forced upon and developed by local authorities and RSLs, outlined above, are evidence of greater sensitivity toward equality issues among social landlords. Indeed, recent reports suggest a growing demand for social housing amongst minority ethnic households, traditionally assumed to prefer owner-occupation (Tomlins 1999). However, evidence that minority ethnic households are being excluded from council housing or channelled into less desirable stock because of the discriminatory influence of the (sometimes well-intentioned) actions of individual officers and institutional processes continues to accumulate (Birmingham City Council 1998; Bowes *et al.* 1997, 1998; Hawtin *et al.* 1999). Meanwhile, although the RSL sector increasingly caters for households on low incomes and minority ethnic households are more likely to be financially worse off and living in poorer conditions than white counterparts, the proportion of RSL tenants from minority ethnic groups remains static at around 10 per cent. It appears, as Jeffers and Hoggett (1995, p.325) conclude, that even after a programme of what they refer to as 'institutional hygiene', enforced through equal opportunity policies and increased staffing from minority ethnic communities, the stereotypes that discriminate against minority ethnic households, such as the assumption that all minority ethnic applicants wish to live close to their community and are unwilling to consider living outside traditional ethnic clusters, continue to exist.

The BME housing movement can be seen as a response to the ongoing failings of mainstream, white-run social landlords to satisfy the housing needs of minority ethnic communities. Supported by government initiatives during the 1980s and 1990s, there has been a dramatic growth in registered BME associations, from 18 organisations in 1986 to 64 in 1999. The sector is now championed as 'one of the most successful examples of BME business in Europe' (Housing Corporation 1998, p.14), and there is no doubt that the contribution of BME-led RSLs to directly meeting the needs of minority ethnic households and increasing cultural competence across the whole sector has been significant (for a more detailed discussion see Chapter 7 of this volume). Drawing 60 per cent of their tenant base from minority ethnic communities, BME RSLs have begun to overcome the negative experiences and perceptions of the social rented sector among minority ethnic communities, which, as Bowes *et al.* (1998) point out, have been important in shaping the choices and actions of minority ethnic households. They have also increased the involvement of minority ethnic communities within housing provision, for example, by providing effective channels for local participation and creation of opportunities for training and work within the sector (Harrison 1992). Working in tandem with mainstream, white-run associations, BME RSLs have also improved cultural sensitivity and competence in provision across the sector (Harrison 1991). Long-term additions or amendments to mainstream services, often provided on a commercial basis by BME RSLs, include language skills, interviewing and outreach work and advice. Examples of shorter-term arrangements include training aimed at facilitating the involvement of more black tenants or involving local people in anti-harassment work. These are significant gains but they remain under threat, the desire to see the sector grow being increasingly tempered by concerns about the financial viability of smaller RSLs in the harsh economic climate within which RSLs now operate (Marshall *et al.* 1998). It should also be noted that the majority of RSL tenants from minority ethnic communities are still housed by mainstream, white-run associations.

## The consequences of exclusion

Despite the various initiatives actioned in response to evidence of racialised inequalities in the allocation of social rented housing, discriminatory practices continue to promote the exclusion of minority ethnic households from the sector. Failure to adequately tackle racial harassment in and around the home, for example, has been shown to foster reluctance among certain communities to consider residing in the social rented sector; among individual officers to nominate minority ethnic households to traditionally white estates; and among social landlords to consider developing housing opportunities for minority ethnic communities outside traditional ethnic clusters. However, the policies of successive governments, and shifting cultural trends and social forces, have undermined the appeal and reputation of social housing and left local authorities and housing associations to provide little more than an increasingly stigmatised safety net for households unable to enter or survive in the market-place (Robinson 1998). So why is exclusion from social housing a cause for concern? Other than it being a moral concern that 'race', colour or ethnic origin impact upon a household's ability to exercise choice in satisfying their housing needs, there are at least three key reasons. First, social housing can still provide housing of a quality and standard better than many people experience in the private sector. Second, local authorities and RSLs are increasingly providing a range of services above and beyond bricks and mortar in acknowledgement of the disadvantage and deprivation facing many of their tenants. Third, policy makers are closely identifying social exclusion with social housing and targeting responses, in particular, at concentrations of social rented housing. Discrimination in the allocation process and racialised inequalities in housing outcomes are excluding minority ethnic communities from equal access to these tangible benefits of living in the social rented sector.

Taking the first of these points, the experiences of people at the bottom of the owner-occupied sector are not dissimilar, and in some aspects are often worse, than those of households living in the social rented sector. Analysis of the British Social Attitudes Survey, for example, reveals that home-owners in the lowest council tax band reported more neighbourhood problems, such as rubbish on the streets, vandalism, burglary, cars being broken into and stolen, than council tenants (Lee and Murie 1999). Neither are households in the private sector necessarily better off, as analysis of Census data has revealed (Lee and Murie 1997). High rates of home-ownership among some minority ethnic communities should not, therefore, be read as an indication of relative wealth and prosperity. In fact, as Bowes and Sim illustrate in Chapter 3 of this volume, these properties are often at the bottom of the market and in a poor state of repair; and according to the English House Condition Survey, Pakistani, Bangladeshi and 'Black' households are considerably more likely to be living in poor housing conditions than white households (DETR 1998).

As well as being more likely to be living in poor conditions, the limited evidence available suggests that minority ethnic communities also experience a disproportionate level of homelessness. Homelessness is the lack of a home. A home might reasonably be defined as a secure and minimally adequate housing space providing physical and emotional security. People living in overcrowded or unsafe accommodation, sharing with friends and relatives, reliant against their will on hostel or bed-and-breakfast accommodation or sleeping rough can all therefore be defined as homeless. While homelessness may be regarded as one part of a chain of experiences, influenced by and shaping other events, any explanation of homelessness has to acknowledge that labour market factors and patterns are key, given that the power to secure an adequate dwelling closely reflects incomes and employment status (Harrison 1999). Minority ethnic households are more likely than those of the white population to be unemployed (DfEE 1999) and more likely than the rest of the population to be poor (Berthoud 1998). Minority ethnic populations also tend to be disproportionately young and, as the Social Exclusion Unit (SEU) Policy Action Team (PAT) Report on Young People concludes, young people from minority ethnic communities are at greater risk of various forms of social exclusion due largely to racism and discrimination (SEU 2000b). It therefore comes as little surprise that, particularly young, people from minority ethnic communities have a disproportionate experience of homelessness (Davies *et al.* 1996).

Given these experiences, it would appear that the social rented sector still has a role to play, freeing disadvantaged people from poor living conditions and the threat of homelessness. Discrimination in the allocation process, however, is preventing the sector from fulfilling this role and limiting access for minority ethnic households to an opportunity that could improve dramatically their quality of life. This loss is being compounded by the consequent exclusion of these households from the opportunities provided by the increasing involvement of the sector in 'housing plus' activities, a second reason why exclusion from social housing remains a cause for concern.

The potential of housing services, as providers of housing and organisers of social and environmental responses to tenants' needs, to 'add value' above and beyond the provision of a physical shelter has increasingly been exercised by social landlords in recent years. Arguing that they are on the front line when it comes to social problems, housing a disproportionately high number of disadvantaged households, and that given their commitment to social welfare they have the ability to make a real difference, housing associations and local authority housing departments have promoted their involvement in community development and regeneration as an essential ingredient in the fight against poverty and inequality. Persuaded of this fact, central government has fostered a strategy of regeneration premised on housing plus initiatives and a partnership approach, for example, through the Single Regeneration Budget programme (Cole and Shayer 1998). The added value to community regeneration of additional investment in housing associations remains unclear (Cole 2000) but unequal access to the sector for certain minority ethnic communities means that whatever benefits are forthcoming will not be equally available to all households in need.

A third reason why continued discrimination in the allocation of social housing remains a cause for concern is that a result is to limit access for minority ethnic groups to the opportunities provided by the emerging social exclusion agenda. Social exclusion has been closely identified with social housing estates. Indeed, the social rented sector is increasingly viewed as an agent of exclusion, rather than merely a sector accommodating poverty. Lee and Murie (1999) argue that the conflation of social exclusion and social housing reflects the increasing emphasis in public policy on neighbourhood deprivation, related to the view that concentrations of deprivation represent a burden and damage competitiveness. As they point out, the policy agenda pursued in the 1990s, before and after the election of the New Labour Government in 1997, has spotlighted the need to tackle concentrations of deprivation. The Prime Minister's Social Exclusion Unit (SEU), for example, given the task of producing 'joined up solutions to joined up problems', has targeted attention on 'poor neighbourhoods' which have 'poverty, unemployment, and poor health in common, and crime usually comes high on any list of residents' concerns' (SEU 1998, p.13). Within these neighbourhoods, or 'worst estates' as Tony Blair refers to them (SEU 1998, p.7), RSLs and council housing have featured predominantly. Although the Policy Action Teams (PATs) commissioned to report on housing management (PAT 5) and unpopular housing (PAT 7) have tended toward more of a neighbourhood than a tenure focus, the concentration on levers for change has inevitably focused the debate on the role to be played by social rented housing.

Evidence of continuing discrimination in the allocation of social housing undermines the focus of the social exclusion agenda on neighbourhoods dominated by social housing in two key ways. First, racialised inequalities in access to social housing are witness to the fact that the relationship between deprivation and housing tenure is not as simple as assumed. Social exclusion is not isolated, or even concentrated, in council or RSL estates, as the SEU policy agenda appears to believe. Second, the danger of ignoring this fact and focusing action on social housing estates is that policy will target neither the most deprived areas nor the households in greatest need and will perpetuate discrimination in the distribution of resources against minority ethnic communities, failing to reach, for example, the large number of deprived Pakistani households resident outside the social rented sector.

The social exclusion agenda has refocused the attention of policy on areas and people suffering problems such as unemployment, poor skills, low incomes, poor housing, high crime rates, poor health and poverty. Acknowledgement of the growing divisions within society, that have so long been ignored, is welcome. Yet, as long as the social exclusion agenda focuses on issues that are not key causal factors, such as housing tenure, the real causes of social exclusion, such as racism, will go unchecked.

## Conclusion

This chapter has set out how discrimination in the allocation process promotes racialised inequalities in access to social rented housing and reviewed the various initiatives employed to limit the impact of racism on minority ethnic housing opportunities. It has questioned the effectiveness of these responses and pointed out that, despite institutional efforts to eradicate discriminatory practice, minority ethnic communities are still discriminated against in the allocation process.

The opportunities offered by RSLs and council housing might not be as attractive as they once were. Indeed, social housing is increasingly viewed as an agent of social exclusion. Racialised inequalities in access to social housing remain a cause for concern, however. Councils and RSLs can still provide housing of better quality than many people experience in the private sector, while the housing plus agenda ensures that entry to the sector affords access to a range of services above and beyond bricks and mortar. Efforts to tackle social exclusion, meanwhile, are increasingly targeted at social housing estates. Discrimination in allocations deny minority ethnic households equal access to these significant benefits.

The concept of social exclusion suggests that people are disempowered and unable to make choices, take charge of their life and thereby enjoy the same rights and life-styles as others (Clapham and Evans 2000). The consequences include poor living conditions, poverty, poor health and unemployment. Tackling social exclusion must therefore involve enabling minority ethnic communities to make their housing choices within a system free from racist influence. An important start has been made with efforts to tackle discrimination in the allocation of social housing. Policy, however, must look beyond discrimination issues and respond to the particular, deep-rooted and pervasive influence of racism on the life experiences, and thereby the housing opportunities, of minority ethnic communities.

## References

Ballard, R. (1992) 'New clothes for the Emperor? The conceptual nakedness of the race relations industry in Britain.' *New Community 18*, 3, 481–492.

Berthoud, R. (1998) *Incomes of Ethnic Minorities.* Colchester: Institute for Social and Economic Research.

Birmingham City Council (1998) *Black and Minority Ethnic Communities' Access to Outer City Housing.* Birmingham: Birmingham City Council.

Bowes, A., Dar, N. and Sim, D. (1997) 'Tenure preference and housing strategy: An exploration of Pakistani experiences.' *Housing Studies 12*, 1, 63–84.

Bowes, A., Dar, N. and Sim, D. (1998) *'Too White, Too Rough, and Too Many Problems': A Study of Pakistani Housing in Britain.* Research Report No.3. Stirling: Department of Applied Social Science, University of Stirling.

Clapham, D. (1989) *Goodbye Council Housing?* London: Unwin Hyman Limited.

Clapham, D. and Evans, A. (2000) 'Social exclusion: The case of homelessness.' In I. Anderson and D. Sim (eds) *Social Exclusion and Housing: Context and Challenges.* Coventry: Chartered Institute of Housing.

Cole, I. (2000) 'The changing role of housing associations.' In I. Anderson and D. Sim (eds) *Social Exclusion and Housing: Context and Challenges.* Coventry: Chartered Institute of Housing.

Cole, I. and Shayer, S. (1998) *Beyond Housing Investment: Regeneration, Sustainability and the Role of Housing Associations.* Sheffield: Centre for Regional Economic and Social Research, Sheffield Hallam University.

CRE (1984a) *Race and Housing in Liverpool: A Research Report.* London: Commission for Racial Equality.

CRE (1984b) *Hackney Housing Investigated*. London: Commission for Racial Equality.

CRE (1996) *We Regret to Inform You: Testing for Racial Discrimination in Youth Employment in the North of England and Scotland*. London: Commission for Racial Equality.

Dahya, B. (1974) 'The nature of Pakistani ethnicity in industrial cities in Britain.' In A. Cohen (ed) *Urban Ethnicity*. London: Tavistock.

Davies, J., Lyle, S., Deacon, A., Law, I., Julienne, L. and Kay, H. (1996) *Discounted Voices: Homelessness Amongst Young Black and Minority Ethnic People in England*. Sociology and Social Policy Research Working Paper 15. Leeds: School of Sociology and Social Policy, University of Leeds.

DETR (1998) *The English House Condition Survey 1996*. London: The Stationery Office.

DfEE (1999) *Report of the Policy Action Team 1: Jobs for All*. London: Department for Education and Employment.

Gidley, G., Harrison, M. and Robinson, D. (1999) *Housing Black and Minority Ethnic People in Sheffield*. Sheffield: Centre for Regional Economic and Social Research, Sheffield Hallam University.

Ginsburg, N. (1989) 'Institutional racism and local authority housing.' *Critical Social Policy 8*, 3, 4–19.

Ginsburg, N. (1992) 'Racism and housing: Concepts and reality.' In A. Rattansi and R. Skellington (eds) *Racism and Anti-racism*. London: Sage.

Harrison, M.L. (1991) *Achievements and Options: Black and Minority Ethnic Housing Organisations in Action*. Leeds: Armley Publications.

Harrison, M.L. (1992) 'Black-led housing organisations and the housing association movement.' *New Community 18*, 3, 427–437.

Harrison, M.L. (1999) 'Theorising homelessness and "race".' In P. Kennett and A. Marsh (eds) *Homelessness – Exploring the New Terrain*. Bristol: The Policy Press.

Hawtin, M., Kettle, J. and Moran, C. (1999) *Housing Integration and Resident Participation: Evaluation of a Project to Help Integrate Black and Minority Ethnic Tenants*. London: Housing Corporation.

Hebbert, M. (1999) 'Not dwelling on race.' *Town and Country Planning*, June, 182–183.

Henderson, J. and Karn, V. (1987) *Race, Class and State Housing: Inequality and the Allocation of Public Housing in Britain*. Aldershot: Gower.

Housing Corporation (1998) *Black and Minority Ethnic Housing Policy*. London: The Housing Corporation.

Howes, E. and Mullins, D. (1997) 'Finding a place – the impact of locality on the housing experiences of tenants from minority ethnic groups.' In V. Karn (ed) *Ethnicity in the 1991 Census. Volume Four: Employment, Education and Housing Among the Minority Populations of Britain*. London: HMSO.

Jacobs, S. (1985) 'Race, empire and the welfare state: Council housing and racism.' *Critical Social Policy 13*, 6–28.

Jeffers, S. and Hoggett, P. (1995) 'Like counting deckchairs on the Titanic: A study of institutional racism and housing allocations in Haringey and Lambeth.' *Housing Studies 10*, 3, 325–344.

Lee, P. and Murie, A. (1997) *Poverty, Housing Tenure and Social Exclusion*. Bristol: Policy Press.

Lee, P. and Murie, A. (1999) 'Spatial and social divisions within British cities: Beyond residualisation.' *Housing Studies 15*, 5, 625–640.

Macpherson, W. (1999) *The Stephen Lawrence Inquiry*. Command Paper 4262-I. London: The Stationery Office.

Marshall, D., Royce, C., Saw, P., Whitehead, C. and Woodrow, J. (1998) *A Level Playing Field? Rents, Viability and Value in Black and Minority Ethnic Housing Associations*. York: York Publishing Services.

Modood, T. (1997) 'Employment.' In T. Modood and R. Berthoud (eds) *Ethnic Minorities in Britain: Diversity and Disadvantage*. The Fourth National Survey of Ethnic Minorities. London: Policy Studies Institute.

Niner, P. (1987) 'Housing associations and ethnic minorities.' In S.J. Smith and J. Mercer (eds) *New Perspectives on Race and Housing*. Studies in Housing No 2. Glasgow: Centre for Housing Research, University of Glasgow.

Nixon, J., Hunter, C. and Shayer, S. (1999) *The Use of Legal Remedies by Social Landlords to Deal with Neighbour Nuisance. A Survey Report*. Sheffield: Centre for Regional Economic and Social Research, Sheffield Hallam University.

ONS (2000) *Social Trends 30*. London: The Stationery Office.

Phillips, D. (1986) *What Price Equality: A Report on the Allocation of GLC Housing in Tower Hamlets*. London: Greater London Council.

Phillips, D. (1993) 'Report on Housing Preferences of Black and White Applicants for Housing in the London Borough of Lewisham.' Unpublished report submitted to the London Borough of Lewisham.

Ratcliffe, P. (1981) *Racism and Reaction: A Profile of Handsworth*. London: Routledge and Kegan Paul.

Ratcliffe, P. (1996) *'Race' and Housing in Bradford*. Bradford: Bradford Housing Forum.

Rex, J. and Moore, R. (1967) *Race, Community and Conflict*. Oxford: Oxford University Press.

Robinson, D. (1998) 'Health selection in the housing system: access to council housing for homeless people with health problems.' *Housing Studies 13*, 1, 23–41.

Robinson, D., Iqbal, B. and Harrison, M. (2000) *Allocation of Housing to Black and Minority Ethnic Groups: From Bids to Black and Minority Ethnic Housing Opportunities. A Research Report to the Housing Corporation*. Sheffield: Centre for Regional Economic and Social Research, Sheffield Hallam University.

SEU (1998) *Bringing Britain Together: A National Strategy for Neighbourhood Renewal*. Command Paper 4045. London: The Stationery Office.

SEU (2000a) *Minority Ethnic Issues in Social Exclusion and Neighbourhood Renewal*. London: The Stationery Office.

SEU (2000b) *Report of Policy Action Team 12: Young People*. London: The Stationery Office.

Simpson, A. (1981) *Stacking the Decks: A Study of Race, Inequality and Council Housing in Nottingham*. Nottingham: Nottingham Community Relations Council.

Skellington, R. (1996) *'Race' in Britain Today*. London: Sage.

Smith, S.J. (1987) 'Residential segregation: A geography of English racism.' In P. Jackson (ed) *Race and Racism – Essays in Social Geography*. London: Allen and Unwin.

Somerville, P. and Steele, A. (1999) *Career Opportunities for Ethnic Minorities*. Salford: Department of Housing, University of Salford.

Spicker, P. (1991) *Access to Social Housing in Scotland: A Survey of Local Authorities and Housing Association Allocation Policies*. Edinburgh: Shelter (Scotland).

Tomlins, R. (1999) *Housing Experiences of Minority Ethnic Communities in Britain: An Academic Literature Review and Annotated Bibliography*. Bibliographies in Ethnic Relations No.15. Coventry: Centre for Research in Ethnic Relations, University of Warwick.

TUC (2000) *Qualifying for Racism: How Racism is Increasingly Blighting Career Prospects*. London: Trades Union Congress.

Walentowicz, R. (1992) *Housing Standards After the Act: A Survey of Space and Design Standards in Housing Association Projects in 1989/90*. London: NFHA.

Ward, R. (1981) 'Race, Housing and Wealth.' Paper presented to the policy seminar on race relations. Nuffield College, Oxford, 27 November.

Chapter 7

# Black and Minority Ethnic Housing Associations

## Malcolm Harrison

The development of black and minority ethnic (BME) housing associations in England was one of the housing policy success stories of the 1980s and 1990s. This chapter reviews the period from 1986 onwards, beginning with a discussion of four historical stages, so as to place the associations in the context of politics and national housing policy. The most recent stage, under New Labour, is dealt with in a separate section. After this we discuss roles played by BME housing organisations, and their constraints and opportunities. The chapter then concludes by relating events – albeit briefly – to some general themes about empowerment, incorporation and regulation in the welfare state. Social welfare movements such as the Black Voluntary Housing Movement rarely operate on ground of their own choosing, and may be heavily affected by the policy and practice environment, which shifts over time. The arrival of a New Labour government changed immediate prospects for the associations, but longer-term development remains difficult to predict.

## History and key events from 1986 to 1997

The history and achievements of BME housing associations have now been chronicled extensively in a variety of publications, including the journal *Black Housing* (published by the Federation of Black Housing Organisations, the FBHO). Although most of these associations are still fairly small, their impact has been far more significant than would be suggested simply from the numbers of their dwellings or staff. The growth of the associations has been held to have contributed to empowerment within minority ethnic communities. As has been argued elsewhere (Harrison 1998, p.77), a sense of increased empowerment may be felt through having a voice via a black-run organisation, control of assets or organisational resources, availability of a more culturally sensitive service, access to services where anti-racist practices are the norm, the ability to cross boundaries between housing needs and socio-medical services, black role models of individual and organisational success, or the availability of contracts or employment from a local housing agency to people within its area. BME housing associations have been involved with these aspects of collective empowerment. The growth of the associations brought new voices into the housing policy forum, improved awareness of racism and cultural diversity, provided role models and gave a sense of ownership of assets. Associations have frequently emphasised their community roots and commitment, extending beyond the bricks-and-mortar provision of homes. It has been indicated that many 'have a community development perspective' (Housing Corporation 1995a, para.8.11).

Alongside the associations themselves, the record of the Housing Corporation as their key sponsor in England is also now well understood. Through the second half of the 1980s, and in the 1990s, the corporation encouraged development of housing associations run by black people, in two five-year programmes providing monies and proactive official support. Despite limits on resources, the programmes enabled a large number of new associations to get up and running.

An overview of events up to 1997 is available from Harrison (1995, 1998) and Royce et al. (1996). In 1996 there was a report to the Housing Corporation on the two five-year programmes (Harrison et al. 1996), summarising circumstances near the end of the Conservative period in office when it appeared that Government would no longer support a programme of this kind. Now that New Labour has been in office long enough to amend policies, it is reasonable to think in terms of four overlapping periods during which governmental agency interactions with the BME associations can be considered. First, there was a brief period prior to the 1988 Housing Act when the Housing Corporation encouraged these associations to form or develop within the context of a relatively favourable national financial environment for the housing association sector. Second, there was a period when the corporation continued to encourage the associations, but in an environment which made progress more difficult for small organisations. This was following the 1988 Act, when mixed private sector/public sector funding was emphasised as the way forward for housing associations (Secretaries of State for the Environment and Wales 1987, pp.12–13). During these years the corporation sustained its programme for BME associations successfully into a second five-year period, albeit with some limitations, especially on what could be achieved for new or small organisations. Third, there was a period when official support was diluted, as the second five-year programme ended and the corporation sought an acceptable way forward. The expectations of the Conservative government, especially about provider competition and the ways that needs should be met, left less space for continuing a strategy which had prioritised particular kinds of provider organisations. A fourth period has followed the election of the new government, with a new policy document and strong expectations that the minority-led associations would continue to receive development funding allocations. We will comment below on these four periods, although it is worth noting that there has nonetheless been some degree of continuity throughout. National changes can sometimes be offset or softened by lags in implementation, or by continuity in commitments and practices locally. Furthermore, some problems for small associations have persisted right through since the 1980s.

## The Housing Corporation's first phase

The Housing Corporation's first five-year programme, begun in 1986/87, involved finance for development of housing schemes, supplemented by grants towards start-up and running costs. The justification given for the strategy at that time referred to indications that the housing needs of black and minority ethnic people were 'substantially worse than for other groups', and that people from ethnic minorities were also under-represented in housing association work (see Housing Corporation 1991, p.1). The strategy was tied in with an overall intent to encourage 'racial equality' within the housing association field, and could also be interpreted as having some of the features of a positive action programme (Housing Corporation 1995b). Corporation personnel became involved in the promotion, registration and support of new black-run associations operating in areas of substantial BME population and housing need. The corporation's strategy stimulated growth in the black voluntary housing movement (although there had been some black-run associations in operation before then). (For fuller coverage see Harrison 1995.)

## A new environment

By the late 1980s the programme was operating in a financial and political environment that made progress more difficult for small organisations, and pressed housing associations generally in more commercial directions. With its 1987 White Paper and 1988 Housing Act, the government began to restructure social renting. More of the investment capital for associations' schemes was to come from private finance, rent rises for tenants were likely, and there was an emphasis on value for money seen in terms of rather basic output measures. The Housing Corporation's approach to minority ethnic housing associations took on a more selective character, with perhaps something of a change in emphasis from promotion to consolidation. Nonetheless, as the first five-year period ended, the corporation reaffirmed its commitment. It set objectives for the next five years, with plans for investing £750 million, and encouragement for white-run associations to transfer some existing dwellings to minority ethnic associations (stock transfers). The planned capital allocation represented over 9 per cent of the corporation's expected total investment in new rented housing. These plans were to take effect, however, in the changing environment for association activity, in which it seemed that only the stronger minority ethnic associations would attain a full capacity for independent action without dependency on larger white-run partners. Some smaller associations might remain primarily managing agencies, running but not necessarily owning properties, and without the financial and staffing strengths to undertake scheme development on their own. Some might even disappear or become components of a merger.

Despite difficulties in this period, the two five-year programmes together achieved a great deal. Although most of the Housing Corporation's financial support was for housing development schemes funded very much on their merits, the channelling of this money helped a range of minority ethnic organisations to emerge and grow. Summarising the situation at the end of our second historical period, we can point to the existence of 60 BME associations registered with the corporation, over 2000 units of stock transferred from 1991–92 to 1994–95, and over 13,000 homes in management at March 1995 (Housing Corporation 1995b).

### The retreat

By the mid-1990s, against a backcloth of falling Housing Association Grant rates and a decreased capital programme, prospects looked unfavourable. It seemed that some black-run associations might merge with others, or struggle to survive independently. The second five-year programme was due to end in 1996, raising questions about what would follow. The history we are describing had entered its third phase. The assumption was that the corporation's established approach on BME housing associations would end. Commentators were indicating a likelihood of the strategy being replaced by a series of strategic initiatives, and a probable ending of the existing 'positive action' approach, with capital and revenue funding no longer being 'ring-fenced' for black-led associations (for discussion see Harrison 1998, pp.78–79). Although the term 'ring-fenced' actually may have been less appropriate here than 'indicative targets' (Housing Corporation 1998, p.19), the policy was moving away from supporting and promoting the role of black-run housing associations as such towards supporting black housing needs. As observed elsewhere (Harrison 1998), the crucial driving force now was the national politics of social rented housing. The Conservative government's preoccupations implied competition among providers, cheapness of output, and dependence on private capital. Any 'top-slicing' of capital budgets in the interests of the development of black-run associations fitted poorly with governmental notions about how housing should be provided.

Efforts were made by corporation staff to create something constructive to follow the ending of the second five-year programme, but this was inherently difficult. A consultation document was followed by a policy statement, *Black and Minority Ethnic Housing Needs: An Enabling Framework* (Housing Corporation 1995a, 1996). The new statement emphasised concerns which included improved identification of housing needs, improved performance of providers in responding to priority housing needs, having a flexible and locally sensitive framework, developing the roles of organisations which add value to their housing functions by providing culturally sensitive services, and meeting the corporation's obligations under Race Relations law. There was a change of emphasis, away from establishing and supporting specific housing associations, towards the identifiable needs of minority ethnic communities. Nonetheless, the policy acknowledged 'the particular skills and experience of strategic B & ME associations' (Housing Corporation 1996, p.4), and the 'specialisms developed' within them (p.5), and hoped to build upon those skills. The corporation would also continue to work with some minority ethnic associations that had not yet achieved revenue viability, to help them move forward (p.24). In addition, the corporation's documents took a sophisticated stance on the issue of housing needs, acknowledging differentiation of experiences between different ethnic groups and in differing localities (Housing Corporation 1995a, para.3.4). Given that cultural sensitivity and local community links had been strong features of black-led associations, the corporation's stress on local needs could be seen as very relevant to their potential competitive positions and roles. As the consultation document put it, future planning to meet needs would require greater understanding of, and more analysis related to, particular communities (para.6.5), and the black-run associations could be important partners in the identification of needs and could help local communities evolve more culturally sensitive ideas on need and diversity (para.6.7).

Despite this, the basic change in policy was still a threat to the movement. One possible outcome was that without a share of funds pre-allocated for minority ethnic associations, these associations might have difficulties in competing for scheme development work and might be in danger of being subordinated to larger (usually white-run) counterparts with more assets. It also seemed possible that community development and 'housing plus' aspects of small associations' work might be undervalued in the new climate.

Looking at governmental policy for social renting in general at this time gave few grounds for optimism. The corporation's role was being redefined 'to direct its power away from the promotion of individual housing associations to a consumer-oriented approach, centred on the housing produced and its use in the long term' (1995a, para.4.4). There would no longer be 'a strategy to promote individual associations' as such (para.4.6). As well as facing increased competition among associations for grants, in due course housing associations might not necessarily remain the only providers of new social rented dwellings. The model of housing developer to which many small associations had aspired might no longer be attainable in a climate of fierce competition for reduced funds, making it essential for them to work co-operatively with more powerful partners (as many in any case had done before). The inclusion of probable rent levels in the competitive bidding process might 'limit the ability of small, relatively new associations' to develop housing schemes independently (para.7.9). There could be more 'mergers, groups structures, transfers of engagements, partial rationalisation of ownership and management patterns or contractual partnerships' (para.8.16). Black-run organisations would be operating in the context of shifting local environments in which 'enabling' local authorities, new housing companies, consortia and partnerships were to be the order of the day.

In fact it appears that the immediate impact of the new policy framework on funding allocations was not dramatic, even though there was now no target (Housing Corporation 1998, p.19, para.7.2). It should be kept in mind that it had long been argued that individual allocations via the minority ethnic associations had been made for worthy scheme bids, not for the associations as such; and the shift in policy would not have inhibited officers from continuing to take a positive view of desirable bids in which the associations were involved.

## New Labour: A changed politics?

New Labour's election victory in 1997 led to official confirmation of the significance of the Black Voluntary Housing Movement, within a broader strategy concerned with meeting minority ethnic needs. This followed indications given
before the election in an explicit policy statement (for an outline see Harrison
1998). BME housing associations (by now included under the term registered
social landlords, or RSLs) would play an important part alongside white-run
RSLs and local authorities. There was a new policy statement from the Housing
Corporation in May 1998, *Black and Minority Ethnic Housing Policy* (Housing Corporation 1998). This included an endorsement of the policy, from the Minister
for Local Government and Housing, who referred to the need for housing
services to be 'culturally competent and inclusive' (p.1). As the Minister's
foreword put it: 'RSLs led by black and minority ethnic people will play a crucial
role in the Corporation's policy. They are in themselves an important manifestation of community empowerment.' The policy statement itself covered general
commitments on issues ranging from membership of RSL governing bodies to
the employment of BME contractors. Perhaps of greatest immediate political significance was the statement that in overall terms the corporation expected that
'the proportion of ADP to BME RSLs will remain above 9%, and that there will
be regional variations based on local needs' (Housing Corporation 1998, p.19).

It is important to set the policies on RSLs within a context. New Labour
appears to be encouraging an active official stance on 'race'. In the Housing Corporation's sphere this seems to be facilitating a range of specific commitments: to
regional strategies and advisory groups, to more work on needs, to a raising of
performance standards, to more 'aspirational' targeting on lettings, staffing, and
management committees, and so forth (Cheesman 1999, p.10). Renewed recognition for minority ethnic associations thus forms part of something larger, albeit
something that connects with previous policies. The new policy emphases are
clearly of great significance for the Black Voluntary Housing Movement, and the
FBHO appears to have been put into a more salient political position by the
change of government (see *Black Housing* 1999a). The Housing Corporation's
1998 policy was certainly welcomed when launched (*Black Housing* 1998a, p.18),
even if on certain general issues in Labour public policy there was felt to be a continuity from the Conservative period (note, for example, critical comments about
the government's commitment to competition: *Black Housing* 1998b, p.12). On
the other hand, the policy statement still affirmed that, following the (Conservatives') 1996 Housing Act, corporation policy would support 'consumers rather
than providers' (Housing Corporation 1998, p.3).

As far as grass roots events are concerned, it is difficult to appraise current experiences within the associations without comprehensive up-to-date data and in-depth qualitative material. The Joseph Rowntree Foundation has sponsored work on funding, rents, viability and financial sustainability (Joseph Rowntree Foundation 1996, 1998a and 1998b), and Lemos and Soares have reported on non-housing services being provided by the associations and on their potential (Goodby and Patel 1998). Summarising from the Rowntree studies, Whitehead distinguishes between those minority ethnic associations 'that act basically as mainstream associations' and 'smaller, culturally-oriented, associations that aim to provide services for specific minority ethnic groups' (Whitehead 1998, p.15). She notes that rents are higher than at other (white-run) associations, and indicates that this might particularly affect the smaller culturally-orientated associations. Furthermore, she does not give an optimistic impression of the future financial position for most of the associations, stating that they 'are more vulnerable to external financial pressures and have to operate within tighter constraints' (p.15).

Recently, Cheesman (1999) has given a positive outline of progress from the Housing Corporation's perspective. Noting that the corporation looks 'to BME-led RSLs to set the pace', he observes that 'last year they gave a lead to the entire RSL sector by setting real rent decreases' (pp.10–11). Substantial sums have continued to be allocated to the minority ethnic associations, especially in London (for general figures recently, see *Black Housing* 1999b). In this region, for 1999/2000, £11.08 million was apparently allocated directly to the associations, and £14.23 million to schemes they were involved with via other associations. The total amounted to over 15 per cent of the rented programme. Substantial percentages were also reported for the Yorkshire and Humberside, North West, and West Midlands regions (*Black Housing* 1999b). Regional strategies mirror and amplify national concerns (see, for instance, Housing Corporation London Region 1999). Cheesman summarises the overall position from Corporation Head Office:

> Our support for BME-led RSLs was underlined by the aspiration in our policy document that investment to them should remain above 9% of the national approved development programme (ADP). The figure for 1999/00 was in fact 11.3% – amounting to £47m, to produce 1,040 homes... There are regional variations, reflecting local circumstances. (Cheesman 1999, p.10)

He also reiterates a point that has been made for earlier periods, that allocations were won through competitive bidding. Interestingly, his commentary shows definite recognition from the corporation of ongoing problems, including the concern that councils and white-led RSLs do not always work effectively with minority associations and that some RSLs do not follow through on stock-transfer agreements. As noted above, stock transfers have been encouraged by the corporation, the expectation being that this would expand the stock and asset base of minority ethnic associations. Thus there would sometimes be an agreement that a white-run association would hand over not only management of dwellings but also, perhaps subsequently, ownership. Supporters of minority ethnic associations have stressed the importance of ownership (although properties need to be of the right quality and in the right locations). The incentives for white-run associations to participate, however, have not necessarily been clear. It is worth stressing, furthermore, that involvement of BME associations is now mentioned specifically in relation to the theme of stock transfers from local authorities, a connection which in the present writer's view remained under-explored in the 1990s (see also Housing Corporation 1998, p.16).

The corporation remains concerned with financial viability where, lacking economies of scale and a pool of unencumbered pre-1988 stock across which to spread their costs, and often providing additional housing plus services, some associations apparently 'are struggling' (Cheesman 1999, p.11). Viability has been a long-standing concern and was noted as an issue in the corporation's 1998 policy statement (Housing Corporation 1998, p.8). Some larger (and generally white-run) associations may have an advantage when setting rents if they hold substantial numbers of older properties where debt burdens and costs are relatively low. Although BME-led RSLs have developed strategies to reduce rents, the rents remain higher than average (Cheesman 1999, p.11). In these circumstances partnerships and co-operative cost-sharing arrangements remain very much on the agenda (cf Joseph Rowntree Foundation 1998b; Whitehead 1998). It is worth adding that in some places there might still not even be a 'main player' generally acknowledged within the local policy arena as the actor representing BME interests, or a strong registered minority ethnic association yet able to enter into partnerships on any basis of equality (for possible options in such a situation see Gidley, Harrison and Robinson 1999, pp.73–76). Since white-run housing associations have long worked with unregistered black-led organisations, this need not preclude participation, but can keep it on a different basis and open the door for accusations about patron/client relationships and about manipulation by white-led organisations.

## Roles, constraints and prospects

BME housing organisations are diverse, carrying out a wide variety of tasks ranging from advice work to management of dwellings. Some management committees have held strong perceptions about trying to identify and help with unmet demand for particular kinds of accommodation, and there has also been an interest in specialised needs or in making a link with services on the housing/care boundary. Housing plus activities have often been important (Harrison *et al.* 1996, pp.17–19), indicating strong connections with local communities.

Associations registered with the Housing Corporation have often wished to take on the role of independent housing developer as well as manager, and to acquire ownership of properties. The corporation's policies have facilitated these aims to some extent, but encouragement has been qualified by recurring concerns about organisations' viability, protecting public investments, levels of likely rents, and security of tenants. Partnerships, consortia and co-operation have been perceived as ways forward. The corporation's regional offices have often tried to broker supportive agreements with possible partners from amongst larger and more established white-run associations. This has offered resources and financial safety, but also potential dependencies. Complaints have been voiced about the power of larger white-run associations and about the self-interested nature of some of their apparent support; yet their co-operation has remained important. Perhaps tensions between autonomy and collaboration have been inevitable here because minority ethnic associations have been developing in a field already well-populated with significant provider organisations, so that there could be no 'clean slate' or 'level playing field' in terms of assets.

Differences amongst BME associations themselves can be seen in terms of capacities and working resources, degrees of local political success, available alliances, and assets. One report suggests that those BME RSLs which are 'strong enough to maintain their separate identity' may themselves be tending 'to become more and more mainstream' (Joseph Rowntree Foundation 1998b, p.2). Apparently, the corporation's general approach, 'through competition for grant, local rent restriction and other pressures', bears 'most heavily on the ethnic minority associations', making it difficult for them 'to maintain their special role' (p.2). One implication might be that there is divergence between, on the one hand, growth, managerialism, financial prudence and commercialisation and, on the other, advocacy and continuing community interactions.

We should be a little cautious, however, about concluding that a larger or more established organisation will necessarily become more out of touch or culturally insensitive, or will do less in terms of capacity-building within the community. Local circumstances could be crucial. For example, recent small-scale research with some tenants of a well-established Yorkshire minority ethnic association did reveal worries about some of the rent levels but also provided an observation that the association had learned from earlier mistakes and was in broad terms offering a good service. Its recent specific innovative activities in helping to develop community mutual aid practices were commended strongly (Phillips, Harrison and Karmani 1999). Similarly, looking at non-housing benefits for the wider local community, it can be argued that larger and better-established minority ethnic associations have been likely to be able to do more to involve black contractors than could smaller organisations.

As regards the future, much depends on external factors, including policies on regeneration, housing benefit, and activities that cross boundaries between housing services, social care, economic regeneration and employment. Beider (1998) has pointed to a range of possible activities for the associations, and an agenda no longer based so much on building and managing housing units, but a 'more holistic approach that appreciates the connection between housing, regeneration and renewal' (p.14). New organisational structures could emerge, and new tasks develop, linked with employment policy, health services, community development and environmental improvement. At the same time, futures for low-income owner-occupation in inner-city areas and beyond deserve particular thought and, given enough interest from government, minority ethnic organisations might contribute substantially here. The issue of responses to minority ethnic tenure preferences remains a submerged one, never adequately addressed. The strong desire for eventual owner-occupation amongst at least some of the potential client groups of RSLs has not been matched fully or systematically by the development of facilitating or partnering roles for minority ethnic associations with occupiers who would like to own, or to upgrade the houses they already own. Practices in meeting specialised housing needs (such as those of single young people) might also benefit from more resources being channelled through BME associations. More generally, ability to represent minority voices and sensitivity to the needs of specific communities give associations a strong case for roles in those local strategies which invoke the notion of partnerships with the community. Increased official emphasis on understanding diverse housing needs has confirmed the desirability of local authorities and other housing bodies involving BME organisations. Such involvement might be especially salient in contexts such as the development and implementation of strategies to revitalise local authority housing in low-demand areas. Where stock lies on the periphery of existing minority ethnic settlement, there might be scope for partnerships aimed at community development, co-ordinated lettings to groups of minority households, and shared ownership.

For some consumers, household 'need' can of course include being dealt with by a culturally sensitive and anti-racist housing service, and perhaps in some instances by minority ethnic staff. One advantage of minority ethnic RSLs has been their ability to attract some clients who probably would not have sought social rented housing otherwise, and there is potential to act as gateways for entry to social housing in co-operation with white-run partners. In discussions with housing agencies in the 1990s, the present writer sometimes suggested that the outreach potential of minority ethnic organisations could be built on in formal terms through a variety of contractual relationships. Services might be purchased by white-run organisations from BME RSLs and other local organisations. Such strategies may still be well worth pursuing, in contexts ranging from the improvement of local communications and advice services to joint management of specialised services on the housing/care or housing/employment boundaries.

## Conclusions

The BME housing associations have become acknowledged participants in housing provision and strategy in England, despite many still having modest assets and staffing. Their roles and successes have been distinctive, and the Housing Corporation strategy which supported their growth was virtually unique in public policy as an explicit and sustained programme for prioritising the funding of service-providing organisations run by black people within a large 'mainstream' budget. Yet policy history here should not be reviewed independently of its broader setting. Growth of the associations should be located, partly at least, in the context of Conservative policy for housing associations (alongside other landlords) to supersede local authorities in providing social rented housing. The Housing Corporation pursued its support for the associations, however, within an overall financial environment that was less favourable after 1988, and a political climate that was definitely unsupportive by the mid-1990s. The emphasis in corporation policy, by this time, on diverse needs, reflected governmental leanings towards prioritising the consumer rather than provider, but also offered an indirect way of protecting the position of some provider organisations which could cater for needs in a culturally sensitive manner. The claim to cultural competence provided one means to argue for a continuing role for minority ethnic associations, as the possessors of specialised knowledge and skills.

One feature of the history in this chapter is continuity of constraints. There is a legacy from the Conservatives of low budgets for public investment in social renting activities, and of competitive bidding for resources. Financial constraints remain crucial under New Labour, while the commitment to involving private sector capital has moved from an inheritance from the government of its rivals, the Conservatives, to an essential article of faith. Likewise, the rhetoric of partnerships and contractual relationships appears to continue, while commercial values are applauded. There may be continuing tensions between advocacy and business-style managerialism for some organisations trying to grow from a grass-roots base. Co-operation between large and smaller partners may continue to be affected by the desire of most players to maintain and enhance their own assets in a competitive environment. Yet financial pressures may continue to encourage partnership or dependency. At the same time minority ethnic housing associations, like others, remain subject to general Housing Corporation rules, guidelines, monitoring and viability expectations. This has encouraged adherence to standards of propriety, planning and behaviour designed to protect tenants and assets, secure equal opportunities, and so forth; but it may appear rather demanding for small organisations. Finally (perhaps partly because social rented provision has increasingly become portrayed pejoratively as residual 'welfare' housing), providers and tenants in the sector remain politically vulnerable, with future financial support for both still being unpredictable in the longer term.

The events and achievements outlined in this chapter point to complex relationships between empowerment, incorporation and regulation. Social welfare movements, of which the Black Voluntary Housing Movement has been a leading example, rarely create the key features of the political, financial and social environments in which they emerge and operate. BME groups have mobilised and co-operated with success in the housing policy arena, seeking the empowerment of minority ethnic communities through gaining a voice in policy, control of property and fairer employment opportunities. Meanwhile, however, they have been heavily affected by the administrative, legal, political and financial environment. That environment itself shifts over time, offering different opportunities. There have been two-way processes of interaction, including direct consultations at several levels. Many ideas about needs and solutions have developed from the grass roots, and have figured in policy debates, yet there have also been possibilities of exploitation by white-run organisations. Furthermore, the incorporation of previously excluded interests into the networks of housing policy and practice has brought multiple effects, some of which have clearly been positive for the minorities, but some of which may have involved adjustments in organisations' own targets, roles and self-perceptions.

The continuity of constraints noted above might be interpreted in 'structural' terms. The constraints are contemporary reflections (or manifestations) of broad structural factors that help shape the processes and assumptions through which dissent, need and ethnicity are managed or regulated, and financial support is rationed, in the welfare state. Organisations drawn in or incorporated as housing providers may become party to some of these processes of regulation, directly or indirectly, and may need to conform to specific expectations. Behind some daily processes and practices lie ideological and material forces, which can condition activities or rhetoric, and the choices of politicians and officials. There is scope for innovation or resistance, or the impact of 'human agency'. Over time, dominant ideas and demands affecting institutional activity may shift somewhat, and grass-roots pressures play roles here. This is one reason why today's performance standards acknowledge 'race'. During the Conservative period, however, some housing changes owed more to economic liberalism, and to trends in the broader management of economies, than to grass-roots pressures. Expectations of business management, competition and commercialism affected larger areas in housing practice, in voluntary as well as profit-making sectors. Dependence on private investment became a significant motor of change. Given freer choice, some participants in the BME housing movement might have liked to strengthen their autonomy and strong community links, rather than stressing financial returns, commercial drive or deals with partners. Development as a competitive provider might eventually require limits on autonomy, and a market-style approach to consumers, suppliers, sub-contractors and staff. With expectations of partners and funders to consider, associations might have less scope for independent action. At the same time, core business concerns might revolve around rents, cost minimisation and buildings, rather than community capacity-building exercises or housing plus work for which little funding is available. Today a minority ethnic housing association – like a white-led one – could even run the risk of being characterised by some potential clients as an institution operating for its own financial benefit, especially if rents appear high. Room for manoeuvre is restricted by external financial, political and ideological factors affecting the operating environment and dominant expectations within social housing organisations.

It remains difficult to appraise the likely longer-term effects of the New Labour government, although in the short-term the 1997 general election certainly changed the prospects of the associations and the FBHO. One fundamental long-term test will be on the terrain of organisational cultures and motivations, where the frameworks, values and practices that develop will reflect the extent to which New Labour maintains similar mechanisms for control and competition to those of the Conservatives. A second test will concern access to resources for households and organisations, a factor crucial to the development of black-led RSLs, and to the options available for their tenants. Official endorsement of cultural diversity has been linked with an acknowledgement of distinctive roles played by minority ethnic associations, but this is qualified by recognition that white-run RSLs still have 'the largest impact' on meeting the needs of minority households in many localities (Housing Corporation London Region 1999, p.7, last para.). To achieve a substantially larger BME RSL sector would require considerable investment and co-operation from other providers. Ways forward might include heavier involvement in the regeneration arena, transfers of stock from councils as well as from white-run RSLs, and new involvements across the boundaries with other services and with owner-occupation.

# References

Beider, H. (1998) 'At the crossroads.' *Housing Today* 25 June, 89, 14–15.

*Black Housing* (1998a) 'FBHO members' briefing.' *Black Housing* July/September, 101, 17–18.

*Black Housing* (1998b) 'Black housing futures: A debate among housing professionals.' *Black Housing* July/September, 101, 11–15.

*Black Housing* (1999a) 'Lobbying and campaigning.' *Black Housing* June/July, 106, 13.

*Black Housing* (1999b) 'Allocations to BME RSLs.' *Black Housing* April/May, 105, 7.

Cheesman, D. (1999) 'Race at the centre of the Housing Corporation's BME agenda.' *Black Housing* June/July, 106, 10–11.

Gidley, G., Harrison, M. and Robinson, D. (1999) *Housing Black and Minority Ethnic People in Sheffield.* Research Report. Sheffield: CRESR, Sheffield Hallam University.

Goodby, G. and Patel, G. (1998) 'Roots regained.' *Black Housing* July/September, 101, 6–7.

Harrison, M.L. (1995) *Housing, 'Race', Social Policy and Empowerment.* Research in Ethnic Relations Series. Aldershot: CRER/Avebury.

Harrison, M.L. (1998) 'Minority ethnic housing associations and local housing strategies: An uncertain future?' *Local Government Studies 24*, 1, 74–89.

Harrison, M.L., Karmani, A., Law, I., Phillips, D. and Ravetz, A. (1996) *Black and Minority Ethnic Housing Associations: An Evaluation of the Housing Corporation's Black and Minority Ethnic Housing Association Strategies.* Source Research Report 16. London: The Housing Corporation.

Housing Corporation (1991) *Black and Minority Ethnic Housing Associations. Housing Corporation Policy: A Draft for Consultation.* London: The Housing Corporation.

Housing Corporation (1995a) *Black and Minority Ethnic Housing Needs: An Enabling Framework.* Consultation paper. London: The Housing Corporation.

Housing Corporation (1995b) *Black and Minority Ethnic Housing Association Strategic Review.* Source Policy Guide 2. London: The Housing Corporation.

Housing Corporation (1996) *Black and Minority Ethnic Housing Needs: An Enabling Framework.* Source Policy 4. London: The Housing Corporation.

Housing Corporation (1998) *Black and Minority Ethnic Housing Policy.* London: The Housing Corporation.

Housing Corporation London Region (1999) *Black and Minority Ethnic Housing Strategy for London.* London: The Housing Corporation, London Region.

Joseph Rowntree Foundation (1996) 'Financing black and minority ethnic housing associations.' *Housing Research Findings* 180. York: JRF.

Joseph Rowntree Foundation (1998a) 'Rents, viability and value in black and minority ethnic housing associations.' *Findings* (May). York: JRF.

Joseph Rowntree Foundation (1998b) 'Black and minority ethnic housing associations: Do they have a separate future?' *Policy Options* (May). York: JRF.

Phillips, D., Harrison, M.L. and Karmani, A. (1999) Unpublished material from focus groups research carried out in Bradford.

Royce, C., Hong Yang, J., Patel, G., Saw, P. and Whitehead, C. (1996) *Set Up to Fail? The Experiences of Black Housing Associations.* York: Joseph Rowntree Foundation.

Secretaries of State for the Environment and Wales (1987) *Housing: The Government's Proposals.* Cm 214. London: HMSO.

Whitehead, C. (1998) 'At the crossroads.' *Housing Today* 25 June, 89, 15.

# Chapter 8

# Black and Minority Ethnic Employment in Housing Organisations

## Peter Somerville, Andy Steele and Dianne Sodhi

This chapter looks at the employment of black and minority ethnic (BME) staff by housing organisations in England, with a particular focus on the issue of progression to senior management positions. The chapter aims to convey a sense of the experience of BME staff within these organisations, and draws upon management literature in an attempt to explain the general position of such staff. Various approaches are considered by means of which greater racial equality can be achieved in housing employment, and conclusions are drawn as to the most promising way forward.

## Introduction

In historical terms, it is not so long ago that black and Asian people were excluded from most types of employment in Britain, having been recruited to work only in particular industries such as public transport, the health service and the textile industry. Consequently, black and Asian people gained access to employment in housing organisations only in posts such as cleaners and care assistants – traditionally very low paid and with little or no career prospects. All this was thirty years ago, but how much has really changed since then? This chapter will show that, although the representation of BME people has improved considerably since those early days, a similar pattern can still be detected, whereby BME staff remain concentrated at the bottom of the organisational hierarchy, with apparently few prospects for promotion.

In 1993 the Commission for Racial Equality (CRE) published a report *Housing Associations and Racial Equality* (Commission for Racial Equality 1993). The report was the result of an investigation into the policies and practices of forty housing associations. The purpose of the investigation was to consider the effectiveness of associations' performance in eliminating unlawful racial discrimination and promoting racial equality generally. The CRE found that only a quarter of associations had plans for implementing racial equality policies, indicating a widespread complacency with regard to this issue. In spite of numerous research reports over the years demonstrating that black households typically receive allocations of poorer quality accommodation than white households (Lakey 1997; Pawson 1988), most associations did not monitor the equality of accommodation that people received by ethnic origin, and very few held information about the ethnic origin of their existing tenants. In particular, the CRE report found that the proportion of housing association employees of BME origin was very low, given the representation of these groups within the workforce generally. The CRE concluded that few associations were meeting the Housing Corporation's minimum equal opportunities requirements, as set out in their 1992 Code of Guidance. Tomlins (1994) commented that 'the CRE's housing association investigation demonstrates greater concern amongst housing associations with paper policies and being seen to be doing something, rather than actually doing it' (p.27).

Research carried out by the University of Salford in the north west of England in 1998 found that the situation had not changed significantly since 1993 (Somerville and Steele 1998). Most housing associations still did not have racial equality plans or comprehensive racial equality training programmes for their staff, and still on the whole appeared to be paying only lip service to equality of opportunity. The main difference was that housing organisations were employing more BME staff, but this was true only of a minority both of housing associations and local authorities, and there were still many housing associations with significant under-representation of BME groups within their workforces. It was also notable that the increased employment of BME staff was almost entirely at the lower levels of the organisations concerned. The research found few examples of good practice worth writing up, and these included well-supported black staff support groups and positive action management training initiatives. With the exception of a few outstanding local authorities, non-BME housing associations and the BME-led associations, the overall impression made upon the researchers was one of complacency and indifference to racial equality issues, which often conflicted with the image that the organisation wished to convey to the Housing Corporation.

It seems unlikely that housing organisations are particularly different from other types of employer in Britain. Indeed, the sector seems remarkably close to the average, with BME groups being represented in the housing workforce in almost exactly the same proportion as in the labour market generally, namely 6.4 per cent according to our research. Modood (1997) provides the most comprehensive and up-to-date general picture here. This picture reveals that minority ethnic people are represented in greater numbers and in a greater variety of types of job than, say, twenty years ago. For African-Caribbeans, Indians and African Asians, there has also been a growth in the numbers in intermediate non-manual positions. In general, there has been 'an overall trend of progress in the job levels of ethnic minorities and a narrowing of differentials between the ethnic majority and the minorities' (Modood 1997, p.142). Modood goes on to comment, however, that men in all ethnic minorities are 'substantially under-represented in the most elite jobs, namely as employers and managers in large establishments. This could be said to be a "glass ceiling" that affects all non-white men equally' (p.143).

Statistics from a great variety of sources confirm Modood's general observation about 'glass ceilings'. Interestingly, the proportions of BME staff within an organisation who are at senior management level are remarkably similar in the different employment sectors. Looking at the UK's top 100 firms, for example, the proportion is 1.75 per cent (Pandya 1999a). Our own recently completed research on registered social landlords (RSLs) in England for the Housing Corporation yields a figure for non-BME housing associations of 1.6 per cent (Somerville, Steele and Sodhi 2000). A more meaningful measure here is the proportion of staff at senior level who come from BME groups. Here the situation looks rather better in housing, with BME staff making up 3.7 per cent of senior managers, compared with 1 per cent for the Department for Education and Employment (Bichard 1999) and 1.6 per cent for senior civil servants generally (Pandya 1999b). However, this is still not much more than half the level of representation of BMEs in the total workforce of RSLs (6.4%, as mentioned above). There seems to be a pattern across a wide range of employers in Britain whereby BME staff are restricted to posts at the lower levels of the organisation, though the extent of this restriction is greater in some organisations than in others. It is particularly notable that there are hardly any BME people at the top of the organisation: only one BME chief executive out of the top 100 private firms, and two out of the 72 non-BME housing associations in our national survey.

The Macpherson Report of the inquiry into the murder of Stephen Lawrence (Macpherson 1999) has arguably shaken many British institutions out of their complacency on racial issues, at least temporarily. Macpherson explicitly commented on shortcomings within the housing service: 'Too often housing departments were seen to be slow and bureaucratic in their response to racist behaviour' (p.313). By Macpherson's definition of institutional racism, as our research shows (see below), it was clear that many housing organisations are institutionally racist, in particular because of widespread 'ignorance, thoughtlessness and racist stereotyping which disadvantage minority ethnic people' (p.28). Up to now, however, not a single housing organisation has publicly admitted to being institutionally racist. This is in spite of the fact that the most recent surveys have shown that only one in ten local authorities have workforces that come within 1 per cent of reflecting their local ethnic minority population (Misra 1999, p.10). The culture of racial indifference therefore appears to be endemic in the housing world, as in other sections of British society.

## Institutional racism in employment

In relation to employment issues, it can be argued that institutional racism is expressed in three ways, each of which is considered below. The first is in terms of an organisation's 'central values' or 'core values', which can be in some sense ethnocentric or culturally insensitive. The second is in terms of how management competence, and in particular leadership qualities, are identified and measured within the organisation, which can involve forms of unconscious stereotyping. And the third is in terms of how the discretion of individual managers is exercised in relation to the management of human resources, which can tap a rich vein of ignorance and prejudice. In general, organisations develop cultures that systematically favour certain types of people and are systematically biased against others, and these are often expressed in terms of 'person specifications'. Consciously or unconsciously, organisations build up an 'assumptive world' (Young and Kramer 1978), which defines for their members what is to count as good or effective management.

### Core values

With regard to central values, there seems to be widespread agreement in the management literature: 'The effective organisation has a few central values about which there is a high degree of consensus. Those are supported and put into operation by simple rules and clear procedures, which are subordinate to the values'

(Torrington and Weightman 1994, p.253). The question is, however: is an effective organisation the same thing as a *good* organisation, in the sense of having ethical practices and actively realising social goals such as racial equality and harmony?

This question can be rephrased in a way that makes it easier to answer, namely: can an organisation that does not have equal opportunities as a core value be as effective as one that does? On this question there is no universal agreement. Two approaches that have been influential in recent years are the learning organisation approach and what could be called the 'equality is good for business' approach.

The learning organisation approach arose as a result of attempting to understand the processes whereby the members of an organisation optimise their contribution to the organisation as a whole. Advocates of this approach emphasise the realisation of the potential of every employee, mainly through a supportive culture, through managers who coach and develop their staff, and through enhanced learning opportunities for all (Argyris 1990; Garratt 1987, 1990). According to this approach, therefore, effective management requires the self-development of all staff, and this should be a core value of every organisation.

In practice, the learning organisation approach is capable of being supportive of BME staff, but it is important to point out that this is not necessarily the case. If equality of opportunity is not explicitly identified and lived as a core value within the organisation, it is possible that self-development might be conceived in an ethnocentric way, and the learning that the organisation experiences may not be sufficient for it to escape the charge of cultural insensitivity. From the organisation's point of view, this may not be regarded as a problem, because so far as it is concerned it is managing effectively in its chosen environment. This therefore suggests that it is indeed necessary to draw a distinction between effective management (in the sense of good performance in relation to organisational objectives) and good management (in the sense of good performance in relation to ethical or social objectives).

The 'equality is good for business' approach is supported by a wide variety of agencies in this field (CRE 1995; Into Leadership 1999; Ross and Schneider 1992). The general argument in favour of the approach is that the inclusion of racial (and other; for example, sexual) equality as a core value helps an organisation to improve in a business sense, for example by being more profitable or productive or by providing a better service to its customers. Two main types of evidence are cited in support of this argument: one is that a more open recruitment policy ensures access to a wider pool of talent, and therefore potentially a more productive workforce. The second is that an organisational culture that is more genuinely welcoming of ethnic and cultural diversity is more likely to retain minority ethnic staff and therefore experience overall lower costs arising from staff turnover, and is also more likely to achieve a better performance from existing BME staff. A third point often made in support of the business case, though less well supported by concrete evidence, is that a workforce whose ethnic composition broadly reflects the communities it serves is, other things being equal, likely to deliver a better service to those communities, providing a more appropriate and sensitive response to their diverse needs.

The business case for racial (and other) equality is widely regarded as strong and convincing. The main criticism of it is, however, that many organisations appear to be quite capable of prospering as businesses without taking equal opportunities particularly seriously, especially when there is no shortage of candidates who can all convincingly claim to be able to achieve a good, and indeed excellent, performance. Kandola and Fullerton (1998), who are clearly sympathetic to the business case, have nevertheless concluded, after a review of the arguments, that the benefits for business from a more diverse workforce have been exaggerated. Two points are particularly important here: one is that the costs to most businesses arising from racial discrimination are relatively low (Kandola and Fullerton 1998, pp.33–34), and the other is that for many, perhaps most, organisations racial discrimination may actually be rational and beneficial. For example, as Torrington and Weightman (1994, pp.224–225) point out, it may be 'good business' to favour those employees or potential employees who are already more highly skilled (who may be more likely to be white) rather than spending money on training those who are less well skilled (who may be more likely to be black). By the same token, it may make 'good business' sense to keep members of certain ethnic groups confined to specialised jobs for which they are more skilled rather than promoting them to other jobs for which there exists a wider pool of suitably skilled recruits. A third point is that an organisation which is catering for a mass market or for 'general needs' may not need to concern itself with minority interests in order to thrive as a business – indeed, the opposite may be true in some cases.

It appears that advocates of the business case approach fall into the error of assuming that racial discrimination is just irrational, based on individual prejudice. Unfortunately, although racial prejudice is still important and widespread (CRE 1998), discrimination at work is largely institutional – that is, it is based on well-established and culturally sanctioned ways of doing things. Common sense suggests that, if the business case were really so convincing, discrimination in employment would have been substantially reduced, if not completely wiped out, years ago.

## Competence

The principle of equality of opportunity implies that people should be selected for jobs on the basis of their competence to perform them, and not on the basis of any characteristic they may possess that is not relevant to the quality of that performance. In practice, however, there are two major difficulties with this position. The first, which does not particularly concern us here, is that it is not always possible to determine with any degree of certainty whether or not a given characteristic is relevant in improving or worsening the performance of a given individual – the continuing debate about the relative merits of older and younger workers is a good example of this. The second, and perhaps even more fundamental, difficulty is that, at least for certain types of job, it is not possible to identify or measure the competence on an individual basis. This perhaps surprising claim can be justified on two main grounds, which are as follows.

One is that the precise nature of management competence in particular is highly contentious. Most writers probably agree with Torrington and Weightman (1994, p.332) that managers need to be able to exercise authority, provide leadership and allow a measure of autonomy to their subordinates. Most writers also probably agree on the meaning of these terms; namely, authority is the right to control and judge the actions of others; leadership is the exercise of the power conferred by that right so as to win a willing and positive response; and autonomy is the freedom of action that subordinates see as necessary and reasonable in order to be effective in their roles. Where disagreement arises, however, is on how to identify a good or bad exercise of authority, leadership or delegation of power. In practice, many people recognise, including even some management gurus such as John Harvey Jones and Charles Handy, that the qualities of a good manager vary, not only according to the nature of the organisation, but even according to the work situation in which the manager is placed. What, therefore, can be meant by a competence to achieve a good management performance, apart from infinite flexibility, omniscience and omnipresence, and a similarly god-like quality of allowing subordinates the exercise of their free will while rewarding their good performance and punishing their bad? It seems, therefore, that the competent manager is really just a new version of God, and His ways are probably no less mysterious.

The second argument against the possible identification of individual managerial competence is that its effective exercise depends as much, if not more, on the dispositions of the managed as on the qualities of the manager. The important implication of this finding is that managerial competence cannot be assessed independently of the context in which it is exercised, and this obviously presents major problems for any purportedly objective selection process. To put it in crude terms, the attitudes and actions of staff (including colleagues and superiors as well as subordinates) can make the most gifted manager appear incompetent, and vice versa, they can make an incompetent manager seem excellent. For this reason alone, the idea that managerial competence can be assessed through measuring the effectiveness of the manager's performance has been criticised as a nonsense (Mangham and Pye 1991).

But what happens with selection for managerial positions, if the competence to perform in such positions cannot be accurately assessed? The obvious, if flippant, answer is that incompetent people may be as likely to be selected as competent ones. On the other hand, however, if an incompetent manager is to stay in post, they are likely to have to improve their skills or to have strong support from their superiors in particular. Whatever happens, the opaqueness of managerial competence means that in general selections will be made on the basis of what people believe to be appropriate for the organisation and for themselves, and not on the basis of any sound empirical evidence. In such circumstances, the role of 'gut feelings' (for which read 'ignorance and prejudice') can be very important.

### Autonomy

Jaques (1970) argued that all jobs have a prescribed content and a discretionary content, meeting universal human needs for a combination of routine and novelty. The appropriate balance between the two depends upon the nature of the individual and of the job they do. In general, however, it is argued that managers need to have a considerable amount of discretion (or autonomy) in order to be effective, to give direction to their staff, to themselves, to their peers, and to their organisation as a whole. Discretion is seen to be a good thing because it leads to responsibility and thoroughness, with individuals being less able to blame others for their mistakes and shortcomings. Armstrong and Murlis (1991) have pointed out that giving greater discretion (or autonomy) is at the heart of ideas on empowerment and performance management. This is why there is widespread agreement that giving autonomy (for example, through delegation of power and responsibility) is an essential quality of a good manager.

In considering the role of managers, it can be seen that discretion occurs at two levels: there is the autonomy which every worker requires in order to perform effectively, and there is the freedom on the part of the manager to determine the scope of discretion for each of their subordinates. Such autonomy and freedom, however, carry with them a certain freedom to discriminate. In the case of the worker, such discrimination may occur in relation to the treatment of service users and colleagues, and in the case of the manager it can happen in the process of selecting, managing, training, developing, appraising and promoting staff. It is the latter source of discrimination that concerns us in this chapter.

There is a paradox here, in that increased autonomy brings a risk of greater discrimination, so it could be argued that the way forward is to reduce that autonomy by imposing stricter rules and regulations on all staff, with appropriate performance targets, rewards and sanctions and so on. The reality, however, is that such a top-down approach assumes that the most senior managers in the organisation, who will be responsible for introducing and enforcing this tighter regime, are themselves free from the tendency to discriminate which the new regime is intended to eradicate. Obviously, where this is not the case, the regime will either not be introduced at all, or, if introduced, will exist on paper only and will not be effectively policed. The key problem here is that if equality of opportunity is not a core value for the individual manager or for the organisation, any increase in autonomy is likely to have discriminatory implications.

## What is good management?

Some commentators have effectively given up trying to identify and measure the characteristics of a good manager, but still want to provide a definition and qualitative description of the processes concerned. For example, Watson (1994, p.175) defines good management as being involved in the business and being involved with the people. This definition is helpful in characterising management as based on a dual commitment to individual staff and to the organisation as a whole, but it needs clarification. We would suggest that good management requires primarily involvement with the people, and then being involved with the business to the extent needed to serve the interests of the people – accepting that those interests are served most importantly by the safeguarding of their jobs, which in turn is best achieved by ensuring the survival of the organisation as a whole. The whole art of good management lies in striking the right balance between involvement with individuals and involvement in the broader organisational context, based on an understanding of the complex relationship between the two. But what is meant by 'the right balance' here, and how is it to be identified and struck in practice? We consider below two approaches to answering this question, the 'managing diversity' approach and what we have chosen to call the 'quality' approach. First of all, however, we look at what is meant by 'involvement with individuals'.

Reed and Anthony (1992, p.608) have argued that good management requires norms of reciprocity, trust, obligation and the maintenance of defensible social relationships: 'Reality, both social and economic, resides in the production and exchange of goods and services, and that depends on the dialectics of control and co-operation, on leadership and community and, finally, upon authority, which is essentially moral.' This analysis suggests a way of incorporating equality of opportunity as a core value within an organisation because, in a multi-cultural society, it could be argued that a manager for whom equality of opportunity is not a core value is likely to lack this moral authority in relation to staff who subscribe to another culture, and will therefore not be capable of being a good manager of those staff.

Quinn (1980) has talked similarly in terms of a continuous dialogue between the different levels of the organisation, with strategies emerging from the dialogical process. Watson (1994, p.33) suggests: 'At the heart of the managerial role is the task of orchestrating a series of exchanges with internal and external parties in order to achieve long-term organisational survival.' Fox (1974, 1985) links personal involvement with a sense of trust among people, and argues that this is best achieved by increasing the degree of discretion available to people at work, as discussed above. Widening the sphere of discretion encourages greater personal responsibility, and this in turn promotes increased involvement with fellow workers and with the organisation and its environment generally, and therefore is conducive to good management.

A number of writers have emphasised that good management cannot be forced upon people. Ciulla (1990), for example, has argued that employees must be given the freedom and power to find their own meaning in the work they do, and their personal ownership of this is the best guarantee of their effectiveness. Again, this implies that the discretionary content of their work needs to be increased as far as possible. Torrington, Hitner and Knights (1982), in a commentary specifically on equal opportunities policies, concluded: 'Research has not succeeded in showing the introduction of policy "from the top" as being effective except in situations where the employment of minority employees has produced major problems that needed to be resolved' (cited in Torrington and Weightman 1994, p.230). However, much depends upon the characteristics of those who are at the top, and it could be argued that where senior managers are wholly committed to racial equality, it may be possible to achieve major shifts in the culture of the organisation.

## The managing diversity approach

The managing diversity approach takes the project of involvement with individuals to its logical conclusion. It can be contrasted with the business approach to good management discussed earlier, which naively equates equity with corporate rationality. Advocates of this approach emphasise the responsibility of management to optimise the potential of every individual employee (Kandola and Fullerton 1998). This can therefore be regarded as an extension of the argument in relation to worker autonomy, namely the more discretion an individual has in the performance of their job, the more their potential can be realised. The role of the organisation, and especially of its managers, is then to respond to the variety of needs and choices of individual staff, including their cultural and family needs. The result, it is argued, is a more contented and productive workforce, and an enhanced responsiveness to a changing external environment.

Supporters of the managing diversity approach are sceptical about policies that provide for special treatment of people by virtue only of their membership of a group – for example, policies of positive action and the adoption of racial equality targets. Kandola and Fullerton (1998) pull no punches here: 'Positive action…is no better than applying a sticking-plaster to a festering wound: it addresses the symptoms rather than the causes. It also provides activity without being purposeful' (p.134). In their view, the organisation should be asking why it is failing to attract suitably qualified minority applicants in the first place. Similarly, they regard equality targets as problematic in principle, not only because they single out groups for special attention, but because they are associated with a failure to examine the decision-making processes and skills used by managers and also because they result in tokenism (Kandola and Fullerton 1998, p.141).

The managing diversity approach is obviously very relevant, but it can be criticised on a number of grounds. For example, it is clear that individual potential is being developed within a framework of organisational rules and imperatives, and these are likely to come into conflict with individuals' career aspirations. The needs of the organisation therefore have to be taken into account, and examined critically in the light of the needs of individuals. Similarly, individual freedom of action is essentially limited by the exercise of managerial prerogative and by organisational discipline. The managing diversity approach is therefore naive to the extent that it paints a picture of organisations as serving the needs of individual staff rather than one of staff serving organisational aims and objectives.

The issue of organisational flexibility is perhaps crucial here – the question to be asked is how far it is really possible for organisations to change so as to be, for example, more 'BME-friendly', in the sense of providing sufficiently for the diverse cultural needs of their staff. Clearly, managers need to be persuaded to accept responsibility for the radical employee empowerment that the managing diversity approach aims to produce, without it necessarily leading to successful challenges to their managerial authority. Realistically, however, what are the advantages to managers to be gained from embarking on such a risky enterprise?

The main point to be drawn from this discussion is that the culture of an organisation needs to be changed so that equality of opportunity becomes a core value. Schein (1985), on the basis of a detailed analysis of organisational culture, concluded that there were primary and secondary mechanisms governing the process of culture change. Primary mechanisms included such things as: what leaders pay most attention to; how leaders react to crises and critical incidents; role modelling, teaching and coaching by leaders; criteria for allocating rewards and determining status; and criteria for selection, promotion and termination. Secondary mechanisms were: organisational structure; systems and procedures; space, buildings and facades; stories and legends about important events and people; and formal statements of philosophy and policy. In attempting to change housing organisations, therefore, it seems sensible to concentrate on the roles played by senior managers and on the criteria for hiring, firing, promoting and rewarding staff. It is necessary to examine closely the relevant practices within such organisations in order to identify how equal opportunities values can be integrated more closely into their form and content. This was indeed the focus of our research for the Housing Corporation, which is discussed below.

### The quality approach

Essentially, the quality case for racial equality consists of a combination of involvement with the external environment and continuous evaluation of organisational performance, within a process of ever-deepening penetration of equal opportunities principles into the everyday practices of the organisation. The approach starts from a recognition that organisations are more likely to learn to be better if the pressures from their external environment are such as to push them in that direction. The approach then builds on the criticisms of the business approach and the managing diversity approach by concluding from these criticisms that most organisations are unlikely to take equal opportunities seriously unless there are clear external incentives or sanctions to encourage them to do so. What is required, then, is a system of regulation that is sophisticated and sensitive enough to move organisations forward in the socially desirable directions while at the same time allowing managerial autonomy to be preserved. An example of such a system is the new Best Value regime, and the possible extension of this regime to racial equality in employment is considered at the end of this chapter.

## Organisational culture

Our research for the Housing Corporation involved a postal survey of 106 registered social landlords (RSLs) in England and an interview survey of 52 black and white staff working at different levels in 15 RSLs. Perhaps the most striking finding of the research was that for most RSLs that were not black-led equality of opportunity was not a core value of the organisation, or at least it did not rank on a level equal to those of customer service or meeting stakeholder needs. On the whole, senior managers in non-BME organisations did not pay substantial attention to equal opportunities issues, did not react constructively to racist incidents, and did not provide appropriate role models or career development initiatives. Senior management therefore generally lacked what Schein (1985) called the primary mechanisms for bringing about the required cultural change. Given the lack of BME representation at senior management level, however, how is this dominant culture to be changed?

Schein's research suggests that in the absence of appropriate leadership the main way to effect change in organisational culture is through the criteria for selecting, promoting, rewarding and valuing staff. Our research therefore concentrated on issues of recruitment and selection; promotion; training and staff development; staff appraisal; and encouragement and support for staff generally.

### Recruitment and selection

In relation to recruitment and selection, the research revealed that hardly any non-BME associations consulted with BME communities, and less than a quarter made special efforts to advertise within such communities. Interviews with staff uncovered a wide range of attitudes and practices that could be regarded as amounting to institutional discrimination: victimisation of particular individuals; making individuals change their dress, speech and so on, in order to fit into the organisation and avoid appearing 'different'; culturally sanctioned ignorance of other cultures; general indifference to equal opportunities objectives; failure to deal with overt racism by some staff; reliance on informal recruitment methods; failure to advertise externally or appropriately; the use of inappropriate person specifications; slotting individuals into jobs without public consultation or agreement; taking advantage of BME staff skills (for example, language skills) without official recognition or reward; and using tests that unjustifiably favoured those with a good command of English and who could do formal tests. Typical comments by interviewees included the following:

> 'People pretend to like you but deep inside the structure does not give much opportunity for a BME person to enter the organisation.'

> 'There is little effort to raise awareness of the organisation in the BME community, which has a negative perception of it.'

> 'BME staff are taken on as "tokens", to keep up numbers and make the image of the organisation look good.'

> 'They just want to be seen to be doing something, [equality of opportunity is] not really taken to heart by the organisation.'

> 'Managers need to focus on the needs of the job, not the type of person they want for the job.'

> 'They already have someone in mind for the post, and then they just go through the motions.'

What these comments reveal generally is that most non-BME housing associations do not really care about racial equality, and this is probably the main reason for their poor practice in this area. But how can they be persuaded to care, to incorporate racial equality as a core value in their organisations? Interviewees made a number of practical suggestions, such as the representation of BME staff on selection interview panels and making the process of selection more open and explicit. At the end of the day, however, organisations tend to appoint people in their own image and likeness, and this goes back to the issue of leadership and the key role played by senior managers.

It emerged from the research that the notion of equality of opportunity was itself a contested one. White staff were more likely to hold that equality of opportunity meant that people should be treated equally, and this was reflected in most written equal opportunities policies which were concerned only with achieving such equality of treatment. In contrast, BME staff were more likely to state that equality of opportunity was to do with respecting and valuing the diversity which exists among individuals and groups. The dominant culture's obstinate and persistent refusal to accept the reality of human diversity and its continuing unquestioned assumptive world of idealised cultural homogeneity almost certainly lie at the heart of modern institutional racism (see the concluding chapter in this volume). The adoption of racial equality as a genuine core value involves moving beyond a concern for merely formal equality towards a commitment to fundamental change in the racial bias of most organisations.

## Promotion

In relation to promotion, the research suggested that institutional discrimination could arise in a number of different ways. In most cases, it appeared to be the responsibility of individual staff members to identify their own promotion opportunities. This could give rise to discrimination because some staff are always more likely than others to be aware of promotion opportunities, and this difference in awareness may not relate to their suitability as candidates for the opportunities that arise. For example, staff who are more 'in' with senior managers than others are likely to be advantaged by such an approach compared with staff who appear more as 'outsiders' or more peripheral to the (equal-opportunity-unfriendly) core culture or business of the organisation. In other cases, discrimination could arise because managers actively singled out individual staff and slotted them into more senior positions, thus denying others (both inside and outside the organisation) an opportunity to make a case for their own promotion to these posts. In yet other cases, staff lost out because there were few or no opportunities for promotion at all, due to the small size of the organisation, the low turnover of staff, the flatness of the organisational structure, or the large gap between key levels in the organisation, which made linear career progression impossible.

In only a small minority of organisations did there exist a culture that could form the basis for a non-discriminatory regime. This was typically where managers who were committed to equality of opportunity advised staff of available promotion opportunities and encouraged them to take advantage of them, but did not attempt to influence the outcome of the selection process itself. Some interviewees recognised, however, that managers had the power to provide staff with experience of additional responsibilities that would inevitably improve their promotion prospects if they performed well. In practice, therefore, managers are not only capable of indirectly influencing selection outcomes, but they may regard it as their duty to do so for the sake of racial equality (and similarly with sex equality, etc.). The problem was that in nearly all of these organisations the choice of managers (whether to attempt to create a level playing field for all, or to encourage their favourites and ignore or obstruct those whom they did not wish to see promoted) was not guided in any way by the values of the organisation. Whether or not a manager was influenced by equal opportunities considerations was left entirely to managerial discretion, and was therefore experienced by their staff as something of a lottery. At the end of the day, no organisation in the research appeared to have given serious thought to the question of how managers should act in these circumstances or how their actions should be monitored to ensure that they are fair.

'Good' management, as we have seen, requires managers to be involved with their staff on an individual basis, and this must include creating opportunities for all of those staff to develop and progress. If the organisation lacks equality of opportunity as a core value, however, then it is inevitable that different managers will exercise their discretion in different ways, and the outcomes for the staff affected will then appear arbitrary, inconsistent and unfair. Culturally, therefore, it appeared that most RSLs fell some way short of good management – the organisation as a whole failed to 'give direction' on equality of opportunity in the promotions process.

One interviewee gave a very detailed and vivid account of the difficulties in progressing within a white-dominated organisation:

> First, there is the speech disability, because of the way I talk [the interviewee's accent]. Some managers see this as a weakness, because if someone like me is allowed to reach the position of senior manager, I would sit among other senior managers, and that would tell on the manager who appointed me, in terms of 'where did he get that idiot from?'. The way I speak is not well accepted by a lot of senior managers, and my own senior manager has 'shut me down' very quickly in the past. The second disability is colour. Whilst with [another company] I was the representative for the whole region, and when I went to meetings I was the only black among all the white people, and the other managers said 'what is he doing here?' and I was asked 'are you in the right place, sir?'. I have to be very careful because in the earlier years of my career people were saying I was over-sensitive, and other people were saying 'you have to be professional'. So I am very careful about how I deal with it, and I have to deal with it because I have a mortgage to pay.

A further revealing comment was made by one interviewee who felt that he had been passed over for promotion within his organisation:

> It is how senior management perceive me. They must have thought I could not do the job since they didn't approach me. I have experience, but it is not recognised. They see me differently – they don't see my potential and they have a stereotypical view of black people. The emphasis by senior managers is on giving jobs and responsibility to 'bull-shitters' rather than looking at what staff can actually do.

He saw it as an issue of 'face-fitting':

> They see me as good at my current job and not as fit for promotion – they have pigeon-holed me. They rely on me in my current post, and they would lose this if I were promoted.

The main points of contention centred on the relationship between individual staff members and their managers. In most cases managers were left very much to their own devices in dealing with their staff. Promotion opportunities then depended crucially on the 'luck' of having a good manager. Arguably, however, equality of opportunity is too important to be left to chance in this way.

## Training and staff development

In relation to training and staff development, it was significant that over half of the non-BME associations had no policy at all, and most of them had no positive action practices. Such practices include a wide range of possibilities that provide concrete evidence of commitment to equality of opportunity. Examples are Positive Action for Training in Housing (PATH) schemes, positive action plans, mentoring, personal development plans, specialist trainee posts, and other forms of training and development aimed specifically at minority ethnic groups such as coaching, shadowing, and student and work experience placements. The absence of any such practices again confirms the failure of most RSLs to incorporate equality of opportunity as a core value in their organisations.

As with promotion opportunities, the most common way for staff to identify opportunities for training and development was through their own initiative. The usual procedure was then for them to obtain their manager's approval for the specific forms of training they identified. This method of accessing training can be criticised on the same grounds as those discussed in relation to promotion, in that those staff who are more aware of training opportunities will have an advantage over those who are less aware. In general, however, interviewees were positive about the process in their organisations, being more likely to regard it as fair than unfair. This probably reflected the fact that managers were generally committed to training that clearly enhanced job performance, and it was notable that most training was of this nature. Training that was directed more to personal and career development was very much less in evidence in the research, and this bias was in fact the most common source of complaint among interviewees.

Another common way in which opportunities for training and staff development were identified was through the process of supervision and performance review and through the appraisal process. This could be regarded as more in tune with equal opportunities principles, because it enables training to be more closely matched with the needs of individual staff members. In practice, however, the effectiveness or fairness of this approach depends crucially on the values guiding the processes of performance review and appraisal (further discussed below). If these values do not have equality of opportunity at their heart, then a planned approach to meeting training needs can still fail – for example, by meeting the needs of the organisation conceived in a narrow, technically rational sense, but not providing individual staff with a satisfying and meaningful understanding of their work, of its context, and of their place in this context. Such a planned approach might at best meet the objective of achieving equality of treatment of the staff affected, but it would not equip staff to appreciate cultural diversity and learn how to live more fully in a multi-cultural environment. This was indeed a source of complaint from a number of interviewees in the research.

Comments made by interviewees suggested that the process of accessing training was regarded rather differently by BME and white staff. For example, some organisations had a practice whereby training was 'cascaded' from one individual to their colleagues within the same team. White staff tended to regard this as acceptable and 'normal' practice, where there were difficulties in securing staff cover and there might be pressures on training budgets. On reflection, however, such a system could be argued to be fair only where the staff were more or less the same, with similar needs and skills, and where the training being provided was not specific to individuals or types of staff. Hence one black interviewee referred to 'problems around requests by BME staff to attend the FBHO conference. One black colleague likes to attend, but when a new manager was appointed his request was turned down.' Where members of a work team differ from each other in important respects, therefore, this method of cascading is not applicable. This is another example of the conflict in principle between 'equal treatment as identical treatment' and 'equal but different treatment'.

## Staff appraisal

Staff appraisal could be argued to be a key function as regards equality of opportunity for existing employees within an organisation. This is particularly the case where appraisal and performance review play a major part in determining employees' prospects for promotion. The research found that most RSLs did indeed conduct appraisals of their staff. A fairly typical arrangement was described by one interviewee as follows:

An annual interview with your supervisor, a form to fill in normally two weeks before the interview, discussion of performance targets and areas, identification of training needs, and both parties signing off the form at the end to agree the action points for the next twelve months.

Interviewees' comments suggested that the appraisal process in most RSLs is 'binary' rather than 'ternary' (Mant 1983) – that is, the process is seen as primarily a relationship between manager and managed, an instrument of external control rather than a tool for self-development. Interviewees generally accepted that the process was a fair one in their organisations, but many of them complained about the control aspects of it, or the lack of real development it allowed. Thus, although in practice most managers appeared to conduct their staff appraisals fairly, interviewees expressed concern that managers were not accountable for their actions in this respect, and that therefore some managers might choose to act otherwise.

In a ternary arrangement as opposed to a binary one, appraiser and appraisee work together on a more equal basis, relating to each other through a third point, which is the task on which both are engaged or the stakeholders they seek to satisfy. The process is ideally one of mutual accommodation and adjustment, as the two parties find the most effective way of sharing duties between them. It was clear from the comments of interviewees that this was not the style in which the appraisal process was approached in most organisations in the research. In some cases, the process did consider personal development needs, but always as an add-on to the need for improved performance in the current post, and meeting the latter need was typically understood only in terms of training provision for the appraisee. The idea that managers might need to change their practice in order to improve the performance of their staff did not appear to be part of the culture of any of the organisations for which the interviewees worked. In fact, this issue arose only in relation to mentoring, where some managers recognised that acting as a mentor could help to achieve such improved performance. Even here, however, they tended to see the issue in terms of their receiving appropriate training for being a mentor, rather than in terms of making more substantial changes to their management practice.

A lengthy comment by one interviewee served to highlight the main problems that occurred in so many associations:

> Staff appraisals are conducted once a year, and are one-to-ones with the line manager where you go through what you have done and set goals within your line of work and targets which you have to meet. Previous goals or targets are checked to see if they have been met and you try to find ways to do this if they

have not been achieved. It depends on the line manager as to whether the appraisal is fair. We work in small teams, and as long as you do your work you're OK, there are no problems. If the line manager doesn't like what you do or your approach, they might take the attitude that you're not doing your work and may not put you forward for an increment. The line manager usually does a report for an increment, and this goes to personnel, but this is not part of the appraisal. Also, you are given an opportunity to put your views on the line manager, but if you did make comments on the line manager they might take a hard line, so really you could not comment.

This quote underlines a number of typical concerns: the onus on the appraisee to get their work right with little or no responsibility on the part of their line manager; the over-dependence on the judgement of the line manager in conducting the appraisal; the inevitable linkage with job status and pay, in spite of policy to the contrary; and the lack of realistic opportunity for reciprocal appraisal of one's line manager.

Again, these concerns can be taken as indicating a lack of good management in these organisations. Too many managers appeared to regard themselves as superior to their staff and were insufficiently involved with those staff and their development, exercising discretion in isolation from the wider needs of the organisation and insufficiently committed to equality of opportunity. It would not be fair, however, to blame individual managers alone. Typically, the organisation as a whole failed to give direction on equality of opportunity, conceiving staff appraisal as primarily an individualised relationship between appraiser and appraisee with little or no consideration of the organisational and wider context within which such appraisal operates. In Foucault's terms, appraisal was seen as an expression of monarchical power rather than disciplinary power, with the direction of the process often left entirely up to individual managers (O'Neill 1986). In contrast, an organisation with equality of opportunity as a core value would approach staff appraisal in terms of something like Quinn's process of continuous dialogue (Quinn 1980). Judgements would not be made in isolation, but in the context of the expected contributions of all the parties concerned. Moreover, organisational as well as individual responsibilities would be accepted, and action plans and targets agreed accordingly, in a process of 'discursive democracy' (Dryzek 1990).

There are serious problems, anyway, in attempting to measure the competence of managers, as mentioned earlier in this chapter. Arguably, though perhaps not to the same degree, the same problems beset the measurement of staff competence generally, because the good or bad performance of a staff member could well be largely due to the quality of that individual's manager. The implication of this argument is that individualised staff appraisals are inherently flawed, and good management requires an appraisal process that is more collectively based, focused on the performance of work teams, if not on the organisation as a whole. The ternary-thinking managers described by Mant (1983) would sit more comfortably within such a process.

Another point about appraisal is that arguably it ought to consider the suitability of staff for more senior posts, as an integral part of career development planning. This could be said to be necessary in order to ensure that the talents of staff are not overlooked but encouraged to develop to the full. A minority of RSLs in the research did indeed pay some attention to staff development in this sense, but it seemed to be a matter of giving some consideration to staff aspirations without actually exercising a judgement as to how realistic those aspirations were. This may be a sensible position to adopt in view of the difficulties in assessing managerial competence mentioned earlier. There is a case to be made, however, for providing appropriate encouragement and support for staff aspirations – for example, by providing opportunities for training, secondment and acting up – and care should then be taken to ensure that these opportunities are distributed on an equal basis. There is also a case to be made for the organisation to give direction on what it means to give direction, so that talent can be spotted more effectively and fairly.

## Overall culture

In spite of all the critical comments made by interviewees in the research, it was interesting to find that nearly half of them felt that their organisation was encouraging and supportive of BME staff. They were particularly complimentary about their line managers and about their organisation's active pursuit of an equal opportunities culture that was tolerant of racial and cultural diversity. On the down side, however, nearly a third of interviewees thought their organisation was indifferent or discouraging. These interviewees referred to the gap between rhetoric and reality, the destructiveness of the organisation's management style and culture, the lack of opportunities for staff generally, the failure to understand or tackle issues of cultural difference and diversity, the failure to take equal opportunities seriously and the lack of BME representation in the organisation's policy process. It was also notable that BME staff were far less likely than white staff to regard their organisation's approach as positively supportive and encouraging.

A good example of a discouraging culture was given by one interviewee who reported the following:

A lot is around management style, the type that the organisation wants, and these are [sic] not necessarily the type of manager who are supportive of staff. They want managers who are concerned with outputs and outcomes, not managers interested in developing the confidence of staff and so on. Team managers are not interested in what the staff do, just what they produce. It is all about staff dynamics, and there is a definite management style in the organisation. I think that might be why I didn't get the opportunity to stay in a management role. I was not actively rewarded for supporting staff, who were suffering from racial harassment. I didn't conform to the organisation's management style, and this came out in my performance review. All this has repercussions for BME staff.

## Conclusion

On the basis of our research, we have to conclude that most RSLs fail to embrace cultural and ethnic diversity within their practices and are not wholeheartedly committed to achieving equality of opportunity. The negative implications of this organisational culture can be most clearly seen in their practices on promotion and staff appraisal, where time and again it was seen as perfectly right and proper to treat people the same when in reality they were different, or even to treat people differently without feeling the need to justify it. The concept of equal but different, which still causes difficulty in relation to sex discrimination, did not appear to have even reached the agenda for many of these organisations.

Black-led RSLs are largely exempt from these criticisms. Most of these in the research were strongly committed to a multi-cultural, multi-ethnic approach. Consequently, practices which would be very likely to be racist in a non-BME RSL, such as reliance on informal methods of recruitment, could be successful in achieving equal opportunities targets, for example where the RSL had very good communications with local BME communities. The research did detect a few black-led RSLs where the organisation was perhaps too closely identified with one particular community, but it was not clear whether this identification amounted to a serious problem in terms of fairness in the treatment of its staff.

To avoid the danger of being overwhelmed by negative considerations, it is important to emphasise that there was a significant minority of RSLs apart from black-led ones who did appear to be genuinely committed to racial equality. These were typically ones who were concerned that their workforce should reflect the communities in which the organisation operated, and considered it a problem that those communities were not represented at senior management level. Although on the whole it appeared that these RSLs had done little if anything to address this problem, it does seem likely that they would be receptive to initiatives from bodies such as the Housing Corporation which would help their BME staff to progress in their careers.

## What is to be done?

Most interviewees were seeking promotion within the next five years, and half of the BME interviewees expressed an interest in participating in a positive action management training initiative. The research clearly showed that BME staff were not lacking in qualifications and experience compared with their white colleagues, so these findings suggest that it would be appropriate for the Housing Corporation, in collaboration with other institutions, to launch such an initiative on a national basis. Currently a number of local authorities (Manchester, Haringey, Leicester, Harrow and Lewisham – LGMB 1998; for an outline of the Manchester scheme, see Somerville and Steele 1998) have pioneered such initiatives, North British Housing Association have recently launched their own scheme and PATH (an independent training agency) have developed a similar initiative in London.

Although helpful, positive action management training has inherent limitations (see the criticisms from the managing diversity perspective mentioned earlier). For example, it can be seen as providing special assistance to black staff, when white staff may be equally in need of such assistance. Ideally, organisations should be planning the career development of *all* their staff, and this point echoes that made above about finding ways of spotting talent, irrespective of colour or ethnicity. An emphasis on management training also conveys the impression that it is primarily the development of individual staff members at a lower level that is required, and this tends to deflect attention from the need to change the culture of the organisation, and specifically to change the attitudes and perceptions of senior managers. As Gary Younge has put it: 'The key issue is not whether black individuals will advance, but whether they will lift as they rise' (Younge 1999, p.22).

However, if the positive action management training actually succeeds in its objectives of significantly increasing the representation of BME staff at senior level, then it seems likely that in time this could lead to the desired cultural change – though there is also the possibility that, as has been noted with respect to increased female representation within senior management, promotion to higher positions comes at the cost of accepting the established 'rules of the game'. There is the risk that, in order to get on, the individual black staff member has to act 'whiter than white', and then becomes so accustomed to it that he or she does not change when promoted – indeed, the very fact of promotion may confirm to the individual the correctness of their assimilation to the dominant culture.

Apart from, or perhaps in addition to, positive action management training, therefore, RSLs need to consider ways in which their culture can be changed so as to make it more actively productive of equality of opportunity rather than the 'housing-plus-equal-opportunities' culture that is currently prevalent. For many, perhaps most, RSLs, however, this would involve quite a radical upheaval of their existing practices. It would involve at least the following:

- substantial consultation with the BME (and indeed other) communities in which the organisation operates, in a spirit of mutual learning and partnership – and such communities include their own staff

- a complete review of procedures on recruitment, selection, promotion and staff appraisal, to achieve greater openness, fairness, sensitivity to diverse individual needs, and optimisation of individual and collective self-development

- the adoption of race equality plans, and clear strategies to deliver those plans, based on the conclusions from the comprehensive review of human resources

- targets in race equality strategies for BME representation at all levels of the organisation, including the board of management, and regular monitoring and specific action to ensure that those targets are met, with the aim of achieving accountability to, and representativeness of, the communities which the organisation serves; these targets should also be reviewed in the light of the changing needs of individual staff and the changing human resource needs of the organisation

- a change of management style away from 'blame the victim' towards acceptance by managers of their individual and collective responsibility for the development of their staff

- equal opportunities training for all staff that emphasises the significance and value of cultural diversity within the organisation and within society generally.

Recently, where the problem of BME under-representation in senior management has been highlighted, the tendency has been to go for a 'top-down' approach to organisational change. For example, targets have been adopted for getting BME people into senior posts without extensive consultation with staff or BME communities – 3 per cent within five years in the case of the Department for Education and Employment and 3.2 per cent by 2005 in the case of senior civil servants generally. Such targets might not seem unrealistic in view of the 3.7 per cent comparable figure for RSLs, but without serious commitment to more fundamental organisational change, it seems unlikely that these targets will be met – or, if met, unlikely that they will be sustained. RSLs will certainly need help to achieve racial equality – for example, in terms of guidance from the Housing Corporation and the National Housing Federation on standards of good practice in human resource management – and on how to develop a culture that has equality of opportunity as a core value, but it looks as if the assistance required by central government is significantly greater. But *quis custodies custodiet?* The Housing Corporation itself needs to comprehensively review its existing housing management standards which tend to portray cultural and ethnic diversity as an 'add-on' to the core business of managing housing.

The CRE (1995) Standard defines five levels of progress towards racial equality. In our research, we did not find any mainstream RSLs that were clearly operating above Level 1 (the lowest of five levels, requiring that the organisation have a racial equality policy and a strategy to implement that policy), and a large proportion of these RSLs were not even operating at this level. This has to change. Although there are undoubted risks in forcing the issue, as discussed earlier in this chapter in relation to the limitations of 'top-down' approaches, there is a definite role for the CRE, the Housing Corporation and the National Housing Federation (for all their faults) in ensuring that the practice of RSLs is improved. For example, RSLs could be required to produce reports to the Housing Corporation, on an annual basis, with regard to their progress in meeting the targets in their racial equality plans. Reports that seem unconvincing or problematic in some way could then trigger investigations into the organisations concerned. In addition, random audits of RSLs could be conducted in order to keep RSLs 'on their toes' and perhaps to identify examples of good practice. At the end of the day, there has to be a threat of sanctions, for example the possible withdrawal of investment funding, where an under-performing RSL fails to improve without good reason. The Housing Corporation will need to spell out the details of a new enforcement regime, specifying under what precise conditions sanctions will be applied, the extent of such sanctions, and the provisions made for RSLs to explain and justify their performance on racial equality.

## Best Value – A way forward?

We are currently considering the potential of Best Value approaches as a means of making progress in this area (DETR 1999). Best Value is the government's favoured way of achieving continuous improvement in public services. Local authorities in particular, from April 2000, are required to produce local performance plans, setting out, through consultation, the aspirations for the area and targets for performance improvements to achieve them. Over a four- or five-year cycle, all services will be subject to a fundamental review, challenging the need for each service and the way it is provided, comparing performance with other providers, consulting stakeholders (users, taxpayers, staff, businesses) on the service delivered and what is needed and exposing the services to competition. Performance will be externally monitored by auditors and inspectors, and where an organisation fails to deliver improvements the government will intervene and direct that actions are taken or services will be removed from local authority control. This framework is equally applicable to RSLs, ensuring their continuous improvement and accountability to a wider public, and encouraging them to move forward by comparing their performance with that of other organisations. This last point has a particular resonance in the RSL sector where some organisations are doing so much better than others.

Specifically, the Best Value framework's four Cs – of challenge, consultation, comparison and competition – are applicable to racial equality issues: challenge, in relation to the need for comprehensive review; consultation, with BME communities and with staff; comparison, involving benchmarking with similar organisations as an alternative to crude target-setting; and competition, for example for Housing Corporation investment funding. Racial equality objectives already form an integral part of the Best Value framework for RSLs, although not for other public sector organisations. What now needs to be done is to flesh out the bare bones of this framework in order to arrive at a workable system of regulation that will steer RSLs effectively towards greater racial equality in their employment practices.

To this end, under the headings of the four Cs, we are suggesting specifically:

### Challenge

Possible questions that housing (and other) organisations could ask include:

- Are we delivering quality career opportunities for all our staff?
- Does the composition of our staff reflect the communities we serve?

- Do we respond to the needs of our staff and potential staff as well as we could?

## Compare

Comparisons could be made with other housing organisations, local authorities or other public or private sector bodies. The following could be considered:

- comparing the costs arising from the loss of staff, especially BME staff

- identifying the under-representation of BME staff at different levels and in different areas of work, as compared with other organisations

- learning more effective methods that may lead to better representation of BMEs within the organisation

- learning how to be more accountable to residents, board members and BME communities in terms of achieving racial equality.

Where significant failings are identified, RSLs could be required by the Housing Corporation to produce credible plans to improve their performance. Performance indicators for racial equality could be developed locally, for example through benchmarking clubs.

## Consult

The views of BME residents, and similarly of BME staff, on developing racial equality, along with other residents, could be tested and their involvement in decision-making could be increased. Detailed consultation is necessary in order to ensure that any targets that are adopted are appropriate to both the organisation and the communities it serves. Residents and staff should then be involved in drawing up performance plans, with a clear timetable and arrangements for action and subsequent revision.

## Compete

Mainstream RSLs and local authorities could consider, for example, inviting BME RSLs to provide services on their behalf, on the basis that the latter would be likely to deliver a better service to BME communities. This would enable BME RSLs to grow, resulting in improved career opportunities for BME staff generally.

# References

Argyris, C. (1990) *Overcoming Organisational Defences: Facilitating Organisational Learning.* Boston, MA: Allyn & Bacon.

Armstrong, M. and Murlis, H. (1991) *Reward Management.* London: Kogan Page.

Bichard (1999) 'Search for black Sir Humphreys.' *The Guardian* 14 July

Ciulla, J.B. (1990) 'Can the corporation provide meaningful work?' *NJ Bell Journal* (Fall).

CRE (1993) *Housing Associations and Racial Equality.* London: Commission for Racial Equality.

CRE (1995) *Racial Equality Means Business.* London: Commission for Racial Equality.

CRE (1998) *Stereotyping and Racism.* London: Commission for Racial Equality.

DETR (1999) *Best Value in Housing Framework: Consultation Paper.* London: Department of the Environment, Transport and the Regions.

Dryzek, J. (1990) *Discursive Democracy: Politics, Policy and Political Science.* Cambridge: Cambridge University Press.

Fox, A. (1974) *Beyond Contract: Work, Power and Trust Relations.* London: Faber.

Fox, A. (1985) *Man Mismanagement.* London: Hutchinson.

Garratt, B. (1987) *The Learning Organisation.* London: Fontana/Collins.

Garratt, R. (1990) *Creating a Learning Organisation.* Cambridge: Director Books.

Into Leadership (1999) London: Conference report.

Jaques, E. (1970) *Equitable Payment.* London: Heinemann.

Kandola, R. and Fullerton, J. (1998) *Diversity in Action: Managing the Mosaic.* Second edition. London: Institute of Personnel and Development.

Lakey, J. (1997) 'Neighbourhoods and housing.' In T. Modood, R. Berthoud, J. Lakey, J. Nazroo, P. Smith, S. Virdee and S. Beishon (eds) *Ethnic Minorities in Britain: Diversity and Disadvantage.* London: Policy Studies Institute.

LGMB (1998) *'Evening the Odds': Research into Management Development for Black and Other Minority Ethnic Managers. Main Report.* Appendix 2. London: Local Government Management Board.

Macpherson, W. (1999) *The Stephen Lawrence Inquiry.* Command Paper 4262-I. London: The Stationery Office.

Mangham, I.L. and Pye, A. (1991) *The Doing of Management.* Oxford: Blackwell.

Mant, A. (1983) *Leaders We Deserve.* London: Martin Robertson.

Misra, A. (1999) 'Lawrence lessons.' *ROOF* July/August, 10–11.

O'Neill, J. (1986) 'The disciplinary society: From Weber to Foucault.' *British Journal of Sociology 38*, 1, 42–60.

Pandya, N. (1999a) 'Mentors for black and Asian managers.' *The Guardian* 26 June.

Pandya, N. (1999b) 'Public sector recruitment targets extended.' *The Guardian* 31 July.

Pawson, H. (1988) 'Race and the allocation of public housing.' *Housing Studies 3*, 2, 134–139.

Quinn, J.B. (1980) *Strategies for Change: Logical Incrementalism.* Homewood, ILL: Irwin.

Reed, M. and Anthony, P.D. (1992) 'Professionalising management and managing professionalisation: British management in the 1980s.' *Journal of Management Studies 29*, 5, 591–613.

Ross, R. and Schneider, R. (1992) *From Diversity to Equality: A Business Case for Equal Opportunities.* London: Pitman Publishing.

Schein, E.H. (1985) *Organisational Culture and Leadership.* San Francisco: Jossey-Bass.

Somerville, P. and Steele, A. (1998) *Career Opportunities for Ethnic Minorities.* Salford: University of Salford/Housing Corporation/National Housing Federation.

Somerville, P., Steele, A. and Sodhi, D. (2000) *A Question of Diversity: Black and Minority Ethnic Staff in the RSL Sector.* London: The Housing Corporation.

Tomlins, R. (1994) 'Housing associations and race equality: The report of the CRE into the housing association movement.' *Housing Review 43*, 2, 26–27.

Torrington, D. and Weightman, J. (1994) *Effective Management: People and Organizations.* Second edition. Hemel Hempstead: Prentice-Hall International (UK).

Torrington, D.P., Hitner, T.J. and Knights, D. (1982) *Management and the Multi-Racial Workforce.* Aldershot: Gower.

Watson, T.J. (1994) *In Search of Management: Culture, Chaos and Control in Managerial Work.* London: Routledge.

and Kramer, J. (1978) *Strategy and Conflict in Metropolitan Housing: Suburbia versus the Greater London , 1965–75.* London: Heinemann.

(1999) 'It's the difference that matters.' *Red Pepper* November, 20–22.

*Chapter 9*

# The Diverse Experiences of Black and Minority Ethnic Women in Relation to Housing and Social Exclusion

Fahmeeda Gill

This chapter will consider the diverse experiences of black and minority ethnic (BME) women in relation to housing and social exclusion. However, there will not be scope to cover the full range of experiences. This would require a whole book. The focus has been narrowed, where possible, to link into the government's social exclusion agenda with specific reference to lone mothers.

The chapter is in three parts. The first part will evaluate some of the theoretical explanations of social exclusion and housing in relation to BME communities and women. It will show that too little attention has been paid to the specific experiences of BME women.

The second part will review research conducted to date on the experiences of BME women in relation to housing and social exclusion. It will demonstrate that the growing needs of homeless BME women are not being adequately met by the mainstream social rented sectors. Their experiences of homelessness and poverty are compounded by their poor employment status and welfare reform changes. It will argue that there is a need for more targeted initiatives providing a spectrum of housing and support and preferably delivered by BME RSLs.

The final part will evaluate the extent to which the current government's social exclusion agenda is able to meet the needs of BME women. It will conclude that there has been a lack of 'joined-upness' in the wake of the Stephen Lawrence Report (Macpherson 1999). Current social exclusion priorities are colour-blind and do not sufficiently address the needs of women. They also place too much onus on the need to change individual behaviour as opposed to tackling the root causes of lone parenthood such as high unemployment, which is particularly acute for BME communities. There is also the risk that current programmes are too fragmented, unco-ordinated and will not succeed in isolation from wider housing, economic and welfare reform. The focus on geographical areas as opposed to needs means that current programmes are failing to reach BME communities. There is an urgent need to redress this imbalance if the social exclusion objectives are to be met. More inclusive and sustainable measures are required which are delivered across tenures, are responsive to the diverse needs of BME women and actively engage BME communities.

## Definition

The term 'BME' is used to describe people of colour and, in the main, of African, Caribbean, Asian, Middle East and South East Asian descent. The term 'BME' will be used interchangeably with 'black' in recognition of the shared experience of British colonialism and racism (Mama 1993). This should not ignore the diversity of their experiences in relation to their different countries of origin, socio-economic positions, life-styles and times of migration (Brah 1993; Modood *et al.* 1997).

## The position of BME women in relation to social exclusion and housing

Before describing the position of BME women, it will be necessary to examine how the term 'social exclusion' will be employed. Social exclusion is comprehensive, dynamic and needs to encompass both individual experiences of and collective responses to 'a multi-dimensional process, in which various forms of exclusion are combined: participation in decision making and political processes, access to employment and material resources and integration into common cultural processes' (Byrne 1999, p.22). This includes the inter-relationship with housing as set out by Lee and Murie (1997) in their analysis of poverty and tenure. 'Most importantly, homelessness does not just create social exclusion, it is also a consequence of it' (Anderson and Sim 2000, p.81). However, this definition still suffers from a lack of recognition of the specific dimensions of 'race', gender and disability, and has implications for the explanations of social exclusion and housing which will be examined below. Furthermore, there is a danger of such a definition reinforcing the negative aspect of dependency without adequate attention to more positive concepts of social inclusion and integration

(Anderson and Sim 2000). This will be partly addressed in considering the aspirations of BME women as well as in the policy recommendations to this chapter.

All the available evidence shows that BME communities experience the most acute social and economic deprivation and disadvantage when compared to the wider population. This is likely to be compounded by factors such as gender, class and disability (Mama 1993; Millar 1997). However, this experience is not uniform, as demonstrated by the Fourth National Study of Ethnic Minorities and the most recent Family Resources Survey (Modood *et al.* 1997). This suggests that a range of policy interventions will be required to address their diverse needs.

Older women and lone mothers have the highest risks and longest duration of poverty. These groups are followed by married women with economically inactive husbands and low-paid women (Millar 1997; Oppenheim 1998; Webster 2000). Byrne (1999) does not recognise ethnicity as significant and argues that the increase in lone parents has mainly been in respect of the white population. 'Relatively little attention has been paid to ethnicity in the…discussion of one parent families' (Burghes, cited in Modood *et al.* 1997, p.35). Yet an analysis of the Labour Force Survey found that more than half of all Caribbean families with children had one parent compared with less than a quarter of white families with children (Webster 2000). A report from the Social Exclusion Unit (SEU) on teenage pregnancies stated that African-Caribbean, Bangladeshi and Pakistani teenage women were far more likely to become pregnant than the national average (SEU 1999a, p.19). State dependence was no higher for a BME lone parent than for a BME woman married to an unemployed man (Modood *et al.* 1997, p.57) although in 1996/1997 the weekly income of lone parents was half the level of all households – £160 compared with £325 (Webster 2000, p.111).

Between 1984 and 1995, the employment rate for white women increased from 59 per cent to 68 per cent, while that for black women increased marginally from 44 per cent to 46 per cent (Bloch 1997). Women are more likely to be found in part-time work and still make up the majority of the low-paid (Webb *et al.* 1996; Pile and O'Donnell 1997; Modood *et al.* 1997). One-third of the female workforce is low paid (Walker and Walker 1997). Although female unemployment is generally lower than male unemployment, it follows the same ethnic pattern of inequality. There are low economic activity rates for Pakistani and Bangladeshi women, although Caribbean women are actually far more likely to be in paid employment than Caribbean men. This pattern is not just a result of racial discrimination but is also due to economic restructuring with a loss of jobs in manufacturing and an increase of part-time work in the service sector (Modood *et al.* 1997, p.149). This will have affected Asian women more adversely than African, Caribbean and South East Asian women who are mainly employed within the National Health Service (Mama 1993).

While the BME community constitutes just 6 per cent of the population, it is still over-represented amongst the homeless as shown in a number of empirical studies (Clapham and Evans 2000; Law *et al.* 1999). There are differential housing outcomes for BME groups according to gender, generation and class (Phillips 1998). Low-income Pakistani and Bangladeshi lone parents in Birmingham are six times and four times, respectively, more likely to be in owner-occupation than white lone parents (Chahal 2000). Young Caribbeans and Bangladeshis have higher rates of social renting than other groups. For Caribbeans, this partly reflects the higher proportion of single parents. Housing and neighbourhood disadvantage are compounded by low incomes and a history of settlement in poor areas (Modood *et al.* 1997; Phillips 1998; Sarre, Phillips and Skellington 1989). Women, and BME women in particular, are less visible in terms of street homelessness and are more likely to be found with friends and family (Law *et al.* 1999). More than half of lone mothers live with family (SEU 1999b; Webster 2000). One-third of lone parents had experienced homelessness in the past ten years compared to 6 per cent of all households (Webster 2000). In 1996, 49 per cent of lone parents rented from local authorities/RSLs compared with 22 per cent of all households; 14 per cent were in private rented accommodation compared with 9 per cent of all households; 37 per cent entered owner-occupation compared with 69 per cent of all households (Webster 2000). Rough sleeping is less feasible for women, given their responsibility for children, and BME women are at greater risk of racist/physical/sexual abuse (Jones 1999). BME women are over-represented amongst the residents of hostels and bed-and-breakfast accommodation. Women with children are more likely to be accepted as homeless by local authorities; in 1994, there were about 11 per cent of homeless women and children in bed-and-breakfast accommodation and 23 per cent of homeless women and children in women's refuges (Clapham and Evans 2000). In 1992/1993, a quarter of all homeless applicants to nine local authorities were black (Clapham and Evans 2000).

In sum, BME women are more likely to endure social exclusion, poor housing and homelessness than other social groups as a consequence of racial discrimination and their worse socio-economic position. The wider reasons for this disadvantage will be considered next.

# Explanations of social exclusion and housing in relation to BME women

There are two broad models in the literature that are relevant for our concerns in this chapter. The first considers the differential impact of housing policies in relation to 'race', and the second in relation to gender and the 'remoralisation' of welfare as advocated by Charles Murray (1996) and which underlies current government policy in relation to lone parents.

Phillips (1998) provides the most comprehensive overview of the pattern of BME concentration, segregation and dispersal in Britain over four decades. She argues that there are 'forces for both minority ethnic inclusion and exclusion at work, although these produce different outcomes for different minority ethnic groups according to generation, gender and class' (Phillips 1998, p.1682). These different outcomes are rooted in historical experiences of migration, ethnic clustering, racial discrimination and the impact of wider economic and political changes on the socio-economic status of BME communities. 'Many minority households have found themselves trapped in marginal urban areas of industrial decline' (Phillips 1998, p.1683). While the 1980s brought modest gains to BME communities as a result of race relations legislation, institutionally racist housing policies have persisted along with the risk of racist harassment. For example, although Caribbean households benefited from local authorities opening up their allocations processes, they were allocated sub-standard quality accommodation (Henderson and Karn 1987). Estate agents operating discriminatory practices against BME groups have both restricted owner-occupation to some BME groups and served to reinforce segregation in some geographical areas (Sarre *et al.* 1989; Sim 2000). Various studies have confirmed that both Caribbeans and Asians may prefer to live together both for safety reasons, due to fear of racial attacks, and community reasons, in view of shared cultural/religious practices (Phillips 1998). This is even where there will be overcrowding as shown in a study of Glasgow (Phillips 1998). Asian women in particular may be averse to moving out of cluster regions as they would be at risk of greater isolation and would lose the support of informal networks.

In general, BME groups remain in the poorest urban locations and in the most deprived housing. This is unlikely to change for younger Caribbeans, Pakistanis and Bangladeshis given their poor employment status. The spatial movement that has taken place reflects, in part, the unequal employment status of different BME groups. A small, black, middle class is emerging which is associated with suburbanisation. Pakistanis and Bangladeshis have remained concentrated in poor quality housing though the former are more likely to live in owner-occupied property (with little access to renovation grants – Sim 2000) and the latter in council stock. Younger Caribbean men (women heads of households have fared worse) are more mobile than older generations and have become less concentrated spatially as they have moved into council stock. They remain in poor quality stock, however; few have gained from the Right-to-Buy and they have suffered indirectly from the under-investment in this sector over the past 20 years (Ginsburg 1997). Those with access to housing association accommodation, even where there are BME specialist providers, have had little choice of location since such accommodation is usually located within the inner city (Sim 2000). Only more affluent first generation Indians have been particularly mobile, with professionals moving into rural areas (Phillips 1998).

Byrne (1999) contends that the fundamental principle of segregation is class not ethnicity. He goes on to claim that black British and African-Caribbean populations are assimilating through intermarriage and common residence, a process that has been described as the 'Irish route'. However, class does not in itself explain why even these groups, including the Irish, continue to experience more social and economic disadvantage than their white counterparts. It is therefore arguable as to whether or not these groups can be said to be really assimilating.

Ginsburg (1997) argues that the rise in rents, the worsening of the housing benefit (HB) poverty trap and the overall decline in investment in social housing since 1979 have reinforced gender and ethnic divisions. He shows how successive government policies in relation to the extension of home ownership, the cuts in bricks-and-mortar subsidies and the sell-off of council housing have been particularly disadvantageous to BME communities. Where African-Caribbean families have had the opportunity to buy quality council housing, they have been keener to do so than white people (Ginsburg 1997). However, deregulation of mortgages and cuts in mortgage interest tax relief have hit African-Caribbean and Bangladeshi households the hardest in terms of negative equity, repossessions and mortgage arrears (Walker and Walker 1997, p.147). There has been uneven development of housing association stock, though further increases can be expected with stock transfers. The deregulation of rents and cuts in government subsidies since the 1980s have resulted in an increase of local authority and RSL rents of 36 per cent and 43 per cent respectively. This will have had an adverse effect on women and children, particularly in African-Caribbean and Bangladeshi households (Walker and Walker 1997, p.150). This was followed by a threefold increase in the cost of housing benefit for private sector tenants. Both housing benefit caps along with the restrictions imposed on 16- to 25-year-olds have resulted in an increase in the poverty trap and homelessness (Walker and Walker 1997).

Sim (2000) has argued that racial harassment is the main factor, while unemployment is increasingly important, in explaining homelessness amongst BME communities. He considered the constraints of access and location to be important in explaining the small numbers of BME communities found within the social rented sector. This under-representation was a result of discriminatory practices within both the local authority sector (for example, West Indians in Birmingham – Henderson and Karn 1987) and the RSL sector, involving insensitive lettings policies, residential qualifications and transfer policies which gave, and continue to give, preferential treatment to existing white tenants. This has not been helped by poor or inadequate communication with BME communities.

The larger average household size of some BME communities is also a deterrent for entry into social housing and results in overcrowding (Sim 2000). The size of local authority stock (up to three bedrooms) and of RSL stock as a result of regulation and funding constraints present a barrier to entry for larger BME families. Sim concluded that 'the issues of choice and preference may be largely irrelevant for BME communities whose housing is often determined by forces outside their control' (Sim 2000, p.97).

The second model provides an explanation of social exclusion and housing in relation to gender. Smith (1999) presents a convincing case for how social housing for women has been undermined as a result of changes to housing policy which no longer recognise the housing needs of lone parents and their children. The 1977 Housing Act recognised the importance of housing as a safety net for families including women and children. The principles of the family ethic and work ethic underpinned welfare and housing provision for women and children. In 1991, 45 per cent of divorced or separated female-headed households occupied social housing compared with 28 per cent of divorced or separated men. In the same year, 31 per cent of single women and 18 per cent of single men occupied social housing (Hutson and Clapham 1999, p.110).

Smith goes on to identify three threats to women's access to social housing. The first is the residualisation of local authority housing. This has limited the supply of social housing which is now more often located in isolating and excluded estates, and local authorities in many areas have been forced to continue using temporary bed-and-breakfast accommodation for homeless families. Second, she highlights the change of emphasis in homelessness policy to tackling 'visible' street homelessness, which specifically excludes women and children.

This is despite an increase in homelessness amongst families between 1978 and 1991, from 53,000 to 149,000 (Smith 1999).

Finally, she considers the implications of the 1996 Housing Act, which removed the duty of local authorities to provide permanent housing. This Act was driven partly by a concern that lone parenthood had increased as a consequence of perverse incentives which have encouraged mothers to live without partners, fathers to abandon families and lone parents to depend on benefits (Webster 2000). Only by removing incentives could the state change people's behaviour and stem the tide of 'a growing underclass, characterised by its behaviour – high levels of illegitimacy, crime and labour market drop-out which was threatening the social fabric' (Murray, cited in Walker and Walker 1997, p.18). There was also a widespread belief that lone mothers were getting priority for rehousing over two-parent couples on the waiting list. This period heralded a shift in the political agenda and the beginning of a wider remoralisation of welfare, which sought to shift attention away from recession and major economic restructuring. A number of measures were taken, including cuts to benefits, which have had an adverse effect on women and children and led to the greater feminisation of poverty (Byrne 1999; Millar 1997). Furthermore, the abolition of the Wages Councils and the privatisation of many public services led to job losses and an increase in part-time and discontinuous work patterns, with reduced access to pensions and sickness schemes (Millar 1997). While some measures were taken to assist women, such as family credit, the extension of maternity leave and the provision of nursery vouchers, they did not go far enough. There were no attempts made to improve women's pay and to recognise the needs of working women and difficulties in combining home and family (Millar 1997). Although there has been a growth in the employment of women, gendered dependency remains (Byrne 1999).

There is no evidence that the availability of benefits has promoted single parenthood (Byrne 1999) or that young girls had babies to gain access to housing (Allen and Dowling 1998; Rowlingson and McKay 1998). The two factors that have led to an increase in lone parenthood from 8 per cent to 21 per cent of all households between 1971 and 1996 are changes in household formation (Byrne 1999; Smith 1999) and the growth of unemployment (Byrne 1999). There were 1.6 million lone-parent families in 1996 of whom 92.6 per cent were female (Byrne 1999). The 1991 census showed that three-fifths of lone parents were divorced/separated, one-third were never married and one in twenty widowed (Webster 2000). Half of lone mothers are aged over 33 and teenage lone parents constitute less than one in twenty-five (Webster 2000). Births to unmarried teenagers only rose from 2 per cent to 5.7 per cent of all births between 1964 and 1993 (SEU 1999a; Webster 2000).

The first model has sought to explain the social exclusion and disadvantaged housing position of BME communities as a result of different patterns of migration, changes in socio-economic status and racial discrimination. The second model has focused upon the disadvantaged position of women as a result of wider socio-economic and demographic changes, ideological changes to housing and welfare policies and gender discrimination. Neither model on its own addresses the specific experiences of BME women. However, it is possible to combine the models in order to get a fuller picture of the specific experiences of BME women. This reveals a complex range of factors that have contributed to the social exclusion, impoverishment and inequitable housing position of BME women.

## BME women and homelessness

This section will consider the research conducted to date on homelessness amongst BME women. There has been very little written on this subject and it is a gap in current homelessness research. This is despite the fact that the limited evidence available suggests that homelessness amongst BME women is on the increase. Most of the studies conducted focus exclusively on either the experiences of the homeless as a result of their race/ethnicity or their experiences as a result of their gender. Few studies have examined the specific experiences of homeless BME women. It will therefore be necessary to combine the findings of both studies in order to get insight into their whole experiences. Given the limited scope of this chapter, only an overview of recent research carried out is provided here. It has not been possible to consider the benefits of specific regeneration initiatives for BME women or wider issues of sexuality and disability. The true extent of homelessness amongst women and BME women in particular has tended to be underestimated especially since it is 'hidden' and often difficult to quantify. This has been exacerbated by the narrowing of the definition of homelessness to that of rooflessness, even though women and particularly BME women will not be found sleeping rough given that they are more vulnerable to abuse (Smith 1999).

One recent research project investigated the experiences of young homeless people (53 African-Caribbeans, 46 whites, 46 Pakistanis, 8 Indians and 5 Bangladeshis) in hostels in West Yorkshire and the Midlands (Law *et al.* 1999). BME groups, and women in particular, were over-represented in bed-and-breakfast accommodation. Women made up a third of this latter group, were more likely to have stayed with friends and were less likely than men to have slept rough. The most common reason for homelessness was a crisis of family relationships. One in five of African-Caribbeans reported actual or threats of physical/sexual violence, compared with one in three Pakistani/Indian women; and one-third of Caribbeans had left care, compared with one in six Asians. Their experiences were exacerbated by low income and lack of access to affordable rented housing. Women were under-represented in hostels and this may reflect that many more are likely to be fleeing domestic violence and would be found in refuges. Many expressed dissatisfaction with mainstream hostels and a preference for black-run accommodation. Most were looking for their own self-contained accommodation either close to or away from their community (Asian women fleeing domestic violence preferred the latter), would benefit from some practical/emotional support and were looking to resume their studies (Law *et al.* 1999).

A recent Crisis study of 77 homeless women (20 per cent of the sample were BME women although their ethnic origin is not broken down) in London, Liverpool, Brighton and Bristol found that the most common reasons for becoming homeless were domestic violence (as well as former physical/sexual/emotional abuse as a child) and being thrown out by their families. Over two-fifths had been homeless more than once and 50 reported having slept rough even though they were vulnerable; however, this was far less likely to be the case with younger women and BME women. Only five of the women were employed and the majority were dependent on benefits and indicated that they would seek employment once they had a home. Hostel life was described as stressful with reports of depression and/or alcohol/substance misuse and many women felt trapped and complained of the lack of move-on accommodation. Most wanted women-only hostel provision and eventually a home of their own, with two-fifths needing ongoing support (Jones 1999).

A recent audit of women (very few BME women were represented in the sample), in Key Change's supported accommodation in Exeter (which has received Rough Sleepers Initiative funding) and Reigate, highlighted the following concerns: a shortage of suitable affordable accommodation in these areas along with a recognition that having children would help women get rehoused more quickly; the need for hostel provision for women over 35 as well as more specialist provision for women with substance misuse problems or mental health problems; the difficulties caused for younger people due to inadequate benefits and poor housing benefit administration; the importance of mediation for young people to prevent homelessness; and the need for follow-up support for women who had moved into their own accommodation. This follow-up work is seen as integral to addressing the effects of social exclusion and the difficulty of reintegrating the homeless back into the community, particularly in Exeter (Ravenhill 2000).

Despite the high percentage of homeless women reporting domestic violence, another research project highlighted the crisis of funding for this provision and the need for a national refuge strategy (Frayne and Muir 1994). There is a demand for 74,000 lettings of refuge places a year, which implies a need for 8200 places in 800–900 refuges. Current refuge provision is for 1700 families in 192 refuges, of which at least 24 are for BME women. The study recognised the need for more BME refuges and for further research in this area.

A survey was conducted in seven cities and four London boroughs, over a period of three months in 1996, of 15,000 homeless clients aged from 16 to 25. Although the study included BME women, their experiences are not highlighted. However, it is still useful in demonstrating their shared experiences as homeless women. The study found that half of the homeless in any one city were women. The majority of the homeless were women in five cities apart from Manchester and Glasgow. Most were single women although a high number (25–44%) were single parents. Single mothers had the same rates of unemployment as men. All the women reported the difficulty of finding affordable safe accommodation with a well-paid job/training and childcare (Smith 1999).

The survey also showed that 'women are not jumping the queue (Hutson and Clapham 1999, p.118)'. Thirty-five per cent of lone mothers were rejected by local authorities as not being in priority need and 55 per cent were rejected by RSLs. Homelessness agencies were more likely to classify men than women as homeless (71 per cent compared to 60 per cent). This was because women were less likely to have slept on the streets and more likely to have stayed with friends and/or relatives. African and Caribbean women were least likely to have slept on the streets. Single mothers were more likely to present from emergency hostels (Smith 1999).

Lone parents live in the worst rented accommodation. In 1996, nearly one in five (18%) were living in 'poor' housing conditions (unfit, in substantial disrepair or in need of modernisation) compared to 14.2 per cent of all households (Webster 2000). Unemployed lone parents were worst off, with one in four living in poor housing. They were more likely to have poor security, lack smoke alarms and live in local authority accommodation with no central heating. This is likely to have been compounded by the policy of making only one offer of accommodation to homeless households. Twenty-three per cent of lone parent families lived in flats compared with 6 per cent of all families. Those sharing tended to be overcrowded in the local authority sector. They were twice as likely to be living in poor neighbourhoods (SEU 1999b). Almost two-thirds wanted to move, evidence suggested that they were moving into the private rented sector and they were twice as likely to be dissatisfied with their accommodation as any other type of family (Webster 2000, pp.112–113).

A survey of 180 Pakistani households in Bradford, Glasgow and Luton found that the housing needs of women living either alone or as single mothers were not being met (Bowes, Dar and Sim 1998).

A qualitative study of 41 existing and prospective tenants (Asian, African-Caribbean and white) of a BME RSL looked at the barriers to employment faced by women with children (Third 1996). Knowledge of housing benefit changes as earnings rise was poor, particularly among Asian women. Most women had assumed that they would not get any housing benefit on the amount they said they would work for. This was even though they would have been entitled to housing benefit for half of their rent. Childcare, not rent, was the biggest and most costly barrier to employment. The majority of mothers said it would not be worth working if they did not have free childcare. Despite these obstacles, the majority of women wanted to work even if they were little or no better off (Third 1996).

A recent survey of supported housing accommodation in Lewisham concluded that there was a need to develop more culturally sensitive services for older black women and black women with mental health problems and sickle cell anaemia. BME women made up 70 per cent of the women in supported accommodation. The survey also highlighted the need for provision for women with children, more self-contained accommodation as well as floating support services and the importance of women-only and BME specialist provision (Reading, Raj and Gill 1998).

This section has demonstrated the range of experiences of homeless BME groups as well as those of homeless women. Together, the studies give the collective and shared experiences of homelessness among BME women in respect of their needs as women and as belonging to BME communities. It has also highlighted some of their aspirations and, in particular, their preference for more specialist provision. This collective experience reveals the following key findings:

- the principal cause of homelessness for BME women is abuse

- sleeping rough is not an option for BME women

- many prefer to stay with friends

- existing hostel provision does not cater for their specific needs

- single parents are even more vulnerable as a result of the lack of affordable housing and childcare
- there is a pressing need to develop more specialist provision for BME women, including refuges, which offers them an appropriate level of support and after-care.

This suggests the need for more capital investment for such provision. However, there will also be many BME women who will still prefer to remain with friends or family. In this instance, it will be necessary to arrange revenue funding to meet their support needs as envisaged under Supporting People.[1]

Whilst these findings are useful, they are not sufficient in themselves. There is a pressing need to conduct a separate study into the specific experiences of homeless BME women. This should adopt a different approach in recognition of the fact that many BME women will not be found in hostels. They are more likely to be with friends and family. Such a survey should locate these women and seek to elicit their views on their diverse needs, experiences and aspirations. This would go a long way to addressing the limitations of existing studies.

## How far can the government's social exclusion agenda meet the needs of BME women?

So far, the discussion has shown that BME women are more disadvantaged in respect of social exclusion and homelessness and the reasons are varied and complex. This section will consider how far the government's social exclusion agenda can meet their specific needs and will make some recommendations for future policy in this area. As with the theoretical models and research studies, most of the work written in this area concentrates exclusively on either the experiences of BME communities or the experiences of women and more specifically lone parents. It will therefore be necessary to review work on these two groups separately and then to pull the common themes together in order to draw any conclusions in respect of BME women.

Although the government's agenda for social exclusion, which cuts across health, housing, employment and education, is to be applauded, there is a legitimate concern that the current targeting of the most deprived geographical areas or council estates is in danger of missing out many impoverished BME communities who are located within mixed tenure areas (Chahal 2000). This is confirmed by the SEU's latest report (SEU 2000). In the first three rounds of the Single Regeneration Budget (SRB), only four out of 555 successful bids were led by BME RSLs; only four out of 23 bids for Round 1 of the Challenge Fund included

BME organisations as partners and, of the seven Challenge Fund priorities, BME policy objectives were least likely to be stated as a priority by local authority led SRB bids (SEU 2000).

A government document (Cabinet Office 2000) attempts to provide a guide to the work of the SEU and Policy Action Teams in relation to BME communities. It outlines five types of action as follows: tackling racial discrimination, ensuring mainstream services are more relevant to BME communities, implementing specifically targeted programmes, tackling racist crime and harassment and improving the information available to BME communities. These actions endorse the need for good practice/monitoring and are certainly an improvement on previous regeneration initiatives, which have often overlooked the specific needs of BME communities. However, the actions that apply to health, housing, education and employment do not make any mention of women's needs. Equally concerning is the fact that they lack any teeth. It is not clear what action will be taken against employers and/or landlords who fail to develop more accessible employment/housing policies. The delivery and implementation of the range of recommendations will need to be monitored centrally, including across the relevant government departments, in order to see what concrete outcomes are delivered to BME communities. Similarly, the government's *New Deal for Communities: Racial Equality Guidance* (DETR 2000) is to be welcomed and includes some good examples of employment, health, education and crime projects that have directly benefited BME communities. However, good practice guidance in this area is not enough without a genuine commitment to re-channelling resources to BME communities. More rigorous evaluation of existing programmes in relation to outcome measures is needed, with particular attention to addressing the needs of BME women. The Rough Sleepers Initiative, for example, is designed to redress visible homelessness at the expense of women, and of BME women in particular (Smith 1999).

'Opportunity for All' reports on the government's progress across all its SEU objectives (SEU 2000). The report is 'colour-blind' and there is a lack of regard for the specific needs of BME communities. However, there are some clear indicators of success which will have benefited women, including some BME women. These include the national minimum wage, investment in more affordable childcare, greater parental leave and maternity benefits, the Working Families Tax Credit and the New Deal for Lone Parents (NDLP) and partners of unemployed people. The improved childcare provision, however, has not benefited lone parents (Webster 2000). Furthermore, Blair's 'third way' places undue emphasis on personal responsibility, which is exemplified in recent welfare reforms, most notably Welfare to Work. This approach is also underpinned by tougher sanctions for failing to return into employment. Arguably, however, the onus should not be wholly on an individual to find employment. There are wider factors, such as the labour market, that are out of their control and for whose shortcomings they should not be penalised. The government's approach is short-sighted and is only likely to widen the gap between rich and poor. This will be more disadvantageous to BME communities and to women (Oppenheim 1998).

The 'remoralisation' of welfare and the promotion of two-parent families remain firm within Labour policy. Both the NDLP along with *Teenage Pregnancy* (SEU 1999a) continue to stigmatise lone parents by focusing on the need to change their behaviour. The NDLP, for example, seeks to encourage women back into employment but sees this as primarily a matter of encouraging women to retrain and find jobs. In reality, the success of the programme requires the creation of employment opportunities and adequate childcare provision. In the absence of such developments, 'Lone parents who want to work will get jobs if they are available in the area, otherwise they will not' (Webster 2000, p.124). While *Supporting Families* (Home Office 1998) mentioned the 'lads and dads agenda' in referring to the loss of traditional male labour, the government has not taken sufficient strides to restructure the economy to address the shortfall of jobs following the collapse of manufacturing and mining (Walker and Walker 1997). Consequently, it is not surprising that the outcomes of the NDLP so far have been poor: 163,383 letters have been sent out, a quarter have had an interview, one-fifth have agreed to participate and only 3.8 per cent have been found a job (Webster 2000).

The SEU, through its report on teenage pregnancies (SEU 1999a), gave a great deal of attention to a group who constitute only a tiny proportion of the total of lone parents. Empirical studies have indicated that the provision of sex education is not enough to stem the increase in teenage pregnancies. The proposed removal of single women and their babies from the definition of statutory homelessness and the removal of the duty of local authorities to provide them with permanent accommodation will produce a further distortion of the official definitions and counts of the homeless. The intention is to develop specialist-adapted mother and baby hostels, with funding from the Housing Corporation, which are seen as more desirable than temporary bed and breakfast. While this is to be welcomed as a short-term measure, it fails to address the needs of lone parents in the long term. Besides, it does not seek to improve the quality of offer of accommodation to lone parents in local authority housing. 'Reversing the family ethic, which once protected women with young children, may appear an efficient source of saving on public funds in the short term but in the long term it may prove very costly indeed' (Smith 1999, p.129).

A further government proposal, for extending the remit of the Child Support Agency (CSA) to raise more money from fathers, is unlikely to succeed unless jobs materialise. The CSA approach has already proved to be a costly administrative exercise. The reality is that three-quarters of fathers are in contact with their ex-partners and are paying their way (Webster 2000).

It is unclear how far the Housing Green Paper will lead to significant improvements in the circumstances of homeless families or provide relief for many homeless women who are currently languishing in sub-standard temporary accommodation.

The picture that is emerging is that neither social exclusion measures, recent welfare changes nor existing housing policies are improving the position of BME women. More direct measures will be required to address their specific needs. These include the following:

- more direct support from the Housing Corporation for BME RSLs, as well as funding for larger accommodation and specialist hostel provision

- more sensitive lettings policies from local authorities and RSLs, offering more choice and effective rehousing strategies in the event of racist harassment

- more effective involvement and engagement of local BME communities in regeneration initiatives/community development and preventative work across tenures

- more renovation funding for BME communities in owner-occupation

- the release of capital receipts to enable local authorities to reinvest in their stock to reduce the use of unsafe temporary accommodation

- recognition of the longer-term rehousing needs of single women and lone parents.

The SEU is the central government body charged with the responsibility for tackling social exclusion. Its current remit, however, does not include addressing the specific needs of BME women who are often amongst the most excluded groups in our society. Whilst the creation of the SEU is to be welcomed, it is unlikely to go far enough in tackling the root causes of social exclusion. This is for several reasons: it has a limited life-time, a limited budget and an ambitious work programme that stretches across other government departments for which it has no direct authority. The biggest challenge it faces is in overcoming the absence of political will, deeply entrenched cultures and conflicting agendas within and across government departments nationally, regionally and locally. Consequently, the work of the SEU is in danger of being too fragmented and unco-ordinated. This could be partly overcome by changes to legislation to ensure that joined-up working takes place locally as well as the creation of cross-agency SEU units on a devolved basis with their own budgets and real involvement from client groups (Halpern 1998). Even with these changes, however, the real obstacle to the success of the social exclusion agenda is the failure of central government to introduce more cross-cutting reforms to the economy to address structural inequality in Britain. These could include the following:

- measures to redistribute wealth including taxation

- reinvestment in those parts of the economy that are failing to facilitate greater job creation

- less punitive welfare measures, which would place less onus on changing an individual's behaviour and more on providing a safety net

- replacement of any cuts in housing benefit by greater capital subsidy for social housing, to prevent people spiralling into debt and becoming homeless

- the provision of more effective measures for regulators to take action against employers and housing providers in respect of racially discriminatory policies and practices.

## Note

1. Supporting People is a government policy to encourage the delivery of more flexible packages of cross-tenure support to people in need. This will require combining existing sources of support funding into one pot – a Supporting People grant, which will be administered from 2003 by local authorities.

## References

Allen, I. and Dowling, S.B. with Rolfe, H. (1998) *Teenage Mothers Decisions and Outcomes.* London: Policy Studies Institute.

Anderson, I. and Sim, D. (eds) (2000) *Social Exclusion and Housing: Context and Challenges.* Coventry: Chartered Institute of Housing/Housing Studies Association.

Bloch, A. (1997) 'Ethnic inequality and social security.' In A. Walker and C. Walker (eds) (1997) *Britain Divided – The Growth of Social Exclusion in the 1980s and 1990s.* London: Child Poverty Action Group.

Bowes, D., Dar, N. and Sim, D. (1998) 'Pakistani housing strategies in Britain.' *Findings* 118. York: Joseph Rowntree Foundation.

Brah, A. (1993) 'Women of South Asian origin in Britain: Issues and concerns.' In P. Braham, A. Rattansi and R. Skellington (eds) *Racism and Antiracism: Inequalities, Opportunities and Policies*. London: Open University Press and Sage Publications.

Byrne, D. (1999) *Social Exclusion*. Buckingham: Open University Press.

Cabinet Office (2000) *Minority Ethnic Issues in Social Exclusion and Neighbourhood Renewal: A Guide to the Work of the Social Exclusion Unit and the Policy Action Team So Far*. London: The Stationery Office.

Chahal, K. (2000) 'Ethnic diversity, neighbourhoods and housing.' In *Findings*. York: Joseph Rowntree Foundation.

Clapham, D. and Evans, A. (2000) 'Social exclusion: The case of homelessness.' In I. Anderson and D. Sim (eds) (2000) *Social Exclusion and Housing: Context and Challenges*. Coventry: Chartered Institute of Housing/Housing Studies Association.

DETR (2000) *New Deal for Communities: Racial Equality Guidance*. London: Department of the Environment, Transport and the Regions.

Frayne, B. and Muir, J. (1994) *Nowhere to Run: Under-Funding of Women's Refuges and the Case for Reform*. London: London Housing Unit.

Ginsburg, N. (1997) 'Housing.' In A. Walker and C. Walker (eds) (1997) *Britain Divided – The Growth of Social Exclusion in the 1980s and 1990s*. London: Child Poverty Action Group.

Halpern, D. (1998) 'Poverty, social exclusion and the policy-making process: The road from theory to practice' In C. Oppenheim (ed.) (1998) *An Inclusive Society – Strategies for Tackling Poverty*. London: Institute for Public Policy Research.

Henderson, J. and Karn, V. (1987) *Race, Class and State Housing: Inequality and the Allocation of Public Housing in Britain*. Aldershot: Gower.

Home Office (1998) *Supporting Families*. London: Home Office.

Hutson, S. and Clapham, D. (eds) (1999) *Homelessness: Public Policies and Private Troubles*. London: Cassell.

Jones, A. (1999) *Out of Sight, Out of Mind? The Experiences of Homeless Women*. London: Crisis/Centre for Housing Policy, University of York.

Law, I., Davis, J., Lyle, S. and Deacon, A. (1999) 'Ethnicity and youth homelessness.' In F. Spiers (ed) *Housing and Social Exclusion*. London: Jessica Kingsley Publishers.

Lee, P. and Murie, A. (1997) *Poverty, Housing Tenure and Social Exclusion*. Bristol: The Policy Press and the Joseph Rowntree Foundation.

Macpherson, W. (1999) *The Stephen Lawrence Inquiry*. Command Paper 4262-I. London: The Stationery Office.

Mama, A. (1993) 'Black women and the British state: Race, class and gender analysis for the 1990s.' In P. Braham, A. Rattansi and R. Skellington (eds) *Racism and Antiracism: Inequalities, Opportunities and Policies*. London: Open University Press and Sage Publications.

Millar, J. (1997) 'Gender.' In A. Walker and C. Walker (eds) *Britain Divided – The Growth of Social Exclusion in the 1980s and 1990s*. London: Child Poverty Action Group.

Modood, T., Berthoud, R., Lakey, J., Nazroo, J., Smith, P., Virdee, S. and Beishon, S. (1997) *Ethnic Minorities in Britain: Diversity and Disadvantage*. London: Policy Studies Institute.

Murray, C. (1996) *Charles Murray and the Underclass: The Developing Debate*. London: IEA Health and Welfare Unit.

Oppenheim, C. (ed) (1998) *An Inclusive Society – Strategies for Tackling Poverty*. London: Institute for Public Policy Research.

Phillips, D. (1998) 'Black minority ethnic concentration, segregation and dispersal in Britain.' *Urban Studies* 35, 10, 1681–1702.

Pile, H. and O'Donnell, C. (1997) 'Earnings, taxation and wealth.' In A. Walker and C. Walker (eds) (1997) *Britain Divided – The Growth of Social Exclusion in the 1980s and 1990s*. London: Child Poverty Action Group.

Ravenhill, M. (2000) *Homelessness and Vulnerable Young People: A Social Audit of Key Change Charity's Supported Accommodation*. CASE Paper 37. London: Centre for Analysis of Social Exclusion.

Reading, J., Raj, M. and Gill, F. (1998) *London Borough Lewisham Supported Housing Needs of Women*. London: CV Services.

Rowlingson, K. and McKay, S. (1998) *The Growth of Lone Parenthood: Diversity and Dynamics*. London: Policy Studies Institute.

Sarre, P., Phillips, D. and Skellington, R. (1989) *Ethnic Minority Housing: Explanations and Policies.* Aldershot: Avebury.

SEU (1999a) *Teenage Pregnancy.* Cm 4342. London: The Stationery Office.

SEU (1999b) *Opportunity for All: Tackling Poverty and Social Exclusion.* First annual report. Cm 4445. London: The Stationery Office.

SEU (2000) *Bringing Britain Together: A National Strategy for Neighbourhood Renewal.* London: The Stationery Office.

Sim, D. (2000) 'Housing inequalities and BME groups.' In I. Anderson and D. Sim (eds) (2000) *Social Exclusion and Housing: Context and Challenges.* Coventry: Chartered Institute of Housing/Housing Studies Association.

Smith, J.M. (1999) 'Gender and homelessness.' In S. Hutson and D. Clapham (eds) *Homelessness: Public Policies and Private Troubles.* London: Cassell.

*The Fourth National Survey of Ethnic Minorities.* London: Policy Studies Institute.

Third, H. (1996) *Affordable Childcare and Housing: A Case Study of Tenants of a Black Housing Association.* York: Centre for Housing Policy, University of York.

Walker, A. and Walker, C. (eds) (1997) *Britain Divided – The Growth of Social Exclusion in the 1980s and 1990s.* London: Child Poverty Action Group.

Webster, D. (2000) 'Lone parenthood: Two views and their consequences.' In I. Anderson and D. Sim (eds) *Social Exclusion and Housing: Context and Challenges.* Coventry: Chartered Institute of Housing/Housing Studies Association.

*Chapter 10*

# Black Youth Homelessness

## Andy Steele

Homelessness is now a commonplace feature in many of our towns and cities and it is generally recognised that homelessness has increased substantially over the last few years (Hall 1996). A number of factors have been identified as contributing to this increase, including changing demographic patterns, particularly marital break-up; changes to welfare benefit entitlement, especially for young single people; and changes within the housing market, most notably the sale of council properties and a decreasing rate of production of homes for rent. Murie (1988) comments that underlying all this has been a growth in socio-economic inequalities, which has disproportionately impacted on the most vulnerable groups in society. The growth in homelessness among black and minority ethnic (BME) groups has been even more dramatic. In 1989, a survey of London boroughs found that black households were up to four times more likely than white households to become homeless (Friedman, LHU and LRC 1989). However, this growth in black homelessness is not confined to the capital. There is evidence to suggest that black people are over-represented among the homeless in other parts of the country. A recent survey undertaken for Oxford City Council found that 45 per cent of those accepted as statutory homeless comprised non-white households, with one-third of these describing themselves as being of black origin. This contrasts sharply with estimates of around 10 per cent of the population in Oxford who are of BME origin (Steele 2000).

Youth homelessness is also on the increase (Davies *et al.* 1996 and Law *et al.* 1999). Anderson, Kemp and Quilgars (1993), in considering the use of hostels and bed-and-breakfast accommodation by ethnic minority groups, reported that while 26 per cent of such users were from ethnic minority groups, this proportion increased to 44 per cent of 16- to 17-year-olds and 38 per cent of those under 25.

Smith and Gilford (1993) collected information on 2738 young people in housing need in Birmingham and found that one-quarter were living in hostels or sleeping rough, another four out of ten were homeless or potentially homeless and the remainder were urgently seeking either accommodation or housing advice. Nearly one-third of the sample was from ethnic minority groups. In particular, the study identified young African-Caribbeans as being most at risk of homelessness as they constituted nearly 12 per cent of the survey population but represented only 5 per cent of Birmingham's 16- to 24-year-old population.

It is generally recognised that the causes of homelessness among ethnic minority youths are the same for all ethnic groups (Law *et al.* 1999). One of the most common causes of homelessness is a family crisis or breakdown. In a recent study in Nottingham, it was found that 42 per cent of those interviewed identified disputes with parents as the main cause while a further 15 per cent referred to a dispute with a partner. Over half of the former group were under 21 years of age and were more likely to be African-Caribbean. Law *et al.* (1999) suggest that even though family relationships often improve, many young people want to assert their independence, and this often brings them into conflict with other family members, particularly their parents. A second important cause of homelessness is domestic violence or threats of violence. In the Nottingham study, one in ten of the respondents gave this as the main reason for being homeless. Law *et al.* (1999) suggest that this was 'particularly significant for Indian and Pakistani women where the proportion was one in three' (p.148) and the Nottingham study confirms this. Other causes of homelessness include: failure of the care system – Law *et al.* (1999) noted that one-third of African-Caribbean homeless young people had been in a children's home; high levels of unemployment; and the withdrawal of benefits from 16- to 17-year-olds. Although the causes of homelessness for ethnic minority young people are similar to those for white youths, their experience of homelessness is somewhat different. A number of studies have highlighted the lack of awareness on the part of the statutory and voluntary services of the needs of ethnic minority homeless young people (Patel 1994; Steele 1997) and the lack of a culturally sensitive service for this client group.

This chapter discusses the need for culturally appropriate and sensitive services for young black homeless people, drawing on the author's own recent work, primarily in Nottingham but also Oxford. The study in Nottingham was undertaken in 1997 for Nottingham City Council. A wide range of agencies in the city were approached and asked to promote the study among young black homeless people. A sample of 191 was identified within the age range 16–35. Personal interviews, as opposed to the use of self-completed questionnaires, were conducted with the majority of the group. In addition, semi-structured interviews were undertaken with a range of agencies providing services to this client group (Steele 1997). The Oxford study (Steele 2000) also focused on black homelessness, although not exclusively limited to young people. The research involved a survey of hostel users and those accepted as statutory homeless by the local authority, and semi-structured interviews with agencies providing services in the city to give a 'provider perspective' on black homelessness in the area. In this chapter I will consider a recent initiative established by Nottingham City Council in response to the study findings: the Azuka Befriending Scheme, which is aimed at young black homeless people within the city and draws upon resources from within the ethnic minority community itself (see later in this chapter). This illustrates one possible answer to the criticisms that those agencies dealing with black youth homelessness do not provide a culturally sensitive or responsive service. It then leads to a wider discussion of whether or not it is appropriate to develop ethnic minority-only services alongside existing services, as opposed to encouraging mainstream providers to respond actively to a multi-cultural and diverse client group.

## The visibility of ethnic minority homelessness

On the whole, street homelessness is generally perceived to be a white issue, with little visibility of black homeless youths on the streets. Davies et al. (1996) found that whites were much more likely to have slept rough than Asians or African-Caribbeans, who were more likely to remain as hidden homeless. The Nottingham study found that just 16 per cent reported that they had slept rough. Within this group, there were twice as many men as women and generally they were below the age of 21. The largest group of rough sleepers tended to be African-Caribbeans (36 per cent), followed by Indians (23 per cent) and Pakistanis (13 per cent). Research has shown that ethnic minority homeless young people will initially look to stay with friends and family when they find themselves homeless, and only as a last resort live on the streets. For example, just one in ten of those interviewed in Nottingham stated that they had no fixed abode, while nearly three out of ten were staying with friends or family (Steele 1997). Similarly, a study in Leicester by Ford and Vincent (1990) found that African-Caribbean women relied overwhelmingly on informal processes and shelter (friends and relatives) when they became homeless. This reliance on friends and family is likely to be, at least in part, a reflection of their lack of awareness as to what services are available. The research in Nottingham found that nearly three-quarters of respondents were unaware of the housing options available to young people in the city, especially in terms of the type of accommodation. One young African-Caribbean woman commented that she believed that there was 'only housing available for homeless people who are pregnant – that's it I think' (Steele 1997, p.21). This heavy reliance on informal networks for surviving is also likely to be a reflection of negative perceptions or experiences of sleeping rough. Law *et al.* (1999) found that when questioned about why they would not sleep rough on the streets, the most common replies related to their sense of pride and fear of harassment and physical violence.

It should also be recognised that when young black homeless people do try to access the statutory and voluntary services they find that these services are not sensitive to their needs (Ford and Vincent 1990). As Sarre, Phillips and Skellington (1989) found in their study in Birmingham of ethnic minorities and the home-ownership market, faced with overt racism from estate agencies, they resorted to 'avoidance strategies', preferring to rely on family and friends to identify suitable properties. A similar analogy may be drawn here with homeless young black people. As they experience a lack of sensitivity to their cultural and emotional needs by service providers, they opt to avoid further contact with such agencies. As one young homeless African-Caribbean man from Nottingham commented about his experiences of contacting agencies in the city, 'from past experience, due to institutional racism, I know they are all a waste of time and money' (Steele 1997, p.22), while a 16-year-old Asian man suggested that 'they don't know anything about me or where I'm coming from, or they just don't care' (p.22).

## Mono-cultural service provision

One of the main findings from the Nottingham study was that the services provided were seen to be mono-cultural and dominated by white staff. These organisations were seen as unwelcoming to young black people and, as such, it has been argued, 'can culminate in young black people feeling stigmatised' (Steele 1997, p.42). In this way, young people perceive that the service providers are unsympathetic to their needs and that they themselves are in some way at fault for the situation they find themselves in. This can further reinforce their own sense of pride that they should be able to manage themselves, and many subsequently choose to avoid further contact with these agencies. Perhaps it is not surprising then that, when the homeless in Nottingham were asked which agency, if any, they had contacted to try to find accommodation, one-fifth reported that they had not approached any agency.

One important indication of the extent to which a service is deemed to be welcoming of ethnic minorities is the ethnicity of the staff. 'Most black people want to see another black face. Particularly for young black people, they need to feel that they can identify with the person that sees them' (Steele 1997, p.42). However, as shown in Chapter 8 of this volume, only a small minority of housing organisations have a truly ethnically diverse workforce.

The lack of a culturally sensitive service can manifest itself in a number of important ways for black homeless young people. First, housing providers respond only to the housing needs of individuals without recognising the cultural context of these needs. In Nottingham, for example, black homeless young people were often allocated self-contained accommodation which was away from their existing family and friends and where they felt socially and culturally isolated. Many of these young people had little experience of living independently and did not have the necessary life skills to cope by themselves. In the absence of support structures and advice, many left their accommodation in favour of their previous, albeit more unsettled, life-style. This point is reinforced by the fact that when questioned about the services that they would find useful if they had their own home, 26 per cent referred to budgeting advice and a slightly smaller group (25%) mentioned race/cultural support. Certainly, there was deemed to be a need for some form of ongoing support in the form of either a caretaker/warden or a support worker (Steele 1997).

Second, as a low priority group for rehousing by local authorities, many ethnic minority homeless people are initially directed to hostel accommodation. There is a range of issues here. First, research has shown that ethnic minorities have a particular dislike for such shared or communal accommodation (Steele 1997). The majority of these hostels cater predominantly for white males and are places, therefore, where ethnic minority residents are in a distinct minority. Many young black people have had negative experiences in such institutions, including racial abuse and harassment from fellow residents. Where hostels cater for both men and women, many Asian young women will refuse to use these facilities, fearful of reprisals from their own community for being seen as associating with male strangers. As one young Asian woman commented, 'it is very shameful for me to live in a hostel' (Steele 1997, p.30). Second, many hostels do not cater for the cultural needs of ethnic minorities. A recent study in Oxford showed that only a tiny proportion of the hostels and night shelters provided for even the most fundamental of cultural needs of ethnic minorities, such as appropriate food or a distinct space for the practising of their religious faith. Indeed, as one hostel worker commented, 'black people have to be desperate to want to use this hostel' (Steele 2000, p.36).

One of the main recurring issues is the lack of black hostel staff who would appreciate the cultural needs of ethnic minority homeless people (Law *et al.* 1999). The absence of black staff does not relate just to the lack of provision for a person's cultural needs but goes much deeper. The lack of black staff within the hostels can mean that a significant degree of ignorance exists on the part of service providers about the heterogeneity of cultures among the ethnic minority community and their distinct needs. This lack of understanding of the cultural needs of individual minority groups can have quite devastating effects on black homeless young people. This was the case for one young Asian woman in Nottingham who approached one of the statutory agencies in an endeavour to find alternative accommodation, having expressed her desire to move out of her parents' home (Steele 1997). The member of staff who interviewed her, who was white, later commented to her Asian colleagues about the plight of the young woman. The young Asian woman was subsequently severely reprimanded by her parents and shunned by her community for her lack of respect for her parents. This, albeit unintentional, breach of confidentiality was born out of ignorance of the culture and beliefs of the Asian community. Yet it can seriously undermine young Asians' confidence in the ability of the service to provide sensitive and confidential support. The Nottingham research found that there was reluctance on the part of young Asian women to contact certain agencies for fear of breach of confidentiality. One of these women said: 'I'm scared in case there's someone there I know and they might tell my family that I'm looking to leave one day soon' (Steele 1997, p.22). A second illustration to reinforce this lack of awareness of different cultural beliefs is that of the rehousing of a young Asian woman and her two children above an off-licence (Steele 1997). Because of this lack of sensitivity in the allocation process, the Asian woman was regarded by her community as having rejected her beliefs and values by being associated with alcohol and was subsequently ostracised by the community.

Third, in some cases, this lack of understanding of the cultures and beliefs of BME communities is the result of a perception that youth homelessness is a white problem. Patel (1994), in a study of homelessness among young black people in Newport, Gwent, found evidence of 'colour-blind' racism among agency workers. In Oxford, during interviews with service providers, reference was made to the lack of a visible problem of ethnic minority youth homelessness. Certainly the ethnic monitoring records maintained by hostels on all residents using the facility identified only a tiny proportion of non-white users. However, as suggested earlier, many of the ethnic minority homeless actively avoid using such hostels. This results in a perpetuation of the mono-cultural approach to the needs of hostel users through denying the needs of ethnic minorities on the basis of lack of demand for such a service.

## Developing culturally sensitive services

> Providing a culturally sensitive service is not about making assumptions that all young black people have the same wants and needs. It is about extending choice, for example not being treated the same, but having the opportunity to express a 'black identity' without being accused of having an attitude problem or a 'chip on your shoulder', having access to a black worker, access to an interpreter, able to network with other black people if that was appropriate. Young black people might not want all of these provisions all the time. What is crucial is that they have a choice and are then able to make informed decisions. (Patel 1994, p.38)

The recommendations from the Nottingham study and the findings from similar reports (e.g. Ahmed and Sodhi 2000) identify a number of ways in which a more culturally sensitive service can be established to meet the needs of young ethnic minority homeless people. Certainly, the presence of more front-line black staff as the first point of contact for black homeless young people is seen as important in encouraging black homeless young people to approach the agency. In the case of the Nottingham study the following was advocated:

> The employment of more black workers or the re-deployment of existing black staff would help overcome some of these barriers. The roles of such staff need to be very specific and represent the first point of contact for young black homeless people approaching the organisation. This role could be extended to encompass an 'outreach' function. This would allow greater accessibility to information and, ultimately, suitable accommodation for those young black people who experience difficulty accessing the services in the City centre or who, for whatever reason, are reluctant to do so. (Steele 1997, p.49)

Providing support to young black homeless people is also crucial in terms of both securing accommodation and, subsequently, enabling them to live independently. Given that one of the major causes of homelessness is family/relationship breakdown, providing a family mediation service would assist in either enabling the young person to return home or, at least, to benefit from the continued support of family and friends if returning home is not an option. Such a mediation service would need to be staffed by black workers who would have specialist knowledge of the family and cultural issues within the respective minority communities.

Leading on from this, the Nottingham study also advocated the provision of continuous support whereby an individual worker takes responsibility for organising the support structures for an individual homeless person up to and after securing accommodation.

> The main emphasis would be upon adopting an advocacy role on behalf of the homeless person. Many young homeless people find the prospect of dealing with a number of agencies very daunting. A continuous support worker would be in an ideal position to liaise with the other service providers about the type, level and duration of support required. They would also, over a period of time, acquire a greater insight into the needs of the individual homeless person themselves and as such, resources, in terms of providing support, could be more specifically targeted. This type of role could have a major impact on preventing young people re-entering the homelessness scene which, without adequate support in their own accommodation, is likely to occur. (Steele 1997, p.51)

In response to this latter recommendation, Nottingham City Council has developed a pilot support scheme for black homeless young people, known as the Azuka Befriending Scheme.

## Azuka Befriending Scheme

Funded by the European Social Fund and Nottingham City Council, the Azuka Befriending Scheme ('azuka' is a West African word meaning 'support is paramount') was established in 1999 in recognition of the fact that young black people's experiences of being homeless, although similar to those of their white counterparts, are often exacerbated by racism and by a lack of awareness among agencies of their spiritual and emotional needs. The overriding aim of the scheme is to provide one-to-one support and advice to young black people to enable them to feel positive, regain their self-esteem and, ultimately, take responsibility for their own lives. The mission statement for the scheme emphasises the need to work in partnership with other agencies and to provide a wide range of culturally sensitive support services to enable black homeless people to achieve their goals and realise their full potential. The specific aims of the scheme are:

- to provide black trained volunteers to offer emotional and practical support and advice

- to enable the young person to make a successful transition from dependence to independence, thus breaking the homelessness cycle

- to empower and encourage the young person towards a healthier life-style

- to provide a service that promotes dignity and respect for the individual and that is tailored to individual needs and choices

- to encourage the young person to develop life and employment skills

- to develop a flexible service based on an assessment of need.

Those providing the support – the 'befrienders' – are volunteers recruited from the African-Caribbean and Asian communities in Nottingham. They are expected to have some knowledge or experience of youth work or housing advice and to be able to be seen as a positive role model for homeless young people. All befrienders attend a comprehensive training package which covers a wide range of key issues associated with the needs of black homeless people, such as advocacy, counselling, life skills, mental health issues, welfare rights, homelessness legislation and education, and training and employment opportunities. Ongoing training is also provided during the befriending period. It is interesting to note that the training sessions also cover cultural issues within the African-Caribbean and Asian communities, enabling a greater appreciation of Asian culture by the African-Caribbean befrienders and vice versa.

The scheme has explicit guidelines on the role of the befriender, particularly their relationships with the young black people they will support, as well as on the additional provision that is available from the statutory and voluntary sectors (such as health care specialists). A mentor-supervisor oversees the activities of the befrienders and facilitates regular de-briefing sessions.

Black homeless young people are identified either directly via the city council's homelessness section or by referral agencies. All potential 'befriendees' are interviewed and all but those with highly specialised needs, such as those requiring a high level of mental health care, are given the opportunity to join the scheme. Participation is voluntary. Befriendees and befrienders are 'paired' on the basis of ethnicity, gender, age and needs. The timing and type of support provided are negotiated by both parties at regular intervals during the relationship but the focus is squarely on the needs of the young person. An extract from the befrienders' *Azuka Handbook* emphasises this point:

A young person needs to know that they can depend on you as a Befriender in order to develop the trust that is crucial for a productive one-to-one relationship. As an Azuka Befriender, you should focus on helping to solve the young person's immediate concerns or problems. Doing practical things, such as accessing benefits, furniture assistance or budgeting, will help you to engage with the young person emotionally. You may then look to address the underlying causes of homelessness (if so required by the young person), which may flag up personal issues for the young person. (Nottingham City Council 1999, p.6).

To date, fifteen befrienders have been recruited to the scheme, seven of whom have been paired with young black people. One of the intentions of this pilot study is to identify transferable elements of good practice, which will enable similar schemes to be developed for other social excluded groups; for instance, those with special needs.

## The cultural diversity approach

The befriending scheme represents a major departure from the more traditional alternatives to the mono-cultural mainstream service providers, which have focused on developing services run or managed by ethnic minorities themselves, although generally not restricted to a black clientele. These latter initiatives have generally been favoured by black homeless young people (such as a black-run hostel – see Law *et al.* 1999), as they are perceived to provide a more culturally sensitive environment. The befriending scheme goes further than this in that it is exclusively aimed at young black homeless people. This raises some important questions about the future development of services for ethnic minorities. Does such a scheme serve only to reinforce the social exclusion of minority groups in society by treating them separately, and could denying access to the befriending scheme for white young homeless people be interpreted as another form of prejudice or racism? Perhaps a more important question is the extent to which this type of approach undermines current thinking, which emphasises that service providers need to create an organisational culture that reflects the diverse multi-cultural environment in which they operate. Organisations need to move from an equal opportunities approach to one which emphasises the need to value cultural diversity.

Before considering these issues, it is worth discussing the notion of cultural diversity, which has gained increased publicity since the Lawrence Inquiry (Macpherson 1999) highlighted the extent of institutional racism within the police force and other public services.

'Diversity' is a relatively new concept in the UK but has been in use in the US since the mid-1980s (Agocs and Burr 1996) and is seen as a human resource management intervention commonly referred to as 'managing diversity' or 'valuing diversity'. This approach to discrimination is differentiated from that of equal opportunities. Equal opportunities is seen as being based on a collective, rights-based, legal approach that targets groups who are discriminated against at work or are disadvantaged; for example, disabled people and ethnic minorities. Positive action, including numerical targets for the employment of people from certain groups, is a possible remedy. In contrast, managing diversity acknowledges that there are different forms of discrimination suffered by people at work but each case needs to be addressed individually while fostering the idea that diversity is beneficial to business performance. 'Managing diversity' takes equality beyond the legalistic approach of focusing on an employer's obligations not to discriminate under the law (IPD 1996, p.12). The philosophy is voluntary in contrast to anti-discriminatory legislation (Prasad and Elmes 1997). Equal opportunities is often seen as the responsibility of human resource practitioners, whereas managing diversity is seen to be the concern of all employees, especially managers within an organisation (Kandola and Fullerton 1998). Diversity is not simply a replacement for equal opportunities, it must be a core value of the organisation and integral part of the business strategy. Somerville, Steele and Sodhi (2000) attribute the lack of progress on equal opportunities to a failure of the organisation to make equal opportunities a core value.

Managing diversity is about understanding that there are differences among employees and that these differences, if properly managed, are an asset to work being performed more efficiently and effectively. Differences among employees create a more diversified workforce with a wide range of perspectives. Kandola and Fullerton (1998) suggest that there are proven benefits to managing diversity, debatable benefits and indirect benefits. Among the proven benefits are the potential to recruit from a wider range of talented candidates, retaining talent and associated savings from lower turnover and absenteeism. Additionally, there is enhanced organisational flexibility. The changing profile of the workforce means that organisations that continue to rely on the more traditional pool of white, able-bodied males will be ignoring the valuable potential in the remaining population and run the risk of losing out to their competitors.

The debatable benefits of managing diversity are those thought to result from having a mix of people with a wide range of styles, backgrounds, personalities etc. in the workforce. This combination could lead to improved creativity, innovation, problem-solving and decision-making within organisations, and increased quality and improved customer service. Indirect benefits are those believed to result when the direct and debatable benefits have been achieved, such as improved morale and job satisfaction, improved relations between different groups of workers, competitive edge and better image. However, as Kandola and Fullerton (1998) note, it is difficult to establish firm evidence linking the benefits directly to the change that was implemented.

It is worth picking up on two of those points which are seen as benefits arising from organisations' valuing or managing diversity, and which are particularly relevant in terms of providing a culturally sensitive service to young black homeless people: those of customer service and the image of the organisation. Given that one of the major problems identified above for young black homeless people when trying to access services is that these services are perceived to be unwelcoming and insensitive to their cultural needs, the managing diversity approach would seem to offer a more positive experience. In attempting to ensure that the agencies' workforce reflects the wider community, more organisations would look to employ those sections of the community that are under-represented in the workforce. Not only would this mean that there would be more black staff recruited (as well as people with disabilities and women etc.) but it should follow, according to the managing diversity argument, that all staff within the organisation would gain a greater understanding of the culture and experiences of different minority groups. This should then lead to a more culturally responsive service to black homeless young people. An organisation whose workforce reflects the multi-cultural community at large is more likely to be viewed positively by those who previously felt excluded from such services. Hence, the image of the organisation is more likely to be seen as welcoming.

Positive action strategies (such as Positive Action Training in Housing which has been pursued to increase the representation of ethnic minorities within housing organisations, particularly at senior level) have formed a major tool within equal opportunities policies to address discrimination on the grounds of ethnicity. However, it has been argued that positive action is not compatible with the diversity approach because the focus on particular groups locates the problem within these groups. Kandola and Fullerton (1998) illustrate this point by pointing out that providing assertiveness training for women suggests that women have a problem. Rather, the training should be provided for anyone who needs it. They further comment:

> If managing diversity is truly about creating an environment where everyone feels valued and their talents are being fully utilised then actions ought to be targeted on any individual who has a particular development need and not restricted to individuals who are members of particular groups. (p.126)

If one accepts that the befriending scheme, which is aimed at one section of the homelessness community, is an example of positive action, then it would seem to follow that it contradicts the diversity approach championed by central government and such organisations as the Housing Corporation and local government associations. At the same time, however, it needs to be remembered that the managing diversity approach is not based on any legal requirement. Rather, organisations are encouraged to adopt such an approach based on the perceived business arguments for doing so. In Hunt and Palmer's guidelines for local authorities, written on behalf of the Local Government Association, the Employers' Organisation and the Improvement and Development Agency, the authors comment that 'to date LARRIE – the Local Authorities Race Relations Information Exchange – has only received notice from 60 authorities that they are working on the Lawrence Inquiry. This is disappointing' (Hunt and Palmer 1999, p.4). They go on to say that 'inaction is not an option for any council irrespective of the size of its local black, Asian and ethnic minority population' (p.4). Yet, it would seem that without any real pressure being brought to bear on housing organisations, inaction is what is happening.

More research is needed to identify the tangible benefits of the managing diversity approach together with greater guidance on how cultural change within an organisation can be achieved. If evidence of the benefits of the managing diversity approach is forthcoming, then it is likely that greater pressure, or at least sanctions, will be applied to those organisations that do not respond positively to the diversity argument. This is likely to be some time in the future but when and, of course, *if* this occurs, it follows, from the argument about the benefits of managing diversity rehearsed above, that the resulting service provided should be inclusive of all sections of the community. In this way, the specific cultural needs of young black homeless people (and other minority groups) can be accommodated within mainstream service provision. Until this becomes a reality, it could be argued, in the face of a lack of success of traditional equal opportunities policies, that it is appropriate for organisations to develop positive action initiatives such as the befriending scheme in Nottingham to target specific minority groups that are excluded from accessing mainstream services. One final point that is worth mentioning is that, in the Oxford study of black homelessness, faced with a choice of developing services exclusively for ethnic minorities or developing strategies to ensure that mainstream providers were able to meet the cultural needs of ethnic minorities, the overwhelming majority of black homeless people favoured the latter.

## Conclusion

Black homeless young people are generally being excluded from many relevant and appropriate services due to the inability of organisations to respond to the cultural needs of ethnic minority groups generally and black youth in particular. Where black homeless young people do access the services, their experiences are generally negative and, for many, this reinforces their perception of a white-dominated, mono-cultural service which is not interested in them, either as individuals or as members of an ethnic group. While the managing diversity approach offers, at least in theory, the promise of a more culturally responsive and inclusive service, the pace of change towards embracing the notion of cultural diversity is slow. In the interim, the development of initiatives targeted specifically at ethnic minority groups would seem to be the only option available. However, initiatives such as the Azuka Befriending Scheme must not be allowed to be used to justify inaction by organisations to embrace the principle of managing diversity and thereby legitimise the exclusion of minority groups from mainstream services.

# References

Agocs, C. and Burr, C. (1996) 'Employment equity affirmative action and managing diversity: Assessing the difference.' *International Journal of Manpower 17*, 30–45.

Ahmed, A. and Sodhi, D. (2000) *The Housing and Support Needs of Women Especially Those from Ethnic Minorities*. Rochdale: Rochdale Women's Housing Aid Group.

Anderson, I., Kemp, P. and Quilgars, D. (1993) *Single Homeless People*. London: HMSO.

Davies, J. and Lyle, S., with Deacon, A., Julienne, L. and Kay, H. (1996) *Discounted Voices: Homelessness Amongst Young Black and Minority Ethnic People in England*. Sociology and Social Policy Working Paper 15. Leeds: School of Sociology and Social Policy, University of Leeds.

Ford, J. and Vincent, J. (1990) *Homelessness amongst Afro-Caribbean Women in Leicester*. Loughborough: Department of Social Sciences/Centre for Research in Social Policy/Foundation Housing Association.

Friedman, D. LHU and LRC (1989) *One in Every Hundred: A Study of Households Accepted as Homeless in London*. London: London Housing Unit and London Research Centre.

Hall, J. (1996) *Homelessness: Trends in Homelessness in London in the 1990s*. London: London Research Centre.

Hunt, J. and Palmer, S. (1999) *Further Guidance for Local Authorities on the Stephen Lawrence Inquiry*. London: Local Government Association, Employers' Organisation and Improvement and Development Agency.

IPD (Institute of Personnel Development) (1996) 'IPD says diversity is the next step for equality.' *Property Management 5*, 12–13.

Kandola, R. and Fullerton, J. (1998) *Diversity in Action: Managing the Mosaic*. London: Institute of Personnel Development.

Law, I., Davies, J., Lyle, S. and Deacon, A. (1999) 'Racism, ethnicity and youth homelessness.' In F. Spiers (ed) *Housing and Social Exclusion*. London: Jessica Kingsley Publishers.

Macpherson, W. (1999) *The Stephen Lawrence Inquiry*. Command Paper 4262-I. London: The Stationery Office.

Murie, A. (1988) 'The new homeless in Britain.' In G. Bramley (ed) *Homelessness and the London Housing Market*. Bristol: School of Advanced Urban Studies, University of Bristol.

Nottingham City Council (1999) *Azuka Handbook*. Nottingham: Nottingham City Council.

Patel, G. (1994) *The Porth Project: A Study of Homelessness and Running Away amongst Young Black People in Newport, Gwent*. London: The Children's Society.

Prasad, A. and Elmes, D. (1997) 'Issues in the management of workplace diversity.' In *Managing the Organisational Melting Pot: Dilemmas of Workplace Diversity*. London: Sage.

Sarre, P., Phillips, D. and Skellington, R. (1989) *Ethnic Minority Housing: Explanations and Policies*. Aldershot: Avebury.

Smith, J. and Gilford, S. (1993) *Birmingham Young People in Housing Need Project*. Ilford: Barnardo's.

Somerville, P., Steele, A. and Sodhi, D. (2000) *A Question of Diversity: Black and Minority Ethnic Staff in the RSL Sector*. Research Findings Summary No. 43. London: The Housing Corporation.

Steele, A. (1997) *Young, Drifting and Black: A Report on the Findings and Recommendations of a Study into Young Black Homelessness for Nottingham City Council*. Nottingham: Nottingham City Council.

Steele, A. (2000) *Black Homelessness in Oxford*. Oxford: Oxford City Council.

# Chapter 11

# The Housing of Older Black and Asian People

## Naina Patel and Ballu Patel

The first section of this chapter includes a summary of the views and experiences of the Asian elders with whom we have worked and lived. We wanted to ensure that they had a platform from which to express their views. Our perspective is one that values our elders and their experiences, although we may not agree with everything that they have said. We admire the strength and the determination of many of our elders and hope that in some small way, through face-to-face interviews and discussions we held with them, we have done justice to conveying some of their pioneering spirit.

The second section reflects our concerns and thoughts on the way forward. This comes from a substantial amount of experience on our part, working within Asian communities around the country, including the voluntary housing movement. Essentially, our argument is that the elders themselves need to be at the forefront of the debate rather than being seen as simply recipients of housing services. Our interviews and daily interactions with our elders prove that they are willing to contribute to the housing debate and are more than capable of expressing views and giving their energies in this arena.

The research was carried out by means of a series of interviews with selected individuals. Most of the elders are used to telling life stories in a general way, but to ensure the required depth of content it was decided to adopt a more personal approach. There were three men and three women interviewed, aged 65 and above. Additional information was taken from focus groups that were held within the community, the findings of which will be published later this year (2001).

## Experiences of Asian elders

### Reasons for moving to the UK

The Asian elders now living in this country came from either Asia or Africa. Those who arrived from Asia did so from the 1950s onwards. They were mainly men, who came with the intention of creating wealth that would enable them and their families to live a comfortable life-style upon their return to Asia (Anwar 1979; Robinson 1986). As their partners joined them, however, and they started a family, they became more settled in the UK. While their children grew up, the men and their partners took on additional commitments and leaving the UK became less of a priority (Anwar 1985).

Those who came from Africa did so in the late 1960s and mainly due to political unrest. They arrived in this country as a family, in some cases leaving their wealth behind in the country they had to flee. Consequently, this country has become their new home (Miles and Phizacklea 1979).

### Employment

Many of those who migrated from Africa and Asia had held professional posts in those countries such as accountants, teachers, bankers, doctors, lawyers. Some had been self-employed with well-established businesses and others skilled craftspeople. One of the interviewees in our research undertook his O levels, A levels and engineering degree in Britain and had lived here for almost forty years.

Despite their diverse backgrounds, for many it was clear that it did not matter how highly qualified or talented they were, the opportunity to gain similar employment in Britain was denied to them. This was despite the fact that many of these professional people were fluent in English and had a similar educational background and standard (for example, a Cambridge Examination Board qualification).

One notable feature of these early migrants was their determination to be economically independent, even if for many of them it meant manual work in factories. Some of them had come to this country with families to support and others were supporting their families back in Asia/Africa. One interviewee in our research said he made numerous applications for a post similar to the professional one he had held in Kenya. This was because he could not physically do the heavy work required in factories. He succeeded in getting an 'office job' despite the fact that he was over-qualified for the post. He took it although it was not what he wanted. Unlike many of his contemporaries, he could afford to support his family on arriving in the UK because he had brought some money with him from Kenya, and he was able to buy his home within six months of arrival.

RESPONSE TO RACISM IN THE WORKPLACE

For those who worked in factories it was not easy, especially for women. One woman recounted how they were given extra jobs to do by their white supervisor. These jobs were ones the white girls did not want to do. Asked how she and the other Asian women responded to this, she replied some just got on with it while others 'creeped' up to the supervisors and some, like her, were not so tolerant of the abuse. She recounted the time when India won a cricket match against England and the white workers in her department came up to her one by one making sarcastic remarks about India and the Indians in this country. She was extremely upset but she went up to one of the men and thumped his table hard, saying that 'India may have just won the cricket game, but we Indians will be taking over your country one day!'.

Another time, an older white woman who was working with her continually gave her a hard time about the hours she took off for childcare. One day, the interviewee lost her temper, held onto the older woman's arm, not letting go and making it clear that, just because she was an Indian woman, there was no reason for her to be quiet and take the abuse. She eventually let the older woman go. However, there was a huge scene with people gathered around both of them. The strange thing was that after this incident the two women became good friends.

In the office environment, race discrimination was clearly evident, as one of the interviewees described how white colleagues often refused to co-operate with him, racially abusing him and deliberately going slow when his jobs needed to be finished.

Two of the interviewees were fed up with working in jobs they did not like or enjoy. One of them tried his hand at running his own business but his venture did not go well. One female interviewee worked and ran her business part-time, until she was sure it was going to go well. She recounted how the factory foreman had said that she would end up coming back to the factory but, because she was a good worker, they would be happy to have her back any time. She commented: 'My businesses are still here, but the factory closed years ago!'

## Housing and self-help

Many of the interviewees who arrived in this country came with very little money. The typical experience of some families was that the father came to the UK first and worked extremely hard, staying in lodgings with families or friends. Then the rest of the family would come over a few years later. Usually, once the family came over, they would rent accommodation and then later become owner-occupiers, if economic circumstances allowed. These memories echo the findings of research carried out at the time these families first came to the UK (Rex and Moore 1967). Houses were often chosen that were near to relatives and other support networks, relatively cheap to buy, and in areas regarded as 'safe' from racial harassment. This meant low-cost homes in the inner city for the early settlers.

What is interesting is not so much why they settled in those houses, but how the support and self-help within the communities had enabled so many families who arrived with next to nothing to survive and begin to buy their homes. This strong sense of self-help amongst family and friends was clearly a positive factor in the lives of the interviewees. One stated that their wages in factories had been low, so the banks had not been prepared to give them high mortgages. Indeed, the banks had not always been keen to lend to them at all, as they had no collateral, 'Nor did they trust us to pay up!' Consequently, they worked extremely hard and the extended family network often helped by lending money. Others worked in a factory by day and set up a small business on the side, working evenings and weekends. Some of the interviewees held down two jobs during the week and a different one at the weekend. It was not uncommon for a couple of thousand pounds to be lent to friends or family to help them buy a home. One respondent described himself as one of the 'lucky ones' because his father had sent him money, which he used to buy a decent house and, subsequently, a business. The money he had been given gave him an excellent start and he was lucky that he did not have to work as hard and as long as some of his contemporaries. Another described with fondness sleeping on a family's sofa for several months before he set himself up in rented accommodation at the time of getting married.

## Daily life

The interviewees encountered racist behaviour in all areas of their life. One of them described how, when searching for student accommodation, he and his friend had been turned down by countless landladies. Another described how a walk in the park led to him and his family being stoned and spat at. Verbal racial abuse was commonplace. Another woman described how their front door was bombarded every weekend by a group of white youths: 'It often felt as if the front door was going to crash down, and it would be a matter of seconds before we would be attacked. The police were often called, but they did nothing and often sneered at us with the youths.'

One of the interviewees described how he went into a social security office and courteously said 'Good morning' to the officer. He was ignored, but he continued to say 'Good morning' until the officer said: 'Are you sick? What do you want?' The interviewee said: 'No I am not sick and I don't want you, but I am going to make you sick – I want to see your boss!' The racism was not always overt. One of the interviewees stated: 'British people were very polite, they said "thank you for applying", but you knew they did not really mean it!'

The response to the racism was by no means a passive one. Interviewees were asked how they responded to it and the general verdict was that they had to deal with it in different ways. It was part and parcel of their lot in life. Some of them had been warned prior to coming into this country that the climate and some of its people were going to be hostile to them, especially older people.

The family that was harassed by the youths took the law into their own hands because the police refused to deal with it. One Sunday afternoon, the men in the household ran out and beat up a couple of the youths. The following weekend the bombardment stopped.

The bottom line was that they had come here for a purpose, and this was common to all the interviewees, one of whom spelled it out clearly: 'We came here to build a better life for our children and to give them opportunities we never had.' Surprisingly, perhaps, none of the respondents felt any bitterness or resentment about the treatment they received.

In view of their experiences, however, it is not surprising that some interviewees did not feel as if they belonged here. One interviewee outlined how, for a long time after his arrival 40 years ago, he did not feel as if he belonged in England. He was only now beginning to feel such a sense of belonging, because he detected a decline in the type of arrogant British attitude, of which he was often at the receiving end and which he said was typified by some members of the English cricket team in the past. His spiritual beliefs had also led to him reducing his attachment to India. He viewed his life as being in the here and now, which at this moment in time is in Britain.

Some of the elders interviewed felt that every culture had its good and bad points, and that racism was part of the package of their experience in Britain. Their general approach was one of pragmatic acceptance of the realities of their situation, as newcomers in an alien land, and their attitude, in some cases, amounted to a kind of stoicism.

## Health

Most of the interviewees had problems with their health. The most prevalent complaints were rheumatism and arthritis, and these impacted on their mobility. They did not feel that they suffered more than their white elderly counterparts but, interestingly, they felt that they viewed ill-health differently, because the management of it was going to be problematic for them. This was especially so because it became difficult when they attended hospital appointments or when they were hospitalised. The difficulties were perceived to arise because of language barriers and the different treatment they received from medical staff. If they became seriously ill, therefore, worries about treatment made the whole thing worse. Some of them recounted stories of people they had known who had gone into hospital with cancer and heart problems, some of whom had not received 'fair treatment'. They also talked about some of the husbands of their friends who had passed away.

Loneliness was seen to be a big factor in creating stress when a partner died. Two of the interviewees were widows living on their own. They kept busy by looking after their grandchildren, visiting their temple and through contact with community organisations.

Also mentioned were the challenges they faced when trying to get their homes adapted by social services to meet their changing physical needs. The whole process was lengthy and slow. It was often very difficult to find out what their entitlements were and where to go to for assistance. This is why the community organisations were perceived to be useful and supportive. In some cases, they were a lifeline, as they proved to be an invaluable form of social contact and helped to maintain a sense of belonging.

## Housing

The desire to remain as independent as possible and not to be a burden on the children was expressed quite strongly. Interviewees were, however, finding it difficult as many were on low incomes and savings were being used up trying to maintain homes. Women, in particular, expressed a great deal of concern about their frustration in getting repairs and maintenance sorted out, even for the most minor things. One interviewee described how they were often being ripped off because some workmen saw elderly people as an easy target.

KNOWLEDGE OF HOUSING OPTIONS AND LONG-TERM CARE

The 'home' (sheltered house/nursing home) was seen as the place of last resort, somewhere interviewees definitely did not want to go. One woman said she prayed that God would take her before she ever needed to go to one of those 'homes'. However, the female interviewees cited a number of examples of relatives who had gone into homes and were enjoying them. 'If it meant,' said one or two women, 'that we were becoming a burden to our children, I do not mind going into a home, if I could not take care of myself.' They gave an example of an older woman who was getting frail. She went to live with all her sons, one by one, so each family shared the burden. Eventually she decided she could not go on doing this and chose to go into a home.

The knowledge of what was available in terms of housing options, for example sheltered housing and nursing homes, was based upon anecdotal evidence from friends and relatives. Interviewees did not possess information about housing options. They did not know who provided housing-related care and they had not heard of housing associations. They did know, however, the names of particular housing schemes for the elderly in the city.

Asked for their views on paying for long-term care, the strongest feeling was that the government should pay for care, as they had paid their taxes. Although they did not know how long-term care was financed in detail, they had heard that it was an unfair system. This was because those who had saved and worked were being asked to pay, while those who may not have planned for their old age were being let off.

Equity release schemes as a way of paying for long-term care were scoffed at as being costly and ineffective. One interviewee stated her house was not worth as much as they required. Some of them were dubious about such schemes, especially because the money they paid might run out.

All of the interviewees were quite sure they did not want to retire to India. This is not to deny that they felt a special place in their affections for India, which they still regarded as their motherland. They felt that their home had become the UK because their children and grandchildren were here. They also realised that India was changing rapidly and values towards older people there were beginning to merge with those in this country. Some of them who had kinship ties in India still went on regular trips there.

## Social life and housing

For most of the respondents, community organisations, whether they were local authority funded or based in temples, were an important part of their life. For some it was their source of social contact with their peers. Luncheon clubs played an important role, especially when guest speakers from the local statutory bodies and organisations gave information on benefits and services.

Some of the respondents were active in managing and volunteering for voluntary organisations. It gave them an opportunity to use their professional skills. For example, two ex-teachers provided lessons in the mother tongue languages and information on religion and cultural teachings in local publications. One interviewee was a very enthusiastic community and voluntary worker in his late 60s. He commanded a great deal of respect and admiration across a number of generations.

Some of the respondents made it clear that it was up to the individual how he/she enjoyed his/her life and interests; for example, some people prefered to watch cultural-based Asian TV channels.

As one of the discussions was held in a community organisation, the cost of partaking in trips and outings was discussed. Their ability to pay for many of the trips was declining. In addition, without transport to pick them up and drop them off, many were becoming increasingly isolated as their health began to deteriorate. They knew of many women in the area who wanted to come to the local organisations but could not do so without transport.

The choice of housing in later life was influenced by a number of factors; for example, whether interviewees could live near their children, family, friends, community facilities (temples, luncheon clubs and voluntary organisations) and shopping areas and surgeries. If a number of these were within easy physical access, it helped them to remain independent and retain control of their own lives.

### A changing culture

It was quite clear that Asian culture as they perceived it had changed, but it was not all for the worse. The negative comments centred around children not listening to their parents. One lady remarked how at one time they led and the children followed but 'now we have to follow wherever the children lead us'. This reversal of roles was something some of the elders found hard to get used to. One lady said she thought that children were irreverent about religious beliefs. She cited an example of some children who wore boots at Garba when the practice is to be barefooted whilst dancing.

Values towards sex had changed and this had created changes in the behaviour of the younger generations. In times past relationships between males and females were not discussed. Issues like finding marriage-partners were settled by tradition rather than by 'self-selection' but today, within some family circles, with the second generation becoming heads of household, there seems to be an openness to discuss certain topics.

One interviewee pointed out that Asian women were under a greater amount of pressure as families became more Westernised. He cited alcohol abuse as an example, saying that he felt it had risen and many women were suffering at the hands of alcoholic and adulterous husbands. He also felt it was the women who took responsibility for providing care to the elders. The independence of women was seen as a positive change, especially for those who had worked hard to achieve it. Some of the older people were able to enjoy their independence, free from the family responsibilities that they had when they were younger. One interviewee stated: 'You have to change, in India everything has changed…you have to change, as the world is very small. If you do not change you will make younger generations very unhappy, orthodoxy will have to be wiped out.'

The extended family was still perceived to exist, but it had adapted. People were not physically living together but still helping each other out. One of the interviewees said: 'I still see elderly people being assisted by their children or grandchildren who take them to the doctor's or the hospital.' There was, therefore, a great deal of pride and contact between the generations but there were no guarantees that the younger generations would or could be there for them if they needed care on a long-term basis. Some of the female interviewees recognised that while their children wanted to help or live with their elderly parents, circumstances made it difficult for them to do so. She cited examples such as jobs taking their children to other places and the commitments the children had to their own children. One interviewee outlined the irony of the situation, in that they had worked hard and made sacrifices in their youth for the sake of their children, but circumstances had taken the children away from them.

## Values and personal philosophies

The value of thrift and hard work with purpose was evident in the early lives of the interviewees. The interviews and discussions highlighted the continuing strength and determination of character in many of them. This was expressed in their desire to remain independent and not to be a burden on anyone. Three of the interviewees, who had retired, were still active in community and voluntary work. Many continued to assist their families by undertaking childcare responsibilities. Some of the respondents reported that at least one person in the family had made huge personal sacrifices to enable the rest of the family to progress. In many cases women had laid the foundations for future generations by working extremely hard both within and outside the home. One of the interviewees stressed that she had the responsibility to be 'a good role model' for her children.

The interviewees also strongly believed in the value of a good education and this was emphasised to their children. One of the motivating factors for emigrating to the UK was the opportunity for obtaining a good education for their children. Interviewees were adamant that their children should not go through their experiences of working in a factory environment, and that they had strived for something better for future generations.

Their personal philosophies were interesting and worthy of note. One man (a youthful-looking 67-year-old) said he took good care of his health by maintaining a disciplined approach to his diet, being helpful and giving to others. He stated he was always ambitious to achieve and this kept him young and active. Discipline was also mentioned by another interviewee, as was courage. Both were needed to ensure that confidence in the face of adversity was not lost.

### *Reflections on the interviews*

The above section on the interviews illustrated that some Asian elders are remarkable individuals and have been and still are a pioneering force within their communities for a number of reasons, as discussed below:

- It took a lot of spirit and determination to uproot themselves and their families, in some cases not just once but twice, to start a new life in a country without support and sometimes in a hostile climate.

- It took a lot of confidence and strength of character not to become disillusioned and disheartened from achieving their goals in the face of adversity.

- It took a great deal of humility (in the positive sense of the word) and personal sacrifice to take manual jobs, when those of them who were used to managerial and professional positions were denied opportunities in this country. For the sake of their families and in order to earn more income they had other jobs.

- Their responses to racial discrimination were quite creative and not always either confrontational or passive. Where doors were closed to them in terms of employment opportunities they looked to their entrepreneurial skills.

- In order for the people to settle in Britain, the elders that were interviewed said that they had taken a visionary approach to achieving certain goals for themselves and their children. This required an enormous amount of hard work, focus and endurance on their part. They practised the philosophy of modern management manuals even before that philosophy was written down.

- They continue to be pioneers because they are testing the waters in terms of housing and care provision. They are providing solutions; for example, setting up their own luncheon clubs and temples (in which there is community provision) and providing cultural teachings to the next generations.

- Their dedication to uplifting and supporting the lives of their children has led to the next generations entering professions that were denied them, such as medicine, accountancy, law and management. What is even more remarkable is that those who entered professional occupations had parents who were illiterate in English and had very little or no education *per se*. Technically, therefore, they came from 'working class backgrounds'.

## Evaluation

### Our concerns

There has been a tendency, in the last two decades of 'race' and housing/care literature on elderly Asian people, to concentrate largely on describing the disadvantages they face. As a consequence, one can fall into the trap of seeing them as victims only, passive in the face of adversity. There has been a regrettable tendency to generalise about the condition of this group without asking elderly Asians themselves about their experiences and attitudes. Our interviews and discussions show that the picture of elderly Asians as passive victims is misleading, and has coincided with a failure to listen to the voice of the Asian elderly themselves and the contributions that they have made to this society. It is our contention that we have to move on, from incorrect and/or unrealistic assumptions based on ignorance, towards offering solutions in housing and care that meet the real needs and aspirations of elderly Asians themselves.

Genuine practical solutions will only come from a concerted effort on the part of institutions to tackle racism. What we have seen from the tragedy of Stephen Lawrence's death and the Macpherson report (Macpherson 1999) are knee-jerk reactions that are largely panic-driven on the part of the institutions.

They have not got to the root of the problem and, as a result, it is naive to expect any groundbreaking strategies to tackle racial disadvantage, for example, in housing as a whole. For groups such as the Asian elderly changes are likely to be slow in coming.

Within national forums that have the potential to bring about deep-rooted changes for older people, the discussion around black and Asian elders has not been integrated into the mainstream dialogue. At best it can be described as a bolt-on. As a result, an important opportunity has been lost. For example, there are no black members on the Board of Better Government for Older People, it is arguable that Debate of the Age considered black issues only as an afterthought, and the Royal Commission on Long-Term Care did not build issues of 'race' and ethnicity into its programme from the start.

Where the discussion in housing has moved on, the emphasis has been on cultural differences (see, for example, Chapters 4 and 7 in this volume). In our opinion, this has distracted housing providers from the real issue, which is racism. It has also led to the 'cultural card' being played to divide and rule the Asian communities; for example, by citing a scarcity of resources to meet the allegedly competing 'cultural' needs of different communities. There is also anecdotal evidence, particularly within Asian communities, that progress has been hindered by individuals from within statutory organisations and within Asian communities themselves who have vested interests but purport to have the interests of the community at heart. We believe that these self-appointed spokespersons should be stopped and perhaps 'moved to the sidelines of the debate'.

There is also the 'let me talk to your leader' mentality on the part of some statutory organisations, albeit in some instances arising from a genuine attempt to ascertain information about the issues. More often than not, members of the Asian communities feel that service providers talk to 'community leaders' who do not have a constituency. These 'community leaders' are perceived to be articulate and knowledgeable in a manner that is acceptable to the service providers, because they are an acceptable face of the black communities in a white environment. There are questions that are currently being asked within the community as to who really is a 'community leader'. At present there is no clear answer to this question but such leaders are not always the ones that are contacted and quoted by the media or by other bodies like local authorities. There are genuine black leaders with roots within the Asian communities who, when approached for information, open up access to the communities and work with service providers by engaging in a genuine partnership to deal with the issue of Asian elders' housing needs. It has to be recognised that, for such a partnership to develop and arrive at lasting solutions in housing, statutory organisations will have to be creative and risk-taking rather than being content with half-baked compromises.

The integrated approach to housing provision termed 'housing plus', offered by black housing associations, is arguably a natural way of working for many black voluntary organisations across the board. It is because these organisations are used to operating in this holistic way that it has been possible for them to absorb the failure of mainstream providers.

Black and minority ethnic-led associations, however, are relatively new on the housing scene. They have been successful on the whole, but have become victims of their own success. As expectations from within some communities have grown, the ability of such associations to match these expectations has been hindered by a lack of resources, particularly finance.

If the housing and care needs of Asian elders are to be met, it also requires the commitment of mainstream housing associations and, if they fail in this respect, they need to be made accountable. There is currently a debate about the care of the elderly and the provision that may be necessary in years to come. Discussions on this issue are taking place in homes and within the communities. There needs, however, to be a clear dialogue between the community and service providers so that mainstream housing organisations can plan now for the future needs.

## The way forward

### Diversity as an opportunity

In the US there is now evidence that, where diversity is tackled in a positive manner in areas of employment and service delivery, it has resulted in economic gains and a positive acceptance of solutions from minority communities.

In Britain there are some institutions that are attempting to deal with diversity in a positive way. For example, some banks who operate in areas with sizeable Asian communities are valuing Asian entrepreneurship, changing the way they work and communicate, and staffing levels are beginning to reflect the community in which they are located. In some cases banks are receiving training about the community. It makes commercial sense for them to understand their customer base. There needs, however, to be a stronger will on the part of statutory service providers.

### Diverse ways of working

There is a need to move away from 'top down' solutions, which, in essence, are derived from 'ethnocentric' values, ways of working and service provision. For example, policy makers working with Asian elders need to possess knowledge of cross-cultural ways of working. The elders should be approached in a cultural setting which is comfortable for them and discussions should be entered into with them in that setting. This type of approach should lead to 'organically grown housing solutions'. These are much more likely to result in ownership and control that is vested in the communities concerned.

## An Asian elders' national organisation

We would argue that there is a need for an Asian elders' national organisation, which would address a number of issues and engage in policy formulation. This is because the voice of Asian elders has been missing from the discussion table on housing strategies for the elderly. They are often asked what their experiences and needs are but are excluded from being architects of their own future. More important, the families who are involved in the housing and care of Asian elderly have often been overlooked in the past. It is important that their views are heard.

## Two-pronged approach

National prescriptive solutions to housing for the Asian elderly need to bear in mind the diversity of groups within the Asian communities. One of the obstacles in housing has been to view diversity as a problem and, moreover, as one that is almost impossible to solve. It has also been seen to be a feature of black and Asian communities only when, in reality, diversity is universal. There is diversity in the white community based upon a number of factors such as social class, religion, national/regional/local identity, kinship, life-style and even football teams.

The issue of diversity and racial disadvantage in housing needs to be approached at two levels in order to arrive at locally based solutions: the national, macro-level of policy-making and the local community, micro-level. What may appear to be an appropriate housing strategy for Gujarati elders in Bristol may be far off the mark for Gujarati elders in Leicester. The reason for this variation is that experiences differ for a number of factors, which include the availability of resources, political commitment (on the part of statutory bodies) and the communities' awareness and exposure to housing options.

However, by emphasising diversity we do not want to fall into the trap of ignoring the common features of experience brought about by racial discrimination that have been compounded over a number of years for our elders. As much of the original 'race' and housing literature based upon the national picture has become outdated, these features need to be explored once again in order to inform policy makers at the national level. Our own research, for example, has shown many common features in the experience of Asian people who came to this country in the 1960s and 1970s, notably with regard to the effects of racism and housing careers. Although their experiences have perhaps become more varied with the passage of time, there continue to be important common considerations; for example, in terms of their emphasis on independent living and the value they attach to family and community networks.

### Changing experiences

A diversity of experience has been illustrated in the past twenty years or so amongst Asian communities by some groups who have moved away from the inner cities to the suburbs (Bowes, McCluskey and Sim 1989; Phillips 1998; Werbner 1979). There are also different housing tenures amongst certain Asian communities, but once again patterns of tenureship change (see, for example, Chapter 3 in this volume).

In cases where the Asian elderly have moved with their families to the suburbs, the housing and care issues may be different from those of the elderly in the inner cities. So far there has been a tendency to focus on the aspirations of the Asian elderly who are in the inner city. We just do not know enough about the impact on those who have moved to the suburbs, especially where there may not be a sizeable Asian community (see Chapter 5 in this volume).

Asian elders are at an important crossroads in their lives and it is essential that statutory providers take the opportunity to plan and develop integrated housing and care strategies in conjunction with the communities they serve. It is likely that in the next twenty years things are not going to change for the elderly *per se* unless those organisations, including governments, are made accountable for their policies and, in some cases, the lack of them. The only glimmer of hope on the horizon is the increasing numbers of the elderly, both black and white, predicted over the next twenty years. They have the potential to be a political force to bring about change.

## References

Anwar, M. (1979) *The Myth of Return*. London: Heinemann.

Anwar, M. (1985) *Pakistanis in Britain: A Sociological Study*. London: New Century.

Bowes, A., McCluskey, J. and Sim, D. (1989) *Ethnic Minority Housing Problems in Glasgow*. Glasgow: Glasgow City Council.

Macpherson, W. (1999) *The Stephen Lawrence Inquiry*. London: The Stationery Office.

Miles, R. and Phizacklea, A. (eds) (1979) *White Man's Country*. London: Pluto Press.

Phillips, D. (1998) 'Black minority ethnic concentration, segregation and dispersal in Britain.' *Urban Studies* 35, 10, 1681–1702.

Rex, J. and Moore, R. (1967) *'Race', Community and Conflict: A Study of Sparkbrook.* Oxford: Oxford University Press.

Robinson, V. (1986) *Transients, Settlers and Refugees: Asians in Britain.* Oxford: Clarendon Press.

Werbner, P. (1979) 'Avoiding the ghetto: Pakistani migrants and settlement shifts in Manchester.' *New Community* 7, 3, 376–389.

Chapter 12

# Black and Minority Ethnic Participation and Empowerment

Steve Gayle

## Introduction

The reality of having control and actually making choices, the sense of feeling confident, competent and respected, of being seen as someone who has power and is able to use it, all define the value people have to society as well as for themselves. It is now widely accepted that, for social housing organisations, involving tenants and residents in the design, development and delivery of housing and related services affect and bring change and improvement in the quality and content of those services. Further benefit has been identified in the impact resident involvement and participation processes can have on improving and adding to the ability of complementary service providers to achieve their overall objectives; that is, in the areas of health, education, community development and regeneration. However, the ability to be involved and participate in society and social affairs depends not only on having access and power to inform and influence decisions but also on the confidence, skills and abilities of individuals and the communities within which they live.

Across the social housing spectrum there are a wide range of interests (central and local government, registered social landlords or RSLs, tenants' and residents' organisations) that are concerned with how people are involved, participate and are able to influence positive change and improvement in the overall quality, quantity and control of social housing. Recently, governmental interests in particular have placed great emphasis on the benefit of consulting with communities who will be subject to and affected by the impact of changing housing and social policy.

This chapter explores the practice of participation and empowerment with regard to black and minority ethnic (BME) residents and tenants of social landlords. ('Social housing' is used as a general term to mean rented housing owned by local authorities, RSLs, New Towns and Housing Action Trusts.) By examining the opportunities for BME groups to gain control of their housing for themselves and become involved in decisions affecting their housing, the chapter seeks to identify some of the key building blocks of participation and empowerment; the processes, activities and operations by which policy, professional and personal agendas for participation and empowerment are transformed into practice. Ideological and theoretical perspectives are not considered here. Rather, the chapter focuses and draws on the experiences of the individuals and organisations involved in promoting and developing BME participation in housing and related areas of social policy.

## Tenant participation and empowerment – the national context

In an attempt to enhance public involvement in decision-making, the Labour government under Tony Blair has given public bodies, for example the police and health authorities, a broader and more extensive duty to consult and involve local people in the way that services are delivered overall, rather than just on specific issues.

Local authorities already have a statutory duty to consult and involve tenants on a range of issues to do with the delivery of housing and related services. The Department of the Environment, Transport and the Regions (DETR) and the Housing Corporation have in place regulatory arrangements and guidance for developing policies and procedures aimed at increasing the quantity and improving the quality and content of tenant involvement and participation practice within social housing organisations.

The current legislative framework for RSL–tenant participation is minimal and defined by s105 of the Housing Act 1985, which requires RSLs to consult and involve tenants in the provision of housing services. RSLs are used to a regulatory body, the Housing Corporation, which scrutinises what they do with regard to tenant and resident involvement and participation. In the past this has been very detailed but now concentrates on the overall picture. The Housing Corporation has set Performance Standards for tenant participation (April 1998). According to these standards, all RSLs should:

- have written policies stating their objectives and methods for achieving accountability to their residents

- involve residents in drawing up or amending these policies

- ensure that clear information on services is available to residents

- consult with secure tenants about matters of housing management as required by s105 of the 1985 Housing Act

- provide opportunities for residents to participate in the design and management of housing and related services and to influence the management of the RSL

- encourage, help, set up and assist and work with resident organisations where residents want this.

By contrast, local authority housing departments have been under greater pressure to consult with and involve their tenants as a result of legislation and the requirement to present information to government through the housing investment programme. Specifically, secure tenants have:

- a right to information (s104 and s106 Housing Act 1985)

- a right to be consulted (s105 Housing Act 1985).

In 1998 the DETR agreed a broader package of Section 16 grants (Housing and Planning Act 1986) – now called the Tenant Empowerment Grants – to underpin the developing tenant participation agenda. Since then the DETR have introduced grants for option studies that are short estate-based projects to provide tenants with information and advice about options for involvement in the management of their homes.

The *National Framework for Tenant Participation Compacts* (DETR 1999) aimed at increasing tenant involvement through the negotiation of local agreements – at council-wide and neighbourhood levels – between local authorities and their tenants. Tenant Participation Compacts (TPCs) involve tenants in both strategic and local decisions on housing issues, with the role and scope of council-wide and local TPCs being clearly defined and complementary to each other. TPCs may be based on existing structures or arrangements where, following review, these are found to be capable of truly representing the tenants' views. Alternatively, TPCs may provide for new models and structures to be developed and put in place to ensure that participation arrangements cover both council-wide and local neighbourhood issues. In the eyes of the present government TPCs are a starting point for a new, longer-term agenda to involve local people in shaping the future of their own communities, to make government programmes and initiatives more responsive to local needs and problems and to tackle social exclusion.

In terms of the involvement of BME tenants and residents DETR (1999) strongly encourages the widening of tenant participation in the community and says:

> Councils should consider drawing up equality strategies, negotiated with tenants, which aim *actively* to recruit tenants from ethnic minority and other groups where they are underrepresented. To help with this, councils and tenants will want to review existing participation arrangements to see whether all groups, including ethnic minority tenants, people with disabilities, tenants whose first language is not English etc., are involved. (DETR 1999, p.17)

It then goes on to suggest that these strategies could:

- set equality objectives (including race equality objectives) and standards for consultation, and monitor levels of involvement and representation by all groups, including ethnic minorities, to ensure that no group is significantly under-represented

- develop facilities and procedures to make sure that all groups, including ethnic minorities, are encouraged and able to participate, and that tenant groups are inclusive

- develop training options for tenants, staff and others to raise awareness of equal opportunity issues in housing, including policies on race equality and racial harassment. (DETR 1999, p.17)

In addition to the development of the governmental framework for tenant participation, a substantive range of related social policy initiatives have emerged under this present administration. The number of these initiatives is bewilderingly large and justice cannot be done to them in this chapter. However, the broad unifying themes that can be said to relate to the involvement and participation of BME communities in particular may be summarised as:

- tackling social exclusion and creating sustainable communities

- tackling crime and anti-social behaviour

- reforming the labour market and benefits system

- modernising democratic and public institutions

- integrating services, transferring services out of the public sector and providing 'Best Value'.

There are also a number of national representative pressure groups that have developed in order to promote, develop and defend the interests of tenants and residents of social housing organisations. The Tenants' and Residents' Organisations of England (TAROE), launched in 1997, merged the national bodies for council and housing association tenants. TAROE's key objectives are to campaign for an end to assured tenancies and to encourage housing association and council tenants to work together to lobby landlords and government on housing-related and policy issues. Other national pressure groups include the Association for Tenant Involvement and Control (ATIC), which aims to represent the interests of tenants involved with tenant management organisations, and the Housing Association Residents' and Tenants' Organisations of England (HARTOE), which has been set up expressly to represent the interests of housing association tenants and residents.

The Black and Minority Ethnic Tenants' and Residents' Advisory Network (BME TARAN) was established in 1999 to address concerns raised by BME tenants and staff regarding the absence of black perspectives in resident/customer involvement initiatives such as Best Value for RSLs and tenant participation compacts for local authorities. BME TARAN have also highlighted the lack of training and development support to black tenants and their organisations and have articulated what has been their common experience of 'mainstream' tenants' organisations and landlords, whose policies and practices have often excluded and discouraged BME households from being involved.

BME TARAN operate nationally and work across the range of social housing organisations (local authorities, RSLs, tenant management organisations and tenants' and residents' organisations), providing advice and assistance in developing different approaches to involving BME tenants and residents. BME TARAN also campaigns to bring to the attention of policy makers, regulators and landlords issues that make it hard for BME households to become involved or discourage their involvement.

Inevitably, however, given the numbers of BME households accommodated by social landlords, minority ethnic groups are not as involved or active in these or other mainstream or local groups as the white majority group (Chahal 2000).

## BME participation and empowerment

Tenant participation in its widest sense has existed throughout the history of social housing provision (Grayson 1997). It was common, following the advent in 1919 of mass council housing, for tenants' organisations to emerge on newly built estates. They often assisted in the 'settling down' process, which sometimes took place in the face of hostility from neighbouring owner-occupiers. For the most part, however, and certainly up until the mid-1980s, active involvement by tenants has been in reaction to outside pressures and interests.

The 1991 Census found that black communities accounted for 6 per cent of the total population in the UK. Current predictions show that by 2020 the size of the black community will have increased to 11 per cent (Harris 1998). In 1998 over 3.3 million properties were in the ownership of local authority housing departments, with a further 1.2 million properties owned and managed by housing associations. BME households account for over 7.5 per cent of lettings made by local authorities and over 10 per cent by RSLs (DETR 2000). Although minority ethnic group households are diverse in form, structure and expectations, these figures demonstrate that such households continue to rely heavily on social housing providers in meeting their housing needs.

Black people have been a part of the fabric of British life for at least the last 200 years (Fryer 1984). The efforts of black people to organise around issues of common interest and concern (racial prejudice and discrimination in employment, health and education) have been well documented in the post-war period. It may be surprising to note, then, that as long ago as the middle of the eighteenth century there is evidence of cohesion, solidarity and mutual help among black people in Britain:

> ...they had developed a social life. And they were finding ways of expressing their political aspirations. Black self-awareness took literary shape in autobiography, political protest, journalism and other published writings by Africans who lived in or visited England and wrote in English. (Fryer 1984)

Studies dating back to the 1960s point to entrenched patterns of ethnic minority disadvantage in the British housing system, measured in terms of place, residence, housing standards, mobility and access (Brown 1984; Pahl 1975; Rex and Moore 1967). Racism and racial discrimination have to a large degree set the context for BME tenant collective action and community activity around housing issues, whose origins go back to the 1950s' campaigns for improved housing conditions. From the early 1950s many of the immigrants to Britain had gravitated to the major industrial cities (London, Birmingham, Manchester, Leeds, Sheffield and Coventry amongst others) because these offered increased work opportunities and the prospect of a new life where there could be relief from the widespread underdevelopment, unemployment and poverty they had experienced in their countries of birth. In this period

> almost half of all housing was still in the hands of private landlords and the Rent Act 1957, although not fully implemented until 1961, had a significant impact by decontrolling rents at the next change of tenancy. This permitted landlords

such as Peter Rachman to 'winkle out' established tenants to take advantage of higher rent possibilities. In 1957 private tenants in the North Kensington Tenants Association had started to organise against the Bill, linking up with a West London Rent Bill Action Committee. Out of this campaign two tenants' groups emerged: the St Stephen's Garden Tenants' Association and the Powis and Colville Residents' Association. Both groups stressed anti-racist and anti-fascist policies and the defence of private tenants and council tenants. In April 1960, 11 tenants went on rent strike in one block and in August 1963 a family faced with eviction were barricaded in – the barbed wire barricades were up for six days and a system of alarm bells was rigged up. (Grayson 1997, p.50)

Through their active involvement not only in housing but also education, health and employment-based campaigns, BME tenants and residents have demonstrated that they are as concerned as other households and communities about the polarisation between people in council and other forms of social housing and the rest of the country (Thomas 1995).

BME tenants are under-represented in many tenant groups. Research undertaken for the DETR by Ian Cole of Sheffield Hallam University reported that 'many respondents were frustrated that tenants who did participate did not represent the tenant population as a whole. In particular, it was difficult to involve younger people and members of Black and Minority Ethnic communities' (Cole 2000, p.43). Comments from respondents included the following:

> 'It was the same old faces who were nearly all over 60, retired and white' (Housing officer, rural authority).

> 'We did a housing needs survey. We found that 50% of our households were black and minority ethnic. The trouble is that the people who got involved are the exact opposite of this population – they are elderly and white' (Housing manager, London borough). (Cote 2000, p.43)

In response to this under-representation of BME tenants many authorities are now looking at new forms of involvement. In the Foreword to the Housing Corporation's BME housing policy Hilary Armstrong, Minister of State for Local Government and Housing, states:

> Appropriate action by local authorities will be critical to the success of the Corporation's policy. They set the local strategy within which RSLs work. Many will need to draw up specific sections on Black and Minority Ethnic communities in their plans... Good practice in local authorities with substantial Black and Ethnic Minority communities should certainly include plans for meeting the housing needs of these communities, and for involving them in the provision of housing services. (Housing Corporation 1998, p.1)

Similarly, mainstream tenants' organisations have consistently been ignorant of the need to involve and include members of ethnic minority groups in their membership or to reflect, in their priorities, issues that are of particular concern to ethnic minorities. This has been the case even where ethnic minority households represent the majority group in the local area, estate or neighbourhood.

There are many barriers to active tenant and community involvement by BME households and communities. It is acknowledged that many of these barriers are deep-rooted, with adverse effects that tend to disadvantage BME communities more than mainstream communities. *Mind the Gap* (Steele and Sodhi 1999), a research report into recognising and managing diversity among BME communities, involved an audit of the needs of the African-Caribbean community in relation to housing, health and employment. The needs audit was conducted to provide the basis of future policy and development and ensure that the needs of the African-Caribbean community are met. Barriers to involvement in community activity were to some extent associated with racism but also included the following:

- Affordability, where the costs associated with participation acted as a disincentive for low-income households to become involved. This has been particularly relevant to the provision of childcare facilities and access to transport for the elderly.

- The levels of hostility experienced by BME tenants and residents who have attempted to be involved, raise their issues with or access mainstream tenants' and residents' groups.

- The racist attitudes of some community activists and members of tenants' and residents' groups.

- The incidence of mental health problems among some BME groups.

- The use of appropriate community centres that offer spaces to meet and develop activities that are accessible and offer a safe and secure environment.

- Language barriers and unfamiliarity with the culture of meetings, agendas and formal procedures that can act as a disincentive to get involved in local community affairs.

- Cultural and religious traditions, which can limit the degree of broader social participation possible by some BME groups; for example, South Asian women.

Furthermore, research conducted by the Federation of Black Housing Organisations (FBHO) suggests that the lack of participation by black people is

> not a result of apathy amongst black tenants but due mainly to the exclusion of black households from participation. Exclusion takes the form of blatant refusal to allow black tenants to use communal facilities or to gain access to other available resources such as funding, the non-existence of black workers on tenants federations, activities organised from the perspective of white tenants which had little appeal to black tenants, and the absence of issues of importance to black households on tenant associations' agendas. (Cooper 1991, cited in Cooper and Hawtin 1997, p.253)

It can be seen that many of the agencies involved in delivering regeneration and social housing initiatives are failing to involve fully all sections of the community. If the objectives of the government's housing policy and agenda for tenant participation are to be realised, particularly in these areas, then the views, preferences and aspirations of BME households need to be taken into account. But how is this to be achieved?

The remaining sections of this chapter highlight and discuss some of the key issues for social housing and related organisations in involving residents in decision-making processes. These issues are considered in the context of service delivery to tenants and residents and area regeneration, examining what methods and approaches have been utilised.

## Participation and empowerment – the building blocks

Tenant participation/empowerment is not just about the relationship between tenants, residents and their landlord organisations, or about what happens at a local level. It is also about the way organisations understand and respond to problems at a community, estate or neighbourhood level. The way people are involved in change is as important as the way organisational services and policies change in response to new challenges.

> Landlords have generally employed the more traditional formal methods of tenant participation with Black and Minority Ethnic communities, which are not necessarily appropriate for these communities. Many approaches to participation have been developed from the landlord's perspective rather than the tenants'. The pursuit of participation is often based on predetermined mechanisms. For example, there is little flexibility allowed in the approach to participation by Section 16 agencies in respect of the Right to Manage. Furthermore there has tended to be a heavy reliance on consulting existing 'community leaders', who are seen as pivotal representatives of particular communities. The question should be asked whether or not communities themselves see such indi-

viduals as representing the views of the whole community, including women and young people. (Steele 1999, p.16)

Many landlords are also not suitably equipped to engage BME communities because they lack cultural awareness or they do not employ staff with appropriate language skills. In addition, and given the geographical spread of some communities and the nature of their non-housing concerns, tenant involvement in housing issues is often a low priority for these communities. For social housing organisations intent on involving BME residents and communities serious consideration needs to be given to:

- the methods that are employed, ensuring that these are innovative, creative and above all sensitive to the needs and cultural norms of the communities involved

- the environmental factors that are present and which may impact on the ability of people to become involved

- the qualities of the people who may be involved in providing support and assistance to target groups

- the resources, human and material, that will be needed to plan, develop and implement proposals to involve BME residents and communities.

## Regional development and area regeneration

Area regeneration programmes are predicated upon a premise which seeks to address fundamental social and economic problems through a largely competitive process, in which bids are made, in the main, by local authorities in accordance with their priorities. Large sums of money are then allocated to areas of often acute poverty and extreme need. These areas are defined not by residents but according to the national indicators of need such as DETR (1998). The money has to be spent quickly, in accordance with the timetables and priorities of local and central government (Duncan and Thomas 2000, p.3).

Housing is at the centre of a raft of new government social policy initiatives aimed at tackling deprivation, improving the circumstances of the most disadvantaged in our society and regenerating run-down communities. These initiatives will centre on the key issues of affordability, quality, quantity and control of social housing. Local authorities and housing associations are being encouraged to engage with voluntary and community-based groups and other agencies, to plan and implement environmental and regeneration projects in these areas.

The government has indicated that these policies will have a specific focus on areas where conditions are worst and deprivation is greatest. Government programmes will take a comprehensive approach to tackling the problems that exist in deprived areas of privately rented and owner-occupied housing, as well as on council estates.

The target of much of the government's actions will be inner-city neighbourhoods and estates, with priority given to changes that help those least able to operate effectively in the housing market. In many cases BME households will account for a significant number of the tenants in housing that is owned and managed by local authorities and housing associations in these areas.

Regional Development Agencies (RDAs) have been established, which have taken over the functions of the English Partnerships, the Rural Development Commission and the Government Offices for the Regions (GORs) and have been given responsibility for the Single Regeneration Budget (SRB) and European Structural Funds. The specific task of RDAs is to address issues of regional economic deficit. A number of initiatives have been introduced to meet these aims in the past, but the role of the RDAs is to:

- pull together existing programmes
- develop a regional strategy
- co-ordinate inward investment
- steer initiatives to provide better value.

However, RDAs have no specific powers to force other bodies to fall into line and so have to command the involvement of other regional players in a bottom-up consultative strategy to ensure regional strategies have the desired impact on all stakeholders. The question is whether the scope of the RDAs' remit ensures that they can involve and enable other government departments to give due consideration to the concerns of black communities.

RDA board members are not appointed to represent particular interests but for their broad range of experience. Access to training in developing strategies that champion race equality and social exclusion is necessary for chairs, chief executives and board members of RDAs. It is not yet clear what criteria will be put in place to ensure that black people are represented in appointments to RDA boards or, indeed, how such boards will be regulated for inclusiveness.

There is as yet no 'new' money for RDAs. They have inherited money from all schemes and programmes already in existence; the vast majority of this funding has been allocated up to 2001. Future funding will be dependent on whether the scope and promise of their intended role is realised. If RDAs are serious about inclusion they will need to change the process of allocating regeneration funds to make sure smaller groups, especially black organisations, are included and not penalised by the prescriptive timetable for bidding.

The key roles for black organisations are to influence strategic priorities and to offer mechanisms to link regional policy to local communities. In terms of influence and impact black communities and organisations need to be involved in the RDA strategies as a means of ensuring that race equality and social inclusion issues form the basis of the RDA's regional plans.

Partnerships in regeneration are not solely about obtaining funding. Partnership development is about the added value and mutual benefits a shared vision and strategies can have in influencing the mainstream. The voluntary sector has steadily learned how to work in partnership with local community organisations. For example, the Refugee Council has learnt much in the past few years through working together with smaller refugee projects that deliver at a local level. Larger voluntary organisations must start to think about working in partnership at the local level, rather than merely pulling in resources for themselves (BTEG 1999).

There is a need for more inclusive partnership working at the operational level. Small communities could become deliverers, but they need to know that there are specific outputs for black communities within SRB programmes, which they could be involved in meeting. More information is required on what other parts of the voluntary sector are doing. For example, the sector could come together and submit either joint or distinctive bids – too often, black voluntary sector organisations submit small bids, which compete with other black organisations. A coherent way of joint working is required to avoid competition and fragmentation in the black voluntary sector. There is also a need to realise that there is no one group of individuals who represent the community. Issues of 'race' and gender remain marginalised within regeneration policy despite an increasing emphasis on social exclusion. For regeneration to be sustainable and effective the diversity of communities at which regeneration efforts are targeted must be recognised and used positively to create strategic priorities (Brownill and Darke 1998). The point is less about who represents whom than about what expertise they bring to the table and what their mechanisms are to feedback to, inform, consult and involve BME communities.

The case studies considered for inclusion in this chapter highlight approaches to participation and empowerment that have stemmed from an interest not just in housing but also in wider community issues and concerns.

## Manningham Housing Association, Bradford – strengthening the role of residents

Manningham Housing Association manages over 700 properties in the inner city areas of Bradford, providing accommodation primarily for BMEs; these include African-Caribbean, Bangladeshi, Pakistani, Indian and mixed parentage households. The association employs a number of BME staff, including a service delivery officer to assist with developing their approach to resident involvement, and is gearing up to empowering residents as stakeholders in the homes and communities in which they live by the implementation of Best Value. Best Value is a major government initiative (for further details, see Chapter 8 in this volume), a main plank of which is the involvement of residents in the management of their homes and the development of real and meaningful partnership with their landlords. Manningham's Best Value Plan has already been drawn up by staff and residents and approved by its board of management.

In order to gather the views and concerns of residents, the association held a series of scheme meetings and focus groups. Feedback from these initiatives has been divided into five main areas: neighbourhood problems; security improvements; lack of children's facilities; external improvements; and home ownership. Where attendance at scheme meetings was low, the association utilised the following mechanisms to encourage resident feedback:

- involving the existing members of the Tenants Advisory Group, who had personal and direct links into the target communities, in approaching residents on the estate to set up focus groups and make other arrangements

- direct contact with residents by telephone, to identify the levels of interest among residents in being involved and also to determine why residents had not chosen to become involved

- door-to-door surveys.

At the time of writing, analysis of the feedback is still ongoing. However, it is envisaged the results of this work will aid in identifying the areas of service requiring improvement and will inform how this improvement can be undertaken. This will feed into the development of Best Value performance plans. The issues and concerns raised by residents falling outside of the association's remit will be planned into the Best Value performance plans scheme by scheme and take account of the arrangements the association may need to broker with relevant agencies to ensure these issues are addressed.

One of the distinct and key lessons learned from this experience is that the development of information, consultation and participation arrangements alone is not sufficient to engage residents. The interests of residents need to be stimulated by activities that demonstrate the benefits of involvement and participation, making these benefits clear by investing time and resources in educating residents in the way organisations work, providing information and training regarding their broad objectives, organisational structures and detail of policies and procedures for service delivery.

## 'My home, my work' – UK6 Bordesley Team Builders, Birmingham

Saltley is an inner-city area with a mixed community of predominantly Pakistani, Indian and Bangladeshi origin. It is an area of run-down housing eligible for government SRB measures.

'My home, my work' is a self-build shared ownership co-operative. It was set up, with advice from the Birmingham Co-operative Housing Service (BCHS), by 17 members of the Pakistani, Indian and Bangladeshi communities who were living in bad housing conditions: 4 young people, 8 long-term unemployed, 2 women and 3 single men. The project partners (BCHS, Accord Housing Association and Birmingham City Council) helped the co-operative secure the necessary bank loans through social housing grants and raising the necessary private finance. North, South and East Birmingham Colleges, Queensway training, British Gypsum and Presto Plan provided training to the self-builders, funded by Saltley and Small Heath Single Regeneration Budget 2.

Before coming onto the project, the participants (5 African-Caribbean, 4 Asian and 2 white) were unemployed and suffered from cuts in benefit, no access to benefits and no access to loans. The scheme offered to meet childcare costs, gave them paid work and access to home ownership loans. The self-builders undertook training at South and East Birmingham Colleges and were employed as sub-contractors for the development agent. There was an advisory board to the project which was made up of BCHS with local training providers, the city architect, representatives of the development agencies responsible for the SRB and Urban Renewal, and members of self-build groups.

Social clauses were included in the main contractor's project contract conditions making it an obligation to provide training or employment for the self-builders. Agreements were signed with regional development agencies, which undertook to take a keen interest in the self-build scheme.

Self-build support workers funded by SRB were employed to give support to the self-builders. The appointment of these workers was instrumental in the success of the project, as they came from BME backgrounds and were able to use their personal experience of the problems faced by BME residents to communicate the proposal and act as advocates for residents throughout the process. One self-build support worker remarked:

> 'A self-build project requires negotiation, counselling and organisational skills together with an understanding of the build process, housing finance, fund-raising skills, and a strong character.' 'We are lucky in having no problems with the competence of our team who put a lot of energy and enthusiasm into the projects despite being poorly paid.' 'The fact that adequate and affordable housing can be provided enables a person to plan for the future, it offers security and a good start in life. Having an industry recognised qualification and self-build experience can give them a path into employment. The scheme aims to help them, especially through New Deal opportunities. There is a skills shortage in the building industry.' 'To avoid conflicts and accusations of unfair competition, there must be policies and strict guidelines on the conduct of this type of scheme, which gives real opportunities to people and families living in such difficult conditions.'

## Black and Minority Ethnic Tenants' and Residents' Advisory Network (BME TARAN)

The idea for a BME network had evolved as a result of the concerns raised by BME delegates at recent Tenant Participatory Advisory Service, (TPAS) annual conferences and at the FBHO conference held in October 1998. These concerns centred on the absence of a BME perspective in resident/customer involvement initiatives, like Best Value and the tenant compact, which were being introduced by the government and the Housing Corporation. Anxiety was also expressed about the lack of training and development support to BME tenants and their organisations. This was fuelled by common experiences reported by delegates of 'mainstream' tenants' organisations and landlords, whose policies and practices often excluded and discouraged BME households from being involved in influencing decisions that affected the management of their homes. Although generally no one could point to good practice in BME tenant involvement by mainstream organisations (such as local authorities or RSLs) which was widespread and consistent, some good practice was identified. For example, Birmingham City Council was reported as convening a black customers group as part of its framework for housing liaison and customer involvement, and also provided funding training and capacity-building support to tenants, residents' groups and tenant management organisations. More generally, however:

- many BME staff were concentrated in frontline posts and in areas where there were high numbers of BME households

- there were few BME senior/middle managers

- there were community tensions which centred on the different resource needs of BME communities, for example African-Caribbean, Asian, Chinese

- access to information, interpreting and translation services were key unresolved issues for BME tenants and residents.

What exists of the BME network has to date been developed by a small group of tenants and staff from social housing organisations. In March 1998, in conjunction with TPAS, this group organised a national conference on 'Involving Black and Minority Ethnic Tenants and Residents', where the proposal to establish a network received widespread support from delegates. Those conference delegates who had volunteered their help to develop the network, together with staff who had expressed an interest, attended the meetings that followed the conference.

The network contacted TPAS with a view to including a BME network workshop in their annual conference programme. The FBHO had already been approached by TPAS to facilitate a workshop on 'Institutional Racism in Social Housing' at the conference. TPAS offered the network the opportunity to facilitate the BME fringe meeting at the conference. The fringe meeting was open to BME delegates attending the conference, as well as those who might have a *personal* interest in BME housing issues. The network meeting agreed it would facilitate the fringe meeting, as it offered the opportunity to involve tenants and promote the organisation to landlords and other key voluntary and statutory agencies.

Key tasks for BME TARAN have been identified as follows:

- developing an interim structure to enable the network to apply for funding to resource its development

- involving tenants and residents in the process of developing the network, enabling them to shape its eventual direction and priorities

- deciding the scope and structure of the network – national or regional organisation, perhaps modelled on Housing Corporation/Regional Development Agency boundaries

- identifying structures for decision-making; for example, the roles and responsibilities of the executive council or management committee

- creating mechanisms for inclusion – considering issues of membership, representation and ethnicity, and striking a balance between tenants/residents and staff

- accountability, in terms of delivering on their broader objectives; for example, whose views should the organisation take into account, who should the organisation give account to for its actions and how will it be held to account if the outcomes are unsatisfactory?

## Conclusions

Developing participation is a planned activity and, as such, all practice should be able to be shown to be working towards a community that is better to live in. However, the different problems, resources and priorities of local government and social housing management and development programmes, as well as the environments in which their delivery takes place, can make measurement and evaluation difficult. The challenge for social housing organisations is to actively confront those problems and obstacles that represent the barriers to effectively involving BME tenants and residents; to demonstrate their commitment to a process of empowering communities; and to ensure that the participation process is led not only by strategic objectives and the need to fulfil regulatory requirements, but also by the needs, choices and aspirations of the communities which they are there to serve.

## Acknowledgement

Thanks to the following for their help, guidance and support: Anil Singh, Manningham Housing Association; Harris Beider, Federation of Black Housing Organisations; and Angela Richards-White, Birmingham Co-operative Housing Services.

## References

BTEG (1999) *New Challenges: Regeneration and Black Communities.* London: Black Training and Enterprise Group National Conference Report.

Brown, C. (1984) *Black and White Britain.* Aldershot: Gower.

Brownill, S. and Darke, J. (1998) *'Rich Mix': Inclusive Strategies for Urban Regeneration.* Bristol: Policy Press/Joseph Rowntree Foundation.

Chahal, K. (2000) *Ethnic Diversity, Neighbourhoods and Housing.* York: Joseph Rowntree Foundation.

Cole, I. (2000) *Tenant Participation in England: A Stocktake of Activity in the Local Authority Sector.* Sheffield: Centre for Regional Economic and Social Research, Sheffield Hallam University.

Cooper, C. and Hawtin, M. (1997) 'Community involvement, housing and equal opportunities.' In C. Cooper and M. Hawtin (eds) *Housing, Community and Conflict: Understanding Resident 'Involvement'.* Aldershot: Arena.

DETR (1998) *Index of Deprivation: A Summary of Results.* London: Department of Environment, Transport and the Regions.

DETR (1999) *National Framework for Tenant Participation Compacts.* London: Department of Environment, Transport and the Regions.

DETR (2000) Personal communication.

Duncan, P. and Thomas, S. (2000) *Neighbourhood Regeneration: Resourcing Community Involvement.* Bristol: The Policy Press.

Fryer, P. (1984) *Staying Power: The History of Black People in Britain.* London: Pluto Press.

Grayson, J. (1997) 'Campaigning tenants: A prehistory of tenant involvement to 1979.' In C. Cooper and M. Hawtin (eds) *Housing, Community and Conflict: Understanding Resident 'Involvement'.* Aldershot: Arena.

Harris, C. (1998) Presentation to the Federation of Black Housing Organisations' Annual Conference 1998.

Housing Corporation (1998) *Black and Minority Ethnic Housing Policy.* London: The Housing Corporation.

Pahl, R. (1975) *Whose City?* Second edition. Harmondsworth: Penguin.

Rex, J. and Moore, R. (1967) *Race, Community and Conflict.* London: Oxford University Press.

Steele, A. (1999) 'No more excuses.' *Housing* September, 32–33.

Steele, A. and Sodhi, D. (1999) *Mind the Gap.* Salford: University of Salford/Kush Housing Association.

Thomas, D. (1995) *A Review of Community Development.* York: Joseph Rowntree Foundation.

# Chapter 13

# From Refuge to Exclusion

## Housing as an Instrument of Social Exclusion for Refugees and Asylum Seekers in the UK

### Martyn Pearl and Roger Zetter

## Introduction

Of all the individuals or groups treated harshly by society, refugees and asylum seekers are often amongst the most disadvantaged and marginalised. Excluded from their homelands, often under the most traumatic and disabling circumstances, they are frequently forced to seek shelter in countries with indigenous populations with whom they share little in common. In many cases these differences are multi-faceted, reflecting language, culture, religion and colour. The reality for many asylum seekers is being homeless, stateless and status-less within a system that is far from welcoming. This chapter examines the housing experience of asylum seekers in the UK, within an unfolding scenario of legislative reform and political manoeuvring. Housing is at the very cornerstone of reception and resettlement (BRC 1987; Carey-Wood *et al.* 1995; Majke 1991; Refugee Council 1997; Robinson 1993) and controlling access to housing has become an increasingly important part of the government's asylum and immigration strategy. Without adequate shelter, few other opportunities exist for those unfortunate enough to be destitute. With no permanent address, there is little chance of establishing the minimum rights of citizenship, which offer inclusion into the host society.

Social exclusion has been a reality for many thousands of asylum seekers over a prolonged period of time. This was true even before the more draconian measures introduced in the Immigration and Asylum Act 1999. The prevailing environment of competition, performance review and value for money has had the effect of increasingly marginalising the most vulnerable groups in British society. In all but a few notable exceptions, the needs of asylum seekers have been inadequately addressed by either public or private sectors (Zetter and Pearl 1999a). This has been due to a combination of institutional inertia and political sensitivity – both cock-up and conspiracy. The most recent legislative measures have further exacerbated the process of exclusion, generating additional hardship for an already overburdened group by extending uncertainty and increasing dependency. However, this merely builds on an established pattern of fragmentation and inertia, which characterises the performance of agencies already involved in this area. This chapter reviews the legislative and policy framework within which asylum operates and examines whether exclusion is an inevitable consequence.

The chapter focuses on the impact of legislative change on asylum seekers rather than refugees. This is not to dismiss the problems experienced by refugees, but rather to recognise the difference in substance. In reality, the rights and entitlements of refugees are little changed by the Immigration and Asylum Act 1999. They remain eligible to receive support and assistance in terms of both benefits and housing from the public sector. This is an important distinction from asylum seekers. *Refugees* are individuals or households whose status under the 1951 Geneva Convention has been approved by the UK government: that is, their 'well founded fear of persecution' has been accepted. They are likely to have either permanent or long-term status of residence in the UK and generally share in the usual rights of citizenship. Those with refugee status are eligible for assistance under the homelessness legislation and qualify for the housing register. To a large extent, such households have fewer institutional barriers to overcome than asylum seekers. *Asylum seekers* have no such clarity of outcome, for which they depend on the result of their pending application. While in this state of limbo, they are disqualified from access to employment, benefits or permanent housing, and are thus placed at the very margins of society. Indeed, at certain times within the mid-1990s, large numbers of single asylum seekers were actually destitute.

Yet Britain does have an asylum pedigree, being one of the original 13 states party to the Geneva Convention of 1951 and, until recently, adopting a relatively benign attitude. However, in common with most other developed countries, self-interest and political expedience have heavily influenced Britain's humanitarian stance. UK immigration policy has, in recent years, been at the forefront of a growing European restrictionism towards refugees and asylum seekers (Joly 1996) fuelled by both ideological and economic considerations. Deterrent entry requirements, coupled with a punitive, exclusionary regime for those who do gain access, have formed the mainstream political response to this issue.

Available data relating to the scale of asylum activity provides only a partial picture. Official Home Office figures (see Table 13.1) indicate that between 1985 and 1996, 67,000 heads of households were permitted to stay of whom 12,000 (less than 20%) were granted full refugee status. Due largely to the changes in legislation, asylum applications dropped from 44,000 in 1995 to 29,600 in 1996 (Home Office 1998), in which year over 31,000 applicants were rejected out of 38,960 decisions reached – an increase in rejections of nearly 50 per cent on the previous year (UNHCR 1997).

| Table 13.1 Asylum statistics | | | | |
|---|---|---|---|---|
| | *1996* | *1997* | *1998* | *1999* |
| Asylum applications | 29,650 | 32,495 | 46,020 | 77,270 |
| Decisions made | 38,960 | 29,880 | 31,570 | 32,330 |
| Refusal rate | 81% | 76% | 66% | 54% |
| Applications outstanding | – | 51,795 | 64,770 | 102,870 |

*Source:* Home Office monthly statistics

Some 52,000 cases and 21,000 appeals were pending in mid-1998 at the time of the government's proposals for policy review (Home Office 1998) with a backlog of applications standing at 64,800 on 1 January 1999 (Home Office 1999a). As of October 1997, the average length of time for determinations ranged from 13.8 months for post-1993 Asylum and Immigration Appeals Act applications to 58.2 months for pre-1993 applications. Of the 29,880 outcomes during 1997, 76 per cent were refusals, reducing in 1998 to about 66 per cent. Applications for asylum in 1998 averaged over 3500 per month but this nearly doubled during 1999 to more than 70,000 over the course of the year.

National data obscure the imbalance in the demand exerted on specific geographic locations. In practice, a relatively small number of local authorities have, to date, shouldered the impact of a particularly high level of demand from refugees and asylum seekers. These tend to be areas containing established communities to which specific refugee or asylum seekers belong or have an affinity, or are near ports of entry, or have other facilities or connection with the immigration process, for example detention centres. This demand is largely concentrated in conurbations, with London bearing the heaviest burden along with, to a lesser extent, the rest of southern Britain. In mid-May 1998 the London boroughs supported 9358 adults, 5387 families with children and 855 unaccompanied children (Association of London Government 1998), which had risen, by the beginning of 2000, to 19,000 single adults and 11,500 families comprising 36,000 individuals. These boroughs are traditionally areas in which social housing is in short supply and thus asylum seekers have found access extremely difficult, competing against other vulnerable households for a scarce resource. The need to alleviate the pressures generated from such an imbalance has been uppermost in the government's thinking behind the introduction of a dispersal programme.

An examination of current government proposals towards asylum seekers provides an insight not only into the politics of pragmatism but also into the policy schizophrenia that has characterised the political minefield of immigration. Despite opposing Conservative asylum measures while in opposition, the then Home Secretary, Jack Straw, presided over the development of a new regime that has proven more punitive and draconian than that which he had so vehemently criticised. In addition, despite the Blairite mantra of New Labour's commitment to effectiveness through governmental 'joined-up thinking', the asylum policy appears to be exempted from this, cutting directly across, and therefore diluting, other key proposals designed to tackle social exclusion and defeat racism.

The political reality behind the asylum legislation appears, therefore, to indicate a reliance on two cardinal principles above all other considerations:

- the control and limitation of public expenditure, particularly personal benefits

- the maintenance of an image of political toughness.

These measures are intended to reassure and impress the domestic electorate that the government is effectively policing the boundary between 'us' and 'them' – that is, between 'deserving' British citizens and 'undeserving' foreigners – by deterring so-called 'bogus' and 'economic' migrants. The result is an asylum process that is set to test the resourcefulness and resolve of prospective applicants to the limit, discouraging all but the most committed. The government points to past experience in justification of this approach, citing the high refusal rate of asylum applications as demonstrating the predominance of bogus presentations. However, it seems likely that excessive zeal in investigating applications and a tough interpretation of events has contributed significantly to the low level of acceptances. It is against a backdrop of increasing demand and spiralling cost that successive governments have implemented asylum policy and practice designed, in effect, to deter applications, legitimate or otherwise, for sanctuary in the UK.

## The asylum legislation

Change in government policy in this area has been enacted by a series of key pieces of legislation. The 1993 Asylum and Immigration Appeals Act was followed by the 1996 Asylum and Immigration Act, which was coupled with associated measures contained within the 1996 Housing Act. The primary objective of each of these statutes has been to remove asylum seekers from being the responsibility of the public sector, principally through eliminating access to benefit entitlements and/or public housing.

The 1996 Acts had the practical effect of driving into destitution and homelessness thousands of mainly single asylum seekers who were deemed to fall outside of the protective safety net of the homelessness legislation. Eligibility for income support and housing benefit for in-country and 'on appeal' applicants were initially removed by regulation, restored by the courts and then formalised by statute within the 1996 Asylum and Immigration Act, alongside housing and homelessness restrictions. However, following appeals brought on behalf of asylum seekers, a ruling by the High Court in October 1996, upheld by a ruling in the Court of Appeal in February 1997, decided that local authorities had a duty to provide housing and sustenance to the homeless under s21 of the 1948 National Assistance Act. As a result, the responsibility for thousands of homeless asylum seekers shifted from housing departments to largely unprepared and under-resourced social services departments. The result was that in many local authority areas, chaos ensued, resulting in a scramble for accommodation, which was wholly reactive and initially unco-ordinated. The worst standard of hotels and bed-and-breakfast accommodation was used and, on occasion, asylum seekers were even forced to share beds.

This sequence of events and the accompanying intensification of demand brought the system, in London at least, near to collapse. The number of asylum seekers supported under the 1948 Act had grown from about 900 in late 1996 to almost 7000 a year later. Asylum seekers were in competition with other marginal groups, including statutorily homeless households, seeking cheap accommodation, thus increasing the stigma and rejection they faced. Because of accentuating pressures of homelessness and the burden of high costs of this accommodation on local authorities, some London boroughs started to move asylum seekers out to lower-cost locations outside the capital. This action was checked by a ruling of the High Court in December 1997 when the Medical Foundation and others successfully contested the practice of sending asylum seekers away from their communities to areas of temporary abode. Subsequent rulings on placement outside London have been less favourable to asylum seekers.

Far from easing the situation, the 1996 legislation appeared to be making matters worse. Paradoxically, the effect of the legislative changes was to draw many thousands more people into the dependency net who might otherwise have found their own accommodation and maintained some independence. In terms of expenditure, all that was achieved, some might suggest deliberately, was a switching of the costs of supporting asylum seekers from the central government-funded benefits system to local authorities' revenue accounts. Far from reducing the overall cost of asylum as originally intended, the effect was quite the reverse, with the Association of London Government (ALG) assessing the total cost to London boroughs alone at £120 million in 1997.

It became increasingly clear during 1998 that the status quo could be sustained no longer. Later on in the year, following a prolonged period of policy vacuum, the government set out its proposals for asylum reform in a White Paper (Home Office 1998). In essence, the measures contained within the White Paper were, with some minor amendments, subsequently enacted within the 1999 Immigration and Asylum Bill, which became law in November 1999. This comprehensively overhauled legislation and policy with regard to asylum seekers, following the government's stated objective of establishing a system that discourages and rigorously tests asylum claims.

The Act contained a number of key measures, many of which involved tightening pre-entry measures and increasing penalties on illegal entrants. The government's stated intention in implementing the new Act was:

- to disperse asylum seekers to locations in the UK on a no-choice basis, in order to minimise the incentive to economic migration

- to relieve the current burden on councils in London and the South East in a sensible and pragmatic way

- to avoid adding to problems of social exclusion

- to avoid creating racial tension

- where possible, to take account of the value of linking to existing communities and the support from voluntary and community groups

- to avoid the possibility that asylum seekers would migrate back to London and adopt rough sleeping as a preferred method of survival. (Home Office 1999a)

Some of these objectives appear contradictory. Compulsory dispersal does not sit well with the avoidance of social exclusion, as people generally gravitate to areas where they are most secure and well served. However, the Home Office has justified this menu by proposing measures to curb the further marginalisation of already marginalised areas, and arguing that these measures would also safeguard asylum seekers.

The Act extended the disentitlement of asylum seekers to public funds, completing their virtual exclusion from monetary benefits. Under the new regime, support for asylum seekers is provided outwith the existing statutory benefits arrangements and is no longer founded on cash payments but, instead, through a system of vouchers at 70 per cent of income support levels. When introduced, this proposal caused a great deal of concern from a wide range of sources, in terms of both humanitarian and utilitarian perspectives. Not only were asylum seekers being expected to survive on significantly reduced levels of benefit but the potential for administrative complexity and inequity in the use of vouchers added further pressure to an already unwieldy system.

Far from promising greater effectiveness, the new system promised an even greater level of cost and complexity than that which it had replaced. The government recognised the incongruity of this:

> The Government is aware that there are some who have argued that full cash benefits should be restored to asylum seekers and that this would be cheaper on a per capita basis. The Government considers, however, that cash benefits represent a strong pull-factor and an encouragement to those who seek to come to this country to claim asylum in order to improve their economic well-being… The arrangements set out in this paper which are based on the principle of support in kind with a minimal cash provision are expected to have a significant disincentive effect and the Government believes that the costs of this scheme will be much lower than the overall cost of restoring cash benefits. (Home Office 1999a)

This political commitment to a regime based on toughness and disincentive was largely a result of the government's post-1996 experience. Following the introduction of the 1996 Asylum and Immigration Act and the 1996 Housing Act, the number of asylum applications initially fell from nearly 44,000 in 1995 to under 30,000 in 1996. However, this trend was reversed following subsequent amending court rulings which somewhat softened the impact of the legislation.

The removal of benefits was coupled with a programme of forced dispersal for asylum applicants away from areas of high demand, with no opportunity to state areas of preference or right of refusal to go where they were sent. The logistics of this dispersal were to be controlled by a new government department, the Asylum Support Directorate (ASD), which was renamed, in November 1999, the National Asylum Support Service (NASS). Together with the removal from benefits, the combination of these measures has the potential to perpetuate the most damaging, exclusionary effects. Asylum seekers currently living in London may indeed experience high levels of deprivation. However, removal from the security of existing community networks followed by random relocation into other, deprived areas of the country, with no independent means, offers a bleak outlook.

Significant in the development of the 1999 Immigration and Asylum Act has been the involvement of non-governmental agencies in the process. Several key organisations, most notably the Local Government Association (LGA) and the Refugee Council, have chosen to work alongside the Home Office, ostensibly to devise a practice framework for delivering the most sensitive and effective programme. For the Refugee Council this was, to some extent, an attempt at damage limitation. They perceived a greater potential for exerting influence within the operating framework of the regime, rather than solely agitating from the outside. Very early in the consultation process, the government's intransigence on the core aspects of their asylum proposals had become clear. Those opposing the measures had to take whatever opportunities were available to soften the impact. Such a strategy proved untenable, however, with the Refugee Council ultimately severing their linkage with the asylum measures by pulling out of the partnership.

The motivation of the LGA was rather more utilitarian. Having fought tooth and nail to have their responsibilities under the 1948 National Assistance Act lifted, local authorities made something of an about-turn when a more voluntary role was offered. Councils, working in tandem with the LGA, recognised a number of advantages if they were able to devise a voluntary dispersal scheme ahead of the government's prompting. The first was that they could drive the agenda rather than simply responding as had previously been the case. This would involve exercising greater control over the events in their areas, including potentially deciding or influencing who might be housed and where. Second, the scheme offered local authorities an opportunity to act as providers at a time when they were more accustomed to being cast in the role of enablers or facilitators. Finally, the cluster regions offered an opportunity for local authorities to address the difficult problem of what to do in areas where there were large numbers of empty publicly owned houses. Although this latter point has been vehemently denied by Home Office ministers and NASS, the practical outcome of dispersal activity has proved compelling.

The corollary of LGA involvement was the introduction, on 6 December 1999, of a voluntary interim scheme of dispersal offered in advance of, or in preparation for, the statutory scheme due for introduction on 1 April 2000. The scheme was geographically modelled on the cluster areas detailed later in this chapter and co-ordinated by regional consortia. The latter were corporate vehicles for providing asylum-seeker accommodation and delivering associated services, led invariably by local authorities but including other interested agencies.

## The NASS and dispersal

The process of dispersal has been a core plank of the government's asylum policy and, therefore, immutable. The rationale justifying such an approach is a complex mixture of political expedience, economic necessity and managerial pragmatism. The government case for dispersal is a combination of relieving the unprecedented and unsustainable levels of demand experienced in London and moving asylum seekers to areas where housing is more readily available at lower cost. Additionally, there is, of course, the inherently punitive dimension of linking reception with compulsory relocation.

The balance between effectiveness and deterrence has proved difficult to achieve. Previous experience of forced dispersal has proved negative and ineffective (Hact 1994a). The existing body of academic research delivers largely critical post-mortems on programme refugee resettlement policies, such as for Ugandan Asians (Robinson 1985, 1993), Vietnamese (Duke and Marshall 1995) and Chileans (Joly 1996). Insufficient co-ordination in the provision of support and housing resources have led to significant policy failures, replicated in each of the aforementioned cases. Far from achieving the original dispersal objective, namely the dilution of impacts, the result has invariably been an accentuated process of secondary migration leading to the spatial concentration of refugee communities in areas of their choice, often London. Government policy documents, however, have clearly accentuated the *firmer* over the *fairer*, remaining adamant that dispersal will remain compulsory and that asylum seekers, once accepted into the system, will have no choice of where they are placed: '...accommodation, in such circumstances, will be provided on a no choice basis' (Home Office 1998, s8.21).

The fact that the government has now chosen to cluster (that is, concentrate) asylum seekers in a few locations, rather than thin dispersal over a greater number of geographical locations, shows at least some deference to past experience. The Home Office, in consultation prior to the Act, was at pains to stress its intention that the creation of cluster areas would be based on sound principles and good practice (Home Office 1999b). They would be established within conurbations at several locations within the cluster region. These would all be areas with an adequate supply of suitable accommodation, an existing multi-ethnic community and with appropriate support infrastructure. This is discussed in further detail below.

Aside from the logistical difficulties of developing sustainable clustering away from London, there is also a series of process issues, which undermine the chances of success and give rise to concern about the potential outcomes. Unquestionably, there is an emphasis on output, process and political rhetoric at the expense of sensitivity of outcome and achievability of targets. NASS has, from its inception, experienced problems in addressing the scale and complexity of the asylum situation. This has been particularly complicated by the huge backlog of unresolved cases in the pipeline, the increasingly volatile position in the traditionally favoured areas of London and south east Kent, and the higher than expected number of applications, fuelled by the conflict in the former Yugoslavia.

In an effort to resolve these problems, the government have committed themselves to the task of speeding up the determination process. The stated target is to achieve a first decision within six months, thus reducing the undue hardship and expense caused by extended periods of uncertainty. Few observers, however, believe that such a target is achievable, certainly in the short term. In such an event, where investigations are conducted over extended periods of time, the result will be larger numbers of asylum seekers in the dispersal system. There would also be a considerable impact on the resources of the cluster areas, in terms of support networks and facilities, of a more 'settled' asylum-seeker community. Initial Home Office estimates predicted 41,500 asylum applications in the first full year 2000/1, and this is likely to be a significant underestimate. The expectation was that, over the course of 2000, NASS would need to commission approximately 50,000 new housing units, predominantly for single asylum applicants, which would accommodate the expected level of new presentations. Thus ten cluster regions would each comprise ten smaller areas of 500 units, providing a total of 5000 per region. However, asylum applications during the latter part of 1999 averaged 6000 per month, suggesting a potential annual requirement nearer to 70,000 units of accommodation.

While the scale of the programme is undoubtedly ambitious, the procurement process also promises to be problematic. There is a strong emphasis on competition and economies of scale, with disincentives for providers to over-specify quality and appropriateness. In a series of regional seminars linked to the tendering of accommodation and support contracts, the Home Office made it clear that cost would be a prime concern, with ongoing savings being sought over the life of the contract.

In a further effort to reduce the administrative burden of the dispersal process, NASS has indicated a desire to award a small number of large contracts to providers who can procure packages of around 1000 units. This is to encourage scale economies and minimise management costs. Contracts might run for several years: a minimum of three, but possibly up to ten. This flexibility offers sufficient certainty for providers to develop business plans, which offer commercial viability, while building safeguards for NASS. Expressions of interest were invited in October 1999, with contracts due to be awarded in February 2000. However, this date was not achieved, and the first contracts were not awarded until almost at the 1 April deadline for the full implementation of the dispersal process. The Home Office indicated that 60 per cent of units would be contracted through commercial tenderers, with the remaining 40 per cent delivered through the regional consortia. Virtually all of the tendered contracts are likely to go to commercial organisations, with very little interest having been shown by registered social landlords (RSLs). This comes as little surprise, with RSLs largely unused to tendering at this scale of provision and within the cost constraints involved. The RSL presence, however, is likely to increase over time as they are engaged as sub-contractors of local authority-led regional consortia.

## Cluster areas and social exclusion

Despite the intent of the Home Office to avoid social exclusion, the act of dispersal, even to planned clusters, will at the very least create additional uncertainty and bureaucracy. The potential pitfalls in the wholesale, compulsory relocation of thousands of traumatised individuals about the country can only give rise to limited chances of success. This has certainly been reflected in the experiences of the LGA interim scheme, which has proven largely ineffective in coping with the number of asylum seekers channelled through it since its introduction. This is not due to the inability of local authorities to provide housing but arises largely because these arrangements have failed to produce a coherent strategic response to the dispersal demands placed on them. Not only have the Home Office principles set out for cluster areas failed to be achieved but there has also been little reduction in the *ad hoc* dispersal arrangements entered into by London boroughs, independent of the LGA's efforts.

This situation appears to characterise much of the asylum policy arena. An absence of clear strategic planning and the existence of confused and conflicting objectives and ineffective management have signally failed to resolve the existing shortcomings of the asylum system. This has been evident at both political and executive levels. Far from achieving the government's intention to speed up asylum determinations, there is a danger that the new layers of complexity will only serve to complicate matters further. This has the potential scope for vastly increasing delays and inconsistency, condemning many asylum seekers to even greater levels of marginalisation and exclusion. Such evidence of vacillation and expediency has been clear from the early days of the government's review of the asylum legislation. Having stated their commitment to clusters, the process of identifying the areas that would be thus designated was protracted. This was, in part, for reasons of political expedience, but was also complicated by the accelerated need for a regional dispersal programme created by the emergency airlift of refugees from Kosovo.

The Kosovo airlift had, for the government, the rather fortunate effect of diverting attention away from their asylum legislation, which was, at the time, experiencing a very difficult passage through the House of Lords. Responding to the emergency, a number of local authorities, working alongside the LGA, produced reception arrangements in their areas. These, not surprisingly, tended to be situated outside the pressure points in the south east of England and therefore, by default, offered a sound blueprint for a future dispersal programme. This suited the LGA and local authorities as the system was voluntary and within their control. The government also supported this approach, which avoided the necessity to impose and, by association, be responsible for the relocation process.

However, even following the eventual publication of the main cluster regions late in 1999, the Home Office remained unprepared to provide exact details of the 'clusters within the clusters' within which the bulk of dwellings would be located. This was partly to avoid excessive prescription and partly because of a concern over the potentially negative effect of the glare of publicity, particularly on the local populace. The broad areas which were identified for cluster region status were identified as: North West, North East, Yorkshire, East and West Midlands, South West, South Central, East Anglia, Scotland and Wales. The Secretary of State also has the power, should he/she consider it appropriate, of compulsion, designating, following appropriate consultation, an 'asylum seeker reception zone'. This designation might cover one or more housing authorities for up to three years. It is unlikely that such a measure would be used other than in exceptional circumstances.

The list of cluster areas contained few surprises, with all of them enjoying a crude surplus of housing and much weaker housing demand than in the south east. Underlying these trends, however, are high levels of poverty, unemployment and deprivation, which are key characteristics of these areas. Each of the regions contains a high representation of the most deprived areas in the Social Exclusion Unit's catalogue, with Liverpool, Manchester and Birmingham occupying three of the top five places. An obvious concern, therefore, is that the concentration of dispersal on these cluster areas would serve only to relocate highly vulnerable asylum seekers in areas with communities that are themselves marginalised and disadvantaged. This would not only undermine existing government policies for tackling social exclusion in these areas, it would actively contribute to increased deprivation. The government has acknowledged these dangers:

> The dispersal policies are likely to compound the exclusion of asylum seekers, unless great care is taken in selecting the cluster areas. The targeting of a new and inevitably marginalised group on localities which already accommodate socially vulnerable communities, may accentuate deprivation and exclusion experienced by the host communities without wider programmes of support for those communities. (Home Office 1999a)

In the early establishment of the system, however, there is little evidence that these fears have been acted upon. Nor have the indicators of success for cluster areas yet been published. Acceptable performance outcomes may be relatively few. If so, they are likely to centre on the limitation of secondary migration, an absence of community tension, a deceleration of further social and economic decay and an established control on asylum costs. Yet the true indicators of sustainability, which are far more complex and qualitative, appear outside the scope of the dispersal process. The likely result is that the implementation of the clustering process will be dominated by the logistical challenge of delivering operational coherence within a highly complex system. With a diverse range of contracted providers ultimately controlled by a centralised, and thus remote, NASS, an inevitable emphasis will be placed on the monitoring of contractual arrangements. From past experience, this is likely to be achieved at the expense of the less contractual, and therefore more informal, arrangements. However, it is often the more organic, community-based initiatives that provide the glue of social cohesion. Without them, the government's efforts towards clustering will prove no more effective than previous programmes of dispersal.

The early indications that social exclusion will result from the government's clustering proposals are inescapable. Not only have the criteria necessary to avoid social exclusion been systematically ignored in the lead-in to the statutory scheme but the Home Secretary, Jack Straw, made it clear that his policy was to implement a scheme which deters rather than attracts asylum seekers. It is therefore likely, in its very nature, to be user-unfriendly. To compound this situation further, critical structural failures exist within the agency framework, which is so central to the establishment of the support networks within cluster areas. This is examined further below.

## The agency framework

Quite apart from the failure of political, social and economic manifestos, other, more practical factors have also been responsible for perpetrating exclusionary outcomes. In particular, the absence of effective co-ordination and collaboration between the statutory, RSL and voluntary sectors has often resulted in the delivery of poor and inconsistent services (Zetter and Pearl 1999a). There are few indications that this will markedly differ in this specific instance. Despite the acceptance that sustainable cluster areas will depend on collaboration ('It will also be important to work closely with community organisations to ensure that potential risks of community or racial tensions are minimised' – Home Office 1999a), the development of such partnerships has had limited success. This is due largely to three reasons:

- partnerships have hinged too much on the involvement of national and regional organisations, at the expense of promoting and developing community-based groups at a local level

- there has been insufficient emphasis on developing a sustainable framework for the involvement of the voluntary sector within the regional consortia

- insufficient time or resources have been allocated to the development of voluntary-sector infrastructure within the cluster regions.

Local authorities remain the lead organisations in the asylum process and this is, to some degree, inevitable. Because of their strategic functions, they have a vital part to play in developing a corporate and holistic response to the needs of asylum seekers in their locality. This role, however, has often proved to be constraining rather than enabling. Research undertaken by the authors indicates significant service fragmentation and a largely reactive rather than a proactive, strategic approach. This has often been underpinned by a heightened political sensitivity, which often covertly seeks, as with national government, to discourage asylum-seeker presentations rather than to attract them with additional services. Some local authorities have generated considerable resentment by 'dumping' their asylum seekers in neighbouring boroughs or even further afield (Zetter and Pearl 1999a).

While not all local authorities are openly hostile to asylum seekers, confusion and inconsistency characterises many of the policies and practices that they have adopted. Sporadic examples of good practice may exist within individual departments but rarely do local authorities display evidence of a corporate approach to strategic planning or management of asylum services.

Of the other main protagonists, RSLs have also shown a marked reluctance to commit themselves to the asylum-seeker cause. Caught in a policy vacuum, with ambivalent messages from the Housing Corporation (Housing Corporation 1997, 1998), many RSLs have perceived asylum seekers as too risky a group to house. This has been based on a combination of political sensitivity, financial risk (although this was somewhat tempered by the Court of Appeal judgment requiring support under the National Assistance Act 1948) and more general uncertainty about length of stay, support needs and ultimate status. The RSLs that have provided housing have often been innovative, flexible and more generally community-based. But they have been a minority amongst developing RSLs (Zetter and Pearl 1999c).

The third main group of players in the scenario are the refugee community organisations (RCOs) which in the main comprise members of the communities they seek to serve. They generally have high levels of specialist knowledge and skills and empathy for asylum-seeker groups, but are often poorly trained, ineffectively organised and inadequately resourced. They, in tandem with the asylum seekers they represent, are usually marginalised at the fringes of the strategic and policy process. They are generally valued for their usefulness in dealing with reactive operational issues whilst being rarely drawn into the hallowed corridors of power. The result is that much of the energy of these groups is often dissipated in scrabbling for patronage, resources and influence, forced to compete rather than collaborate (Zetter and Pearl 1999b, 1999c, 2000; Hact 1994b).

The vignettes above illustrate an environment in which a random and shifting series of cleavages serve to significantly reduce the potential for effective cluster partnership. A further difficulty in mobilising RCOs to underpin the dispersal process is that the vast majority of existing groups are concentrated in London. The development of a coherent voluntary sector for the cluster regions is therefore likely to be a long-term project, unsuited to the existing dispersal timetable. The £6.6 million allocated by the Home Office to fund the voluntary sector in relation to the dispersal process, including the development of 20 additional RCOs, has been little in evidence on the ground in the cluster regions.

The prevailing situation therefore remains one in which services to asylum seekers are often provided in spite of the relevant agencies rather than because of them. Many of the success stories that do exist have, in part, been the result of a critical mass of multi-ethnic groups and communities which have generated an impetus to identify and respond to an often diverse range of needs. Examples of this are the Tamil community in Newham, the Somalis in Tower Hamlets and the Polish community in Manchester. The cosmopolitan nature of London, and, to a lesser extent, of cities such as Manchester and Birmingham, has made this possible. The prognosis for the establishment of viable communities in other, less well-served areas of the country appears less hopeful.

## Conclusion: Nothing but the same old story...

Those indicators that have emerged during the first few months of the interim arrangements have served to confirm the worst fears of the most sceptical. Despite the recognition by the Home Office of the need to work closely with the voluntary sector, little of substance has been forthcoming. Committed to a system of one-stop shops modelled on the Refugee Council's facility in Brixton, the infrastructure has been developed at a national and/or regional level rather than in local areas. Little, if any, additional funding has filtered down to enhance, encourage and establish stronger networks of RCOs in the proposed cluster areas. Yet the government continues to acknowledge the essential role to be played by the voluntary sector if the cluster areas are to prove viable propositions.

In addition to the fragile infrastructure, other, perhaps more fundamental factors threaten to derail the viability of the dispersal programme. The first is the underestimation of the scale of provision needed to cater for the demand generated by asylum applicants. The number of new presentations exceeded the government's estimate by almost 50 per cent, reaching over 70,000 in 1999. This has placed a significant strain on the resources of local authorities to respond in the short term.

The excess demand has been further exacerbated by a potential shortfall in supply post-1 April 2000. The negotiations between NASS and the prospective providers have proven more complex than originally envisaged due largely to the difficult commercial terms being offered. This approach has discouraged RSLs from bidding to be major providers, with only nine indicating serious interest.

In the meantime, the impact on the interim arrangement is that the practice of dispersal is proving even more problematic than the policy. Logistical difficulties have emerged over the transportation of asylum seekers away from London, as has the identification of sufficient accommodation that meets the requirements origi- nally laid down by the government. This has resulted in asylum seekers being dis- persed purely according to availability rather than the suitability of the dwellings or the environment. This has already led to tensions with rural and suburban communities where little planning or consultation has taken place. The indica- tions are that the current programme of dispersal appears to offer little more evidence of sustainability than those which have preceded it.

There is little reason to believe that the new regime for asylum applicants introduced under the Immigration and Asylum Act 1999 will be any less exclusionary than its predecessors. Indeed, the basic objectives behind the new measures are geared towards discouraging asylum applicants by subjecting them to a punitive regime of rigorous investigations and insecurity. It is hardly conceiv- able that such outcomes could be delivered through a system that offered a sensi- tive and humane approach, meeting the sort of quality standards now routinely imposed on most public sector services.

Unlike some of its European neighbours, Britain continues to lack a coherent reception policy for asylum seekers. Whereas a structured approach to initial reception is central to an *effective* immigration policy and would be cost-effective in the medium and long terms, the reality is a fragmented and short-termist approach to policing asylum. The government has clearly identified housing as being one factor which offers a mechanism for exercising control, not only of the quality of the asylum experience but of where people live and how much it costs to accommodate them. Indeed, the dispersal programme has been perceived as little more than a massive government exercise in social engineering (*Panorama* 2000).

Despite being an established activity with a constant demand, few facilities have been developed over the years for asylum seekers. Reception continues to remain a reactive, fragmented and grudgingly distributed service. Asylum is still a highly emotive topic, with strong, resource-based arguments ranged against asylum seekers but little political muscle flexed in their favour. There are clearly articulated public perceptions that the UK is too liberal in its acceptance of asylum seekers and those that do enter the country should be 'tested' by being exposed to the most unappealing circumstances. This should fulfil the dual function of probing authenticity and forcing asylum seekers to 'do their time'. To some degree, asylum seekers have been prepared to collude with this view because it often affords anonymity, out of the glare of media publicity and local scrutiny. This, in turn, offers a greater perception of security and privacy.

Not all exclusionary pressures, however, can be laid at the government's door. The so-called 'caring' agencies, namely local authorities, RSLs and RCOs, are often equally culpable and therefore complete the exclusionary picture. There is little evidence of effective partnership between organisations (Zetter and Pearl 1999a, 1999b, 2000) but, in contrast, many tensions generated by competition, parochial interest, political ideology and a lack of knowledge and understanding about how each operates. Asylum seekers are usually left with the task of manoeuvring through this glaring example of 'non-joined-up thinking'. For some protagonists, the failure of the asylum system may, in reality, be perceived a success, if the ensuing chaos dissuades further increases in asylum applications. For asylum seekers, bussed around the country in an *ad hoc* and random fashion, the results can only be further suffering, uncertainty and marginalisation from the society they have approached for assistance.

# References

Association of London Government (1998) *Weekly Statistics of Asylum Seekers Presenting to London Boroughs.* London: London Borough of Hammersmith and Fulham.

BRC (1987) *Settling for a Future: Proposals for a British Policy on Refugees.* London: British Refugee Council.

Buckley, C. (1996) *Safe Havens.* London: London Federation of Housing Associations.

Carey-Wood, J., Duke, K., Karn, V. and Marshall, T. (1995) *The Settlement of Refugees in Britain.* Home Office Research Study 141. London: HMSO.

Duke, K. and Marshall, T. (1995) *Vietnamese Refugees Since 1982.* Home Office Research Study 142. London: HMSO.

HACT (1994a) *Housing Needs of Refugees in the North.* London: Housing Association Charitable Trust.

HACT (1994b) *Housing Issues Facing Refugee Communities in London: A Survey.* By A.Wol, L. Firth and R. Mukherji. London: Housing Associations Charitable Trust.

Home Office (1998) *Fairer, Faster and Firmer: A Modern Approach to Immigration and Asylum.* Government White Paper Cmd 4018. London: The Stationery Office.

Home Office (1999a) *Asylum Seekers Support.* London: The Stationery Office.

Home Office (1999b) *Full and Equal Citizens.* London: The Stationery Office.

Housing Corporation (1997) *Letting to Certain Persons [From] Abroad.* Circular No. R3, 04/97. January. London: The Housing Corporation.

Housing Corporation (1998) *Temporary Lettings to Asylum Seekers.* Circular No. R3, 34/97. January. London: The Housing Corporation.

Joly, D. (1996) *Haven or Hell: Asylum Policy in Europe.* London: Macmillan.

Majke, L. (1991) 'Assessing refugee assistance organisations in the United States and the United Kingdom.' *Journal of Refugee Studies 4, 3,* 267–283.

*Panorama* (2000) 'Human Traffic.' 7 February. London: BBC.

Refugee Council (1997) *The Development of a Refugee Settlement Policy in the UK.* Refugee Council Working Paper. London: Refugee Council.

Robinson, V. (1985) 'The Vietnamese reception and resettlement programme in the UK: Rhetoric and reality.' *Ethnic Groups 6,* 305–330.

Robinson, V. (1993) 'British policy towards the settlement of ethnic groups: An empirical evaluation of the Vietnamese programme, 1979–88.' In V. Robinson (ed) *The International Refugee Crisis: British and Canadian Responses.* London: Macmillan.

UNHCR (1997) *The State of the World's Refugees.* Geneva: United Nations High Commissioner for Refugees.

Zetter, R. and Pearl, M. (1999a) *Managing to Survive.* Bristol: Policy Press.

Zetter, R. and Pearl, M. (1999b) 'Sheltering on the margins: Social housing provision and the impact of restrictionalism on asylum seekers and refugees in the UK.' *Policy Studies 20,* 4, 235–254.

Zetter, R. and Pearl, M. (1999c) *Guidelines for Registered Social Landlords on the Provision of Housing and Support Services for Asylum Seekers.* London: The Housing Corporation.

Zetter, R. and Pearl, M. (2000) 'The minority within the minority.' *Journal of Ethnic and Migration Studies 26,* 4, 675–697.

*Chapter 14*

# Housing Disadvantage in the Inner City
## The Needs and Preferences of Ethnic Minorities in Sub-standard Housing

### Ade Kearns

## Introduction

It is well documented that ethnic minorities in Britain live mainly in urban centres and that, despite some localised dispersal, the degree of metropolitan concentration has increased (Phillips 1998). In addition, we also know that despite the fact that rates of owner-occupation are relatively high for some ethnic minority groups, ethnic minorities generally occupy lower quality housing than whites. Although some gaps are narrowing, there are still notable differences between whites and ethnic minorities in terms of the type and size of dwelling occupied and the presence of amenities. The most often remarked distinctions are that ethnic minorities are more likely to live in flats and terraced houses, to be overcrowded and, especially in the case of Pakistani households, to lack central heating (Lakey 1997; Phillips 1998). While this broad overview of housing circumstances has been increasingly disaggregated to highlight the differential experience of various ethnic groups, it is nonetheless the case that such national statistics cannot convey the way particular housing circumstances are experienced by ethnic minority households, nor how their situations differ from those of white households in similar conditions.

This chapter aims to fill in some of the detail of ethnic minority housing experiences in inner-city locations by reporting on a study of the occupants of sub-standard housing in inner Glasgow. This will allow us to see in detail the nature of the housing needs experienced by ethnic minorities, appreciate how various needs combine and interact, and investigate the extent to which housing needs feed into the preferences and behaviours of ethnic minority households. With a knowledge of ethnic minority needs and preferences, the policy implications of such circumstances can be explored.

## Studying the ethnic minority housing experience in Glasgow

The ethnic minority population in Scotland is different from that in England and Wales. In particular it is smaller, at 1.2 per cent of the total population, and comprises mainly Indian, Pakistani and Chinese people with a much smaller presence of Black Caribbean and African households. A third of Scotland's ethnic minority population live in Glasgow (Corbett 1994), a city in which, according to other studies of the distribution of ethnic minorities in northern cities, one would expect to find an inner urban concentration and relative isolation of ethnic minority groups (Moon and Atkinson 1997; Owen 1994; Rees, Phillips and Medway 1993). Earlier research in Glasgow indicated that the city's ethnic minorities were clustered in a crescent of wards around the west end of the city centre, north and south of the river Clyde, but not in working-class areas to the east of the city and not in outer public housing schemes (Dalton and Daghlian 1989). Although during the 1980s ethnic minority households appeared in middle-class suburban areas (Mercer 1990), the traditional pattern was still strong and residential stability in core settlement areas remains a feature of Glasgow's ethnic minority population.

Glasgow's ethnic minority population numbers around 21,500, representing 3.3 per cent of the city's population of 641,000. Non-whites predominantly comprise Pakistani, Indian and Chinese households, all of whom reside overwhelmingly (between 70 and 80%) in owner-occupation (Thornley 1993). A survey of ethnic minority residents commissioned by Glasgow City Council in the late 1980s found that 'Asian settlement in Glasgow corresponds with extremely poor tenement property' (Bowes, McCluskey and Sim 1989, p.42). A later review remarked that ethnic minority residents in Glasgow were both more likely to inhabit properties requiring repair and more likely to have received improvement grants than ethnic minorities elsewhere in Scotland (MacEwen, Dalton and Murie 1994).

More recent evidence about ethnic minority owner-occupation in Scotland comes from a Scottish Homes funded survey of owners in Glasgow, Edinburgh and Fife carried out in 1996. It was found that ethnic minority householders felt they had less choice about becoming a home-owner than whites but were just as likely to say that their house had everything they wanted when they bought it.

Despite the fact, as we have seen, that ethnic minorities occupy houses in poorer condition than whites, in the Scottish Homes survey ethnic minority respondents were half as likely as whites both to have carried out works to their home in the last year or to be intending to carry out repairs or improvements in the coming year (Third, Wainwright and Pawson 1997).

Although the studies mentioned above give an indication of the circumstances of ethnic minority households, the relative position of ethnic minorities in terms of housing conditions is not very well documented. Surveys tend to be either only of ethnic minority respondents (in which case comparisons with whites cannot be made) or to be general population samples from which reliable statistics for ethnic minorities cannot be extracted for comparison purposes. As part of a consideration of its ethnic minority housing strategy, Scottish Homes in Glasgow, along with the West of Scotland Equality in Housing Forum, commissioned MORI to conduct a survey of residents in inner Glasgow from which it was hoped such comparisons could be drawn. The survey had a particular focus on the worst housing in the city and the sample was drawn from a city council listing of Below-Tolerable-Standard (BTS)[1] housing in four inner-city wards known to have a high concentration of such properties. The wards were also known to contain significant ethnic minority populations. The aim of the survey was to discover whether ethnic minority households were more or less likely than whites to occupy BTS housing, and thereafter how the needs and experiences of the two groups differed. BTS housing can be thought of as the Scottish equivalent of unfit housing in England, and is estimated by the city council to comprise 9 per cent of the city's housing stock (City Housing 1998).

A word of caution must be introduced at this stage. Overall, BTS housing is concentrated in 15 wards within the city, 11 of which contain a large proportion of ethnic minority households. Given the particular construction of the study, the findings will be far more representative of the ethnic minority housing experience in Glasgow than they are of the white experience, for there may be many more whites occupying BTS housing in other parts of the city who would not have been covered by the survey. It is an investigation of the experience and use of poor quality housing in the inner city only. The survey comprised interviews with 1265 randomly selected respondents (including 919 whites and 341 ethnic minorities) and was conducted in Spring 1997; full details of the survey and findings are given in Littlewood and Kearns (1998).[2]

## Making use of Below-Tolerable-Standard housing

Ethnic minority households are found to make disproportionate use of BTS housing in Glasgow. The four wards studied cover five housing association areas of operation; within these five areas, the ethnic minority community represents 14.6 per cent of the total population (Dowie 1995) and yet ethnic minority householders constituted 27 per cent of respondents to the random survey of BTS occupiers. The ethnic composition of BTS occupiers is given in Table 14.1, which shows that in the inner city over a quarter of BTS occupants are ethnic minority households. Compared with the population of the city as a whole, Pakistani households are ten times more prominent as inner-city BTS occupants than they are as city residents.

### Table 14.1 Ethnic profile of Glasgow residents

| Ethnic group | Population of Glasgow 1991 | Households in BTS housing in Glasgow 1997 |
|---|---|---|
|  | Col. % | Col. % |
| White | 96.7 | 72.6 |
| All Ethnic minorities | 3.3 | 27.4 |
| Indian | 0.5 | 3.8 |
| Bangladeshi | 0.003 | 0.3 |
| Pakistani | 1.7 | 18.7 |
| Chinese | 0.4 | 1.7 |
| Other | 0.47 | 2.5 |

Sources: Thornley (1993); MORI Household Survey Ref 10153 (1997)

Note: Col.% refers to the fact that the figures quoted in the table refer to the percentage of the column group showing the characteristic referred to in each row. For example, 96.7% refers to the fact that 96.7% of the population of Glasgow were white in 1991. The same format applies to other tables where col.% is indicated.

Properties can fail the tolerable standard test for a number of different reasons. Table 14.2 gives the main reason for the sample properties being declared BTS by city council surveyors. This shows that ethnic minority houses are less likely than houses occupied by whites to fail the tolerable standard for reasons of underground instability related to past mineral workings, and are more likely than white-occupied dwellings to be declared BTS for amenity and disrepair reasons. Disrepair featured particularly strongly among properties occupied by Chinese and 'other' ethnic minority households.

### Table 14.2 Principal reason for BTS failure

| Reason for failure | White occupants | Ethnic minority occupants |
|---|---|---|
| | Col. % | Col. % |
| Underground instability | 37 | 28 |
| Lacking standard amenity | 21 | 26 |
| Serious disrepair | 19 | 23 |
| Access | 15 | 13 |
| Number of cases (n) | (919) | (341) |

Source: Glasgow City Council BTS database

Note: Columns in the tables do not always total to 100% as not all categories of response to survey questions have been included in the information presented.

White and ethnic minority occupants of BTS housing are very different in household terms (see Table 14.3). While most white households in BTS housing are single people and couples without children, the majority of ethnic minority households in BTS housing are families with children. The number of extended family units among ethnic minority residents was, however, lower than expected: at 7 per cent the rate of extended family units is close to the national rate of 9 per cent (Scottish Office 1991), but much lower than the 25 per cent reported in a mid-1980s survey of inner Glasgow ethnic minority residents (Dalton and Daghlian 1989). Ethnic minority heads of household were found to be slightly older than their white counterparts on average with twice as many middle-aged householders and far fewer young adults aged under 25. Pakistani, Bangladeshi and Indian households were predominantly in the child-rearing stage of life, whereas a higher proportion of white households than ethnic minorities was using BTS housing in youth and old age.

The two resident groups, whites and ethnic minorities, are clearly distinguishable in tenure and residency terms (Table 14.4).

## Table 14.3 Household characteristics of BTS occupants

| Household characteristic | White occupants | Ethnic minority occupants |
| --- | --- | --- |
| | Col. % | Col. % |
| *Household type:* | | |
| Household with children | 16 | 58 |
| Single person | 36 | 15 |
| Couple without children | 30 | 12 |
| Older person(s) | 13 | 9 |
| Extended family | 3 | 7 |
| Mean household size | 2.09 persons | 4.06 persons |
| *Age of head of household:* | | |
| Under 25 | 24 | 6 |
| 25–39 | 41 | 49 |
| 40–64 | 23 | 41 |
| 65+ | 12 | 5 |
| *Economic status of head of household:* | | |
| Employed | 45 | 45 |
| Unemployed | 10 | 12 |
| Homeworker | 7 | 8 |
| Retired | 13 | 11 |
| Disabled/sick | 7 | 8 |
| Education, training etc. | 19 | 15 |

*Source:* MORI Household Survey (1997)

Ethnic minority occupants of BTS housing are one-and-a-half times as likely to be owner-occupiers as whites and half as likely to be in private renting: whites are equally divided between owner-occupation and private renting whereas ethnic minorities are predominantly owners. Furthermore, while half of ethnic minority households have lived in their sub-standard housing for over five years, this is true of only a third of whites, nearly half of whom have resided in their current homes for less than two years. Clearly, in the case of ethnic minorities, BTS housing is being used as long-term family accommodation, whereas whites are using poor quality housing for short-term, pre-family or non-family accommodation.

### Table 14.4 Housing circumstances of BTS occupants

| Housing circumstance | White occupants | Ethnic minority occupants |
|---|---|---|
| | Col. % | Col. % |
| *Housing tenure:* | | |
| Owner-occupied | 46 | 69 |
| Private rented | 49 | 26 |
| Social rented | 3 | 3 |
| Other | 1 | 2 |
| *Length of residence:* | | |
| 2 years | 46 | 27 |
| 2–5 years | 18 | 22 |
| 5–15 years | 16 | 30 |
| >15 years | 19 | 21 |

*Source*: MORI Household Survey (1997)

## Differential housing needs among BTS occupants

Households living in BTS housing in inner Glasgow suffer problems of overcrowding, affordability and lack of amenities and adaptations. The incidence of these problems, however, varies markedly between white and ethnic minority residents (Table 14.5). The most significant problems are those of overcrowding, with almost two-thirds of ethnic minority households (compared with less than a third of whites) either living at a density of more than one person per room or believing that they did not have sufficient rooms for their needs. Overcrowding was generally more prevalent, and more of a problem, in households with dependent children.

## Table 14.5 Housing needs

| Housing need | White households | Ethnic minority households |
|---|---|---|
| | Col. % | Col. % |
| Lack of rooms/over-crowded | 28 | 62 |
| Affordability difficulties | 19 | 34 |
| Shared/lack of amenities | 16 | 5 |
| Need adaptations or facilities for health/mobility reasons | 13 | 23 |
| Housing dissatisfaction | 15 | 17 |

Source: MORI Household Survey (1997)

Nearly a quarter of ethnic minority households (again, almost twice the rate among whites) contained at least one member who had a mobility-related special housing need, most often a need for a dwelling without stairs but sometimes for other facilities, and yet the household did not have any such adaptations in their dwelling. This is particularly a problem in tenemental houses which are difficult to adapt with stair lifts or other facilities. Interestingly, despite the fact that more ethnic minority dwellings than white dwellings failed the BTS test for reasons of amenities (see Table 14.2), fewer ethnic minority respondents than whites identified the sharing or lacking of basic amenities as a problem (Table 14.5), suggesting that they may not even know that their dwelling is below standard, or why.

Around a third of ethnic minority householders, and a fifth of white householders, had experienced affordability difficulties. Furthermore, whereas for whites the problem was mainly one of finding it difficult to afford their housing costs in general, in the case of ethnic minorities the issue was more often one of having actually been behind with their housing payments in the last year. Affordability difficulties were particularly acute for Pakistani households, 40 per cent of whom faced problems in this regard, and yet they had the highest rate of owner-occupation of any ethnic group indicating potentially very serious circumstances faced by this group.

Despite marked differences in the incidence of housing needs between the two groups, the level of housing dissatisfaction was very similar among whites and ethnic minorities, with the largest single factor producing dissatisfaction being poor condition. Yet up to four-fifths of households in poor quality housing in Glasgow appear to be at least fairly satisfied with their housing. This adds support to arguments that satisfaction is inherently problematic to measure (Heywood 1997).

## Social needs among BTS occupants

Although this study focused upon poor quality housing, we should not be surprised if other needs also featured prominently among the experiences of these inner-city residents and Table 14.6 shows that this was indeed the case. Green and Owen (1998) argue that unemployment tells only part of the story of joblessness and that it is necessary to extend our analysis to non-employment which would in addition include the economically inactive (especially those who want a job) who may or may not be available and/or seeking work. In terms of the employment status of heads of household in our survey, white and ethnic minority households were similar, in that among heads of household aged under 65, around 50 per cent of white are non-employed as are 52 per cent of ethnic minority heads. There is a slightly larger gap between the two groups if all adults of working age are considered. Here we find 43 per cent of ethnic minority households and 38 per cent of white households experiencing worklessness in that no one in the household of working age was in part-time or full-time employment. A further, very large group of ethnic minority households (44% compared with only 17% of white households) had at least one adult of working age not in employment. Whilst these higher rates of non-employed ethnic minority adults may reflect life-style choices such as to engage in higher and further education or to perform domestic duties, it is also likely to reflect the existence of groups such as 'discouraged workers' who would prefer to work but who believe no jobs are available for them (Green and Owen 1998, p.9). Clearly, both white and ethnic minority households in sub-standard inner-city housing experience significant non-employment, but the gap between the two groups is greater among adults other than household heads.

## Table 14.6 Social needs

| Social need | White households | Ethnic minority households |
|---|---|---|
| | Col. % | Col. % |
| Not fluent in English | 1 | 21 |
| Long-term health problem | 19 | 32 |
| Worklessness | 38 | 43 |
| Experience of racial harassment | 13 | 28 |
| Neighbourhood dissatisfaction | 22 | 17 |

Source: MORI Household Survey (1997)

Rates of dissatisfaction with the neighbourhood are reasonably high, though not excessively so, being similar to the rate of housing dissatisfaction in the case of ethnic minorities, but being slightly higher for whites. Given that many of the respondents would have chosen, through market mechanisms, to live in the areas in question (and, in the case of ethnic minorities, have selected areas of traditional ethnic settlement), it is understandable that rates of neighbourhood dissatisfaction are not higher. The rate of neighbourhood dissatisfaction among ethnic minorities is, however, slightly higher than that found a decade earlier in a survey of ethnic minorities throughout the city, at 13 per cent (Bowes *et al.* 1989). Given that the majority of the dissatisfied in the earlier survey were in the council housing sector, with the main dislikes being unfriendly neighbours and harassment (Bowes *et al.* 1989, p.43), the current inner-city rate of neighbourhood dissatisfaction is a little surprising, unless it reflects the fact that BTS housing is located in a relatively poor local environment.

In other domains, the experiences of whites and ethnic minorities are significantly different. One in five ethnic minority households has a non-English speaker as its head or as the partner of the head of household. Moreover, linguistic ability was found to be associated with labour market activity. Over 80 per cent of those households who were not fluent in English or who had English as their second language had at least one adult of working age not in employment within the household compared with 55 per cent of households (white and non-white) who spoke English fluently or as their main language.[3]

A third of ethnic minority households in BTS housing (one-and-a-half times as many as among whites) contained someone with a long-term illness or disability that limited their daily activities (including problems associated with old age). Two-thirds of these people with limiting long-term illnesses or disabilities in ethnic minority households were not registered as disabled, perhaps indicating an inability or unwillingness to take advantage of potential assistance and concessions for disability. As we have seen, these health problems often led to particular housing needs which the current dwelling did not meet. More than half the households with long-term health problems needed housing without stairs for the household member in question, but almost all the dwellings in question were traditional tenemental flats.

Last, it was found that 28 per cent of ethnic minority households and 13 per cent of white households contained one or more persons who had experienced racial harassment. Thus, in inner Glasgow, racial harassment is not insignificant for white ethnic groups. This suggests a need to consider the experience of groups such as East Europeans and particularly that of people of Irish descent in a sectarian city. Nevertheless, racial harassment is twice as likely to be experienced by non-whites. The prevalence of racial harassment in the inner city, at 28 per cent, is credible given that an earlier survey, which included a substantial number of ethnic minority residents of council housing areas in the city, recorded 36 per cent of households having experience of 'violence, threats or harassment' (Bowes *et al.* 1989, p.116).

## Household responses and preferences

Inner-city ethnic minority residents, especially those in poor housing conditions, are a focus of housing policy concern, and thus it is important to understand the aspirations of this target group. We have already seen that ethnic minority households have lived in their homes for relatively long periods of time, and that they are mostly satisfied with their homes and neighbourhoods; we would expect these factors to influence their future housing plans and their responses to the current situation. We shall consider the preference for, and the potential efficacy of, four types of response:

- *in situ* repair and improvement of the property
- moving home

- changing the household structure and composition
- tenure change.

## In situ repair and improvement

All the households in the study lived in properties which had been found to be Below the Tolerable Standard, and so in theory one might expect works to be carried out to the properties. There are, however, three evident constraints upon this response. First, many of the problems with the properties in question are large-scale and communal in nature, requiring complex, costly and co-ordinated action between groups of owners in tenemental buildings. This might apply to 40 per cent of the properties involved, where the problems relate to structural instability and access to the building.

Although an individual occupant response might seem more appropriate in the case of those properties mainly suffering from disrepair and inadequate amenities (50% of the total), there are two further constraints to be overcome in these cases. As we have seen, many occupants do not seem aware that their homes have insufficient amenities. Furthermore, at least a third of ethnic minority householders are having difficulty in meeting their housing costs, and thus the prospect of them embarking on repairs and improvements must be slim. In sum, therefore, *in situ* solutions to some of the housing quality issues facing ethnic minority residents are unrealistic unless advice and assistance is offered by the local authority or other agencies.

## Moving home

Another response to living in overcrowded, poor quality and unaffordable housing would be to move home. This would be easier for whites, many of whom are living in private rented housing, than for ethnic minorities in owner-occupation. However, as Table 14.7 shows, slightly more ethnic minorities than whites (in fact over half) had a desire or need to move home. This rate of desired mobility is higher than found in earlier surveys of ethnic minority residents in Glasgow, but is to be expected because all the respondents in the current survey were living in poor quality housing. The rate of desired mobility was particularly high among ethnic minority households without children (60% desired mobility) and among those households with extended family structures (63%).

## Table 14.7 Housing mobility

| Mobility intentions | White households | Ethnic minority households |
|---|---|---|
| | Col. % | Col. % |
| Would like to move | 41 | 45 |
| Need to move | 9 | 11 |
| Total | 50 | 56 |
| Of which: | | |
| Actively trying to move | 39 | 38 |
| | (20) | (21) |
| Very likely to move in 2 years | 53 | 39 |
| | (26) | (21) |

Note. Figures in brackets are percentages of total column populations
Source: MORI Household Survey (1997)

Of course, the reality may be very different to people's desires or needs. As Table 14.7 also shows, only two in five of those people who wished to move were actively trying to do so. Most of the potentially mobile, therefore, had not yet done anything significant about their situation and were unable as yet to meet their own wishes; this was true for whites and ethnic minority households. There was, however, a notable difference between the two groups in terms of their own assessment of the likelihood that they would move home in the next two years, in that whites were more optimistic than ethnic minorities. Just over half of the white respondents who wished to move home thought it 'very likely' that they would do so within two years, compared with two in five ethnic minority respondents. The gap in optimism is greater if one considers only those who need to move: 44 per cent of ethnic minority respondents considered such a move very likely compared with 78 per cent of whites. Despite the fact that over half of ethnic minority residents needed, or would like, to move home, only a fifth thought this was very likely. The likelihood of moving was lower than average among households containing older people and among extended families in general.

We can look in detail at the extent to which moving home is a response to housing needs. Table 14.8 shows, for both whites and ethnic minorities, the proportion of those with particular housing and social needs who consider that they would like, or need, to move home. The rates of desired mobility are very high, at 75 per cent or more, in the case of ethnic minority households with the following needs:

- neighbourhood dissatisfaction
- housing dissatisfaction
- households containing someone with a special need or mobility need for adapted accommodation
- households who had suffered racial harassment
- households having difficulty paying their housing costs.

In the case of all other needs, apart from English language difficulty, it was the case that the majority of people with a need wanted to move home.

### Table 14.8 Desired mobility in relation to needs

| Type of need | Proportion of those in need who wish to move (row pct) | | |
|---|---|---|---|
| | White | Ethnic minority | Difference (em-w) |
| Neighbourhood dissatisfaction | 75 | 96 | +21 |
| Racial harassment | 62 | 75 | +13 |
| English language | 33 | 44 | +11 |
| Housing affordability | 64 | 75 | +11 |
| Long-term health/disability | 55 | 65 | +10 |
| Need for adaptations | 72 | 82 | +10 |
| Lacking amenities | 53 | 56 | +3 |
| Lacking employment | 53 | 56 | +3 |
| Housing dissatisfaction | 90 | 90 | 0 |
| Overcrowding | 70 | 63 | −7 |

Source: MORI Household Survey (1997)

Curiously, the only need where the rate of desired mobility was lower among ethnic minorities than whites was overcrowding. Two in five ethnic minority households who were experiencing overcrowding would prefer to solve this issue *in situ* (if possible) or not at all. It is therefore probable that one of the most serious housing needs among ethnic minorities will remain unresolved in many cases. We cannot tell from the survey whether this is due to housing affordability, availability or other difficulties.

In the case of every other need, the rate of desired mobility among ethnic minorities was higher than among whites with similar needs. This differential was greatest in the case of neighbourhood dissatisfaction which was much more likely to produce a desire to move among ethnic minorities than whites (although it was still the case that most whites dissatisfied with their neighbourhood wanted to move). Neighbourhood dissatisfaction was associated with the highest recorded rate of desired mobility among ethnic minority residents: almost all those ethnic minority respondents dissatisfied with their neighbourhood felt that they would like, or need, to move home. This indicates how important the neighbourhood context is for residential satisfaction among ethnic minorities.

One must be careful, however, not to over-emphasise the importance of the existing neighbourhood to ethnic minorities, especially in the case of households wishing to move home. The issue of clustering versus dispersal, and the tension between them, is clearly a topic of some debate and inadequate understanding among observers and scholars of ethnic minority residency. Although it has been said that 'clustering still performs an important function in the lives of the ethnic minority groups in Britain today' (Phillips 1998, p.1698), and that dispersal to middle-class suburbs can be threatening and fail to convey the same meanings for ethnic minorities as for whites, between these two extremes of inner-city concentration and suburbanisation there is remaining scope for mobility that is little acknowledged. The evidence from other studies on the question of continued clustering is cautious. In reviewing studies of Asians in Preston (Ashiana 1996) and Birmingham (Karn and Lucas 1996), Phillips (1998) tells us that there was a strong continued preference for clustering among *some* ethnic minority group members, that there was resistance to the *breaking up* of centralised ethnic minority communities, and that Asians were unwilling to make *long-distance* moves away (current author's emphasis), all of which leave scope for a significant degree of suburbanisation.

Such opposition to extreme scenarios and tentative evidence of adherence to the status quo should not be surprising, but the extent to which other outcomes are contemplated is also of interest. Among ethnic minority residents in poor housing in inner Glasgow it was found that, of all those people wishing or needing to move home, 55 per cent expected to move out of the neighbourhood in which they currently resided; we do not know whether this would be elsewhere in the inner city or to a suburban location. In total, 30 per cent of the ethnic minority residents surveyed were considering moving home to another neighbourhood. While the attractions of ethnically clustered communities undoubtedly play a part in residential choices (whether a choice to move or to remain) so too do confidence and ability. Among those ethnic minority respondents who had difficulty with the English language and who wished to move home, 60 per cent said that an important residential consideration would be to move to an area where people from their own ethnic community lived. Although this is a high proportion, reflecting a need for co-residency and co-speakers of the same language, it is not an *overwhelming* endorsement of residing in communities of common ethnicity.

## Changing household structures

We have seen that the most common need among ethnic minority householders is one of insufficient rooms for the number of persons in the household, affecting 62 per cent of ethnic minority households. Extended families (containing grandparents, grandchildren, aunts/uncles and cousins) comprise only 7 per cent of ethnic minority households (Table 14.3), so the issue of insufficient rooms arises predominantly among one- and two-generational households and nuclear families. The most difficult housing need to assess is that of hidden households comprising people who are *not* older relatives of the householder (that is, not the father, mother, grandparent, aunt or uncle). In the case of the Glasgow study, an attempt was made to estimate these hidden households by identifying two groups of people within households who might constitute potential separate households willing to move out of the present dwelling if suitable accommodation were available. These were people aged 18–24 who were not the head of household or spouse, and people aged 25 or over who were not the head of household, spouse or older relative.

A third of ethnic minority households (32%) were found to contain such hidden and potential households, consisting either of one person or two or more persons. Considering these people as potentially separate households, we can estimate the effect upon the experience of overcrowding of such persons being enabled to live elsewhere. The results of such an exercise show that overcrowding would not be significantly altered. Among South Asian households (Indian,

Bangladeshi and Pakistani) the relocation of hidden household members would result in a drop from 62 per cent to 46 per cent in the incidence of overcrowding (that is, households with fewer rooms than the number of persons in the household). The remaining high level of overcrowding is explained by the presence of dependent children. Over three-fifths of households with dependent children would experience overcrowding even after hidden households were relocated. Thus, the main problem of space among this group of ethnic minority households in poor inner-city housing is not due to extended families or hidden households but rather to the size of the 'nuclear' household in relation to the number of rooms in the dwellings they occupy. Enabling new household formation from among the ethnic minority community would contribute to some reduction in overcrowding, but would leave the majority of overcrowded households in an unchanged position.

In actual fact, a desire for household restructuring was evident. It was found that among South Asian households with a desire to move home, the majority of moves would involve separate accommodation and new household formation for one or more members of the existing household: 21 per cent of South Asian respondents wanted to move home with all or some of the existing household members, whereas 35 per cent wanted to move home alone (without other household members).

*Changing tenure*

We might expect some occupiers facing problems such as disrepair and affordability difficulties not only to want to move house but also to change tenure out of either owner-occupation or private renting if these are the tenures in which needs are experienced. There was indeed some expectation of changing tenure among potentially mobile households, particularly among the largest ethnic group, Pakistanis. Of those Pakistani households wishing or needing to move home who were currently living in owner-occupation, 11 per cent expected to move to social rented housing, with the rest staying in their original tenure. Nearly half (48%) of those Pakistani households in private renting and wishing or needing to move home also expected to change to social rented housing. Together, these two potential tenure switches produce a situation where it is estimated that around 11 per cent or just over one in ten of *all* Pakistani households living in sub-standard inner city housing expect to move from the private sector into the social rented sector. In contrast, Indian, Bangladeshi and Chinese households did not report any notable expectation of moving into social rented housing.

These findings do not support the notion that the current tenure distribution among ethnic minority households is more the result of constraint rather than choice. Most ethnic minority households in poor housing conditions who wish to move home expect to remain in their original tenure, owner-occupation. However, the survey did not explore alternative preferences beyond respondents' expectations. Of course, any decision to switch housing tenures is partly dependent upon the presence and awareness of suitable alternatives, and here the survey was enlightening. Of those ethnic minority households interested in moving home, half were aware of the existence of local housing associations and half were not. We must remember that the study was carried out in five areas, each of which has an active local housing association. In fact, awareness of housing associations was highest in the one area where the local housing association has for some time been involved in community outreach work to the ethnic minority community, suggesting that this approach was working. Awareness of housing associations was lowest among the Chinese and Black-African respondents.

This pattern of knowledge of housing associations among ethnic minorities was strongly related to fluency in English. Four-fifths of those households not fluent in English had not heard of any housing associations, and this difficulty was concentrated in the Chinese and Black-African groups. This set of evidence on ethnic minority awareness of housing opportunities and associated linguistic barriers is more indicative of subtle processes of social exclusion than of housing constraints imposed by the discriminatory actions and policies of gatekeepers and organisations. Helping ethnic minorities in housing need is partly dependent upon greater levels of outreach work by housing agencies, the translation of information into other languages and wider action to improve upon the ability of ethnic minorities to speak English.

## Conclusions and policy implications

The ethnic minority households studied here, living in inner Glasgow, all experience sub-optimal circumstances with housing needs that are difficult to resolve. They are much more likely than whites to live in housing which has been assessed as sub-standard, often structurally unstable, in serious disrepair or lacking one or more basic amenity. To improve their housing quality in these terms will require assistance, information and advice, resident co-ordination, access to improvement grants and financial support. In this respect, ethnic minority homeowners in inner Glasgow share characteristics with their counterparts in Bradford: 'Reported levels of disrepair were extremely high while the ability and expectation of households to rectify defects was low' (Ratcliffe 1998a, pp.10–11).

While the city council has a programme for tackling BTS housing, the study indicates that there may well be a need for a spatially targeted improvement policy with parts of the city able to benefit from local home improvement agencies. Housing associations, some of whom have knowledge and experience of outreach work with ethnic minorities, are well placed to perform this role on behalf of the city council.

Problems of overcrowding are equally intractable. Tenemental properties are extremely difficult, if not impossible, to extend (though amalgamation of dwellings is sometimes possible) and thus, given that most households are owner-occupiers, policy focuses upon providing separate accommodation for hidden households. In many of the cases studied here, however, such a policy will not solve the overcrowding problem faced by most households since this involves large households with dependent children. New solutions therefore have to be found to assist ethnic minority owner-occupiers to relocate to larger properties, if a solution to overcrowding is desired.

The last qualification is an acknowledgement of the fact that there is a debate as to whether or not the housing outcomes of ethnic minority communities, and especially of Asian households, such as overcrowding, are a reflection of discrimination or of housing choices and cultural preferences (for a review see Tomlins 1998). In a study highly relevant to the topic of this chapter, Dahya (1974) argued that Pakistanis in Bradford had a preference for owner-occupation even of low physical quality because of a desire for a realisable asset and an antipathy to rented housing.

In the current study, it was clearly the case that most, but not all, ethnic minority households experiencing overcrowding wanted to move home. However, the rate of desired mobility was not as high as among whites who were overcrowded, and movement was acknowledged to be difficult by ethnic minority households with extended families and older members. These findings indicate a significant degree of tolerance of overcrowding by ethnic minority households but do not support any generalisation that ethnic minority households prefer to be overcrowded for cultural reasons; indeed quite the opposite.

The present study provides several pieces of evidence that support the notion that ethnic minorities face constrained choices and this might affect their expressed housing needs. Whether or not, as Bowes, McCluskey and Sim (1990) argue, there is a growing acceptance of renting as a tenure is difficult to say for these occupants of inner-city, poor quality private housing. Only among Pakistani residents was there a small willingness to consider social rented housing as an option, to a slightly greater degree than among whites (11% of the Pakistani sample would consider this compared with 7% of whites). In fact, the city council's track record in assisting Pakistani households is extremely poor so one would not be surprised if Pakistanis in housing need did not think readily of social rented housing as an option. The largest minority ethnic group on the city council's housing waiting list is Pakistani, yet the council's success rate in making suitable offers of tenancy to them was among the lowest of any ethnic group at 7.5 per cent of demand met in a year, compared with 21 per cent for whites and 35 per cent for Chinese (City Housing 1998, p.34).

Given the nature and location of city council housing provision in Glasgow (modern, tenemental flats in large estates) it is understandable that ethnic minorities do not find public housing an acceptable option. Bowes *et al.* (1989) found in a survey of Glasgow's ethnic minorities that over half of Pakistanis agreed that minorities are isolated and get harassed on council schemes (Table 5.3, p.60). Thus, the future of social rented housing provision for ethnic minorities in the city most probably lies with the housing association sector since it operates on a smaller scale and in areas closer to neighbourhoods of ethnic minority settlement. In this regard, the study reveals widespread ignorance of housing associations despite their local presence in all the study locations. What is more, there is evidence that language barriers play a part in constraining the identification of housing solutions in two ways. First, language difficulties are associated with a lower awareness of housing associations. Second, for ethnic minorities who are not fluent in English, choosing a location in which the co-ethnic group is significantly present is more important than for other households, which may limit the availability of better housing alternatives for the households in question. Further longitudinal research would be necessary, however, to confirm the extent to which this set of circumstances constituted a manifestation of social exclusion's relativity, as expounded by Atkinson (1998).

Household structures (preferred or not) were found to be another influence upon resolving housing needs. The self-assessed likelihood of moving home among ethnic minority households in BTS housing who were actually interested in moving was at its lowest among those households with extended structures and older members. Yet the survey also showed that in the majority of cases where a move of home was contemplated, this would ideally involve a change in household composition. It would seem that finding a solution to the overcrowding and other housing needs of inner-city ethnic minority households in sub-standard housing is not as simple as finding alternative rehousing options. Family issues also need to be taken into account and therefore a multi-agency approach to the situation is required. Without help with these other matters, ethnic minority households are likely to stay put without resolving their housing needs.

The evidence from this study, such as that in relation to the role of language and the influence of household structures, supports Ratcliffe's (1998b) suggestion of considering exclusionary factors, and processes of self-exclusion, as multi-layered phenomena operating between choice and constraint and across institutional arenas as a means of explaining and understanding the housing positions of Britain's ethnic minority populations.

The operation of indirect processes of exclusion is further indicated by the fact that the study highlights the importance not so much of the discriminatory actions and prejudices of individual housing officers but rather of the stereotyping that may be inherent in housing policies. Contrary to conventional wisdom and expectations, ethnic minorities in poor quality inner-city housing who wanted or needed to move home were found to desire or expect to live in a different neighbourhood to a slightly greater extent than to live in the same neighbourhood (Littlewood and Kearns 1998, table 5.6, p.38), a ratio of 54:46, and in this regard they were no different from whites. In total, nearly a third of all ethnic minority residents were considering moving to another neighbourhood, be it a suburb or another inner-city location. At the same time, Scottish Homes' development funding strategy for ethnic minorities in Glasgow is founded upon making progress in the provision of housing within ten inner-city neighbourhoods containing 70 per cent of the existing ethnic minority population of the city, known as the 'core area' (Dowie *et al.* 1997). Such an approach, which takes little or no cognisance of the fact that a substantial proportion of the ethnic minority population wish to live somewhere other than where they live at the moment, is, like other stereotypical judgements, likely to produce a 'tendency to cement applicants to existing areas of domicile' (Jeffers and Hoggett 1995, p.338, quoted in Tomlins 1998, p.13) when this may not be what some want.

The main difficulty in constructing housing policies to meet the needs of ethnic minority households is a lack of knowledge. This study of inner-city residents of poor quality housing in Glasgow has illustrated this fact on several occasions. For example, we do not know enough about the scope for spatial mobility among the ethnic minority population. Furthermore, we do not know how ethnic minority households would like to respond to situations of overcrowding and what their views on alternative household structures would be if appropriate housing opportunities were available. In particular, we are ignorant of the housing aspirations of the next generation of householders, the young adults and newly forming households currently living in the family home but with housing choices to make in the near future. We rely too much upon conventional wisdom about ethnic minorities and upon proxy information collected from householders who speak, or are asked to speak, on behalf of young adults (their grown-up children). In relation to ethnic minorities in the inner city, we know a lot about housing disadvantages but not much about housing preferences.

## Notes

1. A dwelling is Below Tolerable Standard if it fails to meet one of the following nine criteria: is structurally stable; is substantially free from rising or penetrating damp; has satisfactory provision for natural and artificial light, for ventilation and for heating; has an adequate piped supply of wholesome water within the house; has a sink provided with a satisfactory supply of both hot and cold water within the house; has a water closet available for the exclusive use of the occupants of the house suitably located within the house; has an effective system for the drainage and disposal of foul and surface water; has satisfactory facilities for the cooking of food within the house; has satisfactory access to all external doors and outbuildings.

2. The analysis of the survey was funded by Scottish Homes and carried out by Amanda Littlewood (then of the Department of Urban Studies, University of Glasgow, now of System Three Scotland) with Ade Kearns.

3. It is recognised, however, that further research and analysis would be required to separate the confounding influences of ethnicity and language upon this employment outcome.

## References

Ashiana (1996) *Action Time: Paving the Way for a Brighter Future.* Preston: Ashiana.

Atkinson, A.B. (1998) 'Social exclusion, poverty and unemployment.' In A.B. Atkinson and J. Hills (eds) *Exclusion, Employment and Opportunity.* CASE Paper 4. London: London School of Economics.

Bowes, A., McCluskey, J. and Sim, D. (1989) *Ethnic Minority Housing Problems in Glasgow.* Stirling: Department of Sociology and Social Policy, University of Stirling.

Bowes, A., McCluskey, J. and Sim, D. (1990) 'The changing nature of Glasgow's ethnic-minority community.' *Scottish Geographical Magazine 106,* 2, 99–107.

City Housing (1998) *Glasgow's Strategic Plan for Housing.* Glasgow: Glasgow City Council.

Corbett, G. (1994) *Ethnic Minorities in Scotland.* Scottish Homes Working Paper. Edinburgh: Scottish Homes.

Dahya, B. (1974) 'The nature of Pakistani ethnicity in industrial cities in Britain.' In A. Cohen (ed) *Urban Ethnicity.* London: Tavistock.

Dalton, M. and Daghlian, S. (1989) *Race and Housing in Glasgow. The Role of Housing Associations.* London: Commission for Racial Equality.

Dowie, D.R. (1995) *Ethnic Minority Housing in Glasgow. Scottish Homes Glasgow District Office Development Funding Strategy.* Glasgow: Scottish Homes.

Dowie, D., Dover, G., Hannigan, M., Aslam, N. and McIntyre, S. (1997) *Ethnic Minority Housing in Glasgow. Development Funding Strategy Intermediate Review and Progress Report.* Glasgow: Scottish Homes.

Green, A.E. and Owen, D. (1998) *Where Are the Jobless? Changing Unemployment and Non-Employment in Cities and Regions.* Bristol: The Policy Press.

Heywood, F. (1997) 'Poverty and disrepair: Challenging the myth of ignorance in private sector housing.' *Housing Studies 12,* 1, 27–46.

Karn, V. and Lucas, J. (1996) *Homeowners and Clearance: An Evaluation of Rebuilding Grants.* London: HMSO.

Lakey, J. (1997) 'Neighbourhoods and housing.' In T. Modood, R. Berthoud, J. Lakey, J. Nazroo, S. Virdee, P. Smith and S. Beishon (eds) *Ethnic Minorities in Britain: Diversity and Disadvantage.* London: Policy Studies Institute.

Littlewood, A. and Kearns, A. (1998) *Below Tolerable Standard Housing and Ethnicity in Glasgow.* Glasgow: Scottish Homes and West of Scotland Racial Equality in Housing Forum.

MacEwen, M., Dalton, M. and Murie, A. (1994) '"Race" and Housing in Scotland: A Literature Review and Bibliography.' Research Paper 58. Edinburgh: School of Planning and Housing.

Mercer, J. (1990) 'The Residential Distribution and Housing of a Racialised Minority: Glasgow.' Discussion Paper 28. Glasgow: Centre for Housing Research.

Moon, G. and Atkinson, R. (1997) 'Ethnicity.' In M. Pacione (ed) *Britain's Cities. Geographies of Division in Urban Britain.* London: Routledge.

Owen, D. (1994) 'Spatial variations in ethnic minority group populations in Great Britain.' *Population Trends 78,* 23–33.

Phillips, D. (1998) 'Black minority ethnic concentration, segregation and dispersal in Britain.' *Urban Studies 35,* 10, 1681–1702.

Ratcliffe, P. (1998a) '"Race" and Housing in Bradford.' *Laria News 56,* January, 10–13.

Ratcliffe, P. (1998b) '"Race", housing and social exclusion.' *Housing Studies 13,* 6, 807–818.

Rees, P., Phillips, D. and Medway, D. (1993) 'The Socio-Economic Position of Ethnic Minorities in Two Northern Cities.' Working Paper 93(20). Leeds: School of Geography, University of Leeds.

Scottish Office (1991) *Ethnic Minorities in Scotland.* Edinburgh: Scottish Office Central Research Unit.

Third, H., Wainwright, S. and Pawson, H. (1997) *Constraint and Choice for Minority Ethnic Home Owners in Scotland.* Research Report 54. Edinburgh: Scottish Homes.

Thornley, E.P. (1993) *1991 Census Ethnic Group Data. A Preliminary Analysis.* Glasgow: Race Equality Section, Glasgow City Council.

Tomlins, R. (1998) *Housing Experiences of Minority Ethnic Communities in Britain: An Academic Literature Review and Annotated Bibliography.* Warwick: Centre for Research in Ethnic Relations, University of Warwick.

*Chapter 15*

# The Housing Experiences of Minority Ethnic Groups in Northern Ireland

## Chris Mackay and Jim Glackin

## Introduction

The consideration of 'race', housing and social exclusion in Northern Ireland poses some special problems. The housing and social exclusion issues facing minority ethnic groups are not dissimilar to those in the rest of the UK or Ireland, but any consideration of the issue of 'race' and housing experience in Northern Ireland raises issues which, apart from a certain amount of residual sectarianism, confined almost exclusively to Glasgow and Liverpool, are unique in a UK context. These issues centre on the question of how far the cleavage which exists between the minority Catholic or Nationalist part of the population and the majority Protestant or Unionist part of the population should be considered as an ethnic or racially based division, and whether there are any parallels with ethnic divisions in the rest of the UK.

Within this chapter a brief examination of the proportions of the population in different groups is followed by an examination of the statutory framework for promoting and monitoring equality of treatment. Since the signing of the Good Friday/Belfast Agreement[1] (Northern Ireland Office 1998) these policies go much further than those in the rest of the UK. This is followed by a consideration of the relationship between sectarianism and ethnicity which leads on to an examination of the way in which the sectarian divide has led to a situation where housing, particularly social rented housing, is very highly segregated. The final part of the chapter is concerned with the treatment of other minorities in Northern Ireland, particularly Travellers.

# Demographic pattern

Largely because of its isolation, general pattern of emigration and declining industrial employment, Northern Ireland did not experience any large-scale immigration from New Commonwealth countries in the period after World War II.

The overall population of Northern Ireland in 1999 was 1,691,800 (mid-year estimate 1999 Northern Ireland Statistics and Research Agency). The estimated size of the ethnic minority population is subject to considerable uncertainty, partly because Censuses of Northern Ireland have not contained any questions on ethnicity. The only source of data available from the 1991 Census in Northern Ireland was the question on country of birth. As this does not include those people from minority ethnic groups who were born in Ireland it is of limited value.

Irwin and Dunn (1997, pp.47–49) examined various estimates and projections of the minority populations in Northern Ireland and concluded that the total ethnic minority population was between 6270 and 8270 (see Table 15.1). The largest variations were found in estimates of numbers of Chinese origin, which, depending on the method of calculation, varied from under 3000 to over 8000.

|  |  |
|---|---|
| **Table 15.1 Estimated population of Northern Ireland by ethnicity, 1995** | |
| Chinese | 3125–5125 |
| Traveller | 1366 |
| Indian | 1050 |
| Pakistani | 641 |
| *Total* | *6270–8270* |
| Protestant | 993,000 (60%) |
| Catholic | 662,000 (40%) |
| *Total* | *1,655,000* |

*Sources:* estimates by Irwin and Dunn (1997, pp.47–49) and mid-year estimates (NIHE 1999, p.18)

Irwin and Dunn's figures were criticised by McVeigh (1997) who considered them to be 'unusually low'. McVeigh pointed out that the research project had 'failed to consult properly with minority ethnic organisations'. He estimated that the minority ethnic population was about 20,000, and the Equality Commission considered that the higher figure was the most realistic.

It would therefore appear that, depending on the method of estimation, between 0.4 per cent and 1.2 per cent of the population of Northern Ireland is from minority ethnic communities. The higher figure is similar to the current estimated proportion for Scotland, which stands at 1.28 per cent.

Apart from Travellers, ethnic minorities tend to be concentrated in a very limited range of activities, particularly catering and, to a lesser extent, wholesale and retail business and health (Irwin and Dunn 1997, p.87).

## Statutory framework

Partly because of the small numbers involved and partly because of the focus on issues that divide the community on religious/sectarian and political grounds, for many years Northern Ireland lagged behind the rest of the UK in the development of effective race relations legislation and of strategies to protect those vulnerable in society to discrimination on grounds of 'race'. The Race Relations (NI) Order did not come into effect until 4 August 1997, 21 years after similar legislation, the Race Relations Act 1976, had outlawed racial discrimination in the rest of the UK.

Recently, however, change has become much more rapid. The signing of the Belfast/Good Friday Agreement was followed by the introduction of Section 75 of the Northern Ireland Act 1998. This Act placed a statutory duty on public authorities in Northern Ireland to promote equality of opportunity and to promote good relations, *inter alia*, between people of different religious beliefs and racial groups. This put equality issues at the centre of public policy decision-making. Having lagged behind for so long, the legislative framework is now considerably stronger in Northern Ireland than in Great Britain. This may not last long, however, as the Race Relations (Amendment) Bill due to become law in 2001 will include the adoption of a new statutory duty on public authorities in Britain in relation to racial equality. The Commission for Racial Equality (CRE) will be given increased powers to ensure that they are complied with. This will not apply, however, to religion/political opinion, sex, age, sexual orientation, disability and whether people have dependants or not, as it does in Northern Ireland. This wider scope in Northern Ireland will allow for pan-minority rights alliances to be developed to address discrimination and disadvantage.

Amongst the policies now in place in Northern Ireland is a requirement that an equal opportunity test should be applied to all new and proposed policies. The majority of policies of public authorities will be subject to the requirement to promote equality of opportunity and good community relations. All designated public authorities will be expected to draw up an equality scheme to consult those most likely to be affected and carry out impact assessments. Established policies will have to be lodged with the Equality Commission for Northern Ireland[2] which will be responsible for approving equality schemes and considering complaints from those who believe that public authorities have failed in their duty.

A further effect of the agreement involves the duty of the Human Rights Commission for Northern Ireland[3] to draft a report to the British Secretary of State on the adoption of a Bill of Rights for Northern Ireland. This will go beyond the incorporation of the European Convention of Human Rights, which have already been incorporated in the Human Rights Act 1998.

Another policy initiative, entitled New Targeting Social Need (New TSN), is concerned with addressing the employment needs and employability of those who are long-term unemployed and who live in deprived areas. It has the potential to change the housing, economic and social situation of minority ethnic communities in Northern Ireland. One aspect of this policy is the Promoting Social Inclusion (PSI) initiative. The government has set up a number of working groups to consider the needs of those most at risk of social exclusion, including Irish Travellers and minority ethnic communities. The groups have members from statutory agencies, voluntary and community groups and members of specific communities. The groups will recommend cross-departmental strategies aimed at tackling the causes of social exclusion.

## Other issues

Minority ethnic groups are particularly affected by the democratic deficit in Northern Ireland. Since 1972, under the provisions of Direct Rule, government has been by ministers appointed by the Prime Minister in London. Recently, however, this has changed due to the Good Friday Agreement/Belfast Agreement (Northern Ireland Office 1998) and the setting up of the Executive. In Northern Ireland outsiders feel they are excluded from joining political parties because, apart from the small Alliance party and the Women's Coalition, the membership and core ideology of all the parties are perceived to be based on the sectarian divide. The limited scope for political activity has been replaced by voluntary activity and campaigning on the issues faced outside political parties, and by a process of gaining cross-party support for particular issues. While this may be beneficial in pursuing particular changes in public policy, it leaves those campaigning in a position that is outside the political party machinery and reinforces the concept of minority ethnic groups (MEGs) as outsiders and their needs as peripheral to those of mainstream society.

## The Irish as an ethnic minority

This section examines how far divisions in Northern Irish society are based on an ethnic divide. The CRE published a report in 1997 which proposed that the Irish should be treated as the largest ethnic minority in Britain, forming up to 4.6 per cent of the population as a whole and as much as 11.5 per cent of the population in Greater London (CRE 1997). Following this report the Housing Corporation continued its policy of supporting housing associations that cater specifically for the Irish population; for example, by employing staff from a similar cultural background who could provide a 'culturally sensitive' service to Irish people (CRE 1997, pp.17, 48).

The CRE report (1997, p.143) considers that it is a myth that all the heterogeneous cultures, religions and nations of the UK form a homogeneous whole and that the Republic of Ireland as part of the British Isles is broadly within the same cultural domain. Because historically the Irish have experienced similar degrees of discrimination and degradation to blacks and suffer considerable housing and health problems and various levels of abuse and discrimination, they should in terms of legislation and monitoring be treated as an ethnic minority. The assumption that racism and discrimination are only experienced by people who are *visibly* different is not correct.

## The origins of ethnicity and sectarianism in Northern Ireland

If it is accepted that the Nationalists/Catholic Irish in the UK are an ethnic minority with a coherent claim to a national identity linked with the Republic of Ireland, this raises the issue of how far the Unionist/Protestant community can also be regarded as a distinctive ethnic group and whether the division in Northern Ireland is primarily racial, ethnic or sectarian. McGarry and O'Leary have defined the situation as 'ethno-national' for which any solution must durably satisfy the nationalism of the current minority while protecting the nationalism of the current majority (McGarry and O'Leary 1995a, p.859).

Present ethnic divisions have deep historic roots. Whereas in most of Ireland an English gentry was imposed on the existing peasantry, in Ulster in the 17th century a systematic policy of 'Plantation' led to a unique character and economy in the north (Jenkins 1997, p.92). By 1703 only 5 per cent of the land of Ulster[4] remained in the hands of the native Irish. The combination of the better land, more modern methods of farming and the capital to develop commerce created economic differences between the two communities. The next two centuries were marked by suspicion and alienation between the communities, which at certain times flared up into violence. Stewart (1977) has shown how deeply territoriality has been ingrained in the 'Ulster psyche'. Although it may seem improbable, some fault lines between the communities today are on the precise lines of the boundaries of 17th century walled towns (Stewart 1977, p.145). 'Not an inch' is still a popular rallying cry.

In so far as the plantations were a colonial occupation it would be surprising if there were not some parallels between the attitudes of the Protestants towards the Catholics and the development of racist stereotypes in the rest of the British Empire (Hayes 1996, p.5). At various times the 'Irish' have been categorised as lazy, drunken and ignorant. In the 19th century 'scientific' racists claimed that the Irish had more Negro features than the Anglo Saxons and were lower in the racial hierarchy (Curtis 1984, p.55). De Paor (1971, p.xiii) has asserted that Catholics in Ulster were 'blacks' who happened to have white skins.

Ulster, particularly Belfast, gradually became much more industrialised than the rest of Ireland and there was a substantial influx of largely poor Catholics from the rest of Ireland, particularly from the south west, into what had been a largely Protestant town. There were inter-ethnic tensions in other places, but in the case of Belfast they were to prove most divisive and persistent. Maguire (cited in Boal 1998, p.98) has suggested that these migrations introduced into an urban setting the intense feelings of territoriality and attachment to land which were common in the rural areas of the west of Ireland.

In Northern Ireland ethnicity goes beyond the anthropological roots of the concept and has its origin in politics and power as well as cultural distinctiveness (Fulton 1995, p.344). For the last thirty years the Protestants/Loyalists have been a community in retreat. Having lost control of most of the levers of power they are left with little more than territorial claims and cultural symbols. Within Unionism paradoxes abound, Unionists are loyal to Britain but ready to reject the wishes of the elected British government, they oppose clerical tyranny yet reject secularism, and they revere the law yet are prepared to break it. According to Fulton (1995, p.352), the majority of Protestants no longer aspire to an independent state, they have an ethnic rather than a national aspiration but, because the vast majority of the British are indifferent or hostile to the claims, aspirations and attitudes of the 'Unionists', the latter face a difficulty in deciding how their cultural distinctiveness from Britain and Ireland can be preserved.

There has been considerable debate about the significance of religion in defining the present-day ethnic divide. Although for some it is at the core, there is a general consensus that for the majority, while the conflict is not primarily religious, religion is the most convenient marker for the two groups (Brewer 1992, p.357). Endogamy is seen as the result of social segregation and fear of exclusion and violence, rather than the teaching of the church. Jenkins (1997, p.122) considered that, even though the conflict is primarily about nationalism and the politics of ethnic domination, it does have a religious dimension.

In Northern Ireland, as elsewhere, ethnic segregation has been linked to class and economic discrimination. Throughout the history of Northern Ireland aspects of discrimination in employment have been a central issue. Protestants have traditionally seen themselves to be entitled to better rewards because of their superior culture, racial characteristics and willingness to work rather than rely on the dole. Catholics have been perceived as having contributed to their own exclusion by their disloyalty and, at least initially, opting out of co-operation with the Northern Ireland state (Bruce and Wallis 1987, p.301; Jenkins 1997, pp.103–104).

The belief that the key to the reduction in sectarian strife lies in economics rather than religion has had support from a spectrum that has ranged from hard-line Marxism to reforming Orangeism. Insofar as the more prosperous middle-class neighbourhoods have indeed been less segregated and less violently sectarian than the working-class areas, there is a certain logic in these points of view. McGarry and O'Leary (1995a, pp.164–167), however, believe that it is naive to imagine that the Northern Ireland conflict is primarily a class conflict that can be removed by policies of equal citizenship or the removal of structural inequalities. There are still numerically more poor Protestants than poor Catholics and their local identity, but their modest symbolic gratifications and feelings of superiority over the Catholics have been seen as virtually all they had to lose. However, any improvement in Catholic opportunities has tended to increase Protestant alienation (Bruce and Wallis 1987, p.304). In 1998 Catholics made up 42 per cent of the available-for-work population but only 39.6 per cent of the monitored workforce (Equality Commission 1999, 2000). In 1991 Catholic men were 2.2 times more likely to be unemployed than Protestant men. The corresponding figure for women was 1.8 (1991 Census).

Fulton (1995, p.344) has pointed out that, before groups invented the idea of legitimate targets, there was a long history of violence in defence of community and territory. This is of particular significance in the consideration of housing policy. Although Republican paramilitaries have tended to attack commercial and security forces, random sectarian attacks on civilians, particularly those who have strayed into 'Protestant territory', have been a feature of Loyalist violence. 'Putting them in their place' by the use of violence is perceived by Loyalist paramilitaries as one of the few powers that have not, in their eyes, been surrendered as part of the peace process. Marching through the streets has been a way of asserting territory and reinforcing the ties between various Protestant groups (Fulton 1995, p.351). The majority of such marches are not contentious and, out of nearly 3000 marches across Northern Ireland, restrictions were placed in only about 30 cases. Catholic communities, however, have concerns that some marches are used to assert superiority and dominance over them by the Protestant community. These 30 or so marches have become a focal point in the debate over the legitimacy of cultural identities and their celebration and over the right to live free from sectarian harassment, as embodied in the Good Friday/Belfast Agreement (Northern Ireland Office 1998, p.16).

The allegations that in certain areas there is harassment of the Catholic population by members of the Royal Ulster Constabulary (RUC), and the fact that, as presently constituted, the force is unacceptable to Nationalists, can be seen to have some parallels in attitudes towards the police by ethnic minorities in Britain. The case of Robert Hamill, a young Catholic who died in May 1997 after being attacked by a sectarian mob in Portadown, has some resonance with the case of Stephen Lawrence. It was claimed by witnesses that police watched the incident but did not intervene. There have also been allegations of collusion between the RUC and Loyalist paramilitaries.

Catholics are as under-represented in the RUC as are members of ethnic minorities in British police forces. The latest official figures show that, although Catholics make up 42 per cent of the available workforce, they constitute only 8 per cent of the RUC. This is partly because Catholic RUC officers and their families have been ostracised by their communities and targeted by Republicans, but is also due to the alienation felt by Catholics/Nationalists towards the politicisation of the police in Northern Ireland, its history of protecting the Union and the deep suspicion felt by Catholics/Nationalists towards the organisation (Equality Commission 1999). Nationalist attitudes to the RUC led to the setting up of the Patten Commission[5], which recommended major changes to policing in Northern Ireland, including a change of name and the recruitment of many more Catholics to the force. Many Protestants have perceived such proposals as deeply offensive and unacceptable, partly because they appear to undermine the sacrifices that have been made by the force, including over 300 police deaths attributed to 'the Troubles', but also, more fundamentally, because for

Unionists the RUC and its predecessors have played a central and symbolic role in the foundation and preservation of the 'Protestant State'.

There continues to be a deep cultural divide in Northern Ireland. This has deep historic roots and has been intensified by the 3000 deaths that have taken place in 'the Troubles'. This divide has had a profound impact on the geography of housing and on housing policy.

## Housing segregation in Northern Ireland

The way in which public rented housing is administered in Northern Ireland is very different from that which is found in the rest of the UK.

Allegations of sectarian discrimination in housing construction and allocations on the part of a number of Unionist-dominated local authorities were highlighted by civil rights demonstrations and civil disorder in the early 1970s. In response James Callaghan, as Home Secretary, transferred all housing powers to a single unified housing 'quango', the Northern Ireland Housing Executive (NIHE) in 1971/72. This removed all housing powers from local government and from the Northern Ireland Housing Trust.

Despite 80,000 Right-to-Buy sales, the NIHE still managed over 130,000 properties or 21 per cent of the total housing stock of Northern Ireland in 1998. The housing association movement has also been given government encouragement and financial support since the mid-1970s, but it still accounts for only 2.5 per cent of the housing stock.

Fairness and anti-discriminatory policies have been at the centre of the NIHE's activities and there has never been a proven case of direct discrimination. However, given the geography of Northern Ireland and continuing sectarian strife, it has not been able to avoid a very high degree of residential segregation, particularly in Belfast. In Derry/Londonderry the Foyle divides the communities and only one small Protestant estate remains on the north bank of the river or 'City' side. Many areas, particularly public housing estates, are either Protestant/Unionist or Catholic/Nationalist in character and housing experiences are likely to be affected by this division.

Although the extent of racial segregation and ghettoisation in Britain is not generally comparable to the levels that are found in some areas of the USA, in Belfast the situation is different. More than half the population lives in wards that comprise 90 per cent or more of a single religious group (McPeake 1998, p.529). In 1977, 78 per cent of the population of Belfast lived in streets where the population was over 90 per cent from one community (Boal 1998, p.100).

The level of ethnic segregation has increased over a period of 150 years, not smoothly, but in a series of jolts, with segregation increasing during periods of communal tension followed by periods of stabilisation or even reduction in segregation (Boal 1998, p.100).[6] Segregation has undoubtedly been intensified by recent unrest, but fieldwork by Boal (1969) and Rose (1971), undertaken before the latest round of troubles began, showed that in many parts of Northern Ireland, particularly Belfast, there were two distinctive communities having very little social interaction.

> The two ethnic groups in Northern Ireland can be visualised as composing two distinct societies with only limited interaction between them, both of them essentially normal societies except that the presence of the other group provides an external enemy, increasing group consciousness and enhancing conformity. (Boal 1981, p.64)

Throughout the 1970s segregation increased as members of the community responded to increases in the level of tension and direct threats and harassment. For example, in the three weeks that followed the introduction of internment in 1977, over 2000 movements of up to 10,000 people took place (Black 1972, p.11). Forty per cent of the movers were Protestant and 60 per cent were Catholics. Those who suffered most at the start of the conflict in the late 1960s were those who lived outside their respective ghettos and were affected by an Irish version of ethnic cleansing (McGarry and O'Leary 1995b, p.855).

There are still major difficulties in measuring the degree of segregation in the public housing stock, partly because the NIHE has had a policy of 'not inquiring too closely into the religion of its tenants' (Melaugh 1994, p.2). Despite its origins in allegations of discrimination the NIHE did not introduce religious monitoring until 1992. It had been argued that monitoring would give the impression that religion was part of its decision-making process and that, if it was 'religion-blind', it could not be accused of direct discrimination (Melaugh 1994, p.89). Melaugh has commented that, given the highly segregated nature of estates, local officials were well aware of the religion of their tenants and applicants so that these arguments, already threadbare from their use by authorities that wished to avoid confronting racial issues in Britain, were of limited validity. It was also thought that monitoring would be unpopular, but this had not deterred successive governments from insisting on it taking place in the employment field.[7]

As a base line for their research into the level of segregation, Smith and Chambers (1987, 1991) had to rely on *ad hoc* methods, primarily the knowledge of local housing managers who were constantly aware of ethnic divisions and had a mental perception of each of the estates (Smith and Chambers 1987, p.7).

Within social rented housing, Boal (1998, p.100) has estimated that in 1969 there was a 'dissimilarity index' of 69, around the same level as in other tenures, but by 1977 it had leaped to 92 which was 'high even by American standards'. The dissimilarity index is a mathematical formula that relates the minority and majority populations in a sub-area to the citywide proportions of those populations. (For a detailed examination of various ways of measuring segregation see Chapter 3 in Poole and Doherty 1996.)

Social housing, therefore, bore the brunt of escalating segregation during periods of civil unrest and became the tenure with the highest level of segregation. This may seem surprising because this sector is the one most amenable to central control. The situation appears to have arisen because the public sector had a statutory obligation to rehouse those displaced from mixed or frontier areas, and the latter sought the safety of accommodation in neighbourhoods dominated by their own groups.

Smith and Chambers (1989) have speculated that there appears to be greater segregation in public housing than in other tenures because it is located in discrete lumps with a single identity and many estates were built in areas that already had a specific sectarian identity. There is also clearly a relationship to social class, with lower-income segments of both Catholic and Protestant communities being quite sharply segregated from the higher-income segment of their own group, as well as being affected by a high degree of ethnic segregation (Boal 1998, p.102).

After a major investigation for the Policy Studies Institute, Smith and Chambers (1987) concluded that, although there was no evidence of direct discrimination, the system did not deliver equal opportunities. Smith and Chambers found that in practice 'maximising choice' is hard to implement and the applicants' demands become part of the system (Smith and Chambers 1987, p.39). In Belfast 'freedom of choice' has meant, in effect, freedom to live in a segregated estate. Security considerations rather than life-style differences have driven tenants apart (Russell 1980, p.84). A 'liberal' policy of 'treating people equally' and housing according to individual choice has assisted those who have seen housing as a political battleground and have wanted to impose their authority and control over the community. The social control exercised by Republican groups and, to a lesser extent, Protestant paramilitaries in their areas has parallels with black power control over ghettos in America (Boal 1981, p.61).

For a number of reasons Protestants have a greater propensity to vacate public rented dwellings than Catholics and, consequently, there tend to be more vacancies and better housing opportunities on Protestant rather than Catholic estates

(Smith and Chambers 1987, p.56). In some areas there is pressure on housing, which is regarded as safe by Catholics, close to where there are low levels of occupation or even abandonment in areas traditionally regarded as Protestant. A strong sense of territoriality and intimidation means that in parts of Belfast there are 'peace lines' of walls, fences, factories and stretches of no-man's land which separate the communities. When the government and NIHE have attempted to redress this imbalance by concentrating development and investment in perceived Catholic areas they have often been accused of discrimination and bias by strident Protestant politicians.

Smith and Chambers (1987, p.57) concluded that the current policies tended to promote segregation and proposed that a system of monitoring should be introduced. The issue of segregation/integration has been virtually ignored in many important NIHE or Department of the Environment Northern Ireland (DoENI) policy documents, and there has been considerable official caution about any consideration of a policy of enforced residential desegregation. A number of commentators such as Darby and Morris (1974, p.116), O'Dowd, Rolston and Tomlinson (1980, p.134), Keane (1990, p.10) and Pollak (1993, p.120) have all suggested that the NIHE could have tried harder to positively promote integration.

There are positive and negative aspects of living in an area with a concentration of one's own community. As well as the traditional benefits of environmental support, ethnic entrepreneurship and the preservation of minority culture, segregated areas have provided safety and security in times of communal conflict (Boal 1998, p.95). McGarry and O'Leary (1995b, p.855) have questioned the liberal belief that the consequences of social integration would necessarily be beneficial. They have argued that, in deeply divided areas, increased exposure to others may make the groups more aware of their differences and cement group solidarity rather than diffuse it, while Rose (1973, p.15) considered that mixing would offer hostages to those prepared to intimidate on religious grounds. Such arguments have not gained official support and have been totally rejected at a policy level where there remains a commitment to equal opportunities irrespective of location or community. However, it is virtually impossible to guarantee safety for those who choose to accept property in what are perceived as hostile areas.

In its consultation paper *Towards a Community Relations Strategy* (NIHE 1999) the Executive spells out the difficulties in implementing the proposal in the Belfast/Good Friday Agreement that 'an essential aspect of the reconciliation process is the promotion of cultural tolerance at every level of society including initiatives to facilitate and encourage…mixed housing'. Surveys show that there is a broad measure of support for the policy of ensuring mixed housing. From a housing-management point of view segregation leads to less flexibility, vacant dwellings and real difficulties in finding accommodation for mixed religion households. Nevertheless it is estimated that throughout Northern Ireland 71 per cent of estates are segregated (NIHE 1999, para 7.1). The Executive accepts that this is a sensitive issue and that its current policy initiatives are 'cautious and incremental' (NIHE 1999, para 8.0). As well as making special efforts to address segregationist trends in existing mixed estates, the Executive intends that a number of pilot and research projects to test the limits of action will be initiated and that communities wishing to achieve desegregation will be supported. In addition many initiatives designed to foster cross-community activities, particularly for young people, have been initiated and funded by government, charities and international organisations.

One aspect of residential segregation that cannot be ignored, but has only recently been given serious consideration by the NIHE, is the presence of visual symbols of territoriality such as flags, wall-paintings, slogans and painted kerbstones in many estates, particularly at certain times of the year. The issue of symbols in residential areas is clearly not a simple one. Rollston (1991) has shown that such symbols, particularly wall murals, are an important aspect of Northern Ireland culture. Some paintings date from the early years of the century and have been retouched many times. For the minority community, however, the anniversary of the Battle of the Boyne, celebrated on 12 July with banners, decorated arches and gable-end paintings of King Billy on a white horse, has always been seen as a symbol of triumphalism (Rollston 1991, p.18). The hunger strikes in 1981 galvanised Nationalism and led to a new tradition of wall murals featuring the hunger strikers who were portrayed as martyrs (Rollston 1991, p.34). Republicans have also used wall murals to develop common themes from 'struggles' around the world, with murals linking the imprisonment of black South Africans (including Nelson Mandela) to the imprisonment of Republicans during the 1980s. A more recent mural has depicted the similarities between the case of Stephen Lawrence and that of Robert Hamill. Although some of the graffiti is crude and offensive, other material could be considered to be part of a folk tradition or to have artistic merit, and can be said to brighten up the environment. Nevertheless, however artistic it might be, it is still likely to be considered offensive by members of the other community and to act as a 'chill' factor in mixed estates.

Illustrations in the *Annual Year Books* and other NIHE publications have usually been carefully chosen to avoid pictures of sectarian symbols. In NIHE

(1999) it is proposed that a policy of removing sectarian symbols should be instituted, but it is accepted that it may not be possible to achieve this in all cases, even in the long term, and that cross-community support and safety and public order constraints must be borne in mind.

The comparative lack of action to tackle the issue of sectarian graffiti in housing areas stands in strong contrast to the situation with regard to places of work. Monitoring and the implementation of fair employment practices in the workplace are backed up by strong legislation and considerable penalties. The Code of Practice issued under the Fair Employment and Treatment (NI) Order 1998 (Department of Economic Development for Northern Ireland 1999)[8] suggests that employers will wish to create and sustain a neutral workplace and to discourage an intimidating working environment or atmosphere:

> By prohibiting the display of flags, emblems, posters, graffiti, or the circulation of materials, or the deliberate articulation of slogans or songs which are likely to give offence or cause apprehension among particular groups of employees. (p.39)

This legislation has been largely effective in removing such material from factories and offices.

As in mainland Britain the government has decided that housing associations should play a larger part in housing provision, particularly in the development programme. Housing associations are able to access private finance and to provide more houses for any given input of public funds. The associations have had to comply with the PAFT (policy appraisal and fair treatment) guidelines whereby publicly funded bodies in Northern Ireland are required not only to actively promote fair and equal treatment but also to combat perceptions of potential discrimination. This has encouraged a number of associations to consider mergers or name changes. In addition, in order to allay any fears of discrimination, the associations will in future be obliged to use a common waiting list and allocation policy administered by the NIHE (Mackay, forthcoming).

For a quarter of a century the government and the NIHE have been publicly committed to the imposition of liberal, universalist solutions to issues of sectarianism and discrimination. There has been a general belief that, if discrimination is banned, equal rights will be guaranteed and, if high levels of public investment are made to improve economic opportunity, irrational ethnic bonds will wither away (McGarry and O'Leary 1995a, p.839). In practice, however, the attack on individual discrimination, fully justified in its own right, appears to have done little to reduce the demand for recognition of two separate ethnic and national identities.

Universalistic, religion-blind, equal opportunities policies and enormous public investment in good quality housing have not prevented levels of housing segregation that are amongst the highest in the world. Boal (1981, p.79) has commented that the appropriate comparators for Belfast with regard to the nature and dynamics of residential mixing should be 'Beirut, Nicosia and Jerusalem rather than Birmingham or Chicago'.

## Irish Travellers

There are an estimated 27,000 Irish Travellers in the south of Ireland and 1600 in the north. This is about 0.77 per cent of the population of the Republic but only 0.07 per cent of the population of Northern Ireland. This may be due to the political situation in the north and the hostility Travellers receive there, linked to their Irishness and based on sectarianism. Butler (1985) states that Travellers are at least nominally viewed as Catholics and their 'brogue' (accent) defines them as Irish. This, according to McVeigh (1998, p.21), has meant that, over the last 30 years, Travellers in the north have stopped visiting some 'Protestant' areas, which were historically Traveller sites.

However, Maginn, Paris and Gray (1999, p.531) have suggested that despite increasing numbers, partly because of the measures in the 1994 Act in the rest of Britain and the limited powers of British local authorities, both the levels of expenditure and the proportion of Travellers accommodated on recognised sites in Northern Ireland have been considerably higher than in England and Wales (Maginn *et al.* 1999, pp.526, 543). This may be because the highly centralised administration system and comparative weakness of local councillors means that local protests are less effective in Northern Ireland.

The Race Relations Order 1997 Article 5(2) specifically names Irish Travellers[9] as a distinct racial group. They are described as

> the community of people commonly so-called who are identified (both by themselves and by others) as people with a shared history, culture and traditions including, historically, a nomadic way of life on the island of Ireland.

The description of Irish Travellers in the Order mirrors closely the judgment in *Mandla* v *Dowell Lee* ([1931] IRLR 209) which set out the test for what constituted a separate ethnic group in respect of protection under the Race Relations Act 1976.

The first cases by Travellers to be brought under the Race Relations Order 1997 raised the issue of whether the Order still applied if they had ceased a nomadic or travelling way of life. The unreported view of the judges and tribunal in each case was that the legislation refers to a 'historically' nomadic way of life and thus there is no need to have to be nomadic to claim protection under the Order (*Ward* v *Gardner Merchant Industrial Tribunal* 1999; *Ward* v *Olive Grove* 1999).

Travellers in the south have been subject to open hostility and racist attitudes from the public and some journalists (Fawcett 1999). In Northern Ireland local politicians have been at the forefront of the attack on this group. One former Ulster Unionist Party Chairman of Fermanagh District Council was cited in a local newspaper as saying: 'If I find any more of them [Travellers] in my country I will be tempted to use my shotgun' (*Fermanagh Herald* 1997). The local authorities rather than the NIHE had responsibility for Traveller accommodation but this was not mandatory as in the rest of the UK (Maginn *et al.* 1999, p.528).

The particular hostility towards Irish Travellers can be seen from a consideration of responses to the Continuous Tenant Survey by the NIHE (NIHE 1998). In this study tenants were asked their view on a member of a different racial group moving next door, into their street or estate/area. Twelve per cent would be concerned about a Chinese neighbour, 17 per cent if this were an Indian, Pakistani, Bangladeshi, Caribbean or African neighbour, but 41 per cent stated that they would be concerned if an Irish Traveller were to move next door. The figures were similar for people moving into the respondent's street or estate/area.

In 1998, the Department of the Environment for Northern Ireland launched a consultation initiative into the accommodation needs of Irish Travellers. This has now become a policy document (DOE 1998) that seeks to address the needs of Travellers over a period of ten years. The major result of the review was to give the NIHE an extended role in the provision of Travellers' accommodation. The NIHE will in future be the central strategic agency dealing with Travellers' accommodation needs. They and housing associations will be able to build Traveller-specific group-housing schemes[10] and serviced sites. The new policy states that district councils will retain a duty to provide for nomadic Travellers who regularly stop in areas for only short periods of time. There are legitimate concerns that councils will not comply with their duty unless these responsibilities are made mandatory. This view is based on the failure of many councils to provide for Travellers' needs in the past.

A major issue for the NIHE will be in regard to the need for it to accommodate nomadism. Traveller organisations have argued for the discussion of 'accommodation' as opposed to 'housing' needs of Travellers, as there is a fear of the debate continuing around the sedentarist view of the need to house rather than accommodate Travellers. According to McVeigh (1992) 'sedentarism' should be seen as a specific form of racism constructed out of the interface between settled and nomadic modes of existence, in which 'settled' is the dominant and powerful mode.

Noonan (1998, p.168) argues that there has been a hidden policy agenda focused on the need to contain Travellers as a stage towards assimilation. He quotes an Advisory Committee on Travellers (ACT) Survey (1988),[11] which in summary argues that although there is a commitment from Travellers to their life-style, there is hope within ACT that, if Travellers are given good standards of serviced sites, the experience of an intermediate form of settled living might lead to some of them, especially the young, giving up travelling.

Poor living conditions have had a dramatic effect on the health and welfare of Travellers. A local study of hospital admissions in 1982 showed that Travellers' children had a ten times' higher admission rate to hospital than settled children and that in winter months there could be up to 25 per cent of Traveller children in hospital at the same time (Noonan 1994). Two influential reports (Gordon *et al.* 1991 and Public Health Matters 1990 – Director of Public Health) have measured Traveller life expectancy at between 11 and 15 years shorter than that of the settled community, child immunisation was found to be poor and the death rate of Traveller children under ten was up to ten times that of settled children (Gordon *et al.* 1991).

A small but significant initiative in Northern Ireland, which has the potential to address the range of issues facing Travellers, involves the designation of two Health Action Zones, one of which is North and West Belfast. These zones are similar to those in England and Wales, but in Northern Ireland they have not attracted additional resources. The development of the zones has meant the setting up of a three-year implementation plan to reduce inequalities in health and social well-being and to create a healthier, more prosperous and socially included population, through joint interventions by public agencies, the commu-nity and voluntary and private sector organisations. One of the initiatives is entitled 'Housing and Health Improvements for Travellers'. The newly estab-lished Health and Housing Working Party, led by the NIHE, will carry this forward.

Maginn *et al.* (1999, p.543) have concluded that a range of policy initiatives designed to provide Traveller-specific accommodation types (transit sites, amenity unit sites and group housing) in different tenures (public rented, owner-occupied and private rented) and by specific suppliers (NIHE, housing associations and Traveller organisations such as co-operatives) would be the most realistic way forward. This would provide a wider range of tenure choice and accommodation options.

## The Chinese community

The housing tenure of the Chinese community is closely related to their pattern of economic activity. Up to 90 per cent of Chinese people are employed in the catering industry and their housing is tied to the place where they work – for instance, living accommodation may be above the restaurant/takeaway. Around 20 per cent of Chinese people live in private rented accommodation (Irwin and Dunn 1997) with its disproportionately poor standards and insecurity. Those in tied accommodation, by its nature, are more vulnerable to employer control and 'families that are unrelated are often put together under the same roof, causing emotional strain on the occupants because of the lack of privacy due to sharing limited space' (Manwah, Watson and McKnight 1998, p.136). Sixty-five per cent of Chinese people are owner-occupiers, but no figure is given for those whose home is linked to their employment (Irwin and Dunn 1997, p.136).

Chinese people are under-represented in public sector accommodation. Their knowledge of NIHE advice services is low (NIHE 1995). There have been to date no initiatives to encourage an uptake of applications by the Chinese community to NIHE or other public accommodation agencies, which have tended to assume that this community is self-sufficient in its housing needs. The NIHE survey showed that 13 out of 20 Chinese interviewees had suffered racial harassment. According to Chinese Welfare Association (CWA) research, 26.9 per cent of respondents reported racial harassment as a *regular* crime in their area.

Due to the lack of specialised sheltered accommodation in Northern Ireland, the CWA has helped many Northern Ireland-based elderly Chinese people apply for sheltered accommodation in Scotland (Manwah Watson and McKnight 1998, p.138). This has meant leaving family and friends and therefore raises obvious issues of increased isolation approaching old age. In a survey of Chinese people (CWA 1997) the CWA estimated that there was demand for sheltered housing from at least 300 elderly Chinese people in Northern Ireland. Ninety-five per cent of those households in the survey that contained elderly people expressed an interest in a sheltered housing scheme. At present the needs of this group are largely unknown to the local health and social services trusts.[12] There are plans for Belfast Improved Housing (BIH) Association to provide a 35-bed sheltered scheme. This will make it easier for social services and voluntary organisations such as CWA to provide some facilities for this group.

## Discrimination and other communities

Research has been carried out into racial attitudes and prejudice in Northern Ireland by Connolly and Keenan (2000). The research found that a large proportion of people surveyed supported the need for effective equal opportunities policies in relation to housing and employment. However, more than one in four were unwilling to accept either an African-Caribbean, Chinese or South Asian person as a resident in their local area. This rose to over two in five who were unwilling to accept one of the above as a close friend and more than half who were not willing to accept anyone from the above communities as a relative through marriage. One in five belonged to a social group where racist name-calling occurs, but racist name-calling was not the preserve of a specific social group.

As we have already stated, the most negative attitudes were reserved for Irish Travellers, with 40 per cent stating that they thought the nomadic life-style of Travellers was invalid, a consistently higher proportion refusing to accept a Traveller as a neighbour (57%), and over three-quarters (77%) were unwilling to accept a Traveller as a member of their family.

The research found that racial prejudice was twice as significant as sectarian prejudice, with those stating that they would have a problem mixing with a person from a minority ethnic group being twice as numerous as those admitting to a problem mixing with a member of the other main religious tradition. The report also found that racial attitudes towards specific groups have become 'significantly worse' since 1995/96. In that year 37 per cent of respondents stated that they were unwilling to accept a person of South Asian origin as a relative by marriage. This rose to 54 per cent in the current study (2000). There was also a similar marked increase in relation to Chinese people (Connolly and Keenan 2000, p.45). The report reminds us that there are real race relations issues to be addressed in Northern Ireland if we are to avoid the development of greater hostility towards minority ethnic communities. It is a widely held belief among minority ethnic communities in Northern Ireland that after the ceasefires the attacks on minority ethnic families increased.[13]

## Racial harassment

For all minority ethnic communities in Northern Ireland, racial harassment is a serious and often daily issue. The police have in the past few years developed a scheme for the recording of racial incidents. Such incidents appear to be concentrated in specific areas. However, this may indicate where the efforts of a few liaison officers to gain the confidence of the communities have had success rather than enclaves of racist behaviour.

The NIHE does not have a specific racial harassment policy or procedure nor does it have a system for monitoring incidents of racial harassment. This is partly due to the fact that according to Irwin and Dunn (1997, pp.70–72) less than 10 per cent of the ethnic minority population lives in public housing. These very small numbers may be due to the policy that was applied until 1999, that to qualify for admission to the waiting list an applicant must have been born in Northern Ireland or resident in Northern Ireland for seven years. In addition, because of socio-economic or employment factors, minority ethnic groups in Northern Ireland have traditionally had high levels of owner-occupation. For those in public housing there is less formal protection for those suffering from racial harassment than in the rest of the UK.

## Conclusion

Northern Ireland illustrates a range of issues related to ethnicity and segregation, which are unique in the UK. The development of statutory duties to ensure equality, after lagging behind the rest of the UK, has now moved into the mainstream ahead of the rest of the UK, especially in areas other than 'race'. The pace of change is fortuitous for members of ethnic minorities in Northern Ireland as, due to the concentration on sectarian issues in the province, the problems faced by ethnic minorities have not always been recognised or perceived as having high enough priority to demand action. The incremental approach to developing protection for racial minorities that has occurred in the rest of the UK has been largely absent in Northern Ireland. The experience in Northern Ireland, one of moving away from conflict and the causes of conflict, has meant developing a range of social policies and instruments that protect minorities and the vulnerable. These could benefit others in the UK, the Republic of Ireland and beyond in showing the next steps to be taken towards the development of a non-discriminatory society, including offering a living example of the far-reaching public statutory duty, and its role in a changing society. The 'peace process' and paramilitary ceasefires continue to survive, but society remains deeply divided and, within working-class areas, the influence of paramilitary groups remains strong. There is no evidence that housing segregation has reduced in recent years and NIHE initiatives to remove sectarian graffiti appear to have had little immediate impact. The Agreement reached in Belfast on Good Friday April 1998 states clearly that 'the parties affirm in particular...the right to freely choose one's place of residence…the right to freedom from sectarian harassment' (Northern Ireland Office 1998, p.16).

There has been a considerable amount of research and a number of policy initiatives with regard to the treatment of Travellers, but the very high levels of community hostility to this group may mean that such innovations receive less prominence when such policies are made by locally elected assembly members rather than politicians from Westminster.

The level of hostility towards Travellers amongst settled people and the worsening of racial attitudes in Northern Ireland, as graphically shown in the Connolly and Keenan research, show the potential for serious deterioration in community relations, if racial equality issues are not addressed. In Northern Ireland these tensions stand as warnings from the past. The last thirty years of conflict stand testament to that.

## Notes

1 The terms 'Good Friday Agreement' and 'Belfast Agreement' are the terms commonly in use to describe the agreement that was reached in the multi-party negotiations in Belfast in April 1998. The terms have vecoem politicised, with catholics/Nationalists tending to use the term 'Good Friday Agreement' and Protestants/Unionists the term 'Belfast Agreement'.

2. The Northern Ireland Act 1998 amalgamated the functions of the previous Commission for Racial Equality for Northern Ireland, the Equal Opportunities Commission and the Fair Employment Commission, and incorporated the duties of the Disability Council into the new body.

3. The Human Rights Commission has replaced SACHR (Standing Advisory Commission on Human Rights). There is no corresponding commission covering the rest of the UK.

4 The Commission on Policing for Nothern Ireland (Pattern Commission) was set up as a direct result of the multiparty negotiations in Belfast in April 1998.

5. Ulster was one of four historic provinces of Ireland; as well as the present six counties in Northern Ireland it included the two border counties of Cavan and Monaghan, and Donegal in the north west.

6. In late 2000 there was evidence of a considerable amount of harassment, violence and forced movement within the Protestant Shankhill area of Belfast because of disputes between various Protestant paramilitary groups.

7. Since 1989 employers have been under a duty to monitor the composition of their employees and are under certain duties in respect of achieving fair participation between Catholics and Protestants as laid out in the Fair Employment and Treatment Order (NI) 1998.

8. The Equality Commission for Northern Ireland has produced guidance notes on *Sectarian Harassment*, which are available from the Equality Commission for Northern Ireland: Equality House, 7–9 Shaftesbury Square, Belfast, BT2 7DP.

9. Irish Travellers are recognised as a distinct racial group and as such the word 'Traveller' is always capitalised, as would be other nouns such as African, Chinese etc.

10. The term 'group homes' refers to a small number of residential units built together so as to maintain the extended family structure. For Travellers these will probably also feature an area for light industrial work.

11. ACT was a government-appointed working group set up to address policy issues. It was disbanded in December 1999. There had been much criticism of its effectiveness from Travellers' organisations, and the CRE, amongst others, has called for it to be replaced.

12. Social services and health in Northern Ireland are unified and managed on a local geographical area level but are not under the control of local councils.

13.  The concern in the rise of racism and racial attacks in Ireland, north and south, led the Equality Commission for Northern Ireland and the National Consultative Committee on Racism and Interculturism [Is this the right word?] to hold an all-Ireland round-table meeting. This discussed 'Developing a North/South Agenda for Anti-Racism and Racial Equality Strategies'. A report of the meeting was published in March 2000.

# References

Black, R. (1972) 'Flight in Belfast.' *Community Forum 2*, 1, 9–12.

Boal, F.W. (1969) 'Territoriality on the Shankhill-Falls Divide, Belfast.' *The Irish Geographer VI*, 1, 30–50.

Boal, F.W. (1981) 'Residential segregation and mixing in a situation of ethnic and national conflict: Belfast.' In P.A. Compton (ed) *The Contemporary Population of Northern Ireland and Population-Related Issues*. Belfast: Institute of Irish Studies, the Queens University of Belfast.

Boal, F.W. (1998) 'Exclusion and inclusion: Segregation and deprivation in Belfast.' In S. Musterd and W. Ostendorf (eds) *Urban Segregation and the Welfare State*. London: Routledge.

Brewer, J.D. (1992) 'Sectarianism and racism, and their parallels and differences.' *Ethnic and Racial Studies 15*, 3, 352–364.

Bruce, S.B. and Wallis, R. (1987) 'Ethnicity and evangelicalism: Ian Paisley and Protestant politics in Ulster.' *Comparative Studies in Society and History 29*, 2, 293–313.

Butler, C. (1985) *Travelling People in Derry and Tyrone*. Derry: World Development Group.

Connolly, P. and Keenan, M. (2000) *Racial Attitudes and Prejudice in Northern Ireland*. Belfast: Northern Ireland Statistics and Research Agency.

CRE (1997) *Discrimination and the Irish Community in Britain*. London: Commission for Racial Equality.

Curtis, L. (1984) *Nothing but the Same Old Story*. London: Greater London Council Information on Ireland.

CWA (1997) *Analysis of a Survey of Chinese Households in NI*. Unpublished internal document. Belfast: Chinese Welfare Association.

Darby, J. and Morris, G. (1974) 'Intimidation in housing.' *Community Forum 2*, 7–11.

de Paor, L. (1971) *Divided Ulster*. Second edition. Harmondsworth: Penguin.

Department of Economic Development for Northern Ireland (1999) *Fair Employment in Northern Ireland Code of Practice*. Dd. 0251 5/99 c20. Belfast: Department of Economic Development for Northern Ireland.

Director of Public Health/Eastern Health and Social Services Board (1990) *Public Health Matters*. Second Annual Report of the Director of Public Health. Belfast: EHSSB.

DOE (No Date) *Building on Success*. Belfast: Department of the Environment for Northern Ireland.

DOE (1998) *Accommodation Needs of Travellers*. Belfast: Department of the Environment for Northern Ireland.

Equality Commission for Northen Ireland (1999) *A Profile of Northern Ireland Workforce Summary of Monitoring Returns 1999*. Monitoring Report 10. Equality Commission for Northern Ireland.

Equality Commission for Northern Ireland (2000) Profile of the Northern Ireland Workforce. Belfast: Equality Commission for Northern Ireland.

Fawcett, L. (1999) *Racial Equality Bulletin No 2*. Belfast: Equality Commission for Northern Ireland.

*Fermanagh Herald* (1997) 9 July.

Fulton, J. (1995) 'Ethnicity and state form in the division of Ireland.' *New Community 21*, 3, 341–355.

Gordon, M., Gorman, D,R., Hashem, S. and Stewart, D. (1991) 'The health of Travellers' children in Northern Ireland.' *Public Health 105*, 387–391.

Hainsworth, P. (ed) (1998) *Divided Society*. London: Pluto Press.

Hayes, M. (1996) *Loyalism and the Protestant Working Class. Beyond Ethnicity?* Southampton: Southampton Institute.

Irwin, G. and Dunn, S. (1997) *Ethnic Minorities in Northern Ireland*. Coleraine: Centre for the Study of Conflict, University of Ulster.

Jenkins, R. (1997) *Rethinking Ethnicity*. London: Sage.

Keane, M.C. (1990) 'Segregation processes in public sector housing.' In P. Doherty (ed) *Geographical Perspectives on the Belfast Region*. Jordanstown: University of Ulster.

McGarry, J. and O'Leary, B. (1995a) *Explaining Northern Ireland*. Oxford: Basil Blackwell.

McGarry, J. and O'Leary, B. (1995b) 'Five fallacies: Northern Ireland and the liabilities of liberalism.' *Ethnic and Racial Studies 18*, 4, 837–861.

Mackay, C.J. (forthcoming) 'Other social landlords.' In C. Paris (ed) *Housing Policy and Practice in Ireland.* Coventry: Charted Institute of Housing.

McPeake, J. (1998) 'Religion and residential search behaviour in the Belfast urban area.' *Housing Studies 13*, 4, 527–548.

McVeigh, R. (1992) *Racism and Travelling People in Northern Ireland.* Belfast: Queens University Institute of Irish Studies.

McVeigh, R. (1997) *Just News*, 'Ethnic Minorities and the "Numbers Game"' March. Committee for the Administration of Justice, Belfast, March, 4–5.

McVeigh, R. (1998) 'There's no racism because there's no black people here.' In P. Hainsworth (ed) *Divided Society.* London: Pluto Press.

Maginn, P., Paris, C. and Gray, P. (1999) 'Accommodating Irish Travellers: The public policy gap in site provision and housing in Northern Ireland.' *Housing Studies 14*, 4, 525–545.

Manwah Watson, A. and McKnight, E. (1998) 'Race and ethnicity in Northern Ireland: The Chinese community.' In P. Hainsworth (ed) *Divided Society.* London: Pluto Press.

Melaugh, M. (1994) *Housing and Religion in Northern Ireland.* Coleraine: Centre for the Study of Conflict, University of Ulster.

NCCRI/Equality Commission for Northern Ireland (2000) *Developing a North/South Agenda for Anti-Racism and Racial Equality Strategies.* Belfast: Equality Commission for Northern Ireland.

NIHE (1995) *Housing Needs of the Chinese Community.* Belfast: Northern Ireland Housing Executive.

NIHE (1998) *Continuous Tenant Survey.* Belfast: Northern Ireland Housing Executive.

NIHE (1999) *Towards a Community Relations Strategy.* Belfast: Northern Ireland Housing Executive.

Noonan, P. (1994) *Travelling People in West Belfast.* Belfast: Save the Children.

Noonan, P. (1998) 'Pathologisation and resistance: Travellers, nomadism and the state.' In P. Hainsworth (ed) *Divided Society.* London: Pluto Press.

Northern Ireland Office (1998) *The Agreement: Agreement Reached in the Multi-Party Negotiations.* April. Belfast: Northern Ireland Office.

O'Dowd, L., Rolston, W. and Tomlinson, M. (1980) *Northern Ireland: Between Civil Rights and Civil War.* London: CSE Books.

Office for National Statistics (1999), *Population Mintimated resident population of Northern Ireland.* The Northern Ireland Statistics and Research Agency (website).

Pollak, A. (ed) (1993) *A Citizen's Inquiry: The Opsahl Report on Northern Ireland.* Dublin: Lilliput Press.

Poole, M.A. and Doherty, P. (1996) *Ethnic Residential Segregation in Northern Ireland.* Coleraine: Centre for the Study of Conflict, University of Ulster.

Rollston, B. (1991) *Politics and Painting.* London: Farleigh Dickinson/Associated University Presses.

Rose, R. (1971) *Governing Without Consensus.* London: Faber and Faber.

Rose, R. (1973) 'Where can the people live?' *Community Forum 3*, 1, 15–17.

Russell, J.L. (1980) *Housing Amidst Civil Unrest.* London: Centre for Enviromental Studies.

Smith, D.J. and Chambers, G. (1987) *Equality and Inequality in Northern Ireland 4. Public Housing.* London: Policy Studies Institute.

Smith, D.J. and Charles, G. (1991) *Inequality in Northern Ireland.* Oxford: Clarendon Press.

Stewart, A.T.Q. (1977) *The Narrow Ground.* London: Faber and Faber.

*Ward* v *Gardner Merchant Industrial Tribunal* (1999). Unreported. 29 November.

*Ward* v *Olive Grove* (public house) (1999) Unreported. 9 December.

# Chapter 16

# The Housing Experiences of Minority Ethnic Groups in Western European Welfare States

Ronald van Kempen and A. Şule Özüekren

## Introduction

All over Western Europe housing conditions and housing market options show inequalities between the native-born households and those who have an immigrant origin. This especially holds when the former guest workers are compared to nationals in these countries. These guest workers generally still occupy the less favourable sectors of the labour market, and their resulting low incomes restrict their housing choices and chances of enjoying a progressive housing career. While a typical housing career of native households is from rented to owner-occupied housing, from multi-family to single-family dwellings and from inner city to suburbs, immigrants and their descendants are usually forced to stay put or to make a housing career within the least popular segments of the housing sector. Sometimes the least popular segment is within multi-family rented housing, sometimes it is the dilapidated owner-occupied housing segment. Whatever the type of tenure, a possible housing career is generally limited to certain neighbourhoods in the city: these occupants clearly have a constrained choice. In this chapter we will describe the background to these housing conditions and housing careers. We will try to describe and explain the housing conditions and housing careers of different groups in different countries, drawing on our own work and work of some other scholars. We will conclude the chapter with some ideas on the future. It will become clear that developments in the labour market, developments within demographic and political spheres, and processes of discrimination all result in a bleak picture of the future housing conditions of immigrants. Fortunately, however, there are also some positive developments.

Most of the chapters in this book are about Britain. This chapter is specifically focused on the housing situation of minority ethnic groups in the rest of Europe. It is, however, definitely not our aim to give a complete picture of all groups in all European countries. Of course, this would be an impossible task and would require a few books instead of one chapter. Even in one country, like Britain, as may be seen in the other chapters of this book, large differences with respect to, for example, housing conditions and social exclusion emerge between different groups and between different cities. In order to get a clear picture, we will have to limit our overview. Our first limitation is that we only talk about West European countries belonging to the European Union (EU). This means that we exclude all East European countries. Although some interesting papers about minorities and their housing conditions and spatial segregation in cities in Eastern European countries do exist (e.g. Kovács 1998; Ladányi 1989), data and information about these countries is usually hardly available. In some cases we will even limit our description to only one or two groups or to a small number of countries or cities, again, because of the unavailability and incomparability of data.

## Minority ethnic groups in Europe: An overview

Before we provide an overview of the housing conditions of minority ethnic groups, it is necessary to say something about the terminology and definitions used and about numbers.

### Terminology and definitions

Terms to designate those who cannot be considered as the native population of a country are numerous. Foreigners, migrants, immigrants, minorities, minority ethnic groups, ethnic minorities, aliens are among the terms used in different countries and at different time periods. While some of these terms have been seen as derogatory in some periods in some countries, they are used without any problems in other countries and periods. The term 'minority ethnic groups' is a case in point. While in Britain the use of this term is quite normal, in the Netherlands and in France it has been seen as a derogatory term for quite some time. At present, however, the term is used again frequently in the Netherlands. The term 'minority ethnic group' is convenient to indicate those people that are not only of foreign descent, but can also generally be found in disadvantaged positions in, for example, the labour market and the housing market. In this way, Turks and Moroccans are separated from, for example, Americans, Belgians and English.

Those of 'foreign' descent include all who migrated from another country to the host country. In some countries the children of these people are also counted in this category and even the grandchildren. In some cases, the definition is even broader: the category of 'foreigners' includes all people who are born abroad or who have at least one parent who was born abroad. For example: Dutch children who are born in Australia, because their parents happened to be there for a short time, are counted among those of foreign descent.

Of course there is a clear danger in defining categories in these ways. It might give the impression that all individuals belonging to a specific category behave in the same way and have the same attitudes towards, for example, housing. This is, however, not the case. We should always be very careful to avoid stereotyped narratives of attitudes and behaviour (see also Chapter 2 in this volume). Differences within groups are always present: some individuals and households perform better than others in the labour and housing markets. Categorising people along lines of ethnicity may be helpful for comparing averages and general trends, but deeper analyses are necessary to explain differences between as well as within categories.

## Numbers

Table 16.1 gives an indication of the number of people belonging to minority ethnic groups in a selected group of EU countries. Because in a number of EU countries (former) Yugoslavs, Turks and Moroccans can be seen as the most important groups (in terms of numbers), their figures are depicted here. For comparison, the percentage of citizens from other EU countries is given for 1996.

From this table the following conclusions may be important:

- Percentages are generally not very high. Although these days there is considerable talk in West Europe about multi-cultural societies, we should be aware of the fact that in every country more than 90 per cent of the population are nationals. Of course the picture changes if we look at cities and when a broad definition is applied. Then higher figures emerge. Also, the European figures mentioned in the table do not include minority ethnic groups who have the nationality of the country where they live. This means that many ex-colonials do not show up in the figures.

## Table 16.1: Population by citizenship in selected EU countries

| | Belgium | Denmark | Germany | France | Italy | Nether-lands | Austria | Sweden | UK |
|---|---|---|---|---|---|---|---|---|---|
| Total pop. 1989 (in 1000s) | 9,928 | 5,130 | 61,715 | 54,335 | 57,508 | 14,805 | – | – | 56,847 |
| % (former) Yugoslavs | <0.1 | 0.2 | 1.0 | 0.1 | <0.1 | 0.1 | – | – | – |
| % Turks | 0.8 | 0.5 | 2.6 | 0.3 | <0.1 | 1.2 | – | – | <0.1 |
| % Moroccans | 1.4 | 0.1 | 0.1 | 0.8 | <0.1 | 0.9 | – | – | – |
| Total pop. 1996 (in 1000's) | 10,143 | 5,251 | 81,818 | 56,652 | 57,269 | 15,494 | 7,796 | 8,838 | 57,881 |
| % (former) Yugoslavs | 0.1 | 0.5 | 1.6 | 0.1 | 0.1 | 0.2 | 2.5 | 1.1 | <0.1 |
| % Turks | 0.8 | 0.7 | 2.5 | 0.4 | <0.1 | 1.0 | 1.5 | 0.2 | <0.1 |
| % Moroccans | 1.4 | 0.1 | 0.1 | 1.0 | – | 1.0 | <0.1 | <0.1 | <0.1 |
| % EU15 | 5.5 | 0.8 | 2.2 | 2.3 | 0.2 | 1.2 | 1.0 | 2.0 | 1.4 |

Note: Figures for France are not for 1989, but for 1982. The older figures for Britain are on the basis of surveys between 1986 and 1988.
Source: Eurostat (1991, 1999)

- Some countries have more immigrants than others. This is both in absolute and in relative terms. Germany, in 1996, for example, counted more than two million people with Turkish citizenship (2.5% of the total population), and 2.5 per cent of the Austrian population has a (former) Yugoslavian citizenship. Of course, the number of immigrants has a direct relationship with migration histories.

- Between 1989 and 1996 numbers increased in some countries, but not everywhere. Besides, the increases were not very high. Naturalisation (taking the nationality of the home country) is an important reason for declining numbers.

## Immigration history

Because the former guest workers make up such an important part of the total number of minority ethnic groups, it is useful to pay some attention to their immigration history. This history is also important for understanding their housing conditions. Across the countries of the EU, the history of guest workers has proceeded along similar lines. Basically, three periods or stages can be discerned (Dieleman 1993; Glebe 1997; Martin 1991). Each of these stages more or less coincides with a stage in the housing market (van Kempen and Özüekren 1997, 1998a).

## Stage 1: The labour migrant stage, coinciding with the boarding house stage

At the beginning of the 1960s, labour migration was considered necessary in many West European countries because of a booming economy and a consequent shortage of labour. In those years, governments and employers thought additional labour to be only temporarily needed. The concept of the 'guest worker' was invented. Labour and housing permits were given for only a year or a few years. Large-scale recruitment of guest workers in most West European countries started at this time. In many cases recruitment first took place in northern Mediterranean countries such as Italy, Spain, Portugal, Yugoslavia, and Greece. Later, countries such as Turkey and Morocco became the most important recruitment areas. Between 1961 and 1973, more than half a million Turks came to work in EU countries. More than 90 per cent of these workers were recruited by German companies.

Many guest workers were housed in boarding houses, often located in the older parts of the cities, and in barracks, often specifically built for them. Because the workers were single men, who had subscribed to the idea of a temporary stay, these conditions also fitted their individual strategies: the low housing costs allowed them to transfer their savings to their relatives in the home country.

## Stage 2: The family reunification stage, coinciding with a move to the less desirable parts of the rented (and sometimes owner-occupied) sectors

After a few years, many of the labourers who initially came for a limited period of time were asked to stay longer. For the labour migrants it then became logical to demand that their families come and live with them in the countries where they worked. The major factor behind a continuing migration from Mediterranean to West European countries thus became the family reunification process. Due to changes in the law in many countries, (former) guest workers were allowed to stay and bring their families over. This took place mainly between the mid-1970s and early-1980s. This process gave rise to a new source of housing demand because barracks and boarding houses were not appropriate for families.

The chances of finding appropriate housing for reunified families varied among countries and cities. Housing market conditions and regulations were the two most important factors affecting their prospects in the housing market. In some countries, immigrants had to wait for some time to obtain the right to access social rented housing. In the Netherlands, for example, until the end of the 1970s, guest workers were not eligible for Dutch social housing, simply because they did not have Dutch citizenship (van Kempen 1997). Many guest workers, therefore, had to find private housing in the 19th-century neighbourhoods of Dutch cities. In most of these cities they had to rely on the private rented sector, but in some cases they bought housing because the private rented sector was too small (see also later in this chapter). These people were called 'emergency buyers' (Van Hoorn and van Ginkel 1986) because they had no other choice, and the quality of these owner-occupied dwellings was generally low.

Early arrivals in France had to find their first housing in low-quality inner-city tenements (de Villanova 1997). Immigrants in France could only move to social rented housing during the first half of the 1970s, when French families moved out. In most cases they could only find a dwelling in the suburban public estates built in the 1960s. In Belgium, the foreigners moved into the socio-economic and spatial 'gaps' left by the upper and middle classes (Kesteloot, de Decker and Manço 1997). They also became concentrated in 19th-century neighbourhoods in dwellings vacated by native Belgians. Immigrants in Sweden were probably luckier at this stage compared to their counterparts in other countries. From the beginning they were allowed to live in municipal housing and, accordingly, were in a better position with regard to bringing their families to their new country (Özüekren and Magnusson 1997).

## Stage 3: The settlement stage, coinciding with the will to improve their housing conditions

The third stage in the migration process of guest workers to European countries involved the decision to settle or to return. Throughout western and northern Europe, increasing restrictions were placed on the entry of labour migrants during the 1970s and 1980s. The oil crisis in 1973 and structural economical changes in European countries were important developments in ending the demand for foreign workers. The economic crisis, however, affected many other countries, including the mother countries of the guest workers. Rates of unemployment increased there too, creating valid reasons for emigration or for a prolonged stay in the host country. Many guest workers started to look for better homes in the host countries. At the present time, this third stage is still relevant. Before we outline the current housing situation, however, some theoretical considerations are necessary. This will help us with the interpretation of the figures and developments presented.

## Theoretical backgrounds of housing conditions and housing careers[1]

One way to start explaining housing conditions and differences between groups with respect to housing conditions is to look at elements from the behavioural approach, which includes the preferences, perceptions and decision-making of individuals. Behavioural models focus on the demand side of the housing market. In behavioural approaches, household choices are directly linked to positions and events in the family life cycle (Clark and Dieleman 1996; Clark, Deurloo and Dieleman 1997). Household characteristics are major determinants of housing (and locational) preferences. The age of the head of household and household composition are the two essential characteristics. Leaving the parental home, the decision to stay childless for a few years after that, starting a family, the decision to have more than one child, contraction of the family and the death of a partner are among the situations that influence the household's size and its preferred type of dwelling.

The behavioural approach has been criticised for its emphasis on demand and 'choice' and the concomitant lack of attention to constraints (see, for example, Hamnett and Randolph 1988). Neither the supply of dwellings nor their accessibility (allocation procedures) receives much attention. The same criticism holds true for the ethnic-cultural approach. The general argument within this approach runs thus: housing conditions and residential patterns differ between groups, and these differences can be attributed to cultural differences between these groups. There is a clear theme of 'choice' in this approach, although it also allows for the inclusion of certain constraints in the explanation. The choice of owner-occupied dwellings, for example, can be viewed as a cultural preference, but also as a defensive reaction against racist practices of landlords (Bowes, McCluskey and Sim 1990; Cater and Jones 1987). The danger of reification of ethnic groups is specifically present in this ethnic-cultural approach.

Rex and Moore's *Race, Community and Conflict* (1967) can be seen as the beginning of the neo-Weberian or institutional approach in housing research. This approach is grounded in the idea that housing, and especially desirable housing, is a scarce resource and that different groups are differentially placed with regard to access to these dwellings. People are distinguished from one another by their strength in the housing market (Rex 1968). This strength is determined by the resources available to the household. Resources can take various forms. *Financial resources* refer to income, security of income and capital assets. *Cognitive resources* include education, skills and knowledge of the housing market. *Political resources* refer to the political power people wield, either formally or informally. And *social resources* refer to the contacts people have that may help them to find suitable housing and places in which to live (Bourdieu 1979). Even the present housing situation can be seen as a resource. All these resources are highly influential in explaining the housing market positions of households. Financial resources in particular go far towards explaining the current housing market position of minority ethnic households, as will be seen later in this chapter. Such resources are clearly more important than ethnic-cultural variables. In other words: constraint- (and opportunity-)oriented explanations appear to be generally more applicable than choice-oriented approaches.

Of course, financial means do not explain everything. Specifically in many West European countries, the state has had a strong influence on housing markets. The number (and quality) of social rented dwellings is one of the possible important effects of this influence. By providing social rented dwellings, the state ensures that low-income households have the opportunity to live in decent housing. The size of the social rented sector has been particularly important for housing provision in the Netherlands and Sweden. In other countries, the social rented sector has either been declining very rapidly (for example, in the UK – Meusen and van Kempen 1995; Murie and Musterd 1996) or has never been very large (as in Belgium – Kesteloot *et al.* 1997). With the restructuring of the post-war welfare state, the number of affordable rented dwellings tends to decline, especially in the newly built stock. This process has occurred in most West European countries since the second half of the 1980s (Özüekren and van Kempen 1997). The state restructuring has an obvious effect on the income position of households of all kinds. When governments pursue a policy of cutting welfare expenditure, everyone who depends on state benefits (such as pensioners, unemployed and disabled people) inevitably feels the pinch.

The existence of 'gatekeepers' is evident in all modern bureaucratised societies. The crucial role of these 'managers' was stressed in the work of Pahl (1975, 1977) and Lipsky (1980). These authors examined, in particular, the role of the housing officer in the allocation of resources. Pahl suggested that social gatekeepers (such as housing officers) could allocate resources according to their own implicit goals, values, assumptions and ideologies. This meant that stereotypes and racism might influence their decisions (Tomlins 1997). Discriminatory practices could be found among private landlords as well as among the intermediaries between landlords and prospective buyers or tenants. For instance, landlords might offer a vacancy to a friend or acquaintance rather than rent it to a minority ethnic household. Exclusionary policies of local authorities and private landlords could force ethnic minorities into owner-occupation (Phillips and Karn 1992). Consequently, minority ethnic households might be more or less forced to rent or buy a sub-standard dwelling and to live in neighbourhoods that were not of their own choosing.

While attention to household preferences and constraints and to housing supply is important for explaining situations in the housing market, our standpoint is that the explanation should adopt a wider perspective. Developments at a macro-spatial level can influence the choices and opportunities of households and individuals (Sarre, Phillips and Skellington 1989). Households operate within the societal, demographic, economic and political context of their countries, regions and cities. Therefore, a contextual approach is needed and attention to economic, demographic and political developments is necessary.

## Economic developments

The global restructuring of the economy and the consequent transfer of manufacturing to newly industrialising nations leads to loss of manual jobs in West European countries. The 'post-industrial' transformation of the economy in the late 20th century has affected the traditional goods-processing industries that are the economic backbone of many cities. These industries were particularly important in providing entry-level employment opportunities for the less skilled (Kasarda 1993), including immigrants. As a result of the transformation, employment opportunities in these industries are being decimated. Consequently, the incomes of the households affected have tended to decline.

Eversley (1992) points to an interesting relationship between economic development and immigration. Economically expanding regions tend to attract migrants. In Britain, individuals born in the New Commonwealth and Pakistan (NCWP) were initially concentrated in districts that were economically flourishing. There, jobs were available in low-pay industries, which were not attractive to the British-born. This implies that areas already suffering from high unemployment levels, for example north east England and Merseyside, did not attract NCWP migrants. The economic well-being of a region thus seems to be important as a pull factor. Migrants gravitate to places that offer them the greatest opportunities in terms of both jobs and housing. Chain migration may then add to the number of migrants in a region (Sarre *et al.* 1989, pp.6–7).

## Households and their preferences

The number of households looking for a home is an important variable. It must be taken into account when studying the housing market. Massive growth in the number of households within a relatively brief period may cause shortages if all those households are looking for the same kind of dwelling in the same area. Not only the number of households but also their composition should be taken into account, since some household types have specific preferences. For example, a rise in the number of extended families could boost the demand for large dwellings. Demographic developments may thus increase the competition between households. This can become a problem if more and more households are competing for the same kinds of dwellings within the local housing market.

Newcomers are often among the weakest parties in the competition for housing; typically, they have low incomes and little knowledge. Therefore, migrant labourers tend to settle in cheap residential areas in the poorer sections of the city, close to their place of work (Sarre *et al.* 1989, p.7). This is especially true when they arrive without their families. According to Peach (1968; quoted in Sarre *et al.* 1989), it is not that newcomers generally create a space for themselves; rather, they fill a vacuum. In this way, the choices of others are very important. Other people create vacancies in the existing stock and in particular neighbourhoods. Other people's choices often have to do with rising incomes and new additions to the housing stock.

## Political developments

Political developments affect rights and legislation. They may refer to gaining entry to a country (immigration laws), or they may concern rights to residency and work, social rights and political rights in the place of destination. In many countries, conflicts about these topics emerge for any number of reasons. Conflict may arise when immigrants are seen as competitors for housing, jobs and social benefits. Or they may be seen as a threat to the alleged cultural homogeneity of the indigenous population (Faist and Häußermann 1996).

In some countries (such as Sweden and the Netherlands), immigrants have long since had the right to vote in local elections. In other countries, the immigrants' participation in the political system may be much more restricted. Such differences might affect their integration into the host country and their positions in the housing and labour markets. Laws and regulations may even limit immigrants' opportunities directly (for example, the right to buy a dwelling or the right to occupy a unit in the social rented sector).

If immigrants are allowed to stay in a country for a limited period of time only, it is unlikely that they will invest in their residential situation:

> It seems self-evident that only if immigrants have the assurance of being able to stay permanently in the country of residence will they be prepared to put down roots, to integrate fully into their new society, and to identify with it. (Murray 1995, p.3)

The immigrants' legal status may also affect their housing preferences. Knowing they will have to return to their country of origin within a few years, they will not be interested in obtaining a permanent residence. Political developments in the country of origin may also be influential. According to Knerr (1990), the governments of Bangladesh and Pakistan have purposely promoted the export of their labour. In part, they have done so because of the resultant remittances. This policy also helps those governments to solve their problems of labour surplus; it is also, of course, directly related to the economic circumstances in the country of origin.

## Current housing conditions of minority ethnic groups in Europe

How can housing conditions of minority ethnic groups be characterised? Are they worse than those of majority groups? What can be said of the differences between countries? Questions like these are difficult to answer, for several reasons. First, (recent and reliable) data on housing situations are not always and everywhere available. Second, data are not always comparable, because of different definitions. Third, data limitations generally do not allow for breakdowns by, for example, income. Finally, it is virtually impossible to obtain information about the subjective part of the housing situation; that is, the opinions of the minority ethnic groups themselves about their own housing conditions. In the following we will focus only on tenure, size, rents and housing quality as important aspects of housing situation.

### Tenure

Minority ethnic groups generally concentrate in rented accommodation and are under-represented in owner-occupation. Hardly any Turks, for example, are owner-occupiers. In Denmark and the Netherlands, 92 per cent of Turkish households are tenants, while in Sweden and the German city of Düsseldorf the figure is as high as 98 per cent. Similarly, in Belgium and France, 85 per cent of Turks are tenants. Their low and insecure incomes are generally seen as the background to this pattern (van Kempen and Özüekren 1998a).

We can, however, detect divergent developments among countries. In some countries, such as the Netherlands, the number of Turkish and Moroccan home-owners was larger at the beginning of the 1980s than at the end of that decade. Van Hoorn and van Ginkel (1986) offer a clear explanation for this: by the end of the 1970s and the beginning of the 1980s, many guest workers were more or less forced to buy a dwelling because they were not allowed to enter the social rented sector at that time. During the 1980s, Turks and Moroccans were allowed into this sector and they gradually moved out of the generally poor quality owner-occupied dwellings. In other countries, such as Belgium, France and Germany, there is a clear increase in owner-occupation among minority ethnic groups (de Villanova 1997; Glebe 1997; Kesteloot *et al.* 1997). In Brussels, for example, owner-occupation among Turks increased from 13 per cent in 1981 to 37 per cent in 1991. In the Belgian city of Ghent, the vast majority of Turks are now owner-occupiers. Kesteloot *et al.* (1997) mention three factors that can explain the move from rent to owner-occupation in Belgium:

- People have come to the realisation that they have made a definitive choice to settle in the host country. While a 'myth of return' will probably never disappear wholly, the decision to stay put might also lead to the decision to improve one's position in the housing market. This decision can be reinforced by family reunification.

- Tenure insecurity in the private rented sector, partly as a consequence of discriminatory practices of landlords, pushed Turks into owner-occupation.

- Although the social rented sector is accessible in financial terms, the low number of social rented dwellings available does not offer good prospects for obtaining suitable accommodation.

The first factor may be applicable to many ex-guest worker categories in many countries. The second factor is important only in countries in which the private rented sector has been a major housing sector and where it is poorly regulated. In the Netherlands, for example, the private rented sector has been an important one for the ex-guest workers but, because of the regulation applied to it, tenure insecurity was hardly seen as a very big problem. Entering the private rented sector, however, was more problematic, in all countries, because of the possible discriminatory behaviour of private landlords. Once living within that sector, in most countries tenancies could be insecure because contracts might suddenly expire or rents might go up without prior notice. All of these factors, singly or in combination, might force people to look for a home in the owner-occupied sector. If people do not have the opportunity even to enter the private rented sector, they have to try and find accommodation in other sectors.

Kesteloot et al. (1997) also point to the fact that at present, compared to Turks, Moroccans, another important guest worker category, are clearly less likely to live in owner-occupied housing. In the Netherlands, for example, 3 per cent of Moroccans are owner-occupiers, compared with 15 per cent of Turks. Many Moroccans share the same positions in the labour and housing markets in Brussels (and also in other cities and countries). Kesteloot et al. (1997) state that the difference between the two groups might be explained by reference to the secularisation of the Turkish state, which relaxed the Islamic prohibition on mortgages. It is unclear if this is a good explanation because Turks as well as Moroccans living in Belgium (or in other countries) might well develop norms and values that have no relation to situations and developments in their home country (or the home country of their parents). Alternative explanations, however, are not yet available.

## Number of rooms and household size

Minority ethnic households often have to manage with less space per person in the dwelling than native households. These differences can, again, to a large extent be explained by the lower incomes of the minority ethnic households, which make larger dwellings unaffordable. It also has to do with the fact that minority ethnic households concentrate in cities. Here, dwellings are generally of a smaller size than dwellings, and specifically owner-occupied single-family houses, in suburban and rural areas. The larger household size is another possible explanatory factor. The latter holds true for certain specific ethnic groups, for example Turks and Moroccans, whose household size is, on average, much larger than that of indigenous households, even though it has been declining over the last two decades (see Tesser et al. 1995 for the Netherlands).

Levels of overcrowding are strikingly high in some countries. In 1980, more than 40 per cent of all Turkish households in Sweden lived in overcrowded conditions (defined as a situation in which households live in dwellings with more than two people per room, excluding the kitchen and one room). Corresponding figures for Greeks and (former) Yugoslavs were 40 and 28 per cent respectively.

Other migrant groups lived, on average, in better conditions. For native Swedes the figure was lower than 4 per cent (Özüekren and Magnusson 1997). Within each ethnic category there were clear differences among socio-economic groups, with rates of overcrowding being relatively low among professionals, managers and self-employed. In 1994, for the Netherlands as a whole, the ratio of the household size of Dutch households comprising more than one person to the number of rooms in their dwellings was 0.7. This means that, on average, the number of rooms in a dwelling is larger than the number of people in the household occupying it. Moroccans (1.2) and Turks (1.0) are worse off than average, but the gaps between the groups have definitely narrowed since 1982, when the figures for Dutch, Moroccans and Turks were respectively 0.8, 1.5 and 1.3. Clearly, the situation of these former guest worker groups seems to be improving in this respect, but the differences still persist.

## Rents

Many former guest workers and their descendants live in low-rent dwellings built before the 1960s. In the Netherlands, for example, more than three-quarters of Turkish renters in 1990 had a net rent of less than 450 Dutch florins (EURO 204), while only 55 per cent of the non-immigrant tenants had a rent as low as this. In the four largest cities almost 90 per cent of the Turkish tenants paid less than 450 Dutch florins, compared to 70 per cent of the non-immigrants (van Dugteren 1993). The structure of the dwelling stock largely explains these differences between the country as a whole and the four largest cities. On average, Turks in the Netherlands spend a slightly smaller part of their income on rent than non-immigrants: 15 per cent compared to 18 per cent for non-immigrants. Of course this is a direct consequence of the lower rents the Turks pay for their dwellings.

It is only in Sweden that minority ethnic groups are concentrated in the newer segments of the housing stock, generally built between 1965 and 1974 (as a result of the so-called 'million dwellings programme'). Consequently, there they pay higher rents compared to non-immigrants who live in private rented housing which is on average older and less expensive than the municipal housing stock (Özüekren and Magnusson 1997). The dwellings and areas that were built as a result of the million dwellings programme are considered unattractive by the Swedes, and this largely explains the concentration of minority ethnic groups, specifically Turks. In Austria, access to different dwelling types and the right to different forms of allowances are defined by nationality criteria (Giffinger and

Reeger 1997). Therefore, immigrants pay more than Austrians for the same or lower quality housing (see also below).

## Housing quality

Do lower rents imply lower-quality housing? According to Glebe (1997), many Turkish families in Germany not only have to live in crowded conditions but also in poor quality housing. In 1987, only half of the Turkish households in the city of Düsseldorf lived in dwellings with standard sanitary equipment, such as a bath and/or shower and central heating, compared to 77 per cent of the German households in that city. Of all the Turkish households in the same city, 15 per cent lived in the poorest equipped apartments, without private bath or toilet and without central heating. Only 3 per cent of native German households were found in this housing category.

In Sweden, the rented dwellings where the Turks and other immigrants live are generally of a high standard and do not show significant differences from the municipal rented dwellings where nationals live. Overcrowding and insufficient amenities in the neighbourhood are the main problems. For instance, in many areas of immigrant concentration day nurseries do not have enough capacity to meet the demand (Özüekren and Magnusson 1997).

Housing quality in the Netherlands can be measured by way of so-called quality points. These quality points are calculated on the basis of a large number of criteria such as the number of rooms, the size of the living room, the age of the dwelling, insulation, form of heating (central or not), presence of shower and/or bath and presence of double glazing (Tesser 1993). While the mean number of quality points in the Netherlands in 1990 was 124, the mean number for Turkish households was only 91, and 89 for Moroccans (Tesser 1993; van Dugteren 1993). Part of this quality difference between Turks and natives can be explained by the fact that Turks are concentrated within the cities where, generally, the dwellings have a lower quality and, consequently, a lower rent than in other parts of the country. In his research in the Dutch city of Utrecht, Bolt (2001) has shown that there is no indication that Turks and Moroccans deliberately choose lower-quality dwellings. This might have been expected because, for example, they might choose to pay lower rents in order to send as much money back to their home countries as possible, or because they might be accustomed to bad housing conditions in their country of origin.

In Belgium, the housing conditions of Turks and Moroccans in 1981 appeared to be worse compared to native Belgians (but also, for example, compared to Italians and Spaniards) (Kesteloot *et al.* 1997). Ten years later, however, the situation had improved considerably for both Turks and Moroccans. Larger numbers of both groups now had a dwelling with a toilet inside and a bath or shower. They were also less concentrated in pre-war dwellings, except in Brussels. Still, their housing conditions overall were consistently worse than those of other groups, including native Belgians. The Moroccans were even worse off than the Turks (Kesteloot *et al.* 1997).

In Austria, as in so many other countries, the housing stock as a whole shows strong differences in equipment standards (Giffinger and Reeger 1997). These standards are defined in the Rent Acts ('Mietrechtsgesetz') of 1971 and 1981, which distinguish four categories according to the combination of certain technical and sanitary characteristics of each flat. High-standard dwellings of category A (representing about 67% of the total housing stock in 1991) are equipped with central heating, a bathroom or shower and a toilet. Dwellings of category B (17% of the total stock) are equipped like category A dwellings, but lack central heating. Category C dwellings (5%) have indoor plumbing and a toilet, but no bathroom or shower. Finally, category D dwellings (11% of the total stock) are not equipped with indoor plumbing or a toilet within the dwelling itself. The latter were mainly built in the 19th century and are usually owned by private landlords.

The overwhelming majority of Austrians live in high-standard dwellings. Approximately 95 per cent of native Austrian households live in category A or category B dwellings. Of all the Turkish households, however, only 9 per cent live in category A dwellings, while 79 per cent live in category B dwellings and 12 per cent in category C and D dwellings. Category A dwellings seem to be, at least for the moment, one step beyond the reach of most Turkish households. Moreover, Turkish households generally live in more crowded conditions than native Austrian households both in Austria as a whole and in Vienna.

For France it is difficult to obtain data about housing quality. It is clear, however, that waiting lists for social housing are long. In Paris, for example, Turkish families have to wait between five and ten years to obtain an HLM-dwelling (Petek Salom 1992). In the meantime they are relegated to the private rented sector, where prices are generally high (de Villanova 1997).

## Changing housing conditions

We have already indicated that housing conditions can change. By the late 1980s and early 1990s, evidence had been increasing of up-market moves by more affluent members of ethnic minorities. In some cases, moves from inner cities to suburbs had been detected (Robinson 1990; see also Daley 1998). In other cases, moves from older and generally low-quality areas to newer areas with better housing were becoming a visible trend (as for Turks in some West European countries; see Kesteloot *et al.* 1997; van Kempen 1997). Owner-occupation became more common among Turks in Germany (Glebe 1997) and Belgium (Kesteloot *et al.* 1997). These moves from lower-quality to higher-quality housing and from rented to owner-occupied dwellings typically also involve moves from one neighbourhood to another, resulting in declining rates of segregation.

However, we should not be too optimistic. Moves do not always imply substantial improvements in housing conditions. Bolt (2001), for example, has indicated that most moves by Turks and Moroccans in the city of Utrecht in the Netherlands still take place within the social rented sector. Moves from the social rented sector to owner-occupied dwellings do take place, but they are not very numerous and only for households with at least one full-time earner. When Turks and Moroccans move home, it is generally to larger dwellings, with one or two rooms more than in their previous dwelling, but often, at about the same time, their family expands. Also, moves from multi-family to single-family houses rarely occur. This has partly to do with the scarcity of single-family houses in Utrecht and its surroundings, but also with the high prices of such homes compared to multi-family units. Those Turks and Moroccans who did make the move to a single-family dwelling were, without exception, households with a relatively high income. Bolt (2001) found no proof that divergent aspirations could explain the limited progress made by Turks and Moroccans in the housing market. Discriminatory practices in the housing market itself also did not seem to play any significant role. Again, it appears that low incomes are probably the most important factor in explaining the patterns of residential mobility of these ethnic groups.

## Conclusions and the future: Improvement or consolidation?

We can conclude that in West European countries the housing conditions of minority ethnic households, and especially of the former guest worker categories, differ overall, and on average, from those of nationals. Minority ethnic households generally occupy the more undesirable parts of the housing stock, they are more likely to live in older housing than nationals, they are found more frequently than nationals in overcrowded conditions and, with some clear exceptions (the Belgian cities of Brussels and Ghent), they are less able to penetrate into the better parts of the owner-occupied sector. In some countries (Austria) there are indications that they pay more for the same kind of housing.

Earlier in this chapter we listed theories and factors that might be important in explaining the housing conditions of minority ethnic groups. There are clear indications that low incomes in particular go a long way towards explaining these conditions. The behavioural approach may have some value (for example, it might be expected that a growing family might want to move, and even would move, to a larger dwelling), but the financial resources of households always limit their options. A move, in general, might entail a better situation (for example, an additional room), but in many cases it might be expected that the room would still be too small or too old or both. All choices in the housing market may well be constrained, but for some groups they seem to be more constrained than for others.

The role of the State in West European countries should not be forgotten here. Its declining power may be observed in many fields, but with respect to housing it is still important. Individual housing allowances exist in many countries, enabling households with a low income to live in better conditions than they could otherwise afford, and social housing is still produced in many countries (although the dwellings in this sector are not as inexpensive as they used to be). Moreover, past effects of the welfare state continue to be important. The existence of an extensive social rented sector in countries such as the Netherlands and Sweden still provides opportunities for low-income minority ethnic households.

What can be said about the future housing conditions of minority ethnic groups in West European countries and cities? To answer this question it is necessary to take account of many developments on different spatial levels. These developments form the context within which individuals and households have to take their decisions. Although the course of many of these developments is uncertain (for example, economic and demographic developments), it is possible to examine some of their potential implications.

With respect to *economic developments* it might be expected that the trend towards more service-oriented economies will continue. It may be that processes of globalisation and computerisation will lead to the further disappearance of jobs for low-educated people. These people might then experience increasing difficulties in finding a job. Within minority ethnic groups, especially within former guest worker categories, low educational attainment is more the rule than the exception. Unless radical re-schooling programmes were to appear, many of the older generation would stay or become unemployed. Their resulting low income would limit their options on the housing market.

But this may be too grim a view. Second and third generation immigrants often (though not always) perform better in the labour market. Moreover, there are indications that a growing number of high-qualified jobs and people may lead to a growing demand for low-level services (for example, cleaning, security), which might give opportunities for the currently or potentially unemployed.

How can *demographic developments* influence the housing conditions of minority ethnic households? In general, an increase in the number of households, for example as a consequence of more (young) people wanting to live independently or of immigration, will increase competition in the housing market and in different segments of the housing market. Due to global inequalities, it might be expected that migration from developing countries to Western Europe will continue and maybe even increase. When new households are also low-income households, they compete directly with low-income households that are already present and that are looking for a home or a better home. Minority ethnic groups or households may suffer disproportionately, because in many cases they are found in the low-income categories.

*Political developments* may be crucial too. It is not only policy in the field of housing and spatial planning that is important, but also decisions with respect to, for example, unemployment, older people and social security benefits. The amount of money that people and households out of work receive will continue to be crucial for their prospects in the housing market.

With respect to housing, the role of the social rented sector is currently crucial in many countries. Will this sector continue to exist? Will it be able to house low-income households, among them those belonging to minority ethnic groups? Will many units be sold or upgraded? Or will they be demolished and replaced by higher-priced alternatives? It is at least clear that the building boom in the social rented sector belongs to the past in probably every Western European country. In some countries the percentage of social rented dwellings has either been declining for years (Netherlands, UK) or has never been high (Belgium). In the future it is expected that numbers will further decline because of demolition and upgrading. The risk even exists that the remaining social rented stock will be residualised and will more and more become the last resort of households with low to very low incomes. We should, however, keep in mind that these low-income households are not solely households belonging to minority ethnic groups. Also, we should not make the mistake of assuming that all minority ethnic households are poor forever and have to stay in marginalised housing forever. This chapter, along with others in this book, has provided clear indications that many such households are capable of moving upward in the housing market.

# Note

1.    See van Kempen and Özüekren (1998b) for a more elaborate review of these theoretical backgrounds.

# References

Bolt, G. (2001) *Wooncarrières van Turken en Marokkanen in Ruimtelijk Perspectief.* Utrecht: Koninklijk Nederlands Aardrijkskundig Genootschap/Universiteit Utrecht.

Bourdieu, P. (1979) *La Distinction: Critique Sociale du Jugement.* Paris: Editions de Minuit.

Bowes, A., McCluskey, J. and Sim, D. (1990) 'Ethnic minorities and council housing in Glasgow.' *New Community 16,* 523–532.

Cater, J. and Jones, T. (1987) 'Asian ethnicity and home-ownership.' In P. Jackson (ed) *Race and Racism – Essays in Social Geography.* London: Allen and Unwin.

Clark, W.A.V. and Dieleman, F.M. (1996) *Households and Housing: Choice and Outcomes in the Housing Market.* New Brunswick: Center for Urban Policy Research.

Clark, W.A.V., Deurloo, M.C. and Dieleman, F.M. (1997) 'Entry to home-ownership in Germany: Some comparisons with the United States.' *Urban Studies 34,* 7–19.

Daley, P.O. (1998) 'Black Africans in Great Britain: Spatial concentration and segregation.' *Urban Studies 35,* 1703–1724.

De Villanova, R. (1997) 'Turkish housing conditions in France: From tenant to owner.' In A.Ş. Özüekren and R. van Kempen (eds) *Turks in European Cities: Housing and Urban Segregation.* Utrecht: European Research Centre on Migration and Ethnic Relations.

Dieleman, F.M. (1993) 'Multicultural Hollland: Myth or reality?' In R. King (ed) *Mass Migration in Europe: The Legacy and the Future.* London: Belhaven Press.

Eurostat (1991) *Demographic Statistics 1991.* Luxembourg: Office for Official Publications of the European Communities.

Eurostat (1999) *Demographic Statistics 1995–1998.* Luxembourg: Office for Official Publications of the European Communities.

Eversley, D. (1992) 'Urban disadvantage and racial minorities in the UK.' In M. Cross (ed) *Ethnic Minorities and Industrial Change in Europe and North America.* Cambridge: Cambridge University Press.

Faist, T. and Häußermann, H. (1996) 'Immigration, social citizenship and housing in Germany.' *International Journal of Urban and Regional Research 20,* 83–98.

Giffinger, R. and Reeger, U. (1997) 'Turks in Austria: Backgrounds, geographical distribution and housing conditions.' In A.Ş. Özüekren and R. van Kempen (eds) *Turks in European Cities: Housing and Urban Segregation.* Utrecht: European Research Centre on Migration and Ethnic Relations.

Glebe, G. (1997) 'Housing and segregation of Turks in Germany.' In A.Ş. Özüekren and R. van Kempen (eds) *Turks in European Cities: Housing and Urban Segregation.* Utrecht: European Research Centre on Migration and Ethnic Relations.

Hamnett, C. and Randolph, B. (1988) *Cities, Housing and Profits: Flat Break-Ups and the Decline of Private Renting.* London: Hutchinson.

Kasarda, J. (1993) 'Cities as places where people live and work: Urban change and neighbourhood distress.' In H.G. Cisneros (ed) *Interwoven Destinies: Cities and the Nation.* New York: Norton.

Kesteloot, C., de Decker, P. and Manço, A. (1997) 'Turks and their housing conditions in Belgium, with special reference to Brussels, Ghent and Visé.' In A.Ş. Özüekren and R. van Kempen (eds) *Turks in European Cities: Housing and Urban Segregation.* Utrecht: European Research Centre on Migration and Ethnic Relations.

Knerr, B. (1990) 'South Asian countries as competitors on the world labour market.' In C. Clarke, C. Peach and S. Vertovec (eds) *South Asians Overseas: Migration and Ethnicity.* Cambridge: Cambridge University Press.

Kovács, Z. (1998) 'Ghettoization or gentrification? Post-socialist scenarios for Budapest.' *Netherlands Journal of Housing and the Built Environment 13,* 63–81.

Ladányi, J. (1989) 'Changing patterns of residential segregation.' *International Journal for Urban and Regional Research 13,* 555–572.

Lipsky, M. (1980) *Street-Level Bureaucracy: Dilemmas of the Individual in Public Services.* New York: Russell Sage.

Martin, P.L. (1991) *The Unfinished Story: Turkish Labour Migration to Western Europe.* Geneva: International Labour Office.

Meusen, H. and van Kempen, R. (1995) 'Towards residual housing? A comparison of Britain and the Netherlands.' *Netherlands Journal of Housing and the Built Environment 10,* 239–258.

Murie, A. and Musterd, S. (1996) 'Social segregation, housing tenure and social change in Dutch cities in the late 1980s.' *Urban Studies 33,* 495–516.

Murray, J. (1995) 'Keynote Address.' Paper for the Seminario Europeo Vivienda e Integración Social de los Inmigrantes, Barcelona, 23–25 October.

Özüekren, A.Ş. and Magnusson, L. (1997) 'Housing conditions of Turks in Sweden.' In A. Ş. Özüekren and R. van Kempen (eds) *Turks in European Cities: Housing and Urban Segregation.* Utrecht: European Research Centre on Migration and Ethnic Relations.

Pahl, R. (1975) *Whose City?* Harmondsworth: Penguin.

Pahl, R. (1977) 'Managers, technical experts and the state.' In M. Harloe (ed) *Captive Cities.* London: John Wiley.

Peach, C. (1968) *West Indian Migration to Britain: A Social Geography.* London: Oxford University Press.

Petek Salom, G. (1992) 'Politique française d'immigration et population immigrée originaire de Turquie.' In: *L'Immigration Turque en France et en Allemagne, Cahiers d'Études sur la Mediterrannée Orientale et le Monde Turco-Iranien.* Editions de l'Association Française d'Études sur la Mediterrannée Orientale et le Monde Turco-Iranien.

Phillips, D. and Karn, V. (1992) 'Race and housing in a property owning democracy.' *New Community 18,* 355–369.

Rex, J. (1968) 'The sociology of a zone of transition.' In R.E. Pahl (ed) *Readings in Urban Sociology.* London: Pergamon.

Rex, J. and Moore, R. (1967) *Race, Community and Conflict.* London: Oxford University Press.

Robinson, V. (1990) 'Roots to mobility: The social mobility of Britain's black population 1971–1987.' *Ethnic and Racial Studies 13,* 274–286.

Sarre, P., Phillips, D. and Skellington, R. (1989) *Ethnic Minority Housing: Explanations and Policies.* Aldershot: Avebury.

Tesser, P.T.M. (1993) *Rapportage Minderheden 1993.* Rijswijk: Sociaal en Cultureel Planbureau.

Tesser, P.T.M., Van Praag, C.S., van Dugteren, F.A., Herweijer, L.J. and van der Wouden, H.C. (1995) *Rapportage Minderheden 1995. Concentratie en Segregatie.* Rijswijk: Sociaal en Cultureel Planbureau.

Tomlins, R. (1997) 'Officer discretion and minority ethnic housing provision.' *Netherlands Journal of Housing and the Built Environment 12,* 179–197.

van Dugteren, F. (1993) *Woonsituatie Minderheden: Achtergronden en Ontwikkelingen 1982–1990 en Vooruitzichten voor de Jaren Negentig.* Rijswijk: Sociaal en Cultureel Planbureau.

van Hoorn, F.J.J.H. and van Ginkel, J.A. (1986) 'Racial leapfrogging in a controlled housing market: The case of the Mediterranean minority in Utrecht, the Netherlands.' *Tijdschrift voor Economische en Sociale Geografie 77,* 187–196.

van Kempen, R. (1997) 'Turks in the Netherlands: Housing conditions and segregation in a developed welfare state.' In A.Ş. Özüekren and R. van Kempen (eds) *Turks in European Cities: Housing and Urban Segregation.* Utrecht: European Research Centre on Migration and Ethnic Relations.

van Kempen, R. and Özüekren, A.Ş. (1997) 'Introduction.' In A.Ş. Özüekren and R. van Kempen (eds) *Turks in European Cities: Housing and Urban Segregation.* Utrecht: European Research Centre on Migration and Ethnic Relations.

van Kempen, R. and Özüekren A.Ş. (1998a) 'Ethnic minority housing in the European Union: A case study of Turks.' *Tijdschrift voor Economische en Sociale Geografie 89,* 459–466.

van Kempen, R. and Özüekren, A. Ş. (1998b) 'Ethnic segregation in cities: New forms and explanations in a dynamic world.' *Urban Studies 35,* 1631–1656.

*Chapter 17*

# Conclusion

## Peter Somerville and Andy Steele

The contributions to this book have contained a number of common threads that need to be highlighted. These threads can be listed as follows:

- the presence of constraints upon black and minority ethnic (BME) groups that are additional to those affecting the white majority

- the increasing diversity of BME groups, in terms of their experiences, needs and aspirations

- the shifting and dynamic character of racism in generating and reinforcing social exclusion

- the process of extending choice for BME people and the implications of this for housing organisations.

This concluding chapter examines the social construction of racism in the context of the current British political agenda, which is focused on the extension of choice and on the effective management of that choice in the interests of the white majority (or so-called 'middle England').

## 'Additional' constraints – the reality of white racism

Lewis (1998) has provided a clear description of the process of 'racialisation', whereby groups of people are constructed into 'races'. It is this process that underlies racisms of all kinds:

1.  Human populations are divided into discrete categories on the basis of variations in physical features.

2.     Meaning is ascribed to this physical variation and it is then said to be possible to know the potentialities, behaviours, needs and abilities of a person on the basis of their 'racial' belonging.

3.     This *social* process of categorisation and classification is then said to be a product of nature – that is, racial division is said to be natural. (Lewis 1998, pp.99–100)

This description makes it clear that 'race' thinking belongs within an established tradition of positivism, according to which what is real is what can be measured and classified into discrete observable categories (Hughes 1998) and, correspondingly, what cannot be readily measured (for example, racist intentions or prejudice) is not real. Racisms, therefore, can be understood to a large extent as 'common-sense' expressions of such positivist thinking. Similar processes of construction of 'the Other' occur in relation to women, disabled people, gays and lesbians, young people and old people. The task of research is to challenge this 'common sense' and the positivism that underpins it, and to enhance our understanding of the complexity and fluidity of human nature.

In relation to housing, three types of constraint can perhaps be identified, which stem from processes of racialisation as described above:

- Institutional racism of housing organisations and the housing market, prioritising the needs and demands of the white majority (the 'middle English').

- The disadvantaged position of BME people in the housing market caused by racism outside the housing market itself, in particular in employment and education.

- Racist harassment in certain areas, resulting from 'common-sense' attempts by white residents to maintain what they perceive to be the social or cultural integrity of their neighbourhoods.

## Increasing diversity

The housing experiences of BME people have varied because:

- housing organisations vary considerably among themselves and the housing market is highly changeable and volatile

- the historical backgrounds, skills and cultures of BME people themselves have differed widely

- the response from white residents has never been either uniformly antagonistic or welcoming but always a complex, confusing and unpredictable mixture of sympathy, indifference and hostility.

The diversity of experience commented upon by many contributors to this book has therefore been produced by at least three separate causes: the characteristics of BME people themselves, the nature of the institutions and social structures they have had to deal with and the attitudes of the white people with whom they have come into contact. All of these causes are in a state of flux, mainly as a result of their continual interaction. Typically, black people have to negotiate their way through the various white-dominated institutions, such as the education and employment systems, and the attitudes of both black and white people change as a result of increasing inter-communication and, in some cases, mutual under-standing. Consequently, differences among and within BME communities become increasingly recognised outside the communities themselves.

## The changing character of racism

It should be noted, however, that this newly found public recognition of diversity does not necessarily bring understanding in its wake because it is perhaps just as likely to lead to more sophisticated forms of 'common-sense' racism. The recent moral panic over asylum seekers shows how such 'sophisticated' racism is increas-ingly allied with nationalism, with the 'self/other' boundary being constructed in terms of 'the English' versus 'foreigners'. Of course this is actually a very old and crude boundary-marking exercise but, in its sophisticated version, it allows BME communities already established in England to place themselves on the 'right' side of the boundary, for example, by passing Norman Tebbitt's famous 'cricket test'. This racism is sophisticated because it does not altogether deny the legitimacy of BME citizenship but makes it conditional on forms of allegiance that are seen (by the racists) to be quintessentially English. According to this form of racism, social inclusion is permissible but only at a price, and that price is a rejection of non-English identities. This racism therefore delegitimises the pos-session of multiple national identities, and also the situation of not having a national identity at all. 'Nationalism' becomes a smokescreen for racism, and 'English' becomes a code word for 'culturally white'.

This issue has recently been considered by Lewis (2000). She points out how modern nationalisms involve 'a contradictory articulation of the demands of par-ticular ethnic identifications and the universal claims of social democracy, citizen-ship and capital's "globalizing" market' (p.264). The attempt to fix national boundaries by excluding 'others' then produces the conditions and sites of anxi-eties over national identity, and erects barriers to 'a multiculturalism which would lead to an equality of recognition and valorization of *all* social groups, including those constructed as "minorities"' (Lewis 2000, p.264). The consequence has been the (racist) construction of the 'race relations problem' as an externally gen-erated issue, neither originating within the UK nor as endemic to the internal politics and trajectory of the UK, but as stemming from the incursion of racialised populations of colour (Lewis 2000, p.266). The real problem of white racism is thereby transformed into a pseudo-problem of black immigrant populations, with the 'solution' being constructed in terms of the assimilation or acculturation of the populations concerned.

## The extension and management of choice

Many of the contributions to this book have raised the issue of the choices made by BME people and how these choices are to be extended and managed success-fully. Arguably, social inclusion requires the facilitation of choice so that people can exercise control over their day-to-day lives. Much of the discussion concern-ing choice suggests the existence of a number of guiding normative principles, which can be listed as follows:

- the 'additional' constraints on choice stemming from racism should be removed

- constraints on choice more generally should be equalised and minimised as far as possible

- the legitimacy of choice should be negotiated through the voluntary interactions of individuals

- the management of choice should be answerable to the communities affected by such management.

The rest of this concluding chapter provides some indications as to how these principles can be applied in order to improve housing policy and practice in this area.

## The removal of racist constraints

To counteract the institutional racism of the housing market and housing organi-sations, it is commonly advocated that BME housing strategies should be devel-oped, at national and local levels (Blackaby and Chahal 2000; Housing Corporation 1998). These strategies are intended, among other things, to ensure that the 'common-sense' knowledge of white professionals is better informed about the needs and aspirations of BME communities, resulting in a responsiveness to those needs that is at least equivalent to that for the white majority. Such strategies, however, do not exist in most local authority areas at the present time and, where they do exist, they are very much in an embryonic form. There is also a danger that such 'strategic' approaches can be assimilated by ethnic managerialism (Harrison and Law 1997), as dominant managerialist approaches transform black liberationist struggles into technocratic programmes based on essentialist notions of need and ethnicity. In other words, BME strategies are vulnerable in the face of powerful processes of racialisation.

Probably the most effective way to prevent racial equality strategies from being hijacked by a managerialist agenda is to involve BME people and organisations themselves in the implementation of the strategy in leading roles. At the moment, however, no example exists of such a strategy. Racist discrimination therefore looks set to continue for some time to come. The Social Exclusion Unit (SEU 2000), in attempting to develop a national strategy for neighbourhood renewal, suggests that part of the solution lies in building the capacities of community leaders; but Patel and Patel in Chapter 11 of this volume have expressed scepticism about this being a viable way forward. This may be a chicken-and-egg situation: white organisations have to change in order for black people to be willing to work in partnership with them but white organisations are not changing (enough) because black people may not be (sufficiently) encouraging them to change. Given the structurally weaker position of BME communities in English society, it is clear that something has to give within white organisations in order for any real progress to be made. Without this, there is a danger that resistance to racist oppression will be premised on a Foucauldian acceptance of the 'rules of the game', involving an accommodation to white racism rather than its transcendence.

Lewis (2000) identifies three features of 'New Labour' that make her pessimistic about whether the desired changes will actually occur in the foreseeable future. The first is 'the attempt to proceed *as if* all inequalities deriving from the constitution of differences around axes of "race"/ethnicity, gender, class, sexuality and disability are no longer sources of serious antagonism' (Lewis 2000, p.268). The second is the tendency 'to dissolve or condense all social inequalities...into the notion of *social exclusion* understood as exclusion from waged work' (Lewis 2000, p.268), ignoring other dimensions of social exclusion such as those examined in this book. And the third is the attempt 'to institute a new social settlement with the hetero-normative family at its core' (Lewis 2000, p.268), thus re-asserting the marginality of 'other' domestic and familial arrangements, which are more common among minority ethnic groups. All of these features can be represented as aspects of a form of rule that assumes a fundamental uniformity or homogeneity of politics and culture in England, based on 'banal nationalism' (Billig 1995), structural racism (and sexism, heterosexism, classism and disablism), acceptance of the dominance of generalised commodity production, and commitment to 'traditional' family-centred consumption.

Further indications of 'New Labour' failure to grasp the nettle on racial and other inequalities include:

- Increasing emphasis on making social inclusion conditional upon appropriate performance on the part of the 'Other'; for example, in the Government's 'New Deal' programmes. The message is that socially excluded groups can become included, but only if they abide by the 'rules of the game', and this means assimilation into the dominant culture through compliance with its norms such as the prevailing work ethic, observance of the law, and so-called 'active citizenship'.

- Attempts to ignore or dilute political struggles around the issue of 'race' (and similarly with class, gender, disability and sexuality, though a detailed discussion of all of these is beyond the scope of this book), in order to defuse the threat that they might pose to established political power.

- The continuing pathologisation of socially excluded groups such as refugees and asylum seekers, as part of an ongoing assumption that the problem lies with the 'Other' (because of their 'foreignness') rather than with the native whites (because of their racism). This pathologisation results in exclusionary policies of immigration control and assimilationist policies of geographical dispersal – in the latter case even in the face of evidence indicating the failure of similar policies in the past (see Chapter 13 in this volume).

## The equalisation of constraints in general

The contributions to this book have emphasised the importance of poverty and inability to access opportunities of various kinds as continuing major constraints on BME people in Britain and elsewhere in Europe. The aim of social inclusion requires that these constraints should be no greater than for the white majority, and this in turn means that much more effort has to be invested in dealing with the problems of unemployment, low educational attainment and poor health among BME communities. It should be noted, however, that these are problems that also affect sections of the white population and there is therefore scope for making common cause with other groups in order to resist managerialist strategies of 'divide and rule'. Indeed, alliances across the boundaries of 'race' and ethnicity are arguably essential if racism is to be defeated. Specialist welfare and advice services to BME communities should therefore be seen as an integral part of programmes for empowering socially excluded groups more generally. The stake of 'social citizenship' needs to be rescued from its nationalist interpretation (Jacobs 1985) and its class bias (Faist 1995) and reclaimed for a much wider constituency.

## The management of choice and of difference – legitimacy and accountability

The recent Green Paper (DETR and DSS 2000) places great emphasis on extending choice for housing consumers, especially in relation to the allocation of housing. Its approach is colour-blind and individualist, and takes little account of the needs of specific communities or of the role of racist harassment in shaping the locational choices of BME consumers. Nevertheless, its general stance can be invoked to provide further support for the criticisms of the cultural ignorance and insensitivity of housing organisations recorded in detail by contributors to this book. It provides official confirmation, for example, that it is quite legitimate for members of minority ethnic groups to move beyond their traditional areas of settlement and that it is not legitimate for housing organisations to ignore such aspirations on the grounds that it makes their management task more difficult (in any case, Hawtin *et al.* 1999 have shown how the process can be managed effectively).

Another issue of choice is that of tenure. At present, this issue is still bedevilled by stereotypical assumptions about what different minority ethnic groups prefer. Strictly speaking, it should be a decision for individual households and the aim should be to provide those households with all the necessary information and advice to enable them to make that decision. Currently, however, choice is limited to an unacceptable degree, not only because of racist constraints but also because of a lack of realistic and affordable options in many areas. This lack of real choice is not addressed by either the Department of the Environment, Transport and the Regions (DETR) or the Social Exclusion Unit (SEU), and these criticisms apply even more strongly in the case of BME women and disabled people.

Barnes and Prior (1996) have made the point that choice can be disempowering where information, confidence and consent are lacking. If the problem here is that the management of housing choice on the part of BME people is being conducted without being accountable to those who are affected by it, then it could be argued that the way forward is for BME communities themselves to take charge of their own destiny and control their own housing organisations. This option was considered by Harrison in Chapter 7, on BME-led housing associations. The difficulty with it is that such organisations continue to be heavily dependent upon white institutions for their survival and, therefore, have to 'play the white man's game' and jump through hoops of various kinds in order to attract the necessary funding. They have to become more commercially oriented and business-like, and this may or may not have detrimental effects on the service that they provide to their communities. In spite of their problems, the performance of such organisations compares very well with most white-led housing associations who fail to give any priority to the needs of BME communities or to involve them in the provision of their services (Somerville, Steele and Sodhi 2000).

There are major issues here about how 'choice' should be managed, particularly in the context of multiple, changing and overlapping identities and preferences (Ratcliffe 2000). Given the inevitable continuing dominance of white-led organisations, the key question again is how such organisations are to be changed so as to be more responsive and accountable to their potential BME users. The verdict on new managerialist approaches, such as the 'New Public Management' (NPM), is not encouraging. Mackintosh (2000, p.88), for example, argues that NPM may actually reinforce social exclusion by widening class divisions, denigrating public sector expertise, increasing central control and disempowering more vulnerable users who need advocates in order to be able to exercise individual choice effectively. To counter this, she argues for elements such as:

- more support to socially excluded groups to develop their 'voice' and to voluntary organisations catering for such groups (this would include BME-led housing associations)

- valuing front-line staff and building on and developing their capacities (see Chapter 8 of this volume)

- having a more open process of public debate, in which difference and dispute are valued rather than glossed over. (Mackintosh 2000, pp.90–91)

Eisenberg (2000, p.398) has identified three lessons of cultural pluralism or multiculturalism, which could usefully guide approaches to the management of 'difference' in general:

- The need to tolerate and protect difference must not make group identity essential or impose onerous obstacles to the dissent of individuals from their communities' traditions and values.

- Recognising cultural differences does not automatically enhance social equality and may undermine it. For example, orientalism (Said 1978) sees non-Western cultures as irreducibly 'Other' and therefore not to be included within Western society on an equal basis. The lesson to be learned here is that Western culture needs to change in order for a more equal society to be achieved.

- Many of the means advocated to protect cultural minorities do so by expanding the power of the State and, in the process, adjudicating and regulating their values and thus reinforcing their subaltern status. This is the danger exemplified by the approach known as 'ethnic managerialism'.

## Racist harassment – the denial of choice

A number of contributors to this book have stressed the importance of racist harassment in affecting the housing opportunities of a large proportion of BME households. As government policy moves increasingly towards making individual choice its key guiding principle, without deconstructing the structural biases inherent in such a notion (biases of gender, class and disability, as well as 'race'), it is likely that racists will increasingly exercise their choice to keep 'England for the English' (or, indeed, 'Scotland for the Scottish' or 'Wales for the Welsh') or to lobby more explicitly for 'rights for whites'. This can be understood as an example of what Moreiras (1998, p.98) has called 'neoracism', which 'works in effect as the mirror image of identity politics, that is, as an identity politics of the dominant'. In this way, new dominant cultures of racism can be developed, with a more or less nationalist flavour. The racialising tendency involved is only exacerbated by the communitarian strand in 'New Labour' thinking where 'community' is an abstract and ambiguous notion that is vulnerable to racist capture, resulting in legitimations of racially exclusionary practices, along the lines of: 'If "our" community is constructed as a white one, then black people should not be allowed to be members of it.'

Lemos (2000) has recently summarised the evidence on what organisations in England and Wales are doing to combat racist harassment. He points out that, although what needs to be done was largely agreed in the 1980s, today most organisations are still not doing it. Lemos singles out in particular the inadequacy of victim support in most areas and the failure of housing associations to participate actively in multi-agency approaches. Some organisations get the Lemos seal of approval (including, surprisingly, the Metropolitan Police) but on the whole the picture is not very encouraging. This widespread inactivity, in the face of such an appalling and escalating problem, cries out for an explanation. This book suggests that it is, in fact, a predictable consequence of the continuing predominance of white racism, which has largely reconstructed itself in the light of new political and economic circumstances. The failure of governments to challenge this reconstruction, and indeed to appease it and acquiesce in it (as in the recent row over asylum seekers or in comments on the behaviour of English football fans), is a source of continuing shame for a society that claims to be civilised.

## References

Barnes, M. and Prior, P. (1996) 'From private choice to public trust: A new basis for social welfare.' *Public Money and Management*, Oct–Dec, 51–57.

Billig, M. (1995) *Banal Nationalism.* London: Sage.

Blackaby, B. and Chahal, K. (2000) *Black and Minority Ethnic Strategies: A Good Practice Guide.* Coventry: Chartered Institute of Housing.

DETR and DSS (2000) *Quality and Choice: A Decent Home for All.* London: Department of the Environment, Transport and the Regions and Department of Social Services.

Eisenberg, A. (2000) 'Cultural pluralism today.' In G. Browning, A. Halcli and F. Webster (eds) *Understanding Contemporary Society: Theories of the Present.* London: Sage.

Faist, T. (1995) *Social Citizenship for Whom? Young Turks in Germany and Mexican Americans in the USA.* Aldershot: Avebury.

Harrison, M. and Law, I. (1997) 'Needs and empowerment in minority ethnic housing: Some issues of definition and local strategy.' *Policy and Politics 25*, 3, 285–298.

Hawtin, M., Kettle, J. and Moran, C. with Crossley, R. (1999) *Housing Integration and Resident Participation: Evaluation of a Project to Help Integrate Black and Ethnic Minority Tenants.* York: York Publishing Services/Joseph Roentree Foundation.

Housing Corporation (1998) *Black and Minority Ethnic Housing Policy.* London: The Housing Corporation.

Hughes, G. (1998) *Understanding Crime Prevention: Social Control, Risk and Late Modernity.* Buckingham: Open University Press.

Jacobs, S. (1985) 'Race, empire and the welfare state: Council housing and racism.' *Critical Social Policy 13*, 6–28.

Lemos, G. (2000) 'Race fate.' *Inside Housing* 30 June, 14–15.

Lewis, G. (1998) 'Welfare and the social construction of "race".' In E. Saraga (ed) *Embodying the Social: Constructions of Difference.* London: Routledge.

Lewis, G. (2000) 'Discursive histories, the pursuit of multiculturalism and social policy.' In G. Lewis, S. Gewirtz and J. Clarke (eds) *Rethinking Social Policy*. London: Sage.

Mackintosh, M. (2000) 'Public management for social inclusion.' In M. Minogue, C. Polidano and D. Hulme (eds) *Beyond the New Public Management: Changing Ideas and Practices in Governance*. Cheltenham: Edward Elgar.

Moreiras, A. (1998) 'Global fragments: A second Latinamericanism.' In F. Jameson and M. Miyoshi (eds) *The Cultures of Globalization*. Durham, NC: Duke University Press.

Ratcliffe, P. (2000) 'Is the assertion of minority identity compatible with the idea of a socially inclusive society?' In P. Askonas and A. Stewart (eds) *Social Inclusion: Possibilities and Tensions*. Basingstoke: Macmillan.

Said, E. (1978) *Orientalism*. New York: Pantheon Books.

SEU (2000) *Minority Ethnic Issues in Social Exclusion and Neighbourhood Renewal*. London: Social Exclusion Unit.

Somerville, P., Steele, A. and Sodhi, D. (2000) *A Question of Diversity: Black and Minority Ethnic Staff in the RSL Sector*. London: The Housing Corporation.

# The Contributors

**Alison Bowes** is professor of sociology and head of the Department of Applied Social Science at the University of Stirling. She has research interests in the delivery of effective health, housing and social work services to black and minority ethnic communities and has published widely in these areas.

**Steve Gayle** is a freelance community development practitioner and trainer and has considerable experience of policy development with statutory and voluntary sector housing organisations in both urban and rural settings and specialist work related to the involvement of black and ethnic minority communities.

**Glen Gidley** is senior housing policy lecturer at Sheffield Hallam University. Glen has extensive experience of consultancy and research work over a range of housing and community development policy issues. He recently led the team that looked at BME housing needs within Sheffield. Other publications include works on housing and marginalised communities, leasehold enfranchisement and tenant involvement in rural areas. Consultancy activities include initiating user involvement strategies with a range of agencies and acting as an independent tenant adviser in over twenty large-scale housing transfers across England and Scotland.

**Fahmeeda Gill** is policy officer for the National Housing Federation and is a board member of the Federation of Black Housing Organisations. She is also an independent consultant and most recently wrote a good practice guide and training manual on the support needs of black and minority ethnic people with alcohol problems.

**Jim Glackin** is manager of Advice and Information for the Equality Commission for Northern Ireland. He previously worked for the Commission for Racial Equality for Northern Ireland and with a number of Irish voluntary housing organisations in London. He is currently vice-chairman of Traveller Movement (Northern Ireland) and a member of the Equality Sub-Group of the Committee for the Administration of Justice (CAJ) in Belfast.

**Malcolm Harrison** is reader in housing and social policy at the University of Leeds, and has published widely on 'race', ethnicity and housing policy. His latest book (with Cathy Davis), *Housing, Social Policy and Difference* was published in April 2001.

**Ade Kearns** is professor and head of urban studies at the University of Glasgow. He is also co-director of the ESRC Centre for Neighbourhood Research, having previously been Depute Director of the ESRC Centre for Housing Research and Urban Studies. His main research interests are in neighbourhood change and social processes in the neighbourhood; the evidence base for urban policy and regeneration; urban governance; and housing, residence and health.

**Christopher Mackay** is lecturer in housing studies at the University of Ulster. He undertook research into ethnicity, housing and segregation as the Northern Ireland Housing Executive research fellow at St Catherine's College Oxford. In 2000 he was visiting professor in housing at the University of Central England in Birmingham.

**Şule Özüekren** is a professor of Architecture at the faculty of Architecture, Istanbul Technical University. During the early 1990s she was a guest researcher at the National Swedish Building Research in Gävle, where she studied the housing conditions of Turkish immigrants in Sweden. She is a member of the co-ordination committee of the European Network for Housing Research and one of the co-ordinators of the ENHR's working group on Housing for Minority Ethnic Groups. She has published widely on housing conditions of immigrants in Western Europe.

**Naina Patel** is a graduate of Hull University with a Sociology and Social Anthropology degree and after several years of managing and developing public sector funded projects, Naina has also attained an MBA from de Montfort University. She was the director of a prominent regeneration company in the Midlands and is presently a business community consultant. Naina has extensive experience of research management for blue-chip and multi-national companies. Her interests include cross-cultural management strategies in a business environment.

**Ballu Patel** has extensive experience of working with public, private, and non governmental organisations, at local, regional, national and international levels. Ballu's experience ranges from working with international companies that work on educational turnkey projects in the developing countries supported by the World Bank and United Nations, to physical and community regeneration projects within the UK's inner cities. Ballu is also a non-executive director of Eastern Primary Care Trust and a fellow of the RSA.

**Martyn Pearl** is director of housing studies at Oxford Brookes University. He has an extensive career in both academic and practi    ce environments and has published widely on social housing related themes, including refugees and asylum seekers in the UK.

**Deborah Phillips** is a senior lecturer in the School of Geography at the University of Leeds and deputy director of the Centre for Ethnicity and Racism Studies at Leeds. She has researched widely in the field of ethnicity, 'race' and housing, and is currently engaged in research into South Asian residential mobility and institutional racism in higher education.

**Peter Ratcliffe** is reader in sociology at the University of Warwick. He is the author of many books, reports and articles on 'race', ethnicity and urban inequality. His most recent publication is *Breaking Down the Barriers: improving Asian access to social rented housing* (Chartered Institute of Housing, June 2001).

**David Robinson** is currently principal researcher in housing at the Centre for Regional Economic and Social Research, Sheffield Hallam University. He has researched extensively around the issue of access to and allocation of housing resources to different interests and groups and is the author of numerous academic and policy oriented publications.

**Duncan Sim** is senior lecturer in housing studies at the University of Stirling. He has undertaken research into minority ethnic access to housing, housing histories, and employment and training issues.

**Dianne Sodhi** is a research fellow in the Salford Housing and Urban Studies Unit at the University of Salford with particular interest in 'race' and housing. She has recently been involved in setting up the 'Race and Housing database' at the Ahmed Iqbal Ullah Race Relations Archive in Manchester.

**Peter Somerville** is professor of social policy and head of the Policy Studies Research Centre at the University of Lincoln. He has researched widely in the field of 'race', housing and social exclusion. His most recent publication was *Social Relations and Social Exclusion* (2000).

**Andy Steele** is professor of housing and urban studies and director of the Salford Housing and urban Studies unit at the university of Salford. He has extensive research experience in the fields of race and housing having been responsible for numerous studies on the housing and related needs of black and minority ethnic groups.

**Richard Tomlins** is professor of race, diversity and housing at de Montfort University, Leicester. His recent work includes a major research report, entitled *A Question of Delivery*, assessing how far housing associations are meeting the needs of minority ethnic communities.

**Ronald van Kempen** is associate professor of urban geography at the Urban Research Centre Utrecht, Faculty of Geographical Sciences at Utrecht University, the Netherlands. His current research focuses on the links between spatial segregation, social exclusion, urban policy and the development of cities.

**Rachael Unsworth** is a lecturer in urban geography at the University of Leeds. She focuses on changing city landscapes and land use patterns, especially clustering and migration of different social groupings and economic activities. She is also interested in the attempts to make cities more 'liveable' and less environmentally damaging.

**Roger Zetter** is professor and deputy head at the School of Planning at Oxford Brookes University. Founding editor of the *Journal of Refugee Studies* (1988-2001), Roger Zetter has been researching in the field of refugee studies in the UK, Europe and the developing world for over 20 years.

# Subject Index

*Note: BME stands for black and minority ethnic.*

# Author Index